Haa Léelk'w Hás Aaní Saax'ú
Our Grandparents' Names on the Land

Edited by

Thomas F. Thornton

SEALASKA HERITAGE INSTITUTE

Juneau

UNIVERSITY OF WASHINGTON PRESS

Seattle and London

Printed in the United States of America

Sealaska Heritage Institute gratefully acknowledges support for the editing and production of this book from a donation by Mike Blackwell.

Map design and composition by Matt Ganley with revisions by Ailsa Allen.

Book design, composition, and editing for publication by Michael Travis.

Tlingit proofreading by Jeff Leer, Michael Travis, Yarrow Vaara, and Hans Chester. Richard Dauenhauer and Nora Marks Dauenhauer provided additional assistance.

In the process of collecting and collating thousands of place names gathered in two decades of personal fieldwork by the editor and augmented by a century of documentation from various sources in a variety of spellings and degrees of accuracy, some errors and inconsistencies in the lists, maps, and narratives may have eluded our proofreading.

Library of Congress Cataloging-in-Publication Data

Haa léelk'w hás aaní saax'ú : our grandparents' names on the land / edited by Thomas F. Thornton.
p. cm.
Includes bibliographical references.
ISBN 978-0-295-99217-4 (hardback : alk. paper)
ISBN 978-0-295-98858-0 (pbk : alk. paper)
1. Tlingit Indians — Alaska — Yakutat — Name. 2. Tlingit language — Alaska — Yakutat — Etymology. 3. Names, Geographical — Alaska — Yakutat.
I. Thornton, Thomas F.
E99.T6H2185 2012 979.8004'9727 — dc23 2011052814

The paper used in this publication is acid-free and meets the minimum requirements of American National Standard for Information Sciences — Permanence of Paper for Printed Library Materials, ANSI Z39.48-1984.

University of Washington Press
www.washington.edu/uwpress

Contents

A Note to the Reader

Harold P. Martin

In 1994, after twelve years as the tribal operations officer for the Central Council of the Tlingit and Haida Indian Tribes of Alaska, I was transferred to the position of subsistence director. During my tenure as subsistence director, I was also serving as president of the Southeast Native Subsistence Commission, made up of representatives from all Southeast Native communities and Anchorage.

Shortly after assuming my new position, I was approached about a Native place names project by Dr. Tom Thornton, who had recently left the Alaska Department of Fish and Game, Division of Subsistence, to teach anthropology at the University of Alaska Southeast. Following the in-depth discussion I had with Tom, it dawned on me that we were losing our elders at a rapid pace, and with the passing of each elder, we lost a wealth of cultural knowledge and history. I suddenly felt an urgency to document our Native place names.

Before the Europeans came to our country, we had Tlingit, Haida, and Tsimshian names for our surrounding environment. We had names for creeks, rivers, mountains, bays, reefs, and other places of significance. I believe Tom described well the importance of place names and why they should be preserved: "For Southeast Alaska Natives, the most fundamental subsistence resource is the land itself. Indigenous place names are valuable linguistic artifacts containing a wealth of cultural and environmental information concerning our region's land and waters."

We applied for and received several grants to carry out this work from the National Park Service Historic Preservation Fund. Thus began an exciting adventure into the past. Dr. Thornton coordinated the project and I administered the grant (see Thornton and Martin 1999).

We first traveled to rural communities throughout Southeast and solicited permission to proceed with the project from tribal governments and elders. Native communities are made up of one main clan that settled that particular area, and several other clans that moved in for various reasons.

We took care to not offend anyone by intruding on burial grounds, sacred lands, or important subsistence areas. Fortunately, we received permission from all communities we visited. To my knowledge, we did not offend anyone, and all in all, we received great cooperation.

Several incidents stand out in my mind. First, when we asked about certain areas, an elder might point out that he could not say anything about that area but would tell us who we could talk with because "it was their clan territory." This, to me, showed respect for one another's territory, and that the protocol still exists.

Another incident taught me a lesson about talking to the media. Interviewed by a young lady from the *Fairbanks Daily News-Miner*, I related to her several examples of place names and their significance. I mentioned a mountain in Chapin Bay on Admiralty Island that had a large hole going through near the top called Shaak'w Wool or "Hole in the Small Mountain." I mentioned that from time to time people have observed geese flying through the hole in the mountain. When she wrote it up, she stated that the people of Kake waited each spring until geese flew through the mountain before they began their subsistence gathering and hunting, which was ridiculous.

At a meeting in Kake, we gathered around a table with a chart spread out before us. I had told Tom that I had forgotten many names, yet whenever a name was mentioned I knew exactly where it was located on the map. There was some humor at this same meeting. Tom liked to be precise and exact on his pronunciation of place names, yet there were names that he tried to say that came out like a reference to certain parts of the human anatomy. Another word he tried to say came out like the Tlingit word for lovemaking. I cautioned him to please not say these words in public.

Initially, there was some opposition to the project. There were those who felt that we would be giving away favorite harvest locations for salmon and halibut, as well as aquatic and terrestrial plants. In reality, the Alaska Department of Fish and Game, and the U.S. Forest Service, already had all fish streams, aquatic plants, and forest products identified and documented. Our purpose was to preserve the Native place names and their meaning in various clan territories.

At the completion of the project, Tom and I traveled to the communities and presented the place name charts and booklets to the tribal governments. These documents were received with great enthusiasm.

In my work on subsistence issues, some federal, state, and municipal agencies and environmental groups had stated that there was no evidence that certain areas were ever used for subsistence purposes. Our place name charts prove otherwise. Nowhere in all of Southeast Alaska is there an area that was not utilized by Natives for one reason or another. All you have to do is look at the maps.

In retrospect, I only regret we had not started this type of project many years earlier, when so many elders who have now passed on would have been available for interview. Nonetheless, after much research, we documented thousands of Alaska Native place names that are now a part of a cultural atlas.

I retired in July of 2000. Dr. Tom Thornton continued his work on developing this atlas of place names, which I am certain will be of great value to the education of our children and grandchildren. I will be forever grateful to Tom for his foresight to document and preserve our Native, cultural place names. I feel a great satisfaction in contributing to the preservation of a small part of Native history.

Harold P. Martin was born and raised in Kake. He is Tlingit of the Raven T'ak̲deintaan clan.

Foreword: People of the Land

Rosita Worl

Land is important to the Indians of Southeast Alaska. More often a Tlingit, Haida, or Tsimshian will open their speech to a non-Native audience with the statement, "We have lived in and owned Southeast Alaska since time immemorial." Ceremonial speeches, on the other hand, do not require the assertion of land ownership. A reference by ceremonial participants to clan crests and identification of a site by its place name where the crest originated signifies ownership of land. Crests, stories, songs, and names serve as title to sites. Place names also tie Natives to their land. In our worldview, we belong to the land and the land belongs to us. It is no wonder that land is prominent in Native identity. In ceremonies, one of the most often heard phrases is, *Yee gu.aa yáx̲ x'wán, aan yátx'u sáani,* "Noble people of the land, take courage!"

Indicative of our ancient occupation and land tenure are the place names the Tlingit and Haida have bestowed on significant features of their land. The Tsimshians, who arrived in Alaska from Canada in the historical period, brought with them their singular place name of Metlakatla and gave it to the community they established. Names were given to prominent geographic features from the southern boundary at Cape Fox to the most northern reaches in the Yakutat region. The meanings of these names reflect the worldview of the Tlingit and Haida and simultaneously embody cultural, social, historical, and environmental values and knowledge of the Native peoples of Southeast Alaska. Place names symbolize an enduring and spiritual relationship of Native people to their land. They embody the traditional knowledge of changes in land features and landscapes. Place names also affirm the use of the land and its resources. They record the ancient and historical events through oral traditions, songs, and visual art handed down through generations.

The Tlingit and Haida continue to use their own place names in lieu of the English names that identify many geographical sites. When our dance group, the Marks Trail Dancers, was given the name of G̲eisán, Nora Dauenhauer and I climbed G̲eisán mountain to honor our ancestors who gave this mountain its name. We know it as G̲eisán, and not as Mount Ripinski by which it is officially known. Ironically, Solomon Ripinsky was a friend of Lt. Frederick Schwatka, whose name was taken by the Shangukeidí (thunderbird) clan and transformed to Schwatgi. Lt. Schwatka did not adequately pay the Thunderbirds for transporting goods over the Chilkoot Pass, and thus the clan took his name and naval uniform as payment for his transgression.

Sites and place names continued to be used by the Tlingit and Haida to record their ongoing history even after the arrival of westerners. Perhaps the most widely known and recorded is that of the Peace Rock (G̲uwakaan Teiyí) located on the Chilkoot River in Haines. As its name implies, ceremonies were traditionally held at the Peace Rock to resolve differences between warring clans. In widening the road leading to the Chilkoot Lake, the State of Alaska's highway department demolished G̲uwakaan Teiyí. The Lukaax̲.ádi clan of Haines immediately voiced its objection, and the state ultimately rebuilt the Peace Rock. In addition to its original meaning, the Tlingit now use G̲uwakaan Teiyí as a lesson for their young. Elders cite the destruction and reconstruction of the Peace Rock as a metaphor describing how Tlingit culture was nearly destroyed by western forces and emphasizing the value of a continued relationship to their land as the basis of their cultural survival and vitality.

The case of G̲eisán demonstrates the common historical practice of ignoring Native names and instead honoring a non-Native. The early visitors tended to give their own names to Alaska geographical features and sites. The colonizers ensured that English names would replace the Native names and become permanent as they recorded the English names on their titles and deeds and on their maps. The actions by missionaries and educators, who worked to suppress Native culture and languages, further hastened the loss of ancient place names.

After Alaska became a state in 1958, the new citizens ensured the colonialist practice of using English names would continue. The state adopted a requirement that Alaska Native names for communities and geographic features must be "pronounceable without considerable difficulty." For the most part, Americans generally do not speak anything other than English. With Tlingit being one of the most complex languages in the world and with many sounds that are not present in the English language, the state's requirement guarantees that Tlingit place names will not be considered as geographical names. To add further insult to Native people, the state extended its geographical naming practices to the naming of state maritime vessels. State law requires that state vessels must bear the name of an Alaska glacier. Thus in Southeast Alaska, where nearly two hundred glaciers are named, less than ten are known by a Native name and in a region where communities are dependent on maritime transportation, state law all but ensures that few if any vessels will bear a Native name.

Many of the Tlingit and Haida place names have already been lost, while others undoubtedly would have passed into obscurity or would remain clouded by the corrupted, anglicized interpretation of Tlingit names were it not for the meticulous research of Dr. Thomas Thornton. Dr. Thornton has dedicated eighteen years to this work. He scoured early records kept by the first visitors to Southeast Alaska and studied the records of government officials and early ethnographers, most important of whom is Frederica de Laguna. He interviewed countless elders and pestered many others until they relented and gave him names and stories. This was no easy task as those who have worked among the Tlingit and Haida know that names are owned in the same way as real property and clans jealously guard their clan names. However, through his collaboration with local researchers and elders, he was able to compile more than three thousand place names.

He has become the archival center of place names. When people learn about other names, they often check with him to see if he has the name in his database. As important as the names themselves, Dr. Thornton has captured the meaning of land to Native people through his documentation and analysis of Native place names. Dr. Thornton will readily give credit to the many others with whom he has worked, but he has been the consistent force behind the compilation of place names.

Although we have had a great appreciation and love for our land, Dr. Thornton has made our relationship with our ancestors tangible. As I travel through the waterways of Southeast Alaska, I have felt the presence of my ancestors. I can visualize them paddling their canoes to trade or visit with neighboring clans. It gives one a sense of immortality knowing that we have lived and traveled through the land and seas of Southeast Alaska for thousands of years. However, the place names that are recorded by Dr. Thornton provide a concrete vehicle to reclaim our culture and history and to glimpse into the lives and history of our ancestors.

Dr. Thornton's work is invaluable not only for the deeper knowledge and understanding of an indigenous culture, it also provides an inventory that Native people can use in their efforts to restore Native names to geographical sites. Like the Peace Rock that was nearly destroyed but then reconstructed, we are working to reintegrate our place names onto the landscape of our homeland. Sealaska Corporation, which was created under the Alaska Native Claims Settlement Act of 1971 and which reclaimed a number of our sacred and historical sites, intends to identify these sites by their Native names. Although we may not be able to change other existing English place names to Tlingit or Haida names, we are using various federal legislative acts and policies to identify different sites by their ancient names through the placement of plaques that record the Native place names, history, and significance of the sites to Native people. Additionally, this publication will greatly enhance the Sealaska Heritage Institute's efforts to protect heritage sites and help foster place-based education and language revitalization throughout the region.

We are indebted to Dr. Thornton for his dedicated research and the inventory of place names and for providing the cultural and social context in which these names are used. His work provides an insight into the Native worldview and gives further credence to Native people's assertions of the significance of land to them. We believe the cultural information and historical records inherent in Native place names are of benefit not only to Native peoples but to all humankind.

Rosita Worl, Ph.D., is the president of Sealaska Heritage Institute. She is Tlingit of the Eagle Shangukeidí clan and the House Lowered from the Sun of Klukwan, Alaska.

Introduction

Thomas F. Thornton

Most people who visit Southeast Alaska, even those of us who have lived there, know very little about the Native place names that grace its marvelous lands and waters. In other words, we are *dis*-oriented. To orient means to align or position with respect to a point or system of reference. By ignoring the indigenous toponymy we remain cut off from this vital system of reference, which is itself a technology of orientation every bit as useful as a compass or GPS (geographic positioning system), only more profound. For Natives of Southeast Alaska, the naming of the world begins with its transformation from darkness to light by Raven. Discovering the Box of Daylight at Nass (Naas) River, Raven releases its celestial contents — the moon, stars, and sun — from the stingy Naas Shaak Aank̲áawu (Nobleman at the Head of the Nass) in order to light the world. Preceding Raven, Naas, today the center of Tsimshian/Nishga culture in northern British Columbia, may be the oldest aboriginal name in the region, perhaps in existence ten thousand years or more. Linguistic artifacts like place names can be hard to date, but there is no mistaking their importance. The nobleman Naas Shaak Aank̲áawu is named for Naas because he dwells there, and his wealth, power, and status stem from this place, as do his descendants, including many of the Native people of Southeast Alaska.

Place names are the foundation of every culture's geographic coordinate system, of every individual's sense of place (Thornton 1997a). Without place names our ability to distinguish, distill, and describe elements of the physical and metaphysical landscape is severely compromised. We must struggle to find other ways to orient ourselves. Nothing conjures a place like a good name. Where names are absent humans invent them, whether they be colonizers seeking to claim new lands for possession, pioneers venturing to tame the wilderness, or children building worlds in backyards. That's why place names are so important. Each one is itself a box of daylight illuminating a world!

Yet, few indigenous names appear on modern maps of Southeast Alaska, and those that do are often anglicized in ways that alter their sounds and obscure their meanings. What happened to the real names? In most cases they have simply disappeared from the official cartography through a process of neglect or erasure. The neglect was a result of surveyors, mapmakers, and other officials who could not be bothered to master the Native geographic nomenclature, with its odd sounds and hidden meanings. The erasure was a result of something more pernicious and programmatic: a concerted effort by colonizers, missionaries, and their partners in government to subordinate and dismantle the indigenous world by undermining its language, culture, and environment. Because they occupy the nexus of language, culture, and environment, and signify the earthly (and even cosmic) foundations of the indigenous world, place names suffered enormously under policies of cultural erasure. As a result, we have been disoriented from a Native vision of the landscape ever since. Like most aboriginal peoples, Tlingits and Haidas of Southeast Alaska felt this disorientation like a shockwave. As one Tlingit leader explained to Governor John G. Brady in 1898: "Now we do not know what we are to do, as we are like a certain man in a canoe. The canoe rocks; we don't know what will become of us" (Hinckley 1996).

A century later the disorientation remains. A recent executive proclamation by Alaska Governor Tony Knowles (July 19, 1999) declares in bold, "The Canoe Still Rocks in 1999." Indeed it does. At the dawn of the twenty-first century, nearly every Alaska Native language is threatened or endangered, swamped by the flood tide of English. Tlingit has fewer than five hundred Native speakers and Alaskan Haida fewer than a dozen, nearly all over seventy years of age. Endangered along with these languages are the indigenous geographies that have been built up over millennia by the laying down of place names to define landscapes of significance. We should all be concerned about this loss, for just as the extinction of endangered species may compromise an ecosystem by reducing its biological diversity and resilience, so too may the extinction of Native geographic names compromise our world by reducing its cultural diversity and thus its resilience. Perhaps more than anything else, Alaska Native geographies, as codified in place names, show us alternative ways of seeing and relating to the world around us. Such diversity is critical in

Table 1. Tlingit Technical Sound Chart

Darker gray boxes indicate sounds like English. Lighter gray boxes are sounds like English in some places, but not in others. Boxes with a heavy outline are consonants are found in German *ich* and *ach*, but not in English.

		Stops			*Fricatives*		*Sonants*	
		Plain	Aspirated	Glottalized ("pinched")	Aspirated	Glottalized	Nasal	Semivowels
Front of mouth	Dental	d	t	t'			n	
	Lateral	dl	tl	tl'	l	l'		
	Alveolar	dz	ts	ts'	s	s'		
	Alveo palatal	j	ch	ch'	sh			
	Velar	g	k	k'	x	x'		y
	Velar rounded	gw	kw	k'w	xw	x'w		w
	Uvular	g̱	ḵ	ḵ'	x̱	x̱'		
Back of mouth	Uvular rounded	g̱w	ḵw	ḵ'w	x̱w	x̱'w		
	Glottal	.			h			

Vowels					
	Short	a	i	e	u
	Long	aa	ee	ei	oo

High tone is indicated with an acute accent (´). Low tone is unmarked, except in the Tongass and Klawock dialects, which mark low tones with a grave accent (`) for contrast (see chapters 9 and 10). Throughout this book asterisks (*) are used to indicate uncertain or unconfirmed names or translations.

order to avoid what Vandana Shiva (2000) terms "monoculture of the mind." Indigenous place names, then, constitute an important component of biocultural diversity; for when "you don't know the names," as the great botanist Linneaus said, "your knowledge of things perishes." If indigenous names and languages cease to be known, Native ways of seeing the world likewise may perish.

Fortunately, not all indigenous place names have been lost. On the contrary, many have remained, if not on maps, in the hearts and minds of the Tlingit and Haida people who learned them from their elders while traveling and living on the land. Despite the rocking, erosion, and sedimentation caused by the flood tide of non-Native language and culture, individuals and families have continued to carry on intimate relationships with places named and frequented by their ancestors. In doing so, they have remembered many place names. Thus, Kake (Ḵéex̱') elder Fred Friday told land claims investigators in 1946: "The Native people know all the points and rocks and every little area by name. If I told you all the names of all the places that I know it would fill many pages. These areas were used so much that we were familiar with every little place" (Goldschmidt and Haas 1998, 177). Use bred familiarity and familiarity bred naming and prodigious knowledge of places. It was not just that Fred Friday knew a lot of place names, but that he knew a lot about each named place from experience, and could thus unpack and interpret them with his intimate knowledge of their history and ecology. For him, the names held a certain descriptive force and adaptive advantage that made them both memorable and worth remembering. As Sitka (Sheet'ká) elder Nels Lawson (G̱ooch Daa) remarks, "The land itself [became] our method of documentation" (pers. comm.).

While the flood of cultural change has eroded and buried Native place names in the sediments and cutbanks of Western language and culture, for those who have lived in the names, especially as children, they still have a potent animating force. Fifty years after Fred Friday's statement, I shared a list of Ḵéex̱' area place names with one of his descendants, Doyle Abbot, as part of an interview. Mr. Abbot, who had moved from Kake to Ketchikan, smiled when he heard them, and commented. "At first, I could not remember a lot of those names... But when you started to say them, it came back to me... like I was seeing a picture. I could see those places. I grew up with them." And the memories flowed.

So evocative are indigenous place names, a speaker who has never even been to a particular site may be able to sense — visually, morally, and in other ways — its features and significance. Such was the case for the K̲éex̲' K̲wáan people, as revealed in Johnny Jackson's narrative on the odyssey of his K̲aach.ádi clan. Mr. Jackson recalls how his people retreated to the Interior during the epic Flood at the end of the last ice age, and when they returned generations later, how descendants of the original inhabitants, seeing the land for the first time, could recognize key geographic features because they appeared just as had been described by the elders and vividly evoked by the richly figurative place names. Mr. Abbot had experienced a similar revelation.

Perhaps it is not so astonishing that just hearing "old Indian" place names can stir up vivid images of life and land that may never have been experienced directly, or in Mr. Abbot's case, been buried by the deluge and sediments of a cultural sea change. Native place names are like that. Because they are so potent in their ability "to summon forth an enormous range of mental and emotional associations," anthropologist Keith Basso argues, place names are "among the most highly charged and richly evocative of all linguistic symbols" (1988, 103). Among the Western Apache, Basso (1988, 1996) found that speaking with place names was an important means of conveying moral lessons and wisdom through the perceptual and participatory frame of the land, a process he terms *interanimation*. Tlingits and Haidas speaking with and about place names accomplish similar social ends, while at the same time engaging in broad reflections on their individual, social, historical, and ecological character (Thornton 2004a).

Powerful and resonant as they are, place names live not only in the hearts and minds of individuals, but also in society's collective iconography. We find them organically embedded in the webs and strands of culture that continue to be woven, especially those not frayed or overcome by the Western cultural flood tide. In Southeast Alaska, these include the material culture of regalia and visual art, the oral culture of songs and stories, and the social culture of identity, ceremony, and exchange. Like the subsistence economy, these vital cultural institutions continue to animate and conserve indigenous senses of place in important ways. They extend our understanding of place names beyond mere labels on the land and reveal how names and their cultural associations operate as versatile and resilient *cultural resources* — boxes of daylight from which people derive their sense of identity, belonging, and dependence on the land, and from which they draw strength, comfort, and wisdom.

Let us examine briefly how place names not only define the land but work within cultural systems to maintain people's sense of being and belonging in this place, Lingít Aaní (Tlingit Country), we now call Southeast Alaska.

Language and Naming

Naming systems develop as a function of language, culture, and environment. Anthropological and linguistic research has shown convincingly that, while language and culture are not so arbitrary as to actually constitute the environment, as the extreme form of the Sapir-Whorf or linguistic relativity hypothesis supposes, they do play a powerful role in shaping our perceptions of the land. Thus, cultures inhabiting the same terrain may conceptualize and act on the environment in very different ways (Thornton 1995).

The vast majority of place names in this book are of Tlingit origin or derivation. But there are also Haida place names, especially in the southern Prince of Wales Island area; Tsimshian names, especially in the vicinity of Nass River and Metlakatla; Eyak and Chugach names in the Yakutat area; and Athabaskan (Ahtna, Southern Tutchone, Tagish, Tahltan, Tsetsaut) names in interior areas linked to Tlingit country by water, trade, and travel routes. And, of course, there are overlays of names from American, British, French, Russian, Spanish, and other sources, typically laid down by explorers and settlers in the region. Beyond these, there are local nicknames and pet names for places which are not necessarily part of the conventional Native or Euro-American geographic nomenclature. The etymology of many Euro-American place names can be found in the *Dictionary of Alaska Place Names* (Orth 1971, and updates), but Native names in this dictionary are often omitted, misrendered, or untranslated. Tlingit names fare especially poorly.

One reason for this under representation and bowdlerization is the difficulty speakers of English and other Indo-European languages have in grappling with the Tlingit language. Part of the Na-Dene language family, Tlingit is most closely related to Eyak and to a lesser degree, Athabaskan. A relatively homogenous language, it is comprised of four mutually intelligible dialects or speech areas: the gulf coast, inland, northern, and southern (de Laguna 1972, 15ff.). It has a large vocabulary, and the phonology, or sound system, includes some two dozen sounds not found in English (see table 1, the technical sound chart).

Like other Na-Dene languages, Tlingit is characterized

by its grammatical emphasis on the verb and its complex prefixing and classificatory structures which allow whole phrases to be built out of a single verb stem. Typically the verb stem appears toward the end of word (e.g., "to Juneau [Dzantik'i Héeni] he is going-by-foot") with up to twelve prefixes and three suffixes modifying it. These modifiers can transform the verb significantly, making it hard for a non-Native speaker to distinguish and parse. To further complicate things, Tlingit place names often incorporate nouns and verbs in contracted form, making them even more challenging to analyze and "unpack."

In a verb-centered language like Tlingit, place names may incorporate complex verb phrases which have the capacity to define the environment in terms of its actions, movements, and processes. This linguistic emphasis on action is mirrored in Tlingit metaphysics in that actions are attributed not only to what English speakers would define as "animate" objects or beings, but also to inanimate ones, such as rocks, glaciers, and trees, indeed the earth itself (de Laguna 1972, 21). In addition to this "enlivening" influence of the Tlingit verb, the Tlingit system of incorporating relational nouns and other classifiers into the verb enables the speaker to describe actions with a precision and economy that is difficult to match in English.

To understand how this works, let us look at the Tlingit and English names for Glacier Bay. The English name,

Table 2. Common Landscape Terms in Tlingit Place Names

Feature	*Tlingit generic*	*Example*	*Translation*
bay	g̲eey	Xóots G̲eeyí	Brown Bear Bay
fortified place	noow	Deikee Noow	Far Out Fort
glacial silt, sand	l'éiw	L'éiw Shaayí	[Glacial] Sand Mountain (cutbanks)
glacier	sít'	Sít'k'i T'ooch'	Little Black Glacier
hill	gooch	X̲'aan Goojí	Fire Hill
hole	tuwool	Tuwool Séet	Hole Strait
hole (below freshwater)	ísh	Ishkahít	House on Top of the Fish Hole
hole (below saltwater)	éet	Cháatl Éedi	Halibut Hole
island	x'áat'	L'éiw X'áat'i	Sand Island
isthmus, portage	góon	Aangóon	Isthmus Town (Angoon)
lake/lagoon	áa	Áak'w	Little Lake
mountain	shaa	Nóoskw Shaayí	Wolverine Mountain
point	x'aa	Teey X'aayí	Yellow Cedar Point
rapids	eey	Eey Tlein	Big Rapids
reef	eech	Yées' Eejí	Large-Mussel Reef
river, creek	héen	Til'héeni	Dog Salmon Creek
rock	té	Téyeiyí	Rocks Alongside
rockslide	k̲aadí	K̲áa Tlénx'i K̲aadí	Slide of the Big Men
sandbar	xákw	Xakwnoowú	Sandbar Fort
spring (freshwater)	goon	Tinaa Gooní	Copper Shield Spring
strait, channel	séet	Taan Té Séet	Sea Lion Rock Strait
trail, road	dei	Deishú	End of the Trail (Haines)
valley	shaanáx̲	S'eek Shaanáx̲	Black Bear Valley
village, settlement, land	aan	Kasa.aan	Beautiful Town (Kasaan)

Glacier Bay, is said to be a translation of the Tlingit Sít' Eetí G̲eeyí (which John Muir [1895] also recorded and helped make part of the official cartography, though it is rendered on maps as Sitakaday [Narrows]) applied by L.A. Beardslee, who surveyed the bay with a Tlingit guide in 1880. Glacier Bay is a classic binomial compound name, consisting of a generic physical feature of the landscape (bay) with a descriptor, in this case a noun (glacier), preceding it. A great many English place names conform to this pattern. The Tlingit name, Sít' Eetí G̲eeyí (Bay in Place of the Glacier), also is typical in its construction. Like the English, the Tlingit includes a generic (*geey*, or "bay"; see table 2 for a list of common generics found in place names), but the descriptor is not an adjective or a noun, as is commonplace in English; rather it is a relational noun (*eetí*) implying action in time (i.e., "taking the place of") and relative location. This place name reflects well the capacity of the Tlingit place names to communicate complex geographic phenomena succinctly.

More intriguing than its grammatical construction, however, is the idea that the Tlingit name conveys. While the English name implies only the *presence* of glaciers, the Tlingit name denotes a historical, geographic *process*—a process of glacial recession and the consequent formation of a bay in its place. Unlike the English name, the Tlingit toponym clues us into important geological and hydrographic events that have occurred in this place. The Tlingit names for Johns Hopkins Inlet, Tsalx̲aan Niyaadé Wool'éex'i Yé ([Passage] Which Broke Through toward Tsalx̲aan [Mt. Fairweather]), and Hugh Miller Inlet, Anax̲ K̲uyaawal'ix'i Yé (Where the Glacier Ice Broke Through), are other examples of this kind of action-oriented naming, describing a process which has occurred, or is occurring, over time. The first name requires a seven word English sentence to express the same idea! From this example we can see how important information can get lost in translating Tlingit place names into English.

Another key to the descriptive power of Tlingit place names lies in the fact that multiple relational nouns and directionals can be incorporated into names to describe position and location even more precisely. The place name Geesh K'ishuwanyee (Place below the End of the Edge of the Base of the Kelp) exemplifies this polysynthetic or "stacking" quality of Tlingit by accommodating no less than four relational nouns to indicate a specific place (a reef) in the sea (in relation to a kelp bed) where halibut can be caught. Literally translated, the name can be decomposed as follows: *geesh* (kelp) *-k'í* (base) *-shú* (end) *-wán* (edge) *-yí* or *yee* (place below). Relational nouns commonly incorporated into place names are summarized in table 3; they are well suited to describing conditions on both land and sea. English place names typically lack such expressive power because relational terms cannot easily be incorporated into their syntax.

What Is Named?

Like material artifacts, place names lie in particular contexts and assemblages, and their distribution and patterning is not random. Examining what features of the environment are distinguished and labeled by place names enables us to assess basic issues of environmental perception and classification as well as environmental change and land use over time.

As we might expect, many similar geographic features tend to be named across cultures, although not with the same frequency. For example, Tlingits name more hydrographic and shoreline features of the environment, such as islands, bays, and streams, while Euro-Americans name more upland features, like mountains, as a proportion of their total name set (see Thornton 1995). Why? One reason is that in oral cultures a "mental economy" (Hunn 1996) seems to exist, whereby not every landscape feature is named, but rather only those worth remembering. To label all features, regardless of cultural interest, would be both superfluous and taxing on memory. Especially among societies without written records, where names and other knowledge have been passed down through oral tradition, cultural interests influence not only the selection of sites to be named but also their retention in the collective memory. Thus, salient cultural sites, including productive hunting, fishing, and gathering locales; refuges; and key navigational and historical landmarks, are populated with names, while places in between remain a "relatively undifferentiated landscape" (de Laguna 1960, 20). In contrast, in literate societies blank spaces on the map seem to stimulate the naming impulse and the map itself is an aid to memory.

Cultural interests and orality also influence the density of names we find on the land. Where they had strong cultural interests and large populations, Tlingits applied place names thickly, often achieving much higher densities than the corresponding Euro-American toponymy. On the other hand, at the regional level, the density of Euro-American names (just over six thousand) is roughly twice that of the indigenous toponymy (just over three thousand). Is this a function of the literate society's impulse to fill empty spaces on maps (often with nondescriptive biographical names in honor of individuals), or is it the result of cultural loss of Native place names? This question is not easy to answer. If all Tlingit territories were as thickly named as those documented around Ketchikan and Saxman by Thomas Waterman in 1922, then the density of Tlingit names in Southeast would seem to have been comparable to the Euro-American name set today, or perhaps even greater (assuming Waterman's data was itself not complete). On the other hand, it may be that southern Southeast Alaska, with its deeper historical roots and higher population densities (which tend to correlate with toponymic densities; see Hunn 1994), supported a higher density of names. In the course of our research, Tlingit elders often lamented that "a lot of the names have been lost." Undoubtedly this is true, but if the loss of Native place names is 50 percent or less (assuming minimal loss as of 1922), that would mean that, as a domain of language, Tlingit place names have proven more resilient than we might have expected.

What's in a Name?

Beyond their distribution and structure, understanding place names entails examining their semantic elements to determine what they mean. Semantic patterns are especially important in evaluating place names as sources of traditional knowledge — boxes of daylight — because they tell us why sites were significant and how they fit together. Meanings are not always obvious, however, and for this reason it is always best to "unpack" place names with local experts who have the traditional knowledge to interpret them.

Table 4 provides a basic breakdown of semantic categories in Tlingit place names, along with the percentage of Tlingit place names (based on a regional sample) that fit them. The table shows that the vast majority of names refer to elements of the physical topography (hydrographic and terrestrial) and biological environment (plants, animals, etc.), and human cultural landscape (e.g., historical and habitation sites, etc.). In contrast, the English name set can include up to 50 percent biographical names (Thornton 1995) honoring people, which do not describe the character of the land.

The majority of semantic associations in Native names are metonymic, meaning that the places are characterized by the presence of a particular thing — an animal, plant, mineral, or other phenomena — often in abundance. Such abundance often reflects a subsistence interest, as in G̲aat Héeni (Sockeye Salmon Creek), or Yaana.eit Xágu (Wild Celery Sandbar), K'wát' Aaní (Bird Egg Land), or X̲áat Áa Dug̲ich Yé (Pitching the Fish Place), the latter being a classic "activity name." Anomalous occurrences of species are also referenced. For example, the toponym Kals'ak̲sk'i (Little One That Has Yews) signals an unusual concentration of these hardwood trees, patches of which are rarely found in Southeast. And sometimes metonymy references not abundance, but rather just one individual animal, as in the activities of a certain bear that are commemorated in the name Daak̲ Uwahuwu Xóots (Brown Bear Who Swam In[land]), or the many toponyms that memorialize the activities of the trickster-demiurge Raven on the land (e.g., Yéilch Yaawax̲ut'i X'aa T'éi, "Raven Adzed [Three] Notches in a Rock Point"). Raven, too, has an abiding interest in subsistence and the names tell how he shaped much of the present landscape in his omnivorous quest for food, as evoked in places like Yéil Nées' Akawlishaa (Raven Ate Sea Urchin), Yéil G̲eiwú ("Raven's Fishnet," an imprint of the net he left on some sloping rocks at the entrance to a bay) and Yéil K̲'wádli ("Raven's Cooking Pot," a set of rocks said to be the remains of a halibut meal he cooked; see de Laguna 1960, 49). In total, mythological names including Raven names constitute about 3 percent of Tlingit toponyms.

Another important type of semantic association is metaphor. Metaphors help us understand landscape features in terms of other things we know. Thus a certain hill formation might resemble a "Whale's Little Head" (Yáay Shaak'ú) or a "Steller's Jay Crest" (Shalax̲'éishx'w). By far, the most important metaphoric schema for landscape is the human body. This is not surprising when we consider that our bodies are the original, primal landscapes that we inhabit, and our most basic tool of measure. Thus, as in English, body analogs are readily found in the landscape — the head of a bay, the mouth of a river, and so on. Even generic topographical references may be couched in terms of the body. For example, a Tlingit word often used to describe a point of land is *lutú*, which means nose or nostril, as in Ltu.áa (Inside the Nostril [point] Lake), a wonderfully apt name that today is rendered as "Lituya Bay" on maps (Thornton 1995). Anatomical references characterize about 8 percent of Tlingit place names. A related metaphoric paradigm is that of kinship, which describes how geographic features, as bodies, are related. The most common of these is the "child of" metaphor, which defines a small feature proximal to its larger "parent," as in Kein, an important island landmark near Kake, and Kéin Yatx'i (Children of Kéin), the smaller islands that trail it. Such a pattern of naming helps establish not only the character of places but their relatedness, weaving disparate names into meaningful wholes, or ensemblages (Thornton 2008).

A semantic analysis also reveals the synaesthetic quality of Tlingit place names, which employ the full panoply of human senses to render places meaningful. Thus Tlingit names reflect not only the visual sense (i.e., what places look like), but also the auditory (Dàalagàaw, "Hollow Sound"), olfactory (Téey Chan Gèeyak'w, "Little Bay Smelling of Yellow Cedar"), and even gustatory senses (X'alinukdzi X'àa, "Sweet-Tasting Point"). Even the play of light and shadow is commented upon. This contrasts with the English toponymy in the region, which tends to favor the static and the visual, and the terrestrial over the hydrographic. As suggested earlier, the English name set is also topographically impoverished in comparison to the Tlingit because of its overwhelming emphasis on biographical naming—places named for people—a phenomenon that is rare in Tlingit, where people are commonly named for places rather than vice-versa.

Much more can be said about place name semantics (see Thornton 2008). The following chapters explore a variety of other semantic themes in further detail.

Place and Culture Intermeshed

Place is culture and culture is place. Not only do the two animate each other but they are intricately intermeshed. In her magisterial study of the Yakutat Tlingit, Frederica de Laguna (1972, 58) emphasizes:

> The ties between the people and the land are close, and no mere geographical description is adequate unless it attempts also to display the associations which make the Lingít-aní [Tlingit-land] a Lebensraum [living space]. These associations are in part conveyed by the names given to places, sometimes descriptive of the locality, sometimes referring to historical or legendary events which have occurred here. Even when the names are in a foreign tongue they serve as

Table 3. Common Relational Nouns Found in Tlingit Place Names

Relational noun	*Translation*	*Example*	*Translation*
a daa	around or about it	Táas' Daa	Double-Headed Tide around It
a eetí	place where it was (or taking the place of)	Sít' Eetí Geeyí	Bay in Place of the Glacier
a ká (shakée)	on top of it (on top of the hill/mountain)	L'awshaa Shakee.aan	Town on Top of the [Glacial] Sand
a k'í	at the base or foot of it	Dzantik'i Héeni	Flounder at the Base of the Creek*
a seiyí	below it; in its shelter	Neixinté Seiyí	Area below the Blue-Green Claystone
a shá	at its head	Taan Shaayí	At the Head of the Sea Lion
a t'áak	back inland from it	L'éiw T'aak Héen	River behind the [Glacial] Sand
a t'aak	beside/inside it	Yat'ak Héen	River beside the Face of It
a t'éik	behind it	Tayx'aayí T'éik Geeyí	Bay behind Garden Point
a t'iká	out toward the open sea from it	Shee At'iká	Ocean Side of Shee (Baranof Island)
a wán	edge of it	Wanachích	Back (edge) of a Porpoise (an island)
a xoo	amidst, among	X'áat'x'i Xoo	Among the Islands
a x'áak	between them	Tsaa Takdi X'áak	Between Which Seals Are Harpooned
a x'é	its mouth	Xukxu Séet X'aka.aan	Village at the Mouth of Xukxu Séet (Sukoi Inlet)
a yá	front of it	Gil' Yaká	In Front of the Cliff
a yík	inside of it; inside an open container	Shee Kaak Yík	Inside Shee Kaak (Hoonah Sound)

reminder of those who once occupied the land and are now gone...The human meanings of the landscape...involve not simply places visited and transformed by Raven in the mythical past, but places hallowed by human ancestors. For individuals of course, the world has special personal meanings, for there are places about which their grandparents and parents have told them, spots they have visited in their own youth, or where they still go. None of these personal associations are completely private; all are intermeshed through anecdote or shared experiences. Not only is the world the scene of happenings of long ago, yesterday, and tomorrow, but it has human significance for what it offers in food resources, scenery, easy routes for travel, or places of danger.

Subsistence. Historically, the subsistence economy was the most important means of defining and relating the world of indigenous places. In many respects it still is. It is striking how those who grew up living off the land remember indigenous names, even if they are not fluent speakers. I recall in Kake how several of the "junior" elders in their sixties apologized for their lack of toponymic knowledge because they had "given up their language" or "given up their culture," a familiar lament. And yet when senior elders began recalling names from memory, the juniors, without any hesitation or instruction, would be pointing them out (as if they were seeing pictures, like Doyle Abbot) for us to see on the maps. Observing this for a time, I finally said to one of them, my colleague Harold Martin, "Wait a minute. You are always telling me you forgot all these names; how is it then that you can find them on the map when they are mentioned?" His response was, "Of course I know these places; I grew up with them. They are where we did our hunting, fishing, and trapping, and we used to refer to these places by their Tlingit names." Unfortunately, contemporary subsistence laws, though they protect (somewhat) customary and traditional subsistence uses, do not explicitly protect people's relationships to particular subsistence places. One of the Southeast Native Subsistence Commission's goals for this project was to help non-Native land and resource managers understand that the most basic subsistence resource for Natives is the land itself, especially ancestral landscapes where their forebears made their livings. Subsistence projects and pathways, as illustrated in the following chapters, reveal these landscapes through encounters with interconnected, named places, "intermeshed" through lived and shared experiences.

Table 4. Distribution of Semantic Referents in Regional Tlingit Place Name Inventory

Category	%
Biological	30
Animal	(22)
Plant	(8)
Topographical	41
Hydrographic	(32)
Terrestrial	(9)
Anatomical	4
Biographical	1
Habitation	14
Historical	8
Other	2

Percentage of Tlingit names applied to various geographic features.

The well-known myth of the "Salmon Boy" is illustrative of this process. Widely distributed among peoples of the Pacific Northwest Coast, the story concerns a boy's capture and years-long odyssey among the salmon people before returning to his people and becoming a powerful shaman. Since salmon are the most important subsistence resource, the story is worth considering for what it tells us about place. A detailed version rich in toponymy was recorded by John Swanton (1909, 301–10) a century ago at Sitka. In April 2000 I had the opportunity to map this story with elders Herman Kitka Sr. and Ethel Makinen, and Sitka Tribe staff, as part of an effort to retranscribe and retranslate the story for a place-based school curriculum (see Littlefield et al. 2003). We went over the story line by line in both English and Tlingit, with a special eye toward identifying and "getting the story behind" named sites in the narrative. The results were richly illustrative of the resonance that exists between place names, stories, and subsistence, and how an ethnogeographical reading of myth can enrich our understanding of indigenous people's sense of place and the links between language, land, and identity.

Figure 1 maps place names in the Salmon Boy story. Swanton's narrator, Deikeenáak'w, a great uncle of Herman Kitka, assumed that his audience possessed the geographic knowledge to interpret the setting of the story, including the specific places he names or alludes to in passing. As a lifelong salmon fisherman, Herman Kitka had this knowledge, and thus could "unpack" the meaning of the place names in light of their ecological context, including names used exclusively by the salmon people, who see the world from their own submarine perspective. Swanton chose to call the story "Moldy-End," after the unflattering name given to the boy protagonist by the salmon people, whom he insulted by disparaging and casting aside a moldy piece of dried fish offered him by his mother. The proper Tlingit title for the story, the elders agreed, should be "Aak'wtaatseen" (Alive in the Eddy), the honorific name bestowed upon the boy after he returned from his time with the salmon tribe and became a shaman. Significantly, Aak'wtaatseen also embodies a geographic reference, for when the boy returned to his people after having been transformed into a salmon, he seeks out his mother in an estuary, or eddy, at the mouth of the stream, where he attracts her attention by behaving in an especially lively manner.

The legend of Aak'wtaatseen can be read in many ways, but through this story mapping exercise one can see the abundance of traditional ecological and place knowledge that is embedded in the tale, and how our interpretation of the story can be enlivened and enriched by contemporary elders who still possess such knowledge and can thus comprehend the ethnogeographical and ethnoecological "grammar" that underlies the text and gives meaning to the particular ensemblage of places that constitute the story's dynamic and sentient setting. We learn that Tlingit life is not only dependent upon sustainable harvest of salmon but also successful moral engagement with these fish, and an empathetic willingness to see the world as they do. Other traditional stories, localized in named places, reveal similar patterns of engagement with other important marine and terrestrial species upon which Southeast Natives depend (see Thornton 2008).

Social organization. In Tlingit and other Southeast Alaska Native traditions, personal names, titles, and other sacred material and symbolic property (*at.óow*) are passed down from generation to generation through the matrilineal clans (*naa*) and their subdivisions, known as house groups (*hít*). The name Aak'wtaatseen (now carried by Fred Hope, among others) still lives among the Kiks.ádi clan. Like place names on the physical landscape, personal names encapsulate important historical events, figures, and geographies in clan histories and give them resonance in the contemporary social landscape. Thus, it is often said that a knowledgeable Tlingit can identify, from people's Tlingit names alone, where they are from and to what lands and lineages they belong.

The same is true of clan and house group names. Both are inextricably tied to place. While the central importance of the matrilineal clans and house groups in social, economic, and political life is well-described in the literature (cf. de Laguna 1983; Kan 1989; Emmons 1991; Thornton 2002), their multiple ties to place are not as well understood. Two aspects of clan geography are particularly significant: origin and distribution. Origin refers to the location where the clan was founded as a distinct social group and is typically from where the matrilineal group derives its name. The majority of Tlingit clans adopted their names from the geographic areas they inhabited, and the linguistic construction of such clan names invoked a sense of belonging or being possessed by the named place. For example, G̲aanáx̲ (or G̲àanax̲ in southern Tlingit dialect), the Tlingit name for Port Stewart in Behm Canal, was settled by a Tlingit group who then became the G̲aanax̲.ádi, literally the "beings of" (or "possessed by") Port Stewart. An offshoot of this group, the G̲aanax̲teidí settled at the head of the same bay (G̲aanáx̲ Tahéen), and later migrated north as far as Klukwan. These origin sites were often taken as crests by the clan and were considered sacred property (*at.óow*). Clans and house groups not named for natural sites often took their identity from some aspect of the village geography, such as an architectural feature of a clan house (e.g., the Kaagwaantaan or "Charred Timber House People") or its location within the village (e.g., the Deisheetaan or "End of the Trail House People"). The linguistic homology between clan names and sacred geography served to reinforce strong material, social, and spiritual ties to place among matrilineages, and the understanding of these ties was considered to be an essential component of one's heritage and identity (*shagóon*).

In fact it is virtually impossible to properly introduce oneself as a Tlingit person without making some reference to Southeast Alaskan geography. Geographic references are embedded in personal names, clan names, house names, and, most obviously and unavoidably, in *k̲wáan* names, which define community territories. To say you are "Sheet'ká K̲wáan" literally means that you are an organic member of the community of Tlingit people who dwell in the vicinity of Sheet'ká (Sitka), which is itself a geographic name meaning the "Ocean Side of Shee (Baranof Island)." In this way personhood and place are intermeshed.

For convenience, this book is organized by k̲wáan — traditional community territories which roughly correspond

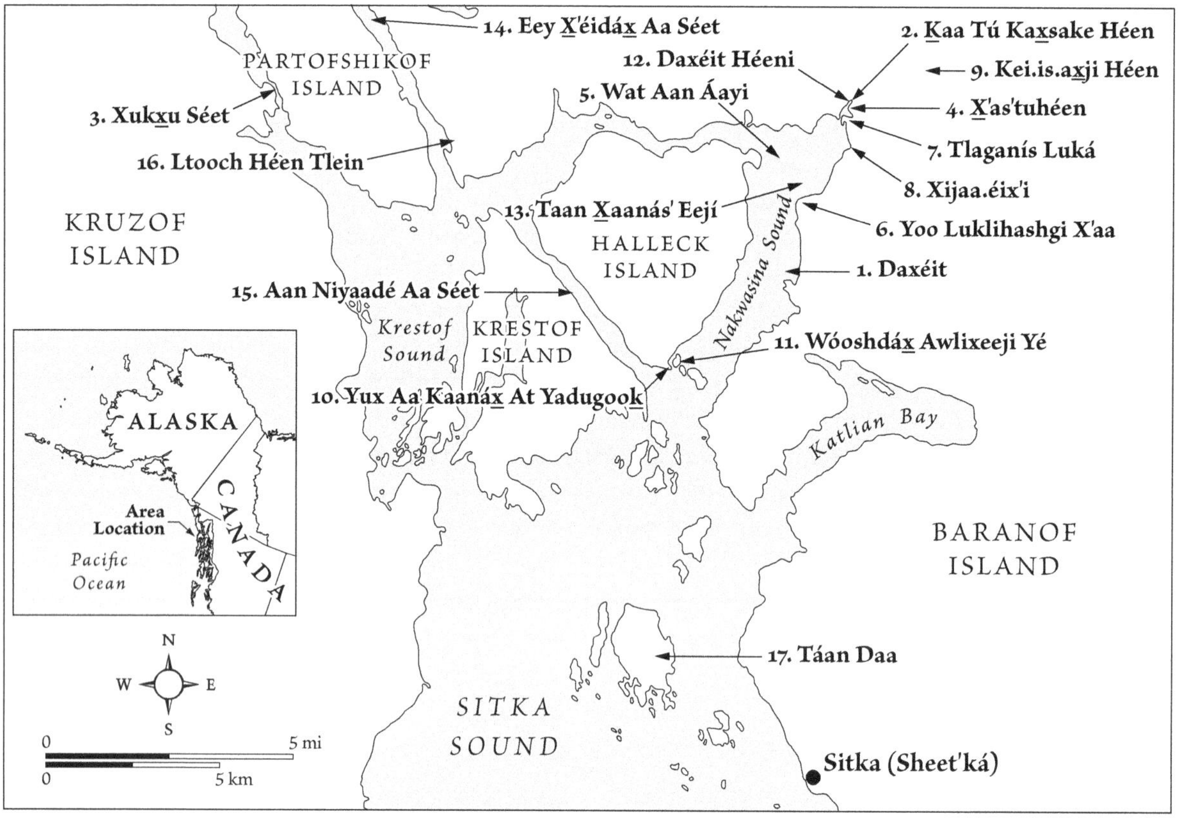

Figure 1. Story map of the Aak'wtaatseen "Salmon Boy" story based on interviews with Sitka elders Herman Kitka Sr. and Ethel Makinen and a version of the tale recorded from Deikeenáak'w in 1904 by John R. Swanton (1909; see also Littlefield et al. 2003). All stories have settings and most Alaska Native stories are localized in named places. These places are often integral to understanding the plot. The Salmon Boy story begins in Nakwasina near Sitka (Daxéit, "Fallen Stunned," #1), an important fishing camp, where a Kiks.ádi boy is taken by the salmon people after he insults them. Subsequent places he visits follow the path of salmon tribe as they journey to the ocean to feed and mature before returning home to spawn. Along the way, we learn something about the way salmon see and experience the world through the names and descriptions of places. For example, the story relates how salmon returning to Nakwasina are buffeted by strong, shifting tides and sometimes scrape against the rocks and become scarred. Herman Kitka identified one place where this occurs as Xukx̲u Séet (Going Dry Strait, #3), a long channel that goes dry at low tide and in which he has seen salmon struggle and sometimes become scarred or trapped. This is followed by another allusion to an unnamed place where salmon went ashore and to them "it appeared like they would throw hot rocks on each other" and "the skin of some of them moved like fish skins being roasted on hot rocks." According to Herman Kitka, this is a reference to the Ltooch Héen Tlein (Big Roasting Creek, #16), another Tlingit fishing camp in Neva Strait where salmon collected and were caught and roasted over a fire on special flat roasting sticks. Nearing Daxéit, the salmon people encounter the herring people at #17, Táan Daa (Jumping Fish Around [Island]), with whom they trade insults and boasts about their relative status as a food source for the people. At the junction of Olga and Neva Strait, according to Herman Kitka, the salmon people divide and tell each other to which stream they will be going. The humpback (pink) salmon say they will be going to X̲'as'tuhéen (Saliva Creek, #4). "That's what the humpy people call it," Herman Kitka explains, because the choicest parts of the spawning rivers are taken by other salmon species, so the "humpies" chose to spawn in the lower reaches of the streams, where the tidal action and foam give the water a saliva-like quality. Finally, Aak'wtaatseen returns to Daxéit where he is landed and recognized by his parents (from a copper necklace he wears) and transformed back to human form. Aak'wtaatseen be-

comes a powerful shaman who educates the people about the salmon and shapes the land in other important ways. The small pond near Daxéit, where Aak'wtaatseen bathes and drums for power, becomes Xijaa.éix'i (Beating Time for Shaman Lagoon, #8); the place where he spears the powerful land otter becomes Yux Aa Kaanáx̱ At Yadugook̲ (The Point It [the Spear] Was Thrown Across, #10); and the place where the he cuts out the otter's tongue and fasts for eight days earns the name Wóoshdáx̱ Awlixeeji Yé (The Place Divided, #11; see Sheet'ká K̲wáan #301 for alternative name and translation). The story gives these places resonance, just as the places animate and make tangible the story. Cartography by Barry Levely with revisions by Michael Travis.

to modern community areas. The term *k̲wáan* derives from the Tlingit verb "to dwell" and refers to the total lands and waters used and controlled by clans inhabiting a particular winter village. Unlike descent-based clans and moieties (the two superlineages which organized clans into Raven and Eagle/Wolf), the k̲wáan is fundamentally a unit of social geography. Accordingly, k̲wáan may be extended to reference communities of persons, or even non-human persons, dwelling beyond the boundaries of Tlingit territory, as in Taagish (Tagish) K̲wáan, a reference to Interior Athabaskans dwelling in the vicinity of Tagish, B.C. Whites often mistakenly assumed that Tlingit k̲wáans had formal governments like those of Western towns and villages, but such governance did not exist among Alaska Natives prior to the development of modern village-based tribes through the Indian Reorganization Act beginning in 1936; rather political authority traditionally was vested in local clans and house groups which owned and managed places (Thornton 2002). Nevertheless, the affinity between traditional k̲wáan territories and modern village and tribal boundaries makes them the most logical unit through which to organize the material.

Ceremonial life. Because named places were foundational to the constitution of subsistence and social organization, they were celebrated in art and ceremonial life. The central symbolic elements of art and ceremony are crests, sacred manifestations of animals, places, and other entities, which are incorporated into artistic designs, regalia, and other cultural forms. Crests, observed de Laguna (1972, 451), "are, from the native point of view, the most important feature of the matrilineal sib or lineage, acquired in the remote past by the ancestors and determining the nature and destiny of their descendants." This combination of heritage and destiny, or *shagóon*, is believed to be embodied in the sacred property of the matrilineage and also in the social group members themselves. Each crest, too, has a story "behind it" that evokes elements of the present landscape in relation to the distant past. When a place is appropriated as a crest, its image serves to link indelibly particular social groups to particular terrains.

Crests are officially "brought out" and sanctified in ritual proceedings, particularly ceremonial parties or potlatches, known in Tlingit as *k̲oo.éex'* (from the verb "to invite"). On such occasions, the stories behind the crests are presented by the hosts and witnessed and validated by the guests. Such investiture empowers crests as sacred property (*at.óow*) and gives them material, social, and spiritual value beyond mere symbols. These values, in turn, are put to a variety of ends, such as to heal grief, build community and solidarity, and even to mediate between time and space. Examples of this kind of mediation are discussed in Dauenhauer and Dauenhauer (1990; see also Thornton 2004a). For instance, in ceremonies in northern Tlingit country, Kaagwaantaan orators still use the phrase *Ch'a tleix' Kax̱'nuwk̲weidí* (We who are still one People of Grouse Fort). Kax'noowú (Female Grouse Fort) refers to the site of the Kaagwaantaan's original house at Ground Hog Bay, among the oldest archaeological sites yielding evidence of human occupation in Southeast Alaska (nearly 10,000 years BP). The phrase is used to achieve at least three objectives: (1) promote solidarity and community among the now dispersed Kax'noowú clans; (2) reiterate inextricable ties to this historic, collective dwelling place; and (3) metaphorically transport listeners to this sacred landscape to be reunited with their ancestors who likewise may be summoned forth by name. In short, Kax'noowú serves as a place where time and space merge and cannot be understood without reference to each other; it is a place that is "brought forth to reconfirm" (*gágiwdul.aat*; cf. Nyman and Leer 1993) *shagóon*, Tlingit geographic, social, and historical being in the world. Unfortunately, studies of Northwest Coast art often focus on the visual aesthetics of design and form in crests and neglect the power of place that underlies them. Looking at crests from the perspective of place opens up new horizons of meaning.

The ceremonial sharing of place is, moreover, a kind of

gift or exchange. It happens not only through art and story but also through song and dance. By sharing their "place intelligence" (Thornton 2004a, 2008) in the context of ritual, Southeast Alaska Natives seek not only to build community, heal, or entertain, but also to make claims about their consubstantial relationships to particular territories. This may even extend to the food that is consumed and the gifts that are given away. When I asked Hoonah (Xunaa) elder Frank White why it is important to have food from Glacier Bay at a memorial party for a Glacier Bay descendant, he responded: "It's hard to explain, but Glacier Bay foods are . . . special. At a party, we like to serve [gull] eggs, salmon, seal, and berries from there not just 'cause they taste the best, but 'cause they're part of who we are. It makes us feel good . . . Even the deceased is fed this food to make him feel good and guide him on his journey . . . The spirits of our ancestors are in Glacier Bay. And when we're there subsisting, we feel them." In presenting and partaking of such gifts of place, hosts renew their organic roots; in bestowing gifts of place, hosts invite guests to share in their experience of place. In return, guests are expected not only to witness and validate hosts' relationships to places, but also to respect them. It was respect that Kaadashaan, the great Tlingit leader, sought when he told Governor Brady at the "canoe rocks" meeting of 1898: "Ever since I was a boy I have heard the names of different points, bays, islands, mountains, places where [we] get herring, [hunt,] and make camps, that is why I think this country belongs to us" (in Hinckley 1970, 270). Unfortunately, Kaadashaan did not get much respect from Brady. Perhaps in a Tlingit ceremonial context, he could have illustrated more fully the many ways that his people were connected to the named sites he mentions.

The "Three Rs" of Native Place Names

Place names are truly boxes of daylight. As such, they can shed immeasurable light on the land, culture, and identity of Southeast Alaska's indigenous peoples. The chapters that follow are an attempt to bring forth some of this light.

While mapping, transcribing, and interpreting place names remain important and fundamental tasks, it is clear that from an anthropological standpoint there are additional issues to consider about the role of place and place naming among indigenous peoples. Particularly among Native Americans, concepts of place and being are intimately linked. These links are expressed in both the patterns of naming and the practical deployment of place names in the context of social and ceremonial life. Thus, place names are not simply linguistic artifacts on the landscape, but basic cultural resources. As such, the conservation of place names, along with physical sites they reference, should be a vital component of land and resource management regimes, and not simply the object of intellectual inquiry. This entails defining a process that involves Native Americans in researching, conserving, interpreting, representing, and naming their own geographies, a process that acknowledges what might be termed the "three Rs" of place.

The first of these is *resilience*. As this book demonstrates, despite the erosion of Native languages in Alaska, place names have shown a remarkable resilience, with a considerable number (Ketchikan, Sitka, Klukwan, etc.) even crossing over into the English geographic nomenclature. Why have indigenous names proven so durable? As suggested above, there are many reasons, from their remarkable descriptive force in capturing the essences of places to the fact they are intimately intermeshed with other cultural institutions that have proven equally resilient, such as subsistence and ceremonial lifeways. It follows from this that threats to these institutions, like threats to the environment itself, will undermine the resilience of Tlingit place names. This we should avoid.

The second "R" is *resonance*. By resonance I mean the intensification and prolongation of meanings that arise from place names. Resonance is contingent upon the salient *interanimation*, as Basso terms it, between geography, culture, and individual experience. In canonical form, place names may signal a whole range of meanings beyond mere geography, including important historical, moral, and sociological messages. In some cases, a single name can stand for a story itself. But this is true only for those who know the land, as elder Fred Friday put it, "so much that we were familiar with every little place" including stories behind the names. Unfortunately, in cases where language and land use patterns have become severely disrupted or threatened, these connections tend to become alienated, abstracted, or abrogated altogether. As place names become decoupled from a story, the story itself may become generalized beyond a certain geographic setting and the links between plot and place may be lost. To a certain extent this has happened to the Aak'wtaatseen story that Swanton recorded from Deikeenáak'w a century ago, especially the shamanic landscape nomenclature. Yet other names continue to have resonance, because people still know them intimately through direct experience and through living cultural institutions (naming, *at.óow*, etc.) that continue to animate them. This we should promote.

Finally, the third "R" is *respect*. Above all, the aim of this book is to promote respect for Native names on the land. Respect not only for their resilience and resonance but for all of their significations — their meanings. Native place names have much to teach us about the landscapes we inhabit, but we must have the patience to unpack their meanings and the willingness to understand the cultural perspectives and natural phenomena that inform them. This is the heart of place-based education, the only kind of education Alaska Natives ever had until little more than a century ago. And for the rich light place sheds, it is the kind of education many still crave, beyond the demands of the dominant society and its schools. This we should remember.

Acknowledgements

This project was, in reality, a dozen smaller projects carried out at the community level in conjunction with Southeast Alaska Native tribal governments. Individual acknowledgements of the many great people and organizations involved are presented at the beginning of each community chapter. For the publication, I am deeply indebted to Michael Travis of Juneau, who not only laid out the entire book but also served effectively as a publisher's editor on matters of style and substance, and also to Ailsa Allen, University of Oxford School of Geography and the Environment, who applied her cartographic skills to improve the final maps immensely. In addition to these acknowledgements, the editor would also like to extend special thanks to two individuals and their respective organizations that helped shape the overall project and this book in fundamental ways: Harold Martin, president of the Southeast Native Subsistence Commission (SENSC), and Rosita Worl, president of Sealaska Heritage Institute. Harold, himself a Tlingit speaker and expert on the Native geography of the Kake community area, was instrumental in guiding the project through all stages: from conceptualization, to funding, to tribal collaborations, to project administration, and dissemination of the results. He took an active role in the research process and made sure the results were personally delivered to the tribes. Upon his retirement from the Central Council of Tlingit and Haida Indian Tribes of Alaska, Harold continued to devote time to the project, working with myself and Gordon Jackson to steer it to completion. Harold has taught me a great deal not only about Tlingit senses of place but about how to follow respectful protocols in conducting research. Rosita, descended from Klukwan and a leading advocate for Southeast Native land and property rights for four decades, was instrumental in seeing that the results of the SENSC project were brought together in a single publication that would serve not only communities but regional and scholarly interests in protecting natural and cultural resources on Native lands. Indeed this has been a key mission of the Sealaska Heritage Institute under her leadership. Without her support and the backing of Sealaska, this publication may never have come to fruition. Finally, I would like to thank the National Park Service Heritage Grant program for funding three separate grants to pursue the place names research between 1994 and 2000.

Although the Southeast Alaska Native Place Names Project is now completed, the effort to document and reincorporate Native place names into contemporary life continues. New names are being generated to mark new places, and old names and their cultural associations are still being unpacked, contemplated and lived. Hopefully, some of place names that we recorded as "uncertain" or only in documentary form (often with peculiar spellings) may yet be re-elicited and reconfirmed by living elders. This is exciting, but also humbling. It means that *Haa Léelk'w Hás Aaní Saax'ú, Our Grandparents' Names on the Land* will have to be supplemented and revised to incorporate new names and new information from new grandparents pertaining to previously-documented names.

But this is as it should be with a *living* indigenous geography. I hope that Sealaska Heritage Institute, working in conjunction with local tribes, clans, and other entities, can facilitate this process, perhaps taking advantage of the multimedia and linking capacities of present technologies to help reorient us to the multidimensional ties that Natives of Southeast Alaska have to their named places.

Haa Léelk'w Hás Aaní Saax'ú

Our Grandparents' Names on the Land

1. *Yaakwdáat K̲wáan, G̲alyáx̲ K̲wáan, and G̲unaax̲oo K̲wáan*

Yakutat territory today is broadly defined as the coastal forelands, waters, and select mountains between Cape Suckling and Lituya Bay. Historically, this large tract encompassed separate but related groups of people centered in three k̲wáan regions: Yaakwdáat (the Native name for Yakutat), G̲alyáx̲ (the Native name for Kaliakh River) and G̲unaax̲oo (the Native name for the Dry Bay area). The matrilineal clans originally inhabiting each k̲wáan are currently centered in Yakutat and, to a lesser extent, in surrounding communities such as Cordova and Hoonah.

As the vanguard of a Tlingit culture that continued expanding northward until the nineteenth century, Yakutat territory was a cultural mixing zone. Some investigators (de Laguna 1972; Krauss 1982) argue that the Tlingit presence north of Yakutat Bay is comparatively recent, perhaps within the last several centuries. This evidence is based primarily on oral traditions and the distribution of Native place names. Archeological evidence is scant due to the dynamic glacial and seismic activities occurring in the region, which destroy material that could potentially speak to earlier origins of Tlingit habitation. Studies of cultural and human remains recently exposed by melting glacial ice, including DNA, cloth, and digestive samples taken from Kwädy Dän Ts'ínchi (Southern Tutchone for "Long Ago Person Found"), the 550–660-year-old aboriginal man unearthed in 1999 in the Interior ice fields east of Yakutat, suggest a continuity of human habitation in this region over many hundreds of years, if not millennia.

Three cultural groups dominated the area between Lituya Bay and Copper River prior to contact: Tlingit, Eyak, and Chugach Eskimo. The Eyak at one time controlled large areas around Yakutat but were increasingly encroached upon by Tlingits moving up from the southeast. Tlingit culture largely subsumed Eyak culture at Yakutat Bay, but there is a transition zone between Yakutat and Cape Suckling. Thus, while both Eyak and Tlingit place names are present in Yakutat, as one moves northwest up the coast, Eyak place names increasingly predominate. In some cases, Tlingits appear to have adopted the Eyak or Chugach names for features of the landscape rather than (or in addition to) applying a new Tlingit name. As a result, some places have more than one Native name and sometimes as many as four (Tlingit, Eyak, Chugach, and Ahtna, not to mention English and Russian), as Tebenkov observed (Davidson 1901b, 44; de Laguna 1972). Tlingitization of other indigenous place names and cultural elements has also taken place. Sorting this out can be difficult, but it also contributes to the richness of the cultural landscapes. Indeed, with its intersection of cultures, unique ecology, world's tallest coastal mountains, Interior trade routes, and dynamic glacial and seismic forces, Yakutat territory is one of the most rugged, diverse, and bountiful landscapes in North America.

We documented more than three hundred place names in this region. Our project was carried out in conjunction with the Yakutat Tlingit Tribe. Key contributors included: Elaine Abraham, Bert Adams, Lorraine Adams, Nora Marks Dauenhauer, Sally Edwards, Sig Edwards, Lena Farkus, Emma Marks, George Ramos Sr., Judith Ramos, Ben Valle, Fred White, and many others who corroborated names, attended meetings, and contributed to the project in a variety of ways. Our task was aided by the pioneering work of Frederica de Laguna, whose *Under Mount Saint Elias* references hundreds of named sites, and the research of George Emmons, Walter Goldschmidt and Theodore Haas, John Harrington, George Johnson, Michael Krauss, Ronald Olson, Louis Shotridge, John Swanton, and others who previously documented indigenous place names. Thomas Thornton coordinated the first phase of Southeast Native Subsistence Commission (SENSC) project fieldwork and mapping with support from Bert Adams and Nellie Vale of Yakutat Tlingit Tribe and Wayne Howell and Maryann Porter of the National Park Service. The editor also would like to thank Jeff Leer, Judith Ramos, Fred White, John Marks, and Hans Chester for their review and input at different stages of the research.

G̲alyáx̲ K̲wáan

G̲alyáx̲ K̲wáan in the north extended from Cape Suckling to Controller Bay, and took its name from the Kaliakh (G̲alyáx̲) River (Emmons n.d.; de Laguna 1972, 98). G̲alyáx̲ people were originally Eyak speakers, but as a result of intermarriage and the expansion of Tlingit culture, most residing in the area spoke both languages well into the twentieth century (de Laguna 1972, 99). Two contemporary Tlingit matrilineal clans identify with places within this region, the Kwáashk'i K̲wáan and the G̲alyáx̲-Kaagwaantaan. The coastline is marked by some of the most rugged features in Tlingit country, including the largest glacier, Bering Glacier, and the highest coastal mountains. This dramatic landscape, with its exposure to the powerful Gulf of Alaska (Yéil T'ooch', "Black Raven," #34), has earned the area the nickname "The Lost Coast." Despite the forbidding terrain, there were numerous habitation sites along the coastline. Descendants of these aboriginal settlements have moved to modern villages at Yakutat, Cordova, and elsewhere, but many still use the area for fish and wildlife harvesting. Connections to these lands remain strong and are celebrated in expressive cultural forms such as stories, songs, and regalia.

Important places within the area included the following sites, moving from southeast to northwest:

Icy Bay (Was'ei Yík, "Inside of Was'ei," or Yas'ei Yík, "Inside of Yas'ei" [Yahtse River], #45). This important refuge and settlement lay in the shadow of Mount Saint Elias (Was'ei Tashaa, "Mountain Inland of Was'ei," #47), and the mountain is named for it. The name for Icy Bay itself, according to de Laguna (1972, 95), may derive from the toponym for Yahtse River, (Yas'ei* Héen, "Swampy* Creek," #48), which may reference the glacial clay (*s'é*) produced by the active glaciers at the head of this watershed. George Ramos (interview) notes that at one time glaciers extended out into the Gulf of Alaska and there are stories of a low island called Grass Island near the mouth of the bay, where hunters used to rest and make camp. This bay was prized especially for its concentrations of mountain goat and seal. In the spring, mountain goats would present themselves on the cliffs above the northwest shore of the bay in such a way that, when shot, they tumbled right down to the water for easy retrieval. Thousands of seals would gather to haul out on the ice, feed, and in springtime, bear their young. Sea-otter hunting in the area was lucrative enough during the Russian fur trade era to attract Tsimshians all the way from Nass River to establish a camp at Mud Bay or Riou Bay. Berries and other plants were also gathered in the meadows below the Chaix Hills, and seagull eggs were abundant on the low island above Riou Bay known as K'wát' X'áat'i (Bird Egg Island, #46.1) in Tlingit (de Laguna 1972, 95–96).

Icy Bay also holds special significance for the Kwáashk'i K̲wáan. Their ancestors, the Gineix̲ K̲wáan (a name derived from a tributary to the Copper River called Gineix̲, possibly the Bremner or Little Bremner rivers), settled just west of Icy Bay at Was'ei Dak, where they made a camp out of bark, named Teey Aaní* (Yellow Cedar Bark Town, #39) which was overrun by a glacier (Judy Ramos, pers. comm.). As a consequence they continued their southeasterly migration to Icy Bay, where they met and intermarried with the G̲alyáx̲-Kaagwaantaan, who were hunting seal in the bay. Mount Saint Elias (Was'ei Tashaa, #47), the tallest mountain on the coast, served as a beacon for seafaring mariners and for land travelers traversing the Bering and Tana glaciers between the Interior and the coast. The Kwáashk'i K̲wáan hold Mount Saint Elias as a sacred crest and symbolize it on *at.óow*, such as ceremonial regalia (see de Laguna 1972, pl. 152).

Cape Yakataga (Tayeesk', "Little Adze," #33) and Cape Suckling.* This cape, named for its adze-like shape, was part of the G̲alyáx̲-Kaagwaantaan territory. It was transformed by Raven, who made a "canoe trail" (Yakwdeiyí, #35) there after quarreling with his wife: "She threw his adze ashore to make the point, and he threw her sewing basket overboard. It is now a rock full of clams and sea urchins, and called [Yéil Naasa.áayi]" (de Laguna 1972, 100; #36).

Yakataga was also the site of a large village. To the west, the cape gives way to the Duktoth River (Dak̲táal,* #31), an important travel and trade corridor to the Interior, and a salmon fishery at the mouth of which were smokehouses (Goldschmidt and Haas 1998). To the east lies the White River (G̣ùtš̓áx̣ʷ,* "Muddy Water," #37), which served as a boundary between the clan territories. Oral history provides clues as to the natural history of the region. G̲alyáx̲-Kaagwaantaan historical narratives refer to a shipwreck in this vicinity of the cape. Based on clues from this story as well as another legend about offshore halibut banks where Raven tricked Bear into killing himself, de Laguna (1972, 99–100) hypothesized that this may be the site of the now-submerged Pamplona Searidge.

Kaliakh River (G̲alyáx̲, #29). In addition to taking their name from this place, the G̲alyáx̲-Kaagwaantaan had a major village on the river's banks. The area was used for hunting, fishing, trapping, and gathering shellfish and seaweed (Goldschmidt and Haas 1998). Today, the Tsiu-Kaliakh watershed supports a lucrative commercial and recreational salmon fishery. Many of the commercial fishing permit holders come from Yakutat and Cordova, maintain camps on the Tsiu, and engage in subsistence fishing and hunting activities in conjunction with their participation in the commercial fishery.

Katalla (*Ḵaataanáa, #5*). Lying just below Eeḵ Héeni, or Copper River (named for its famous native copper; #9), Katalla is the northernmost settlement of the Tlingit. The Galyáx-Kaagwaantaan, Jishḵweidí, and Ḵaanax.ádi clans all had houses there at one time, before the inhabitants moved to Yakutat and Cordova (de Laguna 1972, 104). Just below Katalla, at the mouth of the Bering River in Controller Bay, was another important village, known as Jilḵáat (Cache, #19) where people traditionally fished and smoked salmon and harvested bear, fox, otter, king salmon, and berries (Goldschmidt and Haas 1998).

The area between Cape Suckling and Katalla is another place where Raven was active. Raven stories explain the formation of the Controller Bay area. For example, Kayak Island (Yáay Ká, "On the Humpback Whale," #17) is a whale Raven was hunting, Wingham Island (#13) is Raven's kayak, Okalee Spit (#18) is Raven's harpoon line, and so on. The cave at Cape Suckling is Yéil Hít (Raven's House, #24.1). A large sea cave with rock crystals is here. Susie Abraham states that it was a refuge for women and children while the men were out hunting (Judy Ramos, pers. comm.).

According to de Laguna (1972, 101), "On the cliffs at Cape Suckling are said to be faces some turned sidewise, and also arms and legs. These were made by Raven, who 'did a lot of funny things around here shaping the land,' it is said." Additional Eyak, Tlingitized Eyak, and Chugach terms in this region also are referenced in de Laguna (1972).

Mount Saint Elias is called Was'ei Tashaa (Mountain Inland of Was'ei [Icy Bay], #47), and serves as a landmark and cultural crest for Yakutat Tlingits. It is also known simply as Shaa Tlein (Big Mountain). Photo by Tom Thornton.

Yaakwdáat Ḵwáan (also known as Laaxaayíx Ḵwáan) embraces the area roughly from Malaspina Glacier above Yakutat Bay to the Akwe River in Dry Bay.

Yakutat Bay (Laaxaayík "Inside Laaxaa [from Eyak, 'Near the Glacier']," #61). The lands and waters within Yakutat Bay, especially the eastern shores and islands, were among the most important habitation and resource use areas within Yaakwdáat Ḵwáan. Not surprisingly, it is here that we find the highest density of Native place names, most of which were recorded by Harrington (n.d.) and de Laguna (1972, 58ff.). The present city of Yakutat (Yaakwdáat, "Canoe Rebounded," #62) is located at Monti Bay and incorporates the traditional Native village called Ḵaa Gatsx'áak Aan (Ḵaa Gatsx'áak [#86] Town, #96). Another permanent settlement was located at Port Mulgrave on the southwest end of Khantaak Island. East of Khantaak Island is an important travel route, settlement, and resource harvest area known as Canoe Pass (Dákde Séet, "Channel on the Way to Place Behind," #104). At one time, there was a village here spanning both sides of the channel that was "so huge that ravens trying to fly overhead would be overcome by smoke from the houses" (de Laguna 1972, 64; Yéil Áa Daak Wudzigidi Yé, "Place Where Raven Fell Down," #177). Canoe Pass remains an important travel route and resource harvest area for Yakutat residents.

Subsistence camps and settlements were located at accessible sites with significant patches of fish and wildlife resources, including the Yakutat Islands, Monti Bay (Juwaaník Tá, "Head of Juwaaník,"* #83), Ankau Lagoon (Yaakwdáat Yík, "Canoe Jumps Inside," #74), Redfield Cove (Àtl'at,* from Eyak for "Head of the River," #158), Humpback Salmon Creek (Kwáashk' [Eyak] [Héeni], literally "Humpback Salmon [Creek]," #169), Eleanor Cove / Chicago Harbor (Aasyík Daa, "Around the Area with Trees inside It," #207), Knight Island (Ganawás [Eyak], "Water Extends in an Indefinite Shape," #168; an early village site), and at Disenchantment Bay in the vicinity of Point Latouche (Aanaadi.áak [Eyak], "In Front of the Stone Platform,"* #138). With its glacier-fed, ice-filled waters, Disenchantment Bay was famous as a harbor-seal haulout and rookery. Natives from as far away as Sheet'ká (Sitka) and Jilḵáat (Chilkat) ḵwáans came here to obtain seal oil and other products through trade and kin networks (Grinnell 1901, 158–65; Krause 1956). There were at least four seal-hunting camps between Point Latouche (#138) and Haenke Island and additional hunting camps in Russell and Nunatak fiords, where mountain goat and other resources were prevalent in addition to seal. Yakutat Natives still use these camps as a base for harvesting seal in Disenchantment Bay and seagull eggs on Haenke Island (K'wát' X'áat'i, #181). More detailed information about land and resource use at specific sites in Yakutat Bay was recorded by Goldschmidt and Haas (1998), de Laguna (1972), and Mills and Firman (1986).

Yakutat Forelands. The Yakutat Forelands extend southeast of the bay and are fed by numerous streams where salmon and other resources were harvested from seasonal camps and settlements. These waterways include the Ankau Lagoon system, Lost River (Éix' Yík, #150), Situk River (S'itáḵ, #178), Ahrnklin River (Aan Tlein Héen, #232), Dangerous River (Kulijigi Héen, #237), and the Italio River (Ḵeilxwáa, #243). The lands below Lost River were largely controlled by the Teiḵweidí (brown bear) clan, specifically the Drum House group. The Situk system was renowned for its extraordinarily productive sockeye, king, and coho salmon runs and also for its spring supply of steelhead (*aashát*) and eulachon (*saak*). The uplands of these river systems were prime hunting, trapping, and berrying grounds. Today, the Situk remains the main source of Yakutat residents' subsistence salmon. Among the earliest settlement sites in the Situk watershed is the Lost River settlement, Diyaaguna.éit (#163), which is estimated to be eight hundred to fifteen hundred years old (Davis 1996).

The deep ties of the Yakutat Tlingit to Yakutat Bay and the Yakutat Forelands are manifest in the numerous legends and stories embedded in features of the landscape, many of which were recorded by de Laguna. There are stories not only of Raven's activities but of fights with the "Aleuts" (Chugach) to protect their homeland, and taboos that were violated causing the landscape to change. Humpback Salmon Creek holds special significance for the Kwáashk'i Ḵwáan who were given their name from this place after receiving title to the stream from its original owners. Similarly, as de Laguna (1972, 80) attests, Ahrnklin country is rife with historic and symbolic associations for the Drum House Teiḵweidí:

> Not only was it purchased because the people from Dry Bay found it so beautiful, but later, it was a hunter from 'Antłen [Aan Tlein, "Big Village"] village who encountered a wounded Golden Eagle in the mountains, learned its song … and from it obtained [for] the Drum House people

> the right to use the Golden Eagle as a crest. On the river, half a century ago, the older brother of one of my informants was drowned, but because the Wolf was a Teqwedi [Teik̲weidí] crest, the wolves guarded his body. This story, as well as the Teqwedi [Teik̲weidí] claims to the river, are symbolized in a magnificent beaded blanket (pl. 151). Lastly, a [potlatch?] song composed by Olaf Abraham . . . interprets the mountains at the head of the Ahrnklin River as symbolic of all the ancestors of the lineage.

The landscape is thus part of their *at.óow* and *shagóon.*

G̲unaax̲oo K̲wáan

The third k̲wáan within the Yakutat territory is G̲unaax̲oo K̲wáan, centered in Dry Bay. Dry Bay is the outlet of the Alsek River (Aalséix̲, #273), an important migration and trade route to the Interior. Indeed, the Tlingit name for the k̲wáan means "Among the Interior Natives (Athabaskans)," signifying the nearby presence of the southern Yukon Athabaskans and the importance of the area as a trade nexus. Annie Ned, a Southern Tutchone (G̲unanaa), relates how the groups first made contact at Noogaayík* (not mapped), a subsistence camp on Tatshenshini River in southern Yukon:

> At Noogaayík, Tlingit people first saw chips coming down from upriver. People making rafts, I guess, and the chips floated down.
>
> "Where did this one come from?" they asked. So that time Coast Indians [went in] wintertime to Dalton Post. That's the way they met these Yukon Indians. Yukon people are hunting, and they've got nice skin clothes — Oh, gee, porcupine quills, moose skins, moccasins! Everything nice.
>
> Coast Indians saw those clothes and they wanted them! . . . Coast Indians traded them knives, axes, and they got clothes, babiche, fish skin from the Yukon. (Cruikshank 1990b, 280)

According to de Laguna (1972, 82), this "territory, particularly the Akwe [Aakwéi] River region was claimed by the Athabaskan Raven Lukaax̲.ádi, with whom the Tlingit Raven L'uknax̲.ádi mingled and came to dominate." With them lived other Raven groups, including the X'at'ka.aayí, a branch of the L'uknax̲.ádi that moved to Lituya Bay and later to Sheet'ká, who take their name from an island at the mouth of the Alsek River. The Jilk̲áat Shangukeidí, Sheet'ká Kaagwaantaan, and Teik̲weidí of the Eagle/Wolf moiety also established houses at Dry Bay. These groups are now localized at Yakutat and other communities, and there are no longer permanent settlements at Dry Bay, though seasonal camps are maintained by hunters and fishers. Although Dry Bay is some sixty miles from Yakutat Bay, with no sheltered bays in between, it was accessible from Yaakwdáat via an intertidal canoe "trail" beginning at Ankau Lagoon and wending through sloughs, creeks, and coastal waterways protected from the surf by sandbars that formed at the mouths of the major rivers (see de Laguna 1972, 82–83). This canoe trail includes many portages and is why people of Dry Bay are known as "people who stick their head into canoes" (George Ramos, pers. comm.).

Dry Bay (*G̲unaax̲oo,* #255). Dry Bay is a landscape of profound mythological, historical, and contemporary significance. Raven helped shape this land, which became a great mixing zone for peoples of the coast and interior. Major salmon runs in the Cannery Creek (Sduheenák'w, #251), Muddy Creek (K'aagán Héeni, #253), Akwe (#244), Tanis-Ustay (#254, 248), Alsek (#273), East Alsek (#277), and Doame (#288) rivers supported Native settlements at these places, including the famous village at Gus'eix̲ (#250; see "The Lost Village of Gus'eix̲" below). In the springtime, Dry Bay erupts with eulachon, attracting large numbers of seal and sea lion which prey on them. The area was also rich with terrestrial wildlife, especially mountain goat (and, more recently, moose), brown and black bear, furbearers (marten, wolf, wolverine, fox, and land otter), and berries and other plants (de Laguna 1972, 85; Goldschmidt and Haas 1998). Today, the area supports a healthy commercial salmon fishery, though permits are limited and access to the fishery has been tightly controlled by the state. A protracted lawsuit pitted Native "surf" fisherman, who fish the "intertidal trail" leading to Dry Bay, against the State of Alaska and those largely non-Native fishers who hold state net permits inside the bay, over access to these stocks (Gmelch 1990).

Cape Fairweather (*Laak̲'ásgi X'aayí, "Green Seaweed Point,"* #297). Below the Deception Hills, south of Dry Bay, lies Cape Fairweather, an important landmark and stopping place between Dry Bay and Lituya Bay, the southern boundary of the G̲unaax̲oo K̲wáan and of the Yakutat region. Like Cape Yakataga, Cape Fairweather provides shelter from the southeasterly winds, and small boats can land there by following "Raven's Canoe Trail" (Yéil Yakwdeiyí, #298) which, like the landing at Yakataga, was said to be fashioned by the trickster himself.

Lituya Bay (Ltu.áa, "Lake inside the Point [nostril]," #309). Lituya Bay was an important settlement for the L'uknax̱.ádi, T'aḵdeintaan, and X'at'ka.aayí, the latter two being offshoots of the original L'uknax̱.ádi owners of the bay (de Laguna 1972, 91). The Ḵoosk'eidí clan also report-

edly had a village in this vicinity which Emmons (n.d.) recorded as "Scar-ta-heen" and placed near Sea Otter Creek, though de Laguna's (1972, 91) informants put it further south. The descendants of these groups are now localized in other communities, especially Yakutat (largely L'uknax̱.ádi) and Hoonah (largely T'aḵdeintaan), and thus the bay is used by both communities. When Yakutat proposed to extend its city borough south to Cape Spencer in the early 1990s, Hoonah, then led by a T'aḵdeintaan mayor, objected, and leaders of two Native communities agreed to draw the boundary through the middle of Lituya Bay, in accordance with the Tlingit territoriality.

Like Dry Bay, the Cape Fairweather – Lituya Bay region was rich in fish, wildlife, and plant resources. Especially important were the high concentrations of sea mammals found in this vicinity, as attested by Hoonah (Xunaa) elders in the land claims investigations of Goldschmidt and Haas (1998, 56):

> The Hoonah people went up the coast as far as Yakwdeiyitá [#298.1], a place near Dry Bay [Cape Fairweather]. I have gone up there and shot seal. This place is claimed by the T'aḵdeintaan, but they will let all the people hunt there … Lituya Bay was a place with many camp houses. It was one of the main places they hunted sea otter.

The narrow entrance into Lituya Bay generates strong tidal rips which have claimed the lives of Natives and non-Natives alike (see La Pérouse 1799; Emmons 1911, 25; de Laguna 1972, 92–95). These conditions, combined with the history of glacial and seismic events (including glacial advances and major earthquakes causing landslides and tsunamis that destroyed Native settlements) which have rocked the bay, have made it the subject of much lore. The eighteenth-century explorer, La Pérouse (1799, 1:390) observed that the Tlingit paddlers only approached the bay during slack tide, and upon entering the passage, the leader "arose, stretched out his arms toward the sun, to which he appeared to address a prayer, while [the rest] paddled away with all their strength." Landmarks, including a rock at the entrance called Taan Teiyí (Sea Lion Rock, #306), were used to align a course through the perilous passage known as Tuwool Séet (Hole Strait, #305.1), the name being applied, according to Herman Kitka Sr., not for its narrowness but for the holes that appeared in the crests of the waves during certain phases of the tide. Below these waters dwells Ḵáa Ltu.áa (Man of Lituya Bay), who, according to Emmons (1911, 295),

---

Places Tell the Story of the World around Us

Tlingits believed everything in the world had a spirit (*yéik*) — the mountains, the water, the sky, glaciers, and even certain rocks had a spirit called *té ḵwaaní*. Many landmarks in the Dry Bay area are associated with Raven. Here Raven opened the Box of Daylight; he pulled ashore a house or "ark" (canoe) filled with animals [#270]; Bear Island is the whale that Raven flew out of [#271]; here Raven tricked the king salmon into coming ashore; and Raven threw away his wife's sewing basket and a big king salmon stomach. Art on blankets, house screens, and dance staffs, as well as other *at.óow* commemorate Raven's and other mythological beings' activities on the land.

— *Judith Ramos*

This Shangukeidí house screen represents the Thunderbirds, clouds, a storm, thunder, and lightning and the little boy who was adopted by the Thunderbirds on the Alsek River after he was accidentally left behind by his family. Photo courtesy of Judith Ramos.

> resents any approach to his domain, and all of those whom he destroys become his slaves, and take the form of bears, and from their watch towers on the lofty mountains of the Mt. Fairweather [Tsalxaan, #308] range, they herald the approach of canoes, and with their master grasp the surface water and shake it as if it were a sheet, causing tidal waves to rise and engulf the unwary.

This legend is recorded in a ceremonial wooden pipe obtained by Emmons from a Hoonah T'akdeintaan leader who claimed the bay as his sea-otter hunting ground. Káa Ltu.áa is represented by a frog-like figure who, with his bear slaves, holds the entrance to Lituya Bay, "and the two brass-covered ridges are the tidal waves they have raised, underneath which, cut out of brass, is a canoe with two occupants, that has been engulfed" (1911, 295). Similarly, the descendants of the L'uknax.ádi group who lost their lives in a canoe wreck at Taan Teiyí claim this place as a crest and use a representation of the rock on ceremonial robes and as a face painting for ritual occasions (de Laguna 1972, 94).

Perhaps more than anywhere in Tlingit country, the form and content of the Dry Bay–Cape Fairweather landscape is tied to Raven's doings. Dry Bay is one place (Nass River being another) where Raven opened the Box of Daylight, which "so frightened the people that they ran away and turned into various sea and land animals according to the furs they were wearing" (de Laguna 1972, 84); even the rocks tried to run away (George Ramos, interview; see also "Places Tell the Story of the World around Us" box). Bear Island (Yáay X'áat'i, #271), known today for its high concentrations of bears, has the appearance of a beached whale because it "is in fact the Whale down whose blowhole Raven flew, and which he caused to wash ashore at Dry Bay" after first creating "a fine sandy beach"—the Alsek delta—on which to strand him (de Laguna 1972, 84). Here Tlingit ancestors butchered the humpback whale at Yáay Taayí (Whale Fat, #261) but were outwitted by Raven and thus received none of the blubber. A moral lesson is also inscribed here in the form of five rocks off Bear Island, representing an adolescent girl, her two brothers, and their two dogs. All were turned to stone because the girl violated her puberty rites by looking at the boys. This event is also commemorated in a carved ceremonial hat possessed by the L'uknax.ádi (de Laguna 1972, 84). Other sites farther upriver signify more of Raven's exploits. Likewise, important events in the origin of Athabaskan-Tlingit contacts are embodied in the narrative concerning the travels of Kaakeix'wtí, who killed his sleep in the form of bird and then, unable to rest, ventured north until he made contact with the Athabaskans at Alsek and Copper rivers with whom he exchanged knowledge and goods and intermarried, cementing ties between the interior and coastal peoples of the region (Swanton 1909, tales 32 and 104; Hall 1962; de Laguna 1972, 270–72; Thornton 1997b).

Final Thoughts

The Yakutat area place names project reveals how Tlingits expanded into this country, mixed with other cultures, and produced a richly textured cultural landscape as resonant and dynamic as the geophysical forces that shaped it.

Today, the Yakutat Tlingit Tribe is using the results of the place names project to maintain tribe members' ties to the land through education, language and culture camps, and appropriate management of local, natural, and cultural resources that are defined by named sites.

The Lost Village of Gus'eix̱

Bertrand J. Adams Sr. (Kadashan) is a L'uknax̱.ádi Tlingit leader from Yakutat with ties to named sites in Dry Bay (Gunaax̱oo). He wrote this after participating in a 1996 field trip to locate the historic village of Gus'eix̱ (#250) on Akwe River. This investigation, supported by the National Park Service and the U.S. Forest Service, was a logical sequel to the place names project, which had identified numerous historic sites.

"It's the largest village ever in the Dry Bay area," Grandma Minnie said. "It's a L'uknax̱.ádi village. That's what you are — a L'uknax̱.ádi. The last time I saw the village was forty years ago." She described the tribal houses as if she remembered her hindmost visions of them only yesterday. "Far Out House, that's the one Yéil (Raven) pulled in from the ocean. That's why it got that name — Daginaa Hít. When a house gets too small another one is built and it gets new name. That's how Shaa Hít (Mountain House), Taan Hít (Sea Lion House), Yáay Hít (Whale House), Ta Hít (Sleep Man's House) and X̱íxch'i Hít (Frog House), Eech Hít (Boulder/Reef House) got built."

In 1950 my dad made a gallant decision to move his commercial fishing venture from the Alsek River to the Akwe River thirteen miles, as Yéil would fly, from Dry Bay toward Yakutat. When Grandma Minnie learned we were making the move, she told us about Gus'eix̱. I was thirteen years old then, and my brother, Walt, three years behind me.

The Akwe River originates from Akwe Lake near the mountains and winds its way toward the Pacific Ocean. However, something very irregular happens when it reaches about two miles from the ocean: it turns to the left and then sweeps into a right turn and then makes a beeline for about eight miles before it spills its tea-colored water into the ocean. About five miles from the mouth was a clearing we called the sand dunes, but in Tlingit history and myth, this is where Yéil pulled Daginaa Hít from the ocean; the dunes are his footprints and the place is called Yeil ax̱ yaa wu gudi ye [Yéil Áx̱ Daaḵ Uwanugu Yé, #260].

Going the other way, about parallel from the lower part of the river and a mile and a half across the foot prints of Yéil, the river takes a right turn toward the mountains. Then it makes a sharp turn left and another right to where it winds and turns to its original source. It is somewhat below the turn that Grandma Minnie pointed on a map where she said Gus'eix̱ was located.

In time, we learned the best time to look for the site was early spring or late fall when the vegetation wasn't so thick. Oftentimes our father would take us up the river; while he and my brother fished for cutthroat trout I would dash up and down the river searching for the tribal houses. When Grandma Minnie saw it last, she said the houses had moss growing on the logs. I really didn't know what to look for in those days; for the sixteen years I fished on the Akwe, we were never successful at finding the location. I fished my last year on the river in 1966, chancing my future to greener pastures in favor of a permanent paycheck and pursuing an education.

When I left the Akwe, I gave up any hope of ever finding Gus'eix̱. Yet as I grew older there were times that my soul was forlornly stirred at the thought of never finding the site. Here lay hidden in this rain forest were my heritage, my history, my identity.

Gunaax̱oo is an Athabaskan name and the name is derived from Gunanaa. The Gunanaa traveled from the Interior on the Alsek River to Gunaax̱oo to fish for the salmon and hunt seal during the spring hunts and summer salmon runs. We are talking about a long time ago, probably back into the millennia. They were never permanent settlers, so when the L'uknax̱.ádi settled in Gunaax̱oo, they eventually became the principle inhabitants. From that time on whenever the Gunanaa, or any other groups, came to fish and hunt they had to obtain permission from the L'uknax̱.ádi leader.

Remnants of the Gunanaa eventually became the Lukaax̱.ádi (Sockeye People). When the Tlingits migrated from Southeast Alaska to this area, they eventually became the dominant tribe. These were a group of the Raven moiety identified as the L'uknax̱.ádi (Coho People).

Gus'eix̱ is also a Gunanaa name. Gus'eix̱ grew into the largest L'uknax̱.ádi village in the Gunaax̱oo (Dry Bay) area. On one occasion the Jilḵáat people from the Haines (Deishú) area received permission to hunt seal and fish for salmon. When their expedition was over, it was discovered that they took too many seal and more than their allotted salmon; to add insult to injury, one of the chief's daughters ran off with one of the young Jilḵáat men. The following spring the L'uknax̱.ádi from Gus'eix̱ went to trade with the Haidas and Tsimshians in the southern panhandle. On their way back home they paddled their canoes into Lynn Canal toward Jilḵáat territory to take revenge on them for their misdeeds. The engagement took place along the banks of the Chilkat River. There was this shaman who had a friend with no hair on his head. Whenever a L'uknax.ádi killed a Jilkáat, they would take a scalp as evidence of his kill. The bald-headed sidekick became a casualty and, since he didn't have any hair, his head was cut off. The head was among the scalps taken after the battle was over when the L'uknax.ádi commenced their journey back to Gus'eix.

Always, whenever the Tlingits traveled, they would stop at Lituya Bay. Here, they would take a day or two to rest and then continue on with their journey. It is said that the Jilkáat shaman was a very powerful one, and, as he mourned the loss of his bald-headed friend, he caused what looked like a giant clam to open in the mountain which, in turn, spilled a huge rush of water into Lituya Bay. All six or seven canoes were destroyed and every one of the men perished. Each canoe carried about twenty people; this translates to 120 to 140 warriors, about half the population of Gus'eix, where the elderly, women, and children were left to fend for themselves.

Eventually the survivors of Gus'eix moved to Dry Bay, where the Frog House and Boulder House were rebuilt. These were L'uknax.ádi tribal houses. Two Eagle/Wolf moiety houses also were constructed in Dry Bay, the Thunderbird House of the Shangukeidí clan and the Box House of the Kaagwaantaan.

When commercial fishing was established in Dry Bay during the late eighteen hundreds and early nineteen hundreds, a cannery was built on a place called Stu-heen-nuk [Sduheenák'w, #251] (Cannery Creek); a railroad track was constructed between the cannery and the Akwe where a train hauled salmon from the Akwe River. No one, however, fished as far up as Gus'eix on the Akwe, so its location was overlooked and the site eventually dissipated into wilderness.

In May of 1957 our father "walked into the forest" after a long winter battling cancer. Going back to the Akwe River was very tough on us. The following year our mother remarried, but even then things didn't seem right anymore. When our father was alive it seemed that the only important thing was that we were together in a country we treasured very much. Now the motivation shifted to economics, and our vision moved away from things of nature.

In 1996 a small group of Dry Bay people began to do a place name study of the Dry Bay area supported by the National Park Service and U.S. Forest Service. The purpose was to take about fourteen people who had roots from Gunaaxoo and visit areas where the former people had resided and to recollect some of the place names in the area. My wife, Lorraine, Sigurd and Sally Edwards, Fred White, and George Ramos were some of the key people who spoke the Tlingit language and knew the history of the area. We dedicated the days to walking around the areas; we discovered some tribal house sites and machinery from the old cannery and found the railroad track that linked to Akwe and the small train that hauled salmon; and we shared stories and experiences about Gunaaxoo.

On the second day an extraordinary discovery was made by Vincent Johnson. We were stomping in the forest around Kaa-gun-hee-nee [K'aagán Héeni, #253] (Muddy Creek), when he came upon a rectangular indentation in the ground. It measured about forty feet wide and perhaps sixty feet long. After Forest Service archeologist Kathy Brown took some soil samples from the mound, she found charcoal in a layer of the soil, evidence of fire and human occupancy. She drilled into the core of a healthy tree and counted the rings. The site was over 180 years old!

Immediately, for me, the light bulb turned on. "I bet you if we were to go to Akwe, I could take you to Gus'eix," I told Kathy and Wayne Howell (of the National Park Service, Glacier Bay).

"Oh yes?" they both said simultaneously.

"Yep," I replied. "The only thing different about my previous searches is that we won't be looking for actual structures. We'll be looking for something like this."

Kathy got the funds to take a few people to look for Gus'eix the following year. L'uknax.ádi members George Ramos and Daryl James (who also works for the Forest Service in Yakutat); the district ranger of the Forest Service in Yakutat, Meg Mitchell; Mary Ann Porter from the National Park Service office in Yakutat; Wayne Howell; Kathy Brown; and I were guided by Hippie John, who had a camp on the upper Akwe.

The first day we spent looking on the lower part of the river where it bends and turns toward the straight line to the ocean. We found evidence of a settlement that might have been a small site for a couple of tribal houses of earlier days, but barbed wire fence and an old saw blade revealed that it had latter-day western influence, possibly stuff that had been taken after the battle at the Russian fort in Yakutat in 1805. Or it might be the site that Grandma Minnie said that was very small and was on a hill. The thing that was unsettling about this was that it was alongside the river, not on a hill. We looked further around the area but could not find any evidence of a settlement on a hill.

The next day we headed upriver where Hippie John thought he might have seen some indication of where Gus'eix̲ might be. We went there first; however, I told Wayne that he might be taking us too far upriver. We spent the morning tramping through thick alder brush and devil's club but found nothing. I looked at the map of the river and told Wayne that we needed to stop at a place further down the river. We stopped at the spot I indicated on the map.

Wayne was standing at the edge of the bank beside a tree, writing something in a notebook. I looked upriver and saw this rectangular indentation in the ground. It was about twenty or twenty-five feet wide and perhaps forty feet long.

"Hey, what's this?" I pointed with my stem of *yaana.eit* (wild celery).

Wayne looked and said, "Hey, it looks like we got something here."

The others caught up with us and Kathy took some soil samples and found evidence of charcoal. We looked around for more sites but found none. According to Frederica de Laguna's history of Yakutat, *Under Mount Saint Elias,* Mountain House was separate from the other tribal houses. It was upriver from the main settlement. I was convinced this was, indeed, Shaa Hít. We tried to move through thick alders, but it was getting late. I had to catch a plane back to Yakutat. Wayne and Kathy promised that they would look further downriver the next day.

I reluctantly returned to Yakutat. Early the next day the expedition went on without me. About four hundred yards from Shaa Hít, they located four other tribal house sites.

Gus'eix̲ was found. All those years I had been looking, only the spirits of Gus'eix̲ know how many footprints I had left on these ancient tribal house foundations. Now this could be put to rest.

What will be done in the future with Gus'eix̲ remains to be seen; however, you can be assured that this ancient village will somehow be commemorated for the predominant influence it had on the history of the G̲unaax̲oo people, most notably on those people of Gus'eix̲ who still have roots in that remarkable era.

Yakutat community place names project work session at the National Park Service office in Yakutat, 1997. From left to right: David Ramos (standing), Emma Marks, Nora Marks Dauenhauer, Jeff Leer, Tom Thornton, George Ramos (also standing), Sally Edwards, and Lorraine Adams. Photo courtesy of Bert and Lorraine Adams.

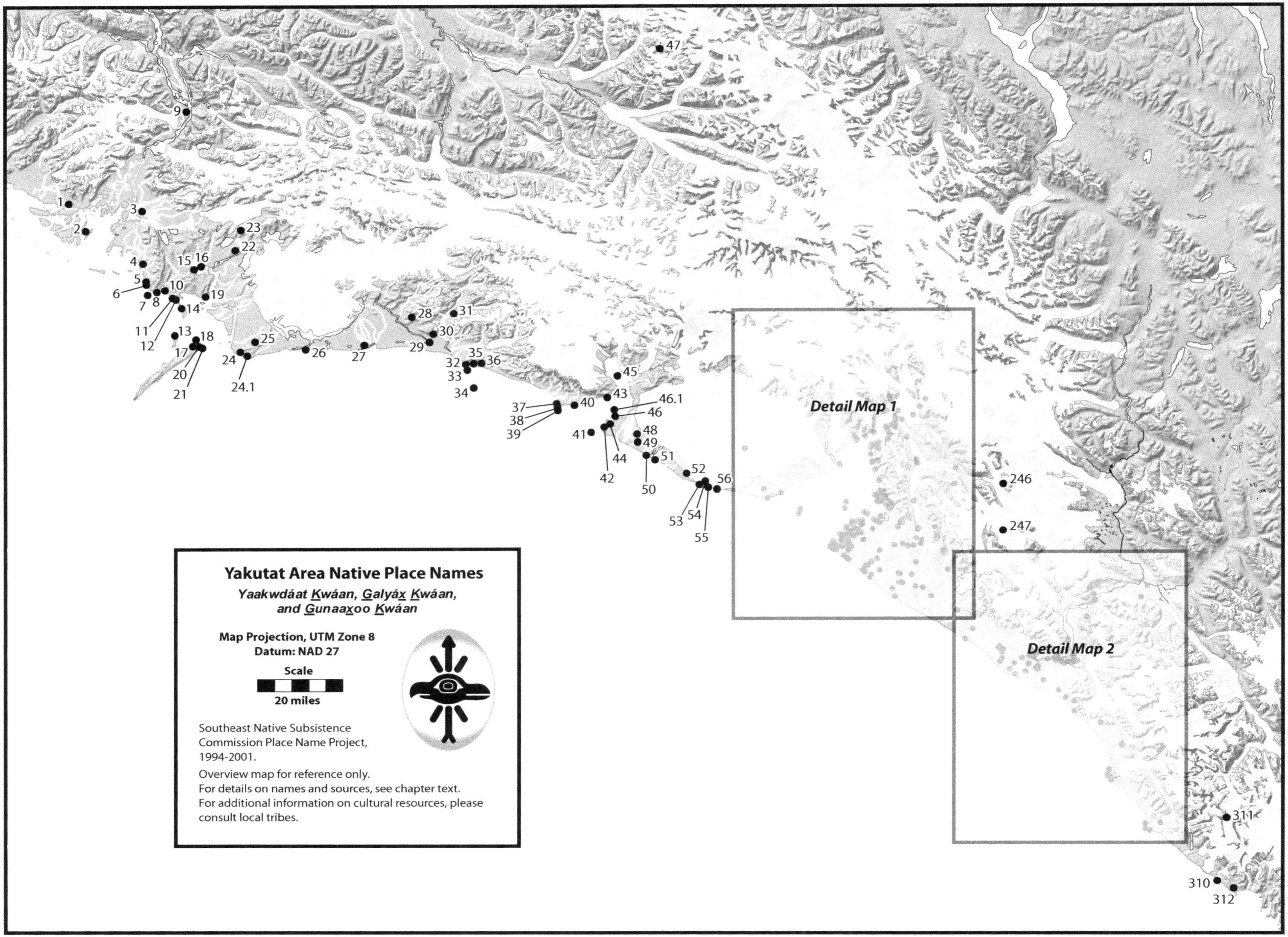

Yakutat Area Native Place Names
Yaakwdáat Ḵwáan, Galyáx̱ Ḵwáan,
and Gunaax̱oo Ḵwáan

Map Projection, UTM Zone 8
Datum: NAD 27

Scale

20 miles

Southeast Native Subsistence
Commission Place Name Project,
1994-2001.

Overview map for reference only.
For details on names and sources, see chapter text.
For additional information on cultural resources, please
consult local tribes.

Detail Map 2

Detail Map 1

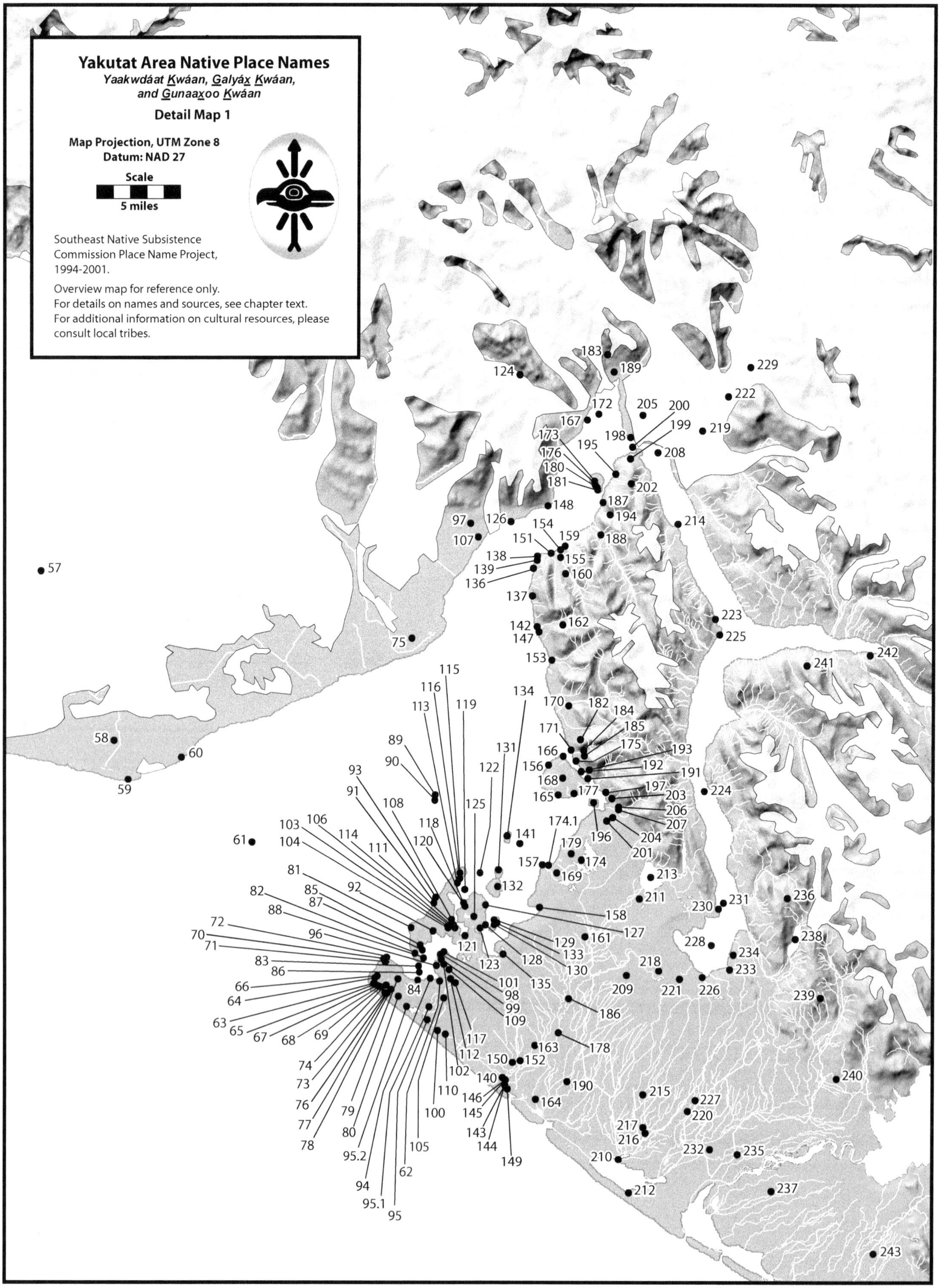

Yakutat Area Native Place Names
Yaakwdáat Ḵwáan, Galyáx̱ Ḵwáan,
and Ḡunaax̱oo Ḵwáan

Detail Map 1

Map Projection, UTM Zone 8
Datum: NAD 27

Scale

5 miles

Southeast Native Subsistence
Commission Place Name Project,
1994-2001.

Overview map for reference only.
For details on names and sources, see chapter text.
For additional information on cultural resources, please
consult local tribes.

256

243

245

244

249
250
248
260.1   254
252
253   265   264   266
263   269
259   267   274
260   261   273   276   285
251   262   275   279   286   290
257   270.1   268   270   278   283   287
255   271   284
258

272

277

282
288

289

296

280
281

291

292   295
293
294

303

302

301

307   308

298.1

298
297
299
300

304   309
305
306
305.1

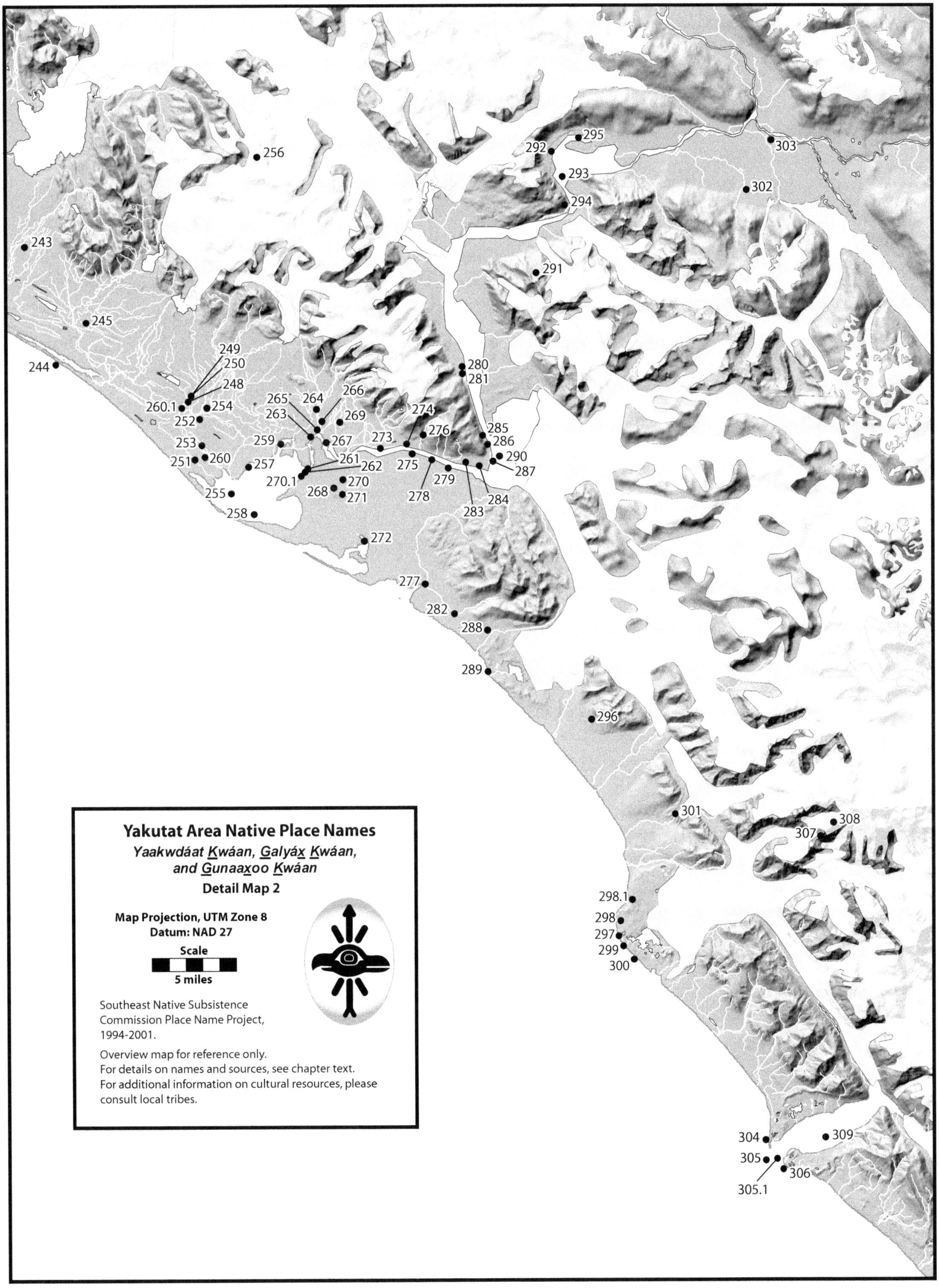

Yakutat Area Native Place Names

Yaakwdáat Ḵwáan, Galyáx Ḵwáan,
and Gunaax̱oo Ḵwáan

Detail Map 2

Map Projection, UTM Zone 8
Datum: NAD 27

Scale

5 miles

Southeast Native Subsistence
Commission Place Name Project,
1994-2001.

Overview map for reference only.
For details on names and sources, see chapter text.
For additional information on cultural resources, please
consult local tribes.

Yaakwdáat K̲wáan, G̲alyáx̲ K̲wáan, and G̲unaax̲oo K̲wáan Place Names

Asterisk indicates uncertain, unconfirmed, or partial; NM = not mapped.
Some names have more than one pronunciation or translation.
Nonstandard orthography from the following pages of de Laguna (1972) is used for these table entries: #4 (p. 105), #13 (p. 103), #23 (p. 104), #26 (p. 101), #28 (p. 101), #31 (p. 100), #37 (p. 97), #58 (p. 59), #59 (p. 59), #107 (p. 59), #114 (p. 62), #122 (p. 64), #125 (p. 64), #127 (p. 64), #130 (p. 64), #133 (p. 64), #142 (p. 67), #147 (p. 67), #158 (p. 65), #161 (p. 79), #186 (p. 79), #201 (p. 65), #233 (p. 70), #239 (p. 80), #300 (p. 90), NM (p. 105). See de Laguna (1972, 11) for explanation of her orthography.

Map #	*Name*	*Translation*	*Location*
1	Anax̲anák̲	Mistake (Wrong Turn) (from Eyak, originally Alutiiq)	Western branch of Copper River
2	K'aagán Héenák'u	Stickleback Creek	Mouth of Copper River
3	K̲aa Yahaayí	Ghosts	Near Copper River
4	Tš̓a’di·q̓*	On the Place of [Frequently Absent*] Mud Flats (from Eyak, Ts’a’di:q’)	Camp on Martin River
5	K̲aataanáa	——* (from Eyak, Qa:ta:lah)	Katalla settlement
6	Saaxw T'áak	Behind the Cockles	Village on Softuk Lagoon
7	Gixdák̲ [X'áat'i]	——* (from Eyak, originally Alutiiq, Qikertaq) [Island]	Fox or Kiktak Island
8	K'ix̲óoliyaa	Teeth (from Eyak, K’uxu:łiyah)	River between Katalla and Cape Martin
9	Eek̲ Héeni	Copper River	Copper River
10	Gixdák̲lak̲	Behind Gixdák̲ (#7)	Village at Cape Martin
11	Gixdák̲ [X'aa]	Gixdák̲ (#7) [Point]	Strawberry Point
12	X̲aat Áa Duls'el' Yé	Where They Dig Spruce Roots	Cordova
13	Thaattł’aát*	Small Kayak* (from Eyak or Athabaskan)	Wingham Island
14	Ginák̲	Egg Island (from Eyak, originally Alutiiq)	Kanak Island
15	Kanaltalgi X'áat'x'i Sáani Dax̲ Nalháshch*	Spongy Islands Are Floating*	Bering River Delta
16	K̲aasheishx̲áaw Áa	Dragonfly Lake	Bering Lake
17	Yáay Ká	On the Humpback Whale	Kayak Island
18	Yéil Xákwdli	Raven’s Harpoon Line	Okalee Spit
19	Jilk̲áat	Cache (from Eyak)	Below Cordova
20	S'igeek̲áawu Hídi	Dead Person House	Cave on Kayak Island
21	Yáay Shaayí	Whale Head	Lemesurier Point on northeast end of Kayak Island
22	Anakéi	*	South side of lake near Bering River
23	’Ukʷyanta*	*	Mountain above Bering River
24	Yéil Katsees	Raven’s Float	Between base of Okalee Spit and Cape Suckling

Map #	*Name*	*Translation*	*Location*
24.1	Yéil Hít	Raven's House	Cave at Cape Suckling
25	Axdalée	Place with Lots of Whales (from Eyak, A:xdalih, originally Alutiiq, Arwertuli)	Settlement at Okalee River
26	She-ta-ha-na-ta*	Northward (upstream) He Lives*	Seal River area
27	Ts'iyuh*	Black Bear (from Eyak)	Tsiu River
28	Djuk̓e*	——* (from Eyak)	Stream entering Kaliakh River
29	Galyáx	The Lowermost (from Eyak, Gałyax)	Kaliakh River
30	Ch'awáax'	Robin Mountain	Robinson Mountain
31	Daktáal* (G̣exta'ał*)	Cooked* (from Eyak, Daqta:ł)	Duktoth River
32	Yéil X'us.eetí	Raven's Footprints	Cape Yakataga
33	Tayeesk'*	Little Adze*	Cape Yakataga
34	Yéil (Yeil) T'ooch'	Black Raven	Gulf of Alaska (Pacific Ocean)
35	Yakwdeiyí	Canoe Road	Inside Cape Yakataga
36	Yéil Naasa.áayi*	Raven's Bentwood Box*	Cape Yakataga area
37	G̣ùtšáx̣^{w}*	Muddy Water (from Eyak)	White River
38	Héen Tlein	Big Creek	Big River
39	Teey Aaní* (Was'ei Dak)	Yellow Cedar Bark Town (Outside of Was'ei [#45])	West of Icy Bay
40	Ligaasi Áa	Tabooed Lake	Icy Bay
41	Ts'ootsxán X'aayí	Tsimshian Point	Point Riou
42	Ts'ootsxán Geeyí	Tsimshian Bay	Riou Bay
43	Ana.óot Gíl'i	Aleut Bluff	Icy Bay
44	Sít' Kaxóowu	Piles of Rock on the Glacier	Icy Bay
45	Was'ei (Yas'ei) Yík	Inside of Was'ei/Yas'ei (see #48)	Icy Bay
46	Geesh K'ishuwanyee	Place below the End of the Edge of the Base of the Kelp	Halibut fishing bank, Icy Bay
46.1	K'wát' X'áat'i	Bird Egg Island	Gull Island, Icy Bay
47	Was'ei Tashaa (Shaa Tlein)	Mountain Inland of Was'ei (#45) (Big Mountain)	Mount Saint Elias
48	Yas'ei* Héen	Swampy* Creek	Yahtse River
49	Ligaasi Héen	Tabooed Creek	Yana Stream
50	Galgox* (Galyáx)	Muddy*	Yahtse River tributary
51	Nasaaxíx*	*	Malaspina Glacier
52	Kwalaxuk'w*	Dry Up Water [Little One]*	Malaspina Glacier
53	Sít' X'aayí	Glacier Point	Front of Malaspina Glacier
54	Sít' Tlein Shaa Ká	On the Mountain of the Big Glacier	Sitkagi Bluffs
55	Taan Teiyí	Sea Lion Rock	At Sitkagi Bluffs
56	Sít' Lutú	Glacier Point (nostril)	Malaspina Glacier, beach in front
57	Sít' Tlein	Big Glacier	Malaspina Glacier
58	Kık*	*	Manby Stream or Kwik Stream

Map #	Name	Translation	Location
59	Yaat'áak* (Yaťak*)	*	Point Manby
60	Shaanáx̱ Héen	Valley Creek	Creek behind Point Manby
61	Laax̱aayík	Inside Laax̱aa (#90) (from Eyak, Ła'x̱a', "Near the Glacier")	Yakutat area
62	Yaakwdáat	Canoe Rebounded (or bruised) (from Eyak, Di:ya'guda't, "Mouth of Body of Salt Water")	Yakutat Bay (and town of Yakutat)
63	Gus'k'iyee Ḵwáan Aaní	Under the Clouds People's (white people's or Russians') Community	Ocean Cape
64	Yakwdeiyí	Canoe Road	Inside the berm on Ocean Cape
65	Goox̱ Áa Shakdut'ex̱'x̱i Yé	Place Where They Conk Slaves over the Head [with a Stone Hammer]	Ocean Cape
66	Anax̱ Tanaashuwu Yé	Where the Rock Sticks Up	Lagoon north of Ocean Cape
67	Anóoshi Noowú	Russian Fort	Kardy Lake
68	Anóoshi Áayi	Russian Lake	Kardy Lake
69	Kadzitéix'i Áa	Rocky/Pebbly* Lake (from Eyak, originally from Alutiiq)	Kardy Lake
70	Anax̱ Daaḵ At Ḵuwdzitiyi Yé	Place Where a Monster Emerged	Point Carrew at mouth of Monti Bay
71	Tayeex̱nák	Spit (from Eyak, originally Alutiiq, Tangirnaq)	Point Carrew (whole area)
72	Tayeex̱nák Lutú	Point (nose) of Spit	Point Carrew (the point itself)
73	Xaas Geiyí Tá	Inside Xaas geiyí (#76)	Ankau
74	Yaakwdáat Yík	Canoe Jumps Inside* (Inside Where the Boat Is*)	Ankau area
75	Tsaa Héeni	Seal Creek	Grand Wash
76	Xaas geiyí	Cow Bay	Ankau
77	Gooch Shakee Aan	Village on Top of the Hill	Kardy Lake
78	Ḵaa Gukk'iyík	Inside the Little Ear	Ocean Cape / Ankau Saltchucks
79	Aanḵáawu	Man of the Town (Chief)	Ankau Creek
80	Áa Ká	On the Lake	Aka/Summit lakes
81	Léin X'aayí	Low Water Point	Khantaak Island
82	Kawdzigani Yé	Opening/Clearing	Port Mulgrave
83	Juwaaník Tá	Head of Juwaaník (from Eyak)	Monti Bay (whole)
84	Tawanyík Tá*	Head of Tawanyík	Monti Bay
85	Ganawaaník Tá	Wild Rhubarb* (from Eyak)	Pyramid Point
86	Ḵaa Gatsx̱'áak	Between a Person's Thighs	Monti Bay
87	Di.aank'i Yé	Place with a Little Village (in front of the road)	Reef opposite Point Turner (Village Shoal)
88	Ts'óos (S'óos') Ká*	*	Port Mulgrave
89	Yaakwdáat geeyí	Canoe Rebounded Bay	Yakutat Bay
90	Laax̱aa	Near the Glacier (from Eyak, Ła'x̱a')	Yakutat area
91	S'ús'	Harlequin Duck	Dolgoi Island area

Map #	*Name*	*Translation*	*Location*
92	Yúxch'i G̲eiyí	Sea Otter Bay	Large bay which nearly bisects Khantaak Island to the east
93	Ganták̲w	Lupine* (from Eyak, G̲a:ndak̲)*	Khantaak Island (see also #115)
94	Taan Teiyí	Sea Lion Rock	Monti Bay
95	Anóoshi Aadé Ayawdihaani Yé	Place That the Russian [Man] Retreated To	Site on/near Ophir Creek
95.1	Tada.áaw*	Having a Strap at the Bottom*	Fish hole (*ísh*), Ophir Creek
95.2	Kadzitéix'i Áa	Rocky/Pebbly* Lake (from Eyak, originally from Alutiiq)	Waterway from Ophir Creek to Aka Lake
96	K̲aa G̲atsx̲'áak Aan	K̲aa G̲atsx̲'áak (#86) Town	Old Village (between two rocky headlands)
97	Ch'áak' Aaní	Eagle Town	Yakutat Bay
98	Tléik̲w Tlein	Big [Salmon]berries	Larger island east of Old Village
99	Yaakw X'áat'i	Canoe Island	Mouth of lagoon north of Old Village island
100	Éil' Áayi	Salt Lake	At head of T'aawáal Yík (#110)
101	Tléik̲wk'átsk'u	Small [Salmon]berries	Just north of Tléik̲w Tlein (#98) near Old Village
102	K̲eik'uts'inatá*	*	Lagoon which runs behind and opens north of Old Village
103	Áx̲ Géel' Wuduwatax'i Yé	Place Where Crunchy Fish Eggs Were Chewed	Shores of Canoe Pass
104	Dákde Séet	Channel on the Way to Place Behind	Canoe Pass
105	K̲ux̲jeeník	*	Ophir Creek
106	Héendt Yatáni Yaakw Shoowú	Half a Boat That Used to Face the Water	Canoe Pass
107	Yat'a S'é.aa* (Yat̓a-sé'a, Yàtà-sí'à')*	Beside the Face of the Muddy Lagoon*	Esker Creek estuary
108	Daak̲ Uwahuwu Xóots	Brown Bear Who Swam In[land]	Rock in Canoe Pass
109	Tatóok	Cave	Puget Cove
110	T'aawáal Yík	Inside ——*	Salt Lake
111	Daag̲aadlaani Aan	Deep-All-Around Village	Island in Johnstone Passage
112	Sgóon Yaká	In Front of the School*	Lutheran Evangelical Mission
113	X̲einda.áax̲'	Strawberry Point*	Khantaak Island
114	Tc̓Áx̲qatłata*	Inside on the Mountain* (as applied to a bay)	Landlocked lagoon just south of Canoe Pass
115	Kanták̲w (G̲andák̲)	Lupine (from Eyak, G̲a:ndak̲)	Khantaak Island
116	K'ulat'áalk' Yaká	In Front of K'ulat'áalk' (#119)	Gilbert Spit
117	Tandaa Áak'w	Jumping Fish Little Lake	An *ísh* (fish hole) in Ophir Creek above highway bridge
118	Gáaxw Áa Dusg̲eiwu Yé	Place Where They Used to Net Ducks	Lagoon west of Dolgoi Island
119	K'ulat'áalk'	Shaking Their Wings (from Eyak)	Crab Island in Johnstone Passage near Khantaak Island
120	Deikée Séet	Out-to-Sea Pass	Ahdahk Bay Pass

Map #	*Name*	*Translation*	*Location*
121	G̲unakadeit Séedi	G̲unakadeit's (Sea Monster's) Pass	Johnstone Passage
122	Qiyakʷ*	Open Place (from Eyak)	Open water between Khantaak and Kriwoi islands
123	Shadat'éix̲'	Busted Head	Hatchet Pass
124	Sít' Kusá	Narrow Glacier	Turner Glacier
125	WÀxÁq* (Goťeẋ 'ayi*)	——* (Aleuts' Lake)	Lake/lagoon on Dolgoi Island
126	X'aa Yayee	Below the Point	Yakutat Bay
127	Qiyu-ẋᴀdi-'ák*	*	Dolgoi Island, west shore
128	Asgutu.aan	Village in the Woods	Dolgoi Island
129	Aanilawáak̲*	*	Fitzgerald Island
130	'Iłdıłıyáł*	Close Together (from Eyak, perhaps Iłt Idi'a'ł, "Extends to Touch Each Other")	Fitzgerald Island (Sister Islands)
131	K̲aa Shaayí X'áat'	Human Head Island	Otmeloi Island
132	K̲áa Kayaani X'áat'	Male Plants Island	Leaves Island
133	'Iłdıłıyáł*	Close Together (from Eyak, perhaps Iłt Idi'a'ł, "Extends to Touch Each Other")	Gregson Island (Sister Islands)
134	K'u.éit	Place of Absent Thing (from Eyak, K'u'e't)	Krutoi Island
135	Nex̲kit*	——* (from Eyak, Ne:x̲ki:t)	Broken Oar Cove
136	Laax̲aa Tá	Head of Laax̲aa (#90)	Old sealing camp three miles south of Point Latouche
137	L'awshaa Tlein	Big Sand Mountain	Bluffs at Roosevelt Creek
138	Aanaadi.áak	In Front of the Stone Platform* (from Eyak)	Point Latouche
139	Léin X'aayí	Low Tide Point	Point beyond Logan Bluff
140	K̲aax̲'us.hittaan	Human Foot Village	Lost River area
141	Shagulkeex'*	Head with a Lump on Top	Reef near Krutoi Island
142	Tłáẋátà* (same as #136?)	Dead Trees Inside	North bank of last stream south of Point Latouche
143	At'éik (Atéix̲')	Behind It (At the Heart)	Lost River
144	Ganiyaash Héen*	Creek by the Firewood* (from Eyak, Gani:ya'sh)	Lost River
145	Kadzitéix'i Áa	Rocky/Pebbly* Lake (from Eyak, originally from Alutiiq)	Lake outlet of Tawah Creek (same as #95.2?)
146	Naasoodat (Naasudáat)	*	Lost River
147	Tł'e·tshú·t*	Canyon* (from Eyak, Tł'e:ts-hú:t)	Stream below Point Latouche
148	G̲íl' Shakee Aan	Village on Top of the Cliff	Bancas Point
149	Héen Áa Yéi Léich Yé	Place Where the Water Ebbs	Lost River
150	Éix̲' Yík (Kawli.éx*)	Slough Inside (River Is Meandering)	Lost River
151	Shaanáx̲ Kuwóox̲'	Wide Valley	Valley above Point Latouche

Map #	*Name*	*Translation*	*Location*
152	Wulilaayi Aan	Shallow Water Town	West bank of Little Lost River
153	Giyax̲ak̲* (Geeyax̲'áak̲*)	Biggest Canyon/Ravine (from Eyak, Gi:yax̲'a:k*)	Roosevelt Creek canyon
154	Ayuwaakát Yasatán	Gravel between Two Main Camps*	First sealing camp above Point Latouche
155	K̲eik'uliyáa	——* (probably from Eyak)	Between Point Latouche and Haenke Island
156	K'waats'eelaa	——* (probably from Eyak)	Reef outside Knight Island
157	Wooshdak̲an Té	Stones Quarreling with Each Other	Two big rocks near Humpback Creek
158	'Àtł'at*	Head of the River (from Eyak, A:tł'aht)	Redfield Cove
159	Woogaani Yé	Burned Up Place (shaman's name)	Between Point Latouche and Haenke Island
160	X̲'akoosayi Yé	Place Where the Mouth (entrance) Is Narrow	Double canyon above Point Latouche
161	GíyÀq*	Open Space* (from Eyak)	Situk area
162	Daak Wushix̲'il'i Yé	Place Where It Slid down the Cliff	Wide rockslide near Roosevelt Creek
163	Diyaaguna.éit	Where the Salt Water Comes Up and People Moan for Fresh Water (from Eyak)	Lost River village
164	X̲áat Áa Dug̲ich Yé	Pitching the Fish Place	Landing on Johnson Slough
165	Tlákw.aan	Old Town	Knight Island
166	Ganawás Shadaa	Around the Head of Ganawás (#168)	North end of Knight Island
167	L'éiw G̲eeyí	Sand [Beach] Bay	Beach at head of Disenchantment Bay
168	Ganawás	Water Extends in an Indefinite Shape (from Eyak, Galawas)	Knight Island
169	Kwáashk' [Héeni]	Humpback Salmon [Creek] (from Eyak, Kwa:shk')	Humpback Creek
170	K̲aa Déx̲'de Agaax̲	Dog Crying behind You	North of Knight Island
171	Néix̲' Hít Tá	Back of Marble House	Logging camp at bay
172	At'éik*	Behind It*	Disenchantment Bay
173	Yook̲ Tatóok	Cormorant Cave	On Haenke Island
174	Áa Tlein Tuk̲yee	Outlet (anus) of the Big Lake	Outlet of Redfield Lakes
174.1	K̲uwís'k'	[Fish] Coming into the Cove*	Kooisk Point, Humpback Cove
175	Tsaa Yoowú	Seal Stomach	Shoreline above Eleanor Island
176	X̲áax' Háas'*	Big Cracked Rock	On Haenke Island
177	Yéil Áa Daak Wudzigidi Yé	Place Where Raven Fell Down	Knight Island
178	S'iták̲	——* (from Eyak, Ts'itaq)	Situk River
179	Nás'k' Xala Áa*	Three Lakes (probably from Eyak, Nax̲tłax̲ak 'Á: Ká)	Head of Humpback Creek
180	Daak Léin*	Rock Chute Tide Flats*	Haenke Island camp
181	K'wát' X'áat'i	Bird Egg Island	Haenke Island
182	Xóots	Brown Bear	Mount Hoortz
183	L'éiw Kunag̲eiyí	Sand Little Bay	Yakutat Bay*

Map #	*Name*	*Translation*	*Location*
184	L'éiw Tlein	Big Glacial Sand	Yakutat Bay*
185	L'óox̲'	Silty/Muddy Water	Stream below Mount Tebenkof
186	Gʊdał'-tex̣ł*	——* (from Eyak, K'udałtl'ihix̲ł, "Bird's Nest")	Main branch of Situk
187	Jánwu Noowú	Mountain Goat's Fort	Rockslide cliff between Point Latouche and Haenke Island
188	Shaanáx̲ Tlein	Big Valley	Calahonda Creek valley
189	Wéinaa Tá*	Head of Gypsum [Bay]	Bay at west end of Russell Fiord
190	G̲unayáash	Inside the Woods (firewood*) (from Eyak, Gulayahsh, "Offspring of Liquid")	Kunayash Creek
191	L'óox̲' Wát	Mouth of Silty Water	Cabin at point on mainland near Alex Johnson's
192	Noowk'	Little Fort	Small island opposite middle Knight Island toward shore (or Lost River)*
193	Té K̲aadí	Rockslide	Behind (inland from) Knight Island
194	Shaanáx̲ Kusá	Narrow Valley	Between Point Latouche and Haenke Island
195	X'aa Tlein Jiseiyí*	Area below (in the shelter of) Big Point	Bight on mainland just northeast of Haenke Island
196	Tlákw ——*	Ancient ——*	Xagh Island
197	Shaa Geeyí	Mountain Bay	Behind Mountain
198	Sít' Lutú	Glacier Point	Part of Hubbard Glacier that sticks out into Russell Fiord
199	Néix̲' Áa Daak Kawdzikug̲u Yé	Where Marble Rock Fell Down	Point opposite Hubbard Glacier
200	T'íx' Ka Séet	Ice Overturning Strait	Passage from Disenchantment Bay to Nunatak Fiord
201	Qayuƙotła*	Around the Face	South Point
202	Wéinaa Shaa	Sharpen Knife (Whetstone) Mountain	Gilbert Point
203	L'óox̲' Shaayí	At the Head of Muddy Water	Head of Eleanor Cove
204	Áa Goon	Spring Water Lake	Nettle Lake beach
205	Taasaa* Sít'	——* Glacier	Hubbard Glacier
206	Aasyík Daak'átsk'u	Little Aasyík Daa (#207)	Little Bay inside Chicago Harbor
207	Aasyík Daa	Around the Area with Trees inside It	Eleanor Cove / Chicago Harbor
208	K'wát' X'áat'ik'átsk'u	Little Bird Egg Island	Osier Island in Russell Fiord
209	Ch'áak' Noow	Eagle Fort	Situk River*
210	X̲'é Noow* (X̲'a Noow)	Mouth of the Fort	Ahrnklin River
211	Áa Shuku Áak'w*	Little Lake of the Lake*	Upper Situk River
212	Kóox X'áat'i	Wild Rice Island	Ahrnklin River
213	S'itak̲ Shak Áayi	Lake at the Head of S'iták̲ (#178)	Situk Lake
214	Néix̲' X'aayí	Marble (white quartz) Point	Russell Fiord, Marble Point
215	Tsaa Héeni	Seal Creek	Seal Creek

Map #	*Name*	*Translation*	*Location*
216	Gunatsítsk'w	Narrow Stream (from Eyak, Gulatsitsk)	Ahrnklen River tributary
217	Ch'áal' Gutuhéen	Creek among the Willow	Ahrnklen River tributary
218	Aantlaat*	Village at Head of River (from Athabaskan, Tlaat, "Head of River")	Situk River
219	K'wát' Aaní	Bird (seagull) Egg Land	Eastern moraine, Hubbard Glacier*
220	Héen Aawawal'i Yé	Place Where the Water Broke (a former waterfall)	Ahrnklen River tributary
221	Héen Ta.eetí	Place Where River Bottom Used to Be*	Old Situk Channel
222	Sít' T'ooch'	Black Glacier	Moraine of Hubbard Glacier
223	G̲unakadeit G̲íl'i	G̲unakadeit's (Sea Monster's) Cliff	Cliff at Cape Enchantment
224	Tsaa Eejí	Seal Reef	Reef south of Hidden Glacier
225	Gel' X'áat'ak'u	Little Hilly Island	Small island between Nunatak and Russell fiords
226	K̲útlkw (K̲útlk'w*) G̲eeyí (S'iták̲ Shaayí)	Mud Bay (Head of Situk River [the Situk used to be there])	Mud Bay (head of Russell Fiord)
227	Aan Deiyi Héen	Camp Trail Creek	Ahrnklen River tributary
228	K̲útlkw G̲eeyí	Mud Bay	Bay in Russell Fiord
229	Sít' Tlein	Big Glacier	Hubbard Glacier
230	Laagak̲aal	It's Holding the Glacier in Its Mouth (from Eyak)	Cape Stoss
231	Luyik Éix̲'	Slough inside the Point	Cove inside of Cape Stoss
232	Aan Tlein Héen	Stream of the Big Country [of the Animals]	Ahrnklen River
233	Qudᴇnixł qᴀnɪk* Héeni	—— ——* Creek (from Eyak)	Second stream south of Beasley Creek
234	Wat.lax̲eil	Foam at the Mouth	First stream south of Beasley Creek
235	Aan Tlein	Big Country [of the Animals]	Ahrnklin River
236	S'itak̲ Sháak	Head of S'iták̲ (#178)	Peak between Fourth Glacier and Russell Fiord
237	Kulijigi Héen (Kulix̲éitl'shani Héen)	Tough (Strong) River (Dangerous River)	Dangerous River
238	At T'ika Sít'*	Way Back Glacier	Fourth Glacier
239	Lagut*	Overflowing*	Slate Peak at Russell Fiord
240	Sdax̲éi Yashaak'w	Little Mountain at ——*	Above Harlequin Lake
241	Dáanaa Shaa	Silver Mountain	Mount Draper
242	Yuk̲w G̲íl'i	Cormorants' Cliff	Bird cliffs, Nunatak Fiord
243	K̲eilxwáa	*	Italio River
244	Aakwéi	*	Akwe River
245	Kaligoonx'i Yé	Place of Many Springs	Akwe River tributary*
246	Sit'k'átsk'u	Tiny Glacier	Nunatak Glacier
247	Atéix̲' Sít'i	Glacier at Its Heart	Nunatak Glacier
248	Yoost'ei (Aast'ei*)	——* (Behind the Trees)	Ustay River

Map #	*Name*	*Translation*	*Location*
249	Sax̲'ahéen*	Confluence Creek	Akwe River
250	Gus'eix̲	Sunken*	Village up Akwe River
251	Sduheenák'w	Short Creek	Cannery Creek
252	Dagis (Dag̲isdinaa Aaní)	——* (a creek) (Dag̲isdi Clan Country)	Inland from Alsek*
253	K'aagán Héeni	Stickleback Creek	Muddy Creek
254	Taanís	Jumping Fish	Tanis River
255	G̲unaax̲oo (G̲unanaa X̲oo)	Among the Interior Natives (Athabaskans)	Dry Bay
256	Ta Shaak'ú	Little Mountain Inside	Above Situk
257	Lutu Héenák'w	Water Going Away	Dry Bay area
258	Wuxoogu G̲eey	Going Dry Bay	Large flat in east Dry Bay
259	K'ux̲aach Héeni	K'ux̲aach's Creek (from Eyak, K'uxaach, "Gills")	Williams Creek
260	Yéil Áx̲ Daak̲ Uwanugu Yé	Where Raven Scooted Back [Kicking Up the Sand]	Dunes on Akwe River
260.1	Áa Tuk̲ X'aa	Point at Lower End of the Lake	Island point between Cannery and Muddy creeks
261	Yáay Taayí	Whale Fat	East side of Dry Bay
262	Yáay Taayí Lutú	Whale Fat Nose (point)	Bear Island Point, Dry Bay
263	Shix'aa.aa Noowú	Eddy Fort	Alsek River
264	Stahéenáak'w* (alternative to #251?)	Little Lake Creek*	Split Creek, Dry Bay*
265	Dinetgi Aan	Shaking Village	Gateway Knob*
266	Sít' X'aa Noowú	Glacier Point Fort	Below Canyon Glacier at Split Creek*
267	Gus'eix̲ Yádi / Tsalx̲aan Yádi	Gus'eix̲ (#250) [Village] Child / Tsalx̲aan (#308) Child	Cabin Slough
268	Gal'jinoowú	Clam Hand Fort	Dry Bay, Bear Island
269	Shaanáx̲ Héeni	Valley Creek	Emilie Creek, Alsek River*
270	Kudatankahídi	[Raven's] Repository House	Dry Bay
270.1	Kunaga.áa*	Going into a Lagoon*	Sand flat at mouth of Alsek River
271	Yáay X'áat'i	Whale Island	Bear Island, Dry Bay
272	Til'héeni	Dog Salmon River	Doame River tributary
273	Aalséix̲	Resting	Alsek River, including island at mouth
274	Kawdzinedi Aan	Trembling Village	Dry Bay area
275	Yéil Áa Yoo Akaawajiyi Yé (Yéil Áx̲ Daak̲ Akawujiyi Yé)	Where Raven's Feet Worked into the Mud Dragging (the salmon repository or "food canoe")	Alsek River
276	Jánwu Héeni	Mountain Goat Stream	Mountain at head of Alsek River
277	Diyáayi	Looks like a Whale	East River / Deception Hills
278	T'aaganísk'ex̲	Pressed Roots	Alsek River*
279	Yéil Kínde Akaawatsex̲i Yé	Where Raven Trampled [the Ground Packing It] Upward	Alsek River

Map #	Name	Translation	Location
280	Chookán Náagu	Beach Grass Medicine*	Tatshenshini River
281	Yéil Katooli Yé (Yéilch Uwatuli Yé)	Hole Raven Bored	Near Gateway Knob
282	Kantak̲w Héeni	Lupine River	Stream east of Dry Bay
283	Yéil Yakwdeiyí	Raven's Canoe Trail	Alsek River
284	G̲ílguwaa (G̲ílkw.uwaa)	Pass That Resembles G̲ílkw (#293)	Mountain west of Gateway Knob
285	Yadagwált	Raven's Rocks Falling Down	Gateway Knob area
286	Yéil Áa Ludaawdligoowu Yé	Place Where Raven Wiped His Beak Off	Alsek River
287	Yéil Dzoonáyi	Raven's Work	Gateway Knob
288	Gunhéeni	Clear Spring Water	Doame River
289	Shgaadaayi Héen	Moving Creek	Waterfall Creek
290	Yadagwéin*	*	Gateway Knob
291	Sít' X'aayí	Glacier Point	Near Novatak Glacier
292	Yei Wal'ji Héen	Stream That Breaks Downward	Where the Alsek River floods
293	G̲ílkw	Mountain Pass	Near Alsek River
294	T'á Yuwaax̲'éeshi	Dried King Salmon Belly	Alsek River area
295	T'á X̲'éeshi	Dried King Salmon	Alsek River
296	Shgada Héen (alternative to #289?)	——* River	Flows from Grand Plateau Glacier
297	Laak̲'ásgi X'aayí	Green Seaweed Point	Cape Fairweather
298	Yéil Yakwdeiyí	Raven's Canoe Trail	Cape Fairweather area
298.1	Yéil Yakwdeiyí Tá	Area Back of Raven's Canoe Trail	Cape Fairweather area
299	L'idak̲neech	By the Unusual* Beach	Cape Fairweather shoreline
300	Seq̲ayi (Tšaqᴀyᴇ)*	Steep Waterfall*	Southeast of Cape Fairweather
301	Yáx̲wch'i Héeni	Sea Otter Creek	Sea Otter Creek
302	Chaan Yuká*	Ice Field*	Alsek River
303	Sít' X'aayí	Glacier Point	Alsek River
304	Yakwdeiyí	[Raven's] Canoe Trail	Above Lituya Bay
305	Tanagu*	Master of the Fish* (from Emmons n.d.)	Entrance to Lituya Bay
305.1	Tuwool Séet	Hole Strait	Entrance to Lituya Bay
306	Taan Teiyí	Sea Lion Rock	Lituya Bay
307	Ḵées' Kanadaa	High Tide All Around	Peak of Mount Fairweather
308	Tsalx̲aan	Land of the Ground Squirrels*	Mount Fairweather
309	Ltu.áa	Lake inside the Point (nostril)	Lituya Bay
310	Ltu.áa Watyee	Area below the Mouth of Ltu.áa (#309)	Lituya Bay
311	Yéil Nées' Akawlishaa	Raven Ate Sea Urchin	Mount Crillon or Mount La Pérouse
312	Kaháakw Héeni	Salmon Egg Creek	Lituya Bay
NM	Aalséix̲ Yík	Inside Aalséix̲ (#273)	Settlement on upper Alsek River

Map #	*Name*	*Translation*	*Location*
NM	Gooch Tatóogu	Wolf Cave	Ahrnklen River
NM	ʼÌ·yáq*	Eyak (from Alutiiq)	Cordova and separate town of Eyak
NM	Kaknagu (Kaknigu)	Summer Village*	Akwe River*
NM	Noogaayík*	Inside of ——* (possibly Eyak or Athabaskan)	O'Connor River / Tatshenshini River confluence*
NM	Tínx Kayaaní	Bearberry/Kinnikinnick Leaves	Sediment Creek / Tatshenshini River confluence

2. *Xunaa K̲áawu*

Xunaa K̲áawu (Dwelling Place in the Lee of the North Wind) is the only Tlingit geographic community that is not referred to as a k̲wáan, the term *k̲áawu* being a synonym for (human) dwelling place. Emmons (n.d.) reports that this name was bestowed on local Tlingits by a Sheet'ká (Sitka) leader who attempted to journey to their territory for a visit but was delayed for days by strong north winds, prompting him to exclaim, "I wonder when I will be able to see these men from the direction of the North Wind." Xunaa (#218), from which the present day town of Hoonah and the Huna (Xunaa) Tlingits draw their names, is short for Xunniyaa, meaning "Lee of the North Wind," and neatly describes the community's sheltered location within Port Frederick.

Xunaa K̲áawu encompasses the vast majority of Glacier Bay National Park, except for the area north of Sea Otter Creek, which is claimed by G̲unaax̲oo K̲wáan. The territory also extends east of the park to include Excursion Inlet, Homeshore to Point Couverden, and across Icy Strait and Cross Sound to include the northern part of Chichagof Island from Lisianski Strait on the west coast to Freshwater Bay on the east coast, including the northwestern portion of Tenakee Inlet which connects to Port Frederick via the legendary portage said to have been created by the killer whales (Kéet Góoni, #238). George Emmons (n.d.) believed that the Xunaa region was home to the first wave of migrants from the south who "later contributed to the peopling and formation of all of the more northern Tlingit tribes." This hypothesis has been bolstered by more recent archeological excavations at Ground Hog Bay, in the vicinity of the historic Tlingit settlement known as Kax'noowú (Female Grouse Fort, #181), suggesting human habitation in the area dates back nearly ten thousand years (Ackerman 1968, 67–72; Ackerman, Hamilton, and Stuckenrath 1979).

Glacier Bay and Dundas Bay were also early settlement sites in this territory, and many northern clans trace origins or early history to these places, including the T'ak̲deintaan and L'uknax̲.ádi on the Raven side and the Chookaneidí, Kaagwaantaan, and Wooshkeetaan on the Eagle/Wolf side.

We documented more than 250 place names in the vicinity of Xunaa K̲áawu. Our project was carried out in collaboration with the Hoonah Indian Association (HIA) and supplemented earlier place name work in Glacier Bay National Park carried out by the tribe in conjunction with the Alaska Department of Fish and Game, Division of Subsistence, and the National Park Service. Key contributors included: James Austin, Ken Austin, Richard Dalton, Nora Marks Dauenhauer, Eva Davis, Ken Grant, Sam Hanlon, Charles Jack, Wilbur "Jumbo" James, Mary Johnson, Andrew Johnnie, Herman Kitka Sr., Gilbert Mills, Katherine Mills, Emma Marks, John Marks, Amy Marvin, Alfred McKinley, George Obert, Mary Rudolph, Frank See, Richard Sheakley, Winnie Smith, Kelly St. Clair, Lilly White, Frank White, Frank O. Williams, Bill Wilson, and many others. We also recognize the contributions of past researchers, including Nora and Richard Dauenhauer (1987, 1990, 1994), Frederica de Laguna (1960, 1972), George Emmons (1991, n.d.), Walter Goldschmidt and Theodore Haas (1998), George Hall (1962), Ronald Olson (1967), Eliza Scidmore (1896, 1899), Louis Shotridge (n.d.), John Swanton (1908, 1909), and others who documented indigenous place names in the area over the years. Robert Schroeder and Thomas Thornton coordinated the original (1992–94) research on behalf of the Alaska Department of Fish and Game, Division of Subsistence. These data were supplemented by additional interviewing and documentation of place names by Thornton and local research coordinator Bill Wilson through a National Park Service (NPS) grant with the Southeast Native Subsistence Commission (SENSC) in 1995–96. All named sites were digitized using GIS technology and reconfirmed by Glacier Bay National Park staff under the supervision of Wayne Howell; this process also generated additional place names which have been incorporated into this map.

A separate, larger and more detailed map produced by the National Park Service and Hoonah Indian Association is available through HIA for purchase (HIA 2006). Linguistic review was provided by Jeff Leer (Alaska Native Language Center), Ken Austin (NPS), Ken Grant (NPS), and Nora Marks Dauenhauer (Sealaska Heritage Institute).

Some Important Named Sites

Cape Spencer (*Naguk̲.yadaa, #190*). The mainland coast between Lituya Bay and Point Carolus on the west entrance of Glacier Bay, including grand Mount Fairweather, was claimed by the T'ak̲deintaan clan. The human geography of the Cape Fairweather–Lituya Bay region is described further in the G̲unaax̲oo K̲wáan section of chapter 1 (see also de Laguna 1972). Moving southeast, the next important place was the Icy Cape–Cape Spencer region. Numerous productive salmon streams lay here, including sockeye streams with settlements at Graves Harbor (L'ewtá, #160) and between Point Villaluenga (Naguk̲ K'i, #187) and Dicks Arm (Naguk̲ Héen, #175), as well as hunting, trapping, shellfishing and berrying grounds, and halibut banks. Of Graves Harbor, T'ak̲deintaan elder Kendall Williams observed you "[c]ould get everything there—gumboots, strawberries, salmonberries, cohos, king salmon, ribbon and black seaweed, and hair seal" (Goldschmidt and Haas 1998, 57). The sheltered areas along this coast also were used for sea-otter hunting and were the source of contention between the Tsimshian market hunters and the Xunaa Tlingits during the fur trade era (Beardslee 1882).

East of Icy Point, the arch at Boussole Head was called G̲aanax̲áa (#134) and the creek in Boussole Bay where the T'ak̲deintaan had fish camps was known as G̲aanax̲aa Héen (#134.1). It was here that a group from this clan drowned, save for one woman who was rescued by seabirds (Swanton 1909, 57–58). The incident is memorialized in a crest hat, a blanket, and in the T'ak̲deintaan house name, G̲aanax̲aa Hít. The creek inside Point Villaluenga (G̲aat Héeni, #183.1), at the entrance to Cross Sound, was the site of Ta.aan (Sleeping Town, #179) where the legendary hero K̲aakeix'wtí killed his sleep in the form of a bird before journeying to the Interior (see Hall 1962; Dauenhauer and Dauenhauer 1987, 153; Thornton 1997b).

Taylor Bay (*T'íx'aa X̲'aká, #156*). In the wake of the mammoth Brady Glacier (Sít' Tlein, #118), Taylor Bay was known as T'íx'aa X̲'aká (Ice Point at the Mouth) and was home to at least two villages: K̲eix̲itu.aan (Village inside the Brush, #153) and Asgutu.aan (Village in the Woods, #154) (Goldschmidt and Haas 1998). According to Emmons (n.d.), the early occupants of the bay were a branch of L'uknax̲.ádi called the Tikkadi [T'ix'ádi] ("Children of the Ice," taking their name from the bay), who were of southern origin, having migrated from the Tsimshian coast. George Vancouver passed by the bay in 1794 and observed the Native settlement, which was later destroyed by the advance of Brady Glacier. When Lieutenant C. E. S. Wood (1882, 332) visited almost a century later, a new camp had been established just below the glacier where he found Tlingit hunters using toggle harpoons to hunt adult harbor seals and bow and arrow for immature seals, which were taken by young boys. He reported that moss, seal oil, and driftwood were used for fuel due to the lack of trees. S. Hall Young, the missionary who accompanied Muir on his famous 1879 expedition into Glacier Bay, related how the Tlingit leader of the group that owned the salmon stream reacted to Brady Glacier's ominous advances by accepting responsibility for the glacier's "anger" and making various attempts to appease it:

> "Once," he said, "I had the finest salmon stream up on the coast." Pointing to a point of rock five or six miles beyond the mouth of the glacier, he continued: "Once the salmon stream extended far beyond that point of rock. There was a great fall there and a deep pool below it, and here for years great schools of king salmon came crowding up to the foot of that fall. To spear them or net them was very easy; they were the fattest and best salmon among all these islands. My household had abundance of meat for the winter's need. But the cruel spirit of that glacier grew angry with me, I know not why, and drove the ice mountain down towards the sea and spoiled my salmon stream. A year or two more and it will be blotted out entirely. I have done my best. I have prayed to my gods. Last spring I sacrificed two of my slaves, members of my household, my best slaves, a strong man and his wife, to the spirit of that glacier to make the ice mountain stop; but it comes on, and now I want you to pray to *your* God, the God of the white man, to see if He will make the glacier stop!" (1915, 178–83)

Young further notes that, despite proselytizing that turned the Xunaa Tlingits away from slavery, polygamy, and other objectionable practices, this leader "could not get rid of his superstition about the glacier... and about eight years afterwards, visiting at Wrangell, he told me as an item of news which he expected would greatly please me that, doubtless as a result of my prayers, [Brady] Glacier was receding again and the salmon were beginning to come into that stream."

Inian Islands (Dak̲áa X̲oo, #176). The islands of Cross Sound, especially the Inian Islands, were strategically important because the narrow passages between them comprised the gateway to the northern Inside Passage. Like other important geographic sites, the Inian Islands were believed to possess their own agentic spirits, Dak̲áa Kinaa K̲wáani ("Spirits Dwelling above Inian Islands"; see Dauenhauer and Dauenhauer 1990, 126). Enormous concentrations of salmon squeezed through South Inian Pass on their way to their spawning streams, and the powerful tidal currents generated through the narrow opening earned it the nickname "The Laundry." In the historic era, the Xunaa Tlingits became well known for their local knowledge and skill (some even called it *héix̲waa* or "magic") in seining large quantities of salmon in this perilous pass. The Inian Islands were also said to be "the best

Place Names as Linguistic Artifacts in Glacier Bay

Searching for archaeological sites in the temperate rainforests of Southeast Alaska can be a daunting task, where high precipitation, luxuriant vegetation, and a dynamic glacially and tectonically altered landscape can conspire to conceal site locations. But by using ethnographic information in the form of place names, Glacier Bay National Park staff has been successful in locating former village and camp sites where physical indicators, such as vegetation anomalies or subtle alterations to the terrain, give only the slightest hint of former habitation.

The information contained within many names has also proven useful in deciphering the Little Ice Age geological history of Glacier Bay. For example, some of the names we have from lower Glacier Bay, such as S'é Shuyee (Area at the End of the Clay), L'éiw Shaayí ([Glacial] Sand Mountain), or Chookanhéeni (Grassy Creek), describe an ancient landscape very different from the marine bay we know today. Geologists, using these geographic descriptors from ethnography, have begun to relocate remnants of an ancient landscape that fits nicely with these descriptions. The geologists have gathered organic materials from these places to be used for radiocarbon dating—pieces of bark from buried forests, shells from ancient estuaries, mats of grass from ancient meadows. This data will allow us to fit these events accurately into a historical chronology, while they enrich our understanding of the relationship of the Xunaa people to their ancestral homeland.

These names have also proven useful in locating places important in mythology, such as landforms attributed to Raven's activities at the time of creation (e.g., Diyáayi, or "Looks like a Whale") or in clan histories, where cultural alterations to the landscape are entirely lacking, but where the places are imbued with deep cultural significance—the black-legged kittiwake colony at G̲aanax̲áa is a good example of this. Thus, a place such as Mount Fairweather (Tsalx̲aan, or "Land of the Ground Squirrels"*) transforms from merely being an imposing ice-clad mountain to a place of spiritual seeking when we learn that the slopes and peaks around it are called Yéik Yee Aaní, "Land of the [Shaman] Spirits."

These names breathe spirit and life into what is otherwise an inanimate physical landscape. This is perhaps the greatest contribution of these Tlingit place names.

—Wayne Howell, Glacier Bay National Park, archeologist and management assistant

Tsalx̲aan (#27), also known as Mount Fairweather, is the tallest mountain in Xunaa K̲áawu and a sacred site associated with T'ak̲deintaan and other clan histories. This view is from Lituya Bay (Ltu.áa, #64) looking northeast toward the mountain. Courtesy of Glacier Bay National Park.

place for picking salmonberries and drying seaweeds" and good hunting and trapping grounds prior to the establishment of a fox farm there early in the century (Goldschmidt and Haas 1998). The wealth of salmon and other food also attracted large quantities of sea mammals, and a narrow passage called Tsaa T'a<u>k</u>di <u>X</u>'áak (#177) provided ideal conditions for landing them by harpoon. Tlingit sea mammal hunters also camped at Georges Island (<u>K</u>ooshnáa<u>x</u>'i, #191) and Three Hill Island (Kana<u>x</u> Aan <u>G</u>ashú, #198). The largest island, Lemesurier Island (Táas' Daa, #162), housed both a winter village and a fort (Goldschmidt and Haas 1998).

Dundas Bay (*Lanastáak*, #145). Dundas Bay supported a large village with a name our consultants referred to as "old Tlingit" which could not be interpreted (L'istee, #117). A famous fort, Xakwnoowú (Sandbar Fort, #132), was situated on the sandy spit at the mouth of Dundas River. The coho clans that originated at Dundas Bay, including L'ukna<u>x</u>.ádi and Ta<u>k</u>deintaan, sometimes employ the phrase *Ch'a tleix' Xakwnuw<u>k</u>eidí* ("We who are still one People of Sandbar Fort"; see Thornton 1997b, 2008) to reference their common history at this place. According to Native testimony recorded by Goldschmidt and Haas (1998) and Schroeder and Kookesh (1990), Dundas Bay was used for harvesting sockeye, humpback, and coho salmon, brown and black bear, mountain goat, marten, mink, otter, nagoonberries, mountain blueberries, soapberries, highbush cranberries, and other plants. While hunting and subsistence fishing activities are now prohibited or tightly regulated by the Park Service, special trips are still made here to harvest soapberries, strawberries, and nagoonberries during the summer, and the bountiful flats of Dundas Bay are appropriately named Tléi<u>k</u>w Aaní (Berry Land, #123) (Thornton 1999).

Glacier Bay (*Sít' Eetí <u>G</u>eeyí*, #122). Glacier Bay, now the centerpiece of a national park and world heritage site, was once the seat of Xunaa Tlingit culture. The indigenous toponymy in the area highlights their long presence there. As evidence of Tlingit presence there over time, there are three distinct names for the bay which apply to different periods in its geologic history. The first, S'é Shuyee (Area at the End of the Clay, #106) refers to an era (perhaps millennia ago) when the glaciers were advanced almost to Cross Sound and the mouth of the bay was but a small river banked by clay and silt generated by the moving glaciers. As the glaciers receded, a small bay was formed which was choked with icebergs, thus inspiring the second name, Xáatl Tú (Inside the Icebergs, #114). The third and current name, Sít' Eetí <u>G</u>eiyí (Bay in Place of the Glacier), was applied when the glaciers retreated even further, creating a full-fledged bay. Though mangled in transcription, this name can still be found on modern maps as "Sitakaday Narrows." These names reveal the natural history of the glacier, while other names reference its ethnological history. L'awshaa Shakee.aan (Town on Top of the [Glacial] Sand, #103), the original settlement at Bartlett Cove, was once inhabited by all the major Xunaa clans. But all groups were compelled to abandon their settlements after a young Chookaneidí girl, Kaasteen, violated her puberty seclusion by calling to the spirit of the glacier called Sít'k'i T'ooch' (Little Black Glacier, #19), causing it to advance rapidly, thus destroying the village and all in its path (see Emmons n.d.; Hall 1962; Dauenhauer and Dauenhauer 1987, 245–92; see "Do Glaciers Listen?" box). The Chookaneidí and T'a<u>k</u>deintaan moved to Spasski Bay (La<u>k</u>oo<u>x</u>ás' T'aa<u>k</u> Héen, #225) and ultimately to Port Frederick (Xutsgeeyí, #229), establishing a town called Gaaw T'a<u>k</u> Aan (#216) the name being derived from the drum-like sounds made by waves reverberating against a large hollowed-out boulder "tunnel" (Gaaw, #213) at the base of the cliff just north of present day Hoonah (and, unfortunately, partially destroyed by road construction). The Wooshkeetaan settled in Excursion Inlet (<u>K</u>uyei<u>k</u>', #129), while the Kaagwaantaan became centered at Kax'noowú (Female Grouse Fort, #181), and the L'ukna<u>x</u>.ádi established a village at Swanson Harbor (recorded by Emmons as "Koohk keh kee an" [Koo<u>k</u> Keikee.aan*], "In the Front of the Damp Ground Village"*) near Point Couverden. In the historic era, the latter reportedly became a trading village, occupied mainly by Wooshkeetaan, T'a<u>k</u>deintaan, and Kaagwaantaan (Goldschmidt and Haas 1998), the L'ukna<u>x</u>.ádi having largely removed to Jil<u>k</u>áat (Chilkat). These areas were also rich in natural resources, though they did not rival the abundance of Glacier Bay.

The retreat from Glacier Bay was only temporary, however. When the glacier receded, "The Icebox" or "Breadbasket," as Glacier Bay also came to be known by its original inhabitants, was once again settled and used to harvest resources. Though glaciers still choked the mouth of the bay during Vancouver's 1794 visit, fishing and sealing camps were established in the bay as soon as the ice receded, and Tlingits from as far away as Sitka and Pavlof Harbor (Asáank'i, #244.1) were hunting seal there by 1880. It was Tlingits from these camps who guided C. E. S. Wood (1882) and later John Muir (1915) on their "discovery" explorations of Glacier Bay. The seal in Glacier Bay

Do Glaciers Listen?

Do glaciers listen? This question forms the title of a book by Julie Cruikshank (2005), examining the relationship between these rivers of ice and indigenous peoples of Southeast Alaska and southern Yukon in the context of environmental and social change. The answer is, of course, "yes," glaciers do listen. The Chookaneidí story of Kaasteen, set in Glacier Bay and encapsulated in this button blanket (*x'óow*), exemplifies the moral ecology between humans and features of the natural world, like glaciers, which possess agentic spirits. The blanket maps the sacred geography of the story, including L'awshaa Shakee.aan (Town on Top of the [Glacial] Sand), where Kaasteen (bottom center), a young women in menarche, called to the glacier, Sít'k'i T'ooch' ("Little Black Glacier," center), violating her taboo of seclusion, thus causing the glacier to advance and destroy the village. As a consequence, the people were forced to evacuate and composed songs of mourning for their houses and land as they departed (Dauenhauer and Dauenhauer 1987). These powerful songs are still performed today, and Chookaneidí entering Glacier Bay still feed and sing to the spirits of their ancestors who continue to dwell there among the glaciers. The blanket also features other crests of the Chookaneidí, including the brown bear, and serves as a historical and legal record of Chookaneidí ties and rights to Glacier Bay.

Below: On a trip to Glacier Bay, Lilly White, *naa tláa* (clan mother) of the Chookaneidí clan (female members of which are called Chookanshaa), interprets her clan's *at.óow* (sacred possession), a button blanket representing the story of Kaasteen, a young woman of her clan who spoke to the glacier Sít'k'í T'ooch' (#19) in violation of her menstrual seclusion. The glacier responded by advancing and destroying the Tlingit village at L'awshaa Shakee.aan (#103). Photo by Tom Thornton.

were not only plentiful but considered to be easier to harvest and of exceptionally high quality meat, fat, and hides. Similarly, the fish, terrestrial wildlife, and plants in the bay were thought to be of the highest quality, due to the icy waters, cold air, and other unique climatic conditions that prevailed there. The Bartlett River (G̲athéeni, #91) was an especially productive salmon system and the Tlingit established a seasonal settlement on Lester Island, also referred to as G̲athéeni (#98). Bartlett Cove later became the site of a commercial salmon saltery and, eventually, the headquarters for Glacier Bay National Park. Other important sites in the area included the Chookaneidí settlement at Berg Bay (Chookanhéeni, #85) from which the clan took its name, and habitation sites at Point Carolus

Hoonah Indian Association: Putting Our Place Names Back on the Map

Long before Russian, French, Spanish, and British explorers mapped and named the mountains and bays of the Xunaa Tlingit homeland, we identified special places in our own vibrant, descriptive ways. Tlingit place names reflect important natural resources, ancestral stories, sacred places, and major geological and historic events. Our place names describe more than just inanimate locations, for we perceive the mountains, glaciers, and streams to be as alive and aware as ourselves. Rather, they capture the history, emotions, and stories of our enduring relationship with a living, evolving landscape.

Place names such as Tsaa Áayi (Seal Lake), K'wát' Aaní (Bird [seagull] Egg Land), and K̲'aach' X'aayí (Point of the Ribbon Seaweed) convey the respect we hold for the animals and plants whose spirits inhabit and "own" the places where they reside. We named hunting grounds on both land and sea, fish camps at stream mouths, egg-harvesting islands, berry patches, and food-gathering beaches — all places that sustained the Xunaa Tlingit people for countless generations. Some names such as Yéil Nées'kuxli Tashaa (Raven Sea-Urchin Echo Knife Behind-Mountain*) commemorate ancestral stories which describe our world order, ingrain social and spiritual values in our youth, and impart life lessons. Others remind present day clans of social contracts and arrangements still applicable today, such as X̲'aak Takaadé Wuduwak̲ani Yé, or "Place Where the Argument Was Settled." Our place names commemorate not only events of the past, but capture the very emotions our ancestors experienced; we sense the relief ancestral hunters felt when their canoes rounded the rocky point near Cape Spencer at Yaanash Kweix̲, or (loosely) "Take a Deep Breath, You Are Out of Peril," leaving the rough and dangerous waters of the outer coast behind.

Our place names, then, are as alive as the locations they describe. When we speak these names today, we are — quite literally — transformed and transported; we become the ancestors gathering berries, defending territory, and resolving conflicts in our homeland. Through language we continue to participate in the formation, adaptation, and evolution of the rich culture of the Xunaa Tlingit people.

The word *aan* means "land" or "country" and is often associated with Tlingit village sites. Adding an *i* to make *aaní* symbolizes the possessive — that is, the land belongs to the animals or plants that live there and give it its name.

Because place names are so important to the survival of Xunaa Tlingit culture, the Hoonah Indian Association is working with a number of other organizations and agencies to document and share place name information. In 2005, we produced the long-awaited *Tlingit Place Names of the Huna Káawu* poster with assistance and funding from the Alaska Department of Fish and Game, the National Park Service, the U.S. Forest Service, and of course, the Xunaa Tlingit elders. With further assistance from the U.S. Forest Service and the Institute for Museum and Library Services, we produced a twenty-five-square-foot scale topographical model of our traditional territory with descriptions and stories of the place names embedded in our homeland. In cooperation with the National Park Service, we are working to complete a computer-based "talking map" that captures the sounds of elders speaking our place names as well as photographs and stories associated with important locations. We hope these projects — and others — will continue to connect our people to the stories, events, relationships, and emotions embodied in the place names of Xunaa K̲áawu.

(Yáay Shaak'ú Aan, #135) and Beartrack Cove (G̲athéeni Tlein, #72). Xunaa Tlingits continue to assert their rights to harvest key cultural foods within the park despite restrictions, and have shown they can do so sustainably (cf. Hunn et al. 2003).

Lisianski Strait (*K'udeis*, #239). On the Chichagof side of Icy Strait and Cross Sound, Lisianski Strait was the site of perhaps the earliest European contact with the Xunaa Tlingit. It was here that Alexis Chirikov, with Bering's expedition in 1741, sent a boat out to explore the waterway (presumed to be a bay), which failed to return. Later he witnessed two Tlingit boats coming out of the same bay in a canoe which did not approach, but whose passengers waved and shouted "Agai, Agai" before heading to shore. Chirikov assumed that the Natives had killed or detained the men (Golder 1922, 1:296–97). The Tlingit version of the incident recounts that Chirikov's scouts were not captured or slain, but rather feasted as honored guests. It is said that they were invited to stay among the Tlingit and desired to do so because of the privations and other misfortunes they had suffered on their voyage. They remained among the Tlingit, eventually intermarrying and settling in the area.

Chichagof Island. Other important Xunaa K̲áawu settlements and use areas on north Chichagof Island include those at Idaho Inlet (Dak̲áanáx̲, #196), Mud Bay (Xákw Tlein, #192), Port Frederick (Xutsg̲eeyí, #229), Tenakee Inlet (T'einaag̲eey, #251), and Freshwater Bay (Asáani,* #244). In addition to the modern village of Hoonah (Xunaa, #218), which also has several historic names (e.g., Gaaw T'ak̲ Aan, #216), Port Frederick housed numerous seasonal camps and fort sites, as well as the famous Killer

This large format map, *Tlingit Place Names of the Huna Káawu* (K̲áawu), is available through the Hoonah Indian Association (HIA 2006). A Tlingit proverb gracing the map translates as follows: "If you don't know the names, your [Tlingit] way of life will drift away forever."

Whale Portage (#238) to Tenakee Inlet (Goldschmidt and Haas 1998; Swanton 1909). As John Swanton recorded from Sitka Tlingit elder Deikeenáak'w in 1904 (1909, 27):

> On their way to us the first killer whales came into a bay called Kots!ê'L! [Kus'eil', early name for Tenakee Inlet or Port Frederick; see #231] after the first man who came to that bay. They encamped at its head and the day after began digging into the cliff. The land there is not very high, so they were soon through, laid skids down, and carried their canoes across. Some people watched them. The killer whales always used to cross at the place where they laid down these skids, and now people cross there. It is called Killer-whale-crossing place (Kîtgû'nî) [Kéet Góoni].

While not considered part of the Xunaa K̲áawu, Tlingit settlements in Tenakee Inlet were contiguous to the territory and their occupants, including Wooshkeetaan, T'ak̲deintaan, and some Chookaneidí, were closely related to those clans in Hoonah.

Final Thoughts

Nearly a half century ago in his book *Glacier Bay: The Land and the Silence*, David Bohn (1967) reflected soulfully on the loss of Tlingit names on the land:

> Among over two hundred place names covering a land and water area of 4400 square miles, there is exactly one Indian name surviving, and that is Lituya Bay. Other Indian names have been added, about seven of them, one of which — Sitakaday Narrows — is misspelled from John Muir's original rendition of Sitadakay [misrendered from Sít' Eetí G̲eeyí]. What happened to the Hoonah names for Taylor and Dundas Bay and the Grand Pacific Glacier, for example, all of which were intimately known to these people? As far as I know, they are lost as are the native words for all the other inlets and glaciers in Glacier Bay. For perhaps five hundred to a thousand years of Indian history to be represented by several place names in two hundred, speaks rather poorly for the white man, but that is certainly nothing new.

Fortunately, many of these names, including those for Taylor Bay (T'íx'aa X̲'aká), Dundas Bay (Lanastáak), and Grand Pacific Glacier (Sít' Tlein), have not been lost. Though missing from the cartography, they have survived in the culture, minds, and hearts of Xunaa Tlingits. As a result of this cooperative project, a significant portion of Tlingit toponyms in Glacier Bay are now transcribed and mapped. That the names have not been lost is testimony to the vitality of Tlingit culture in this area.

There are good reasons for consulting Tlingit place names as a source of scientific information about Glacier Bay. This knowledge base represents many centuries of direct experience with the land and provides important clues as to the natural and cultural history of the area which can aid and complement Western scientific inquiry. Today, the Park Service is working with Hoonah Indian Association to realize the value of Native place names in understanding the full history and significance of Glacier Bay National Park as a dynamic cultural and physical landscape. In addition, Tlingit language and names are being reintroduced through the schools and place-based cultural programs sponsored by the tribe, Huna Totem Corporation, and Glacier Bay National Park and Preserve. Certainly, knowing the Tlingit place names and their meanings helps us speak better of the rich cultural heritage that is Xunaa K̲áawu.

Comparing English and Tlingit Naming Patterns in Glacier Bay

Analysis of the linguistic structure and topographical distribution of place names provides a partial glimpse of how cultures perceive their environment. A semantic analysis helps to complete the picture by tracing out meanings contained in toponyms. The typology in the table below provides one basis for comparing semantic referents in Tlingit and English place names in Glacier Bay National Park, and is based on a sample of more than one hundred names from each language.

The first category, biological references, includes animals, plants, and anatomical and mythological allusions. Animals are evident in 29 percent of Tlingit place names, referring to nineteen different species of fish and wildlife. In English, animals are evoked in 6 percent of names, referring to ten different species of wildlife but no fish. The majority of these associations in both languages are *metonymic,* meaning that the animals characterize the places by their presence there, usually in abundance. For example, Goose Cove was a name suggested by W. S. Cooper who observed there "a number of young wild geese who, still unable to fly, were flapping over the water" (Orth 1971). The English name, Tlingit Point, is a metonymic association referring to Xunaa seal hunters who camped there. Similarly, the Tlingit called Tidal Inlet Gus'k'iyee Kwáan Geeyí (Under the Clouds People's [white people's] Bay) because of the presence of whites at that place. The Tlingit names for Bartlett River, Gathéeni (Sockeye River), and Beartrack River, Gathéeni Tlein (Big Sockeye River), reflect not only the concentration of this species at these locations but also the Tlingit cultural interest in these fish. On the other hand, the lack of references to fish in the English name set is indicative of a bias toward upland resources, especially those which are easily viewed.

Metonomy also characterizes plant references in both languages. In the English toponymy, Strawberry Island is an example of a metonymic plant association based on abundance. Chookanhéeni (Grassy Creek), Keishísh Aaní (Alder Country), and Wudzidugu Yé (Place Wooded with Cottonwood) are examples of this pattern in Tlingit. The relative dearth of plant names in both toponymies may be a reflection of glacial scouring of the vegetation and the lack of culturally significant plants in Glacier Bay as compared to other habitats.

Not all plant and animal references are metonymic. Some associations may hearken back to a mythological or historical event. Kuts'een Gíl'i (Rat Cliff) refers not to an abundance of ordinary rats at the cliff below Spokane Cove, but rather to a single extraordinary rodent of epic proportions that once, long ago, kidnapped a young Tlingit maiden to be his wife. The villainous varmint eventually had to be subdued by the young woman's brothers in a violent battle at the site. There are also many names commemorating the wanderings and misadventures of the trickster-demiurge Raven. X'as'tuhéen (Creek inside the Jaw) identifies small streams created by the drops of water that spilled from Raven's mouth as he fled from Petrel after stealing his water (Sam Hanlon, pers. comm. 1993). A site where Raven was active on the Alsek River is dubbed Yéil Áa Ludaawdligoowu Yé (Place Where Raven Wiped His Beak) (Nora Marks Dauenhauer, pers. comm. 1999). Such toponymic references serve as historical citations on the landscape, bringing events of the past into the present for new generations to behold. Mythological animal and plant references comprise 5 percent of the Tlingit toponymy in Glacier Bay.

Another set of references found in place names are those that refer to the body. Anatomical references are common in place naming and other referencing systems because the body is in fact our most basic environment and instrument of measure. Place names such as Yáay

Table 5. Semantic Referents in Glacier Bay Place Names

Semantic category	*% Tlingit names*	*% English names*
Biological	43	9
Animal	(30)	(7)
Plant	(13)	(2)
Topographical	59	25
Hydrographic	(43)	(11)
Terrestrial	(16)	(14)
Biographical	1	50
Habitation Sites	12	0
Historical	13	9
Mythological	5	0
Anatomical	7	1
Other	0	6

Some Tlingit names fall into more than one category.

Shaak'ú (Whale's Little Head) display a *metaphoric* association, positing an analogy between a geographic feature and an anatomical feature based on visual resemblance. Body references characterize 7 percent of the Tlingit place names in Glacier Bay. Anatomical metaphors are also invoked in the English toponymy (e.g., Dicks Arm) but less frequently.

A second major category of semantic references consists of topographical associations. Topographical references may be divided into two basic categories: hydrographic, those alluding to aquatic or shoreline features, and terrestrial, those referring to upland features of the landscape. Topographical references other than generics make up 59 percent of the Tlingit name set and 25 percent of the English. Significantly, 42 percent of all Tlingit place names contain hydrographic references, another reflection of the culture's maritime orientation. The majority of non-generic Euro-American topographical referents, in contrast, are associated with upland features.

While these two major semantic categories account for more than 90 percent of Tlingit place names, less than 35 percent of the English toponyms contain non-generic biological or topographical referents. This is because the preeminent category in the English toponymy is biographical naming. English place names refer to explorers (e.g., La Pérouse Glacier, Dixon Entrance, Muir Inlet), scientists (e.g., Geikie Inlet, Reid Glacier, Adams Inlet), missionaries (e.g., Young Island, Brady Glacier), entrepreneurs (e.g., Bartlett Cove, Willoughby Island, Ibach Point), inventors (e.g., Wilbur Mountain, of the Wright brothers), surveyors (e.g., Riggs Glacier, Lars Island, Netland Island), treasurers of the British Navy (e.g., Dundas Bay), and a host of other characters, many of whom never came within a thousand miles of Glacier Bay. Tlingits were not left out either. In addition to Hoonah Glacier, which recognizes the whole group, individual Tlingits also were honored. Sitka Charley (Charley Glacier) and Tyeen (Tyeen Glacier), members of Muir's expedition, were memorialized in glaciers (although not until years after their pioneering voyage), as were the Xunaa leader Kasohto (Kahsoto Glacier) and the Jilkáat leader Koh Klux (Kloh-Kutz Glacier).

Ironically, such honorific naming practices would probably be deemed inappropriate in Tlingit. Indeed, biographical naming is virtually absent from the Tlingit toponymy. Rather than naming places after people, as was the Euro-American tradition, the Tlingit custom was more commonly to name people after places.

—*Adapted from Thornton (1995)*

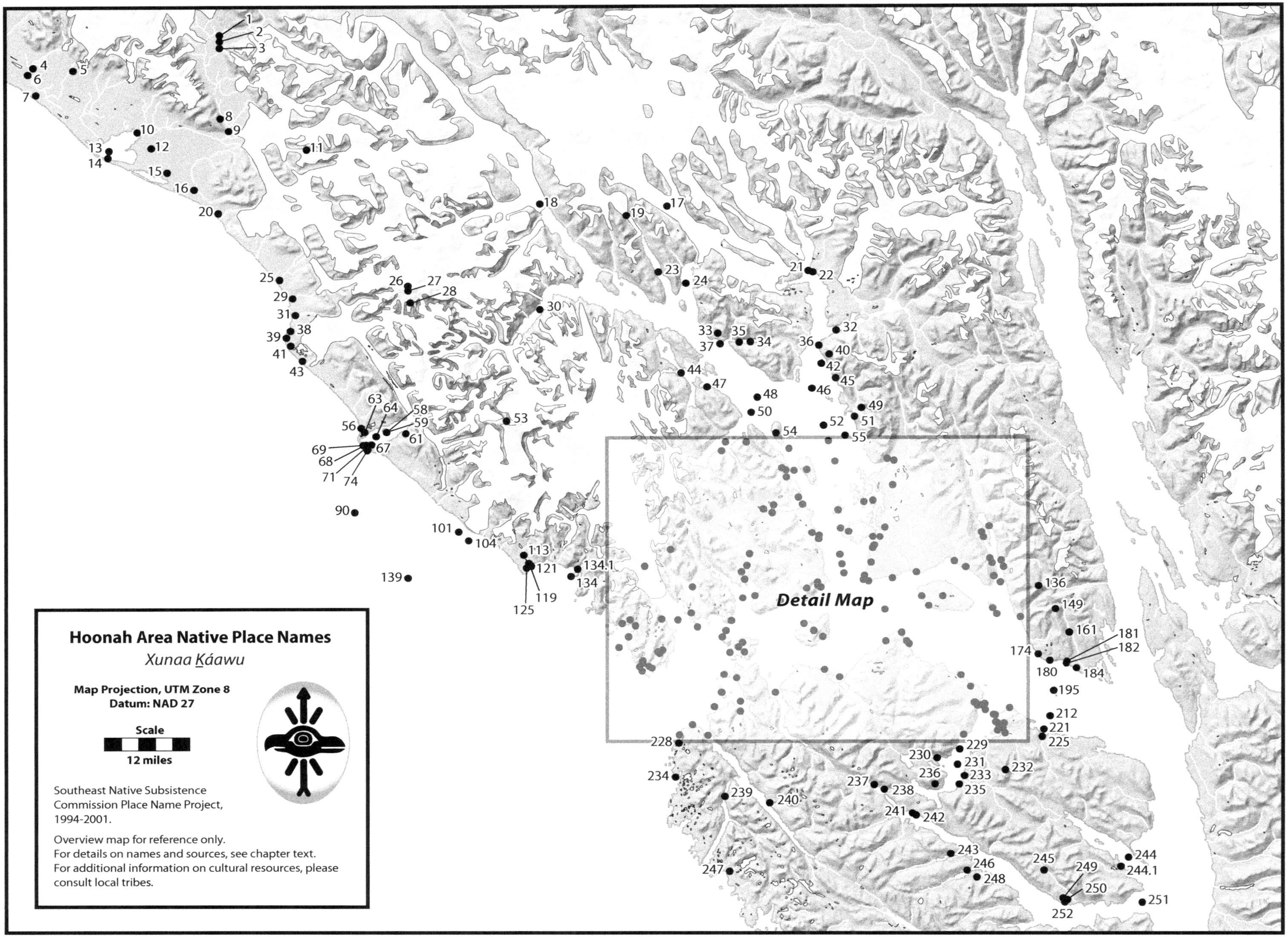
Hoonah Area Native Place Names
Xunaa Ḵáawu
Map Projection, UTM Zone 8
Datum: NAD 27
Scale
12 miles
Southeast Native Subsistence Commission Place Name Project, 1994-2001.
Overview map for reference only.
For details on names and sources, see chapter text.
For additional information on cultural resources, please consult local tribes.
Detail Map
1 2 3 4 5 6 7 8 9 10 11 12 13 14 15 16 17 18 19 20 21 22 23 24 25 26 27 28 29 30 31 32 33 34 35 36 37 38 39 40 41 42 43 44 45 46 47 48 49 50 51 52 53 54 55 56 58 59 61 63 64 67 68 69 71 74 90 101 104 113 119 121 125 134 134.1 136 139 149 161 174 180 181 182 184 195 212 221 225 228 229 230 231 232 233 234 235 236 237 238 239 240 241 242 243 244 244.1 245 246 247 248 249 250 251 252

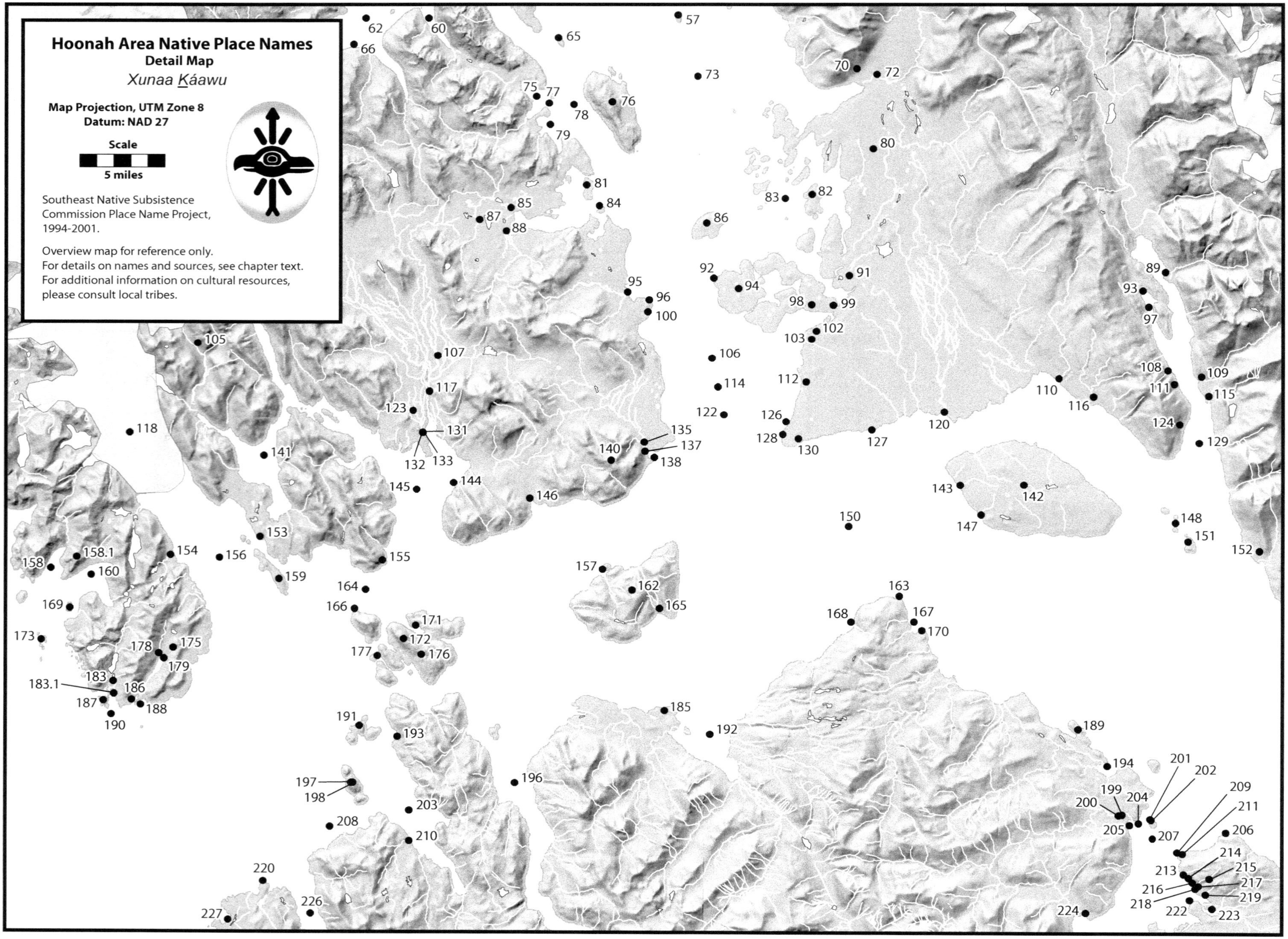
Hoonah Area Native Place Names
Detail Map
Xunaa Káawu
Map Projection, UTM Zone 8
Datum: NAD 27
Scale
5 miles
Southeast Native Subsistence Commission Place Name Project, 1994-2001.
Overview map for reference only.
For details on names and sources, see chapter text.
For additional information on cultural resources, please consult local tribes.
57
60
62
65
66
70
72
73
75
76
77
78
79
80
81
82
83
84
85
86
87
88
89
91
92
93
94
95
96
97
98
99
100
102
103
105
106
107
108
109
110
111
112
114
115
116
117
118
120
122
123
124
126
127
128
129
130
131
132
133
135
137
138
140
141
142
143
144
145
146
147
148
150
151
152
153
154
155
156
157
158
158.1
159
160
162
163
164
165
166
167
168
169
170
171
172
173
175
176
177
178
179
183
183.1
185
186
187
188
189
190
191
192
193
194
196
197
198
199
200
201
202
203
204
205
206
207
208
209
210
211
213
214
215
216
217
218
219
220
222
223
224
226
227

Xunaa K̲áawu Place Names

Asterisk indicates uncertain, unconfirmed, or partial; NM = not mapped.
Some names have more than one pronunciation or translation.

Map #	*Name*	*Translation*	*Location*
1	Aas X̲'áak	Between Trees	On old Alsek River trail*
2	Sít' X'aayí	Glacier Point	Point on Alsek River near Novatak Glacier*
3	Yéil Dzoonáyi	Raven's Bola	Alsek River, Gateway Knob area*
4	Gus'eix̲	*	Akwe River
5	Gaaw Aaní	Time (Drum) Land	Akwe River area, Raven's land of creation
6	Aakwéi	*	Akwe River
7	Yéil Áx̲ Daak̲ Akaawajiyi Yé	Where Raven's Feet Worked into the Mud Dragging (the salmon repository or "food canoe")	Akwe River
8	Yéil Áa Ludaawdlig̲oowu Yé	Place Where Raven Wiped His Beak	Alsek River above Alsek Lake
9	Yadak'wát'	Bird Eggs on the Face	Gateway Knob
10	Aalséix̲	Resting	Alsek River island
11	G̲elk.uwaa (G̲elguwaa)	Looks like a Small Pass	Mountain pass east of Gateway Knob
12	Diyáayi	Looks like a Whale	Bear Island
13	G̲unaax̲oo (G̲unanaa X̲oo)	Among the Interior Natives (Athabaskans)	Dry Bay
14	Kunag̲a.áa	Paddling Hard	Dry Bay*
15	Dinetgi Aan	Shaky Ground Village	Near East River
16	Til'héeni	Dog Salmon River	Doame River
18	Sít' Tlein	Big Glacier	Grand Pacific and Marjorie glaciers
19	Sít' T'ooch'	Black Glacier	Carrol Glacier
19	Sít'k'i T'ooch'	Little Black Glacier	Rendu Glacier
20	Gunhéeni	Spring Creek	Clear Creek
21	Aan Adéli	Village Watchman	Sealers Island
22	Óoxjaa G̲eeyí	Windy Bay	Goose Cove
23	Sít' Eetí G̲eeyí	Bay in Place of the Glacier	Rendu Inlet
24	T'ooch' G̲eeyí	Black Bay	Queen Inlet
25	Kantak̲w Héeni	Lupine River	Between East Alsek River and Cape Fairweather
26	G̲éelák'w	Little Mountain Pass	Small pass over Mount Fairweather
27	Tsalx̲aan	Land of the Ground Squirrels*	Mount Fairweather
28	Yéik Yee Aaní	Land of the [Shaman] Spirits	Area around Mount Fairweather
29	Yáxwch'i Héeni	Sea Otter Creek	Sea Otter Creek

Map #	*Name*	*Translation*	*Location*
30	Tsalxaan Niyaadé Wool'éex'i Yé	[Passage] Which Broke Through toward Tsalxaan (#27)	Johns Hopkins Inlet
31	Shgadaayi (Shgaadaayi) Héen	Lone Creek	Above Cape Fairweather*
32	Héen Xook Geeyí	Dry Stream Bay	Adams Inlet
33	Áak'w Kakúxti	Dried-Up Little Lake	Vivid Lake area
34	Gus'k'iyee Kwáan Geeyí	Under the Clouds People's (white people's) Bay	Tidal Inlet
35	Tsalgi Geeyí	Ground Bay	Tidal Inlet
36	Hinxuka.aaní	Village [Reflected] on the Surface of the Water	Near Muir Point
37	Xóots X'oosí X'aa	Brown Bear Paw Point	Outcrop between Tidal Inlet and Vivid Lake
38	L'idakneech	By the Unusual* Beach	Cape Fairweather shoreline
39	Laak'asgi X'aayí	Black Seaweed Point	Cape Fairweather
40	At Aaní	Wildlife Grounds	Uplands near Mount Wright
41	T'akdein Satán	Sticking Out on the Side*	Cape Fairweather area
42	Wasus X'áat'i	Cow Island	Garforth Island
43	K'atl* Shakee Aaní	——* on Top of Land	Sea-otter hunting grounds, Cape Fairweather
44	Anax Kuyaawal'ix'i Yé	Where the Glacier Ice Broke Through	Hugh Miller and Scidmore inlets
45	Daklashú	Where the Woods End	Bluffs north of Sandy Cove
46	La.aayí Tukyee	Outlet of [La.aayí, "Building the Lake"]	Muir Inlet
47	Gus'k'iyee Kwáan Noowú	Under the Clouds People's (white people's) Fort	Hugh Miller Inlet (head of bay)
48	L'ée Hítk'	Little Blanket House	Lone Island
49	Guchhéeni	Wolf Creek	Wolf Creek in Spokane Cove
50	Ts'agéegi Teiyí	Little Seabird Rock	Geikie Rock
51	Kuts'een Gíl'i	Rat Cliff	Cliff south of Spokane Cove
52	Nánde Néix' X'áat'i	North Marble Island	North Marble Island
53	Yéil Nées'kuxli Tashaa	Raven Sea-Urchin Echo Knife Behind-Mountain*	Mounts Crillon or La Pérouse, or Bald Mountain
54	X'áat' Kulasá	Narrow Island	Drake Island
55	Hintuxu X'aayí	Seagrass Point	Leland Island
56	Yakwdeiyí	Canoe Trail	Portage Creek above La Chaussee Spit
57	Íxde Néix' X'áat'i	South Marble Island	South Marble Island
58	Kanaxdakéen	Flying Over	Cenotaph Island
59	Deikée X'aká	Inside the Mouth at the Outer Coast	Cenotaph Island
60	Wudzidugu Yé Yádi	Child of Wudzidugu Yé (#62)	Shag Cove
61	Yat'ak Héen	River beside the Face of It	Fall Creek (Lituya Bay)
62	Wudzidugu Yé	Place Wooded with Cottonwood	Geikie Inlet
63	Anax'aayí	Passageway* (correct way to go in or out)	Lituya Bay

Map #	*Name*	*Translation*	*Location*
64	Ltu.áa	Lake inside the Point (nostril)	Lituya Bay
65	Shaltláax̱ K'átsk'u	Small Rock Island Covered with Lichen	Francis Island
66	Atx̱'as'i X̱'atá	Inside Corner of Animal's Jaw	Jaw Point, Geikie Inlet
67	Naháayi Goojí	Hill of the Wanderer	The Paps, Lituya Bay
68	Tuwool	Hole Inside	Lituya Bay below Harbor Point
69	Taan Teséet	Sea Lion Rock Strait	Passage Rock (rock with blinker in Lituya Bay)
70	Xutsjíni Hít	Brown Bear Paw House	Inside Beartrack Cove
71	Kaanax̱tí	Being Overcome	Weather watcher's rock, south entrance to Lituya Bay
72	G̱athéeni Tlein	Big Sockeye River	Beartrack River
73	K'wát' Aaní	Bird (seagull) Egg Land	Marble Islands area
74	Taan Teiyí	Sea Lion Rock	Lituya Bay entrance
75	Gíl' X̱'aan Seiyí	Red Cliff Reach	Northwest shore of Fingers Bay
76	Shaltláax̱ Tlein	Big Rock Island Covered with Lichen	Willoughby Island
77	X̱'aan Gooch G̱eeyí	Red Hill Bay	Fingers Bay
78	Gíl' X̱'aan Séet	Red Cliff Strait	Whidbey Passage
79	Aankáawdahaan Tl'átgi	Aankáawdahaan's (man's name) Property	Inside Fingers Bay
80	Áax'w X̱oo	Among the Lakes	Hutchins Bay area*
81	Chookanhéeni X̱'akax'áat'	Island at Mouth of Chookanhéeni (#85)	Netland Island
82	Kadigooni X'áat'	Island That Has Spring Water	Kidney Island
83	X'áat'x'i X̱oo	Among the Islands	Beardslee Islands
84	X̱'atadáa Noowú	Weasel[s] at the Corner[s] of the Mouth Fort	On Lars Islands
85	Chookanhéeni	Grassy Creek	Berg Bay and River
86	L'awx'áat'i	[Glacial] Sand Island	Strawberry Island
87	Chookanhéeni Áax'w X̱oo	Among the Lakes at Chookanhéeni (#85)	Upstream of Berg Bay/River
88	L'ukhéeni	Coho Stream	Berg Bay, south stream
89	Wéitadi Noow	Fort of the Young Woman in Seclusion (in menarche)	Head of Excursion Inlet
90	X̱'oon Kalshaḵx'i Aaní	Out of Breath (exhausted) Fur Seal Land	Fairweather Grounds
91	G̱athéeni	Sockeye River	Bartlett River
92	K'wát' Aaní Luyee	Area below the Point of Bird Egg Land	Westernmost point of Young Island
93	Ḵuyeiḵ' Tú	Inside Ḵuyeiḵ' (#129)	Sawmill Bay in Excursion Inlet
94	S'ax̱x'áat'i	Marmot Island	Young Island
95	Chookanhéeni Yádi	Child of Chookanhéeni (#85)	River above Rush Point
96	Ḵ'aach' X'aayí	Ribbon Seaweed Point	Rush Point
97	Nánde X̱ánk'	Small Place Close Up toward the North	Cove in Sawmill Bay

Map #	Name	Translation	Location
98	Ḡathéeni	Sockeye River	Lester Island fish camp
99	T'aawáḵ Séedi	Goose Narrows	Bartlett Cove lagoon
100	T'ooch' Ḡí'l'i	Black Cliff	In Glacier Bay, perhaps Rush Point or Berg Bay
101	Yant'íká	Out on the Ocean, on the Coast	Another name for the Fairweather Coast
102	L'éiw Shaayí	[Glacial] Sand Mountain	Bartlett Cove area
103	L'awshaa Shakee.aan	Town on Top of the [Glacial] Sand	Bartlett Cove area
104	Yáxwch'i Aaní	Land of the Sea Otter	Fairweather Coast
105	Laxaas'	*	Dundas Bay
106	S'é Shuyee	Area at the End of the Clay	Glacier Bay (first name)
107	Gakakaiwuhéen*	Creek Where Plenty of Fish Come*	Seclusion River
108	Ḵáa Tlénx'i Ḵaadí	Slide of the Big Men	West shore, Excursion Inlet
109	L'ux'uhéen	Murky Creek	Excursion Inlet (above cannery)
110	Katahéeni	Trap* Creek	Falls Creek, Gustavus
111	Yeis Ḵaadí	Autumn Slide	West shore, Excursion Inlet
112	Keishísh Aaní	Alder Country	Point Gustavus to Bartlett Cove
113	Kaháakw Héeni	Salmon Egg Creek	Kaknau Creek at Icy Point
114	Xáatl Tú	Inside the Icebergs	Glacier Bay (second name)
115	Kuyeiḵ' L'e.aan	Kuyeiḵ' (#129) Peaceful* Village	Excursion Inlet (creek south of cannery)
116	Tlaxaneis' Héen	Kingfisher Creek	Creek on Icy Passage shore
117	L'istee	——* (fort name in "old language")	Dundas Bay at Dundas River
118	Sít' Tlein	Big Glacier	Brady Glacier
119	Xaatgutu.aan	Village Nestled in the [Spruce] Roots	Inside Icy Point
120	Wanachích T'aak Héen	Stream Back of Wanachích (#142)	River east of Gustavus
121	Yéil Yakwdeiyí	Raven's Canoe Trail	Safe anchorage inside Icy Point
122	Sít' Eetí Ḡeeyí (Ḡeey)	Bay in Place of the Glacier	Glacier Bay (third name)
123	Tléiḵw Aaní	Berry Land	Dundas River flats
124	Kuyeiḵ' X'aka.aan	Village at the Mouth of Kuyeiḵ' (#129)	Excursion Inlet, west point
125	T'aay X'é	Hot Springs Mouth	Icy Point
126	Ḵ'aach' Xágu	Ribbon Seaweed Beach	Above Point Gustavus
127	L'éiw Tú	Inside the Sand	Gustavus to Point Gustavus
128	S'íx' X'aayí	Dish Point	Point Gustavus
129	Kuyeiḵ'	*	Excursion Inlet
130	S'é X'aayí Lutú	Nostril of Clay Point	Point Gustavus
131	Xunaa Ḵáawu Noowú	Xunaa People's Fort	West bank of Dundas River near mouth
132	Xakwnoowú	Sandbar Fort	Mouth of Dundas River
133	L'éiw Noowú	Sand Fort	Dundas Bay near Dundas River
134	Gaanaxáa	*	Arch at Boussole Head
134.1	Gaanaxaa Héen	Gaanaxáa (#134) Creek	Creek in Boussole Bay

Map #	*Name*	*Translation*	*Location*
135	Yáay Shaak'ú Aan	Whale's Little Head Village	Point Carolus village
136	Shuk Da Doogu*	Strong Person's Mountain	Mountain above Homeshore
137	Wat'aḵhéen (Yat'aḵ Héen)	River alongside the Face/Side	Carolus River
138	L'éiw T'aak Héen	River behind the [Glacial] Sand	Point Carolus
139	Yéil (Yeil) T'ooch'	Black Raven	Gulf of Alaska (Pacific Ocean)
140	Yáay Shaak'ú	Whale's Little Head	Point Carolus
141	Éenaa X̱'atán	Spruce Root Scraper Lying There*	West arm of Dundas Bay
142	Wanachích (Wunachích)	Back (edge) of a Porpoise (an island)	Pleasant Island
143	Wanachích Daa	Beaches around Wanachích (#142)	Beach areas around Pleasant Island
144	Tináak'w	Little Copper Shield	Bight on east coast of Dundas Bay
145	Lanastáak (Lunastáak)	——* (Back of the Nose Ring*)	Dundas Bay
146	S'eek (S'ik) Shaanáx̱i	Black Bear Valley	Bight east of Dundas Bay
147	Koolsaw X'aa	Narrow Sandy Point	Sandy beach on west side of Pleasant Island
148	Ḵuyeiḵ' X̱'aka.aan X'áatx'i	Islands at the Village in Front of Ḵuyeiḵ' (#129)	Porpoise Islands
149	Lulx̱ooshaa	Mountain amidst the Fireweed	Mountain above Homeshore
150	S'íx' Tlein	Big Dish	Icy Strait
151	Kulisawu X'áat'	Slender Island	Porpoise Islands
152	X̱'as'tuhéen	Creek inside the Jaw (saliva)	Streams along Homeshore below Excursion Inlet
153	Ḵeix̱itu.aan	Village inside the Brush	East side of Taylor Bay
154	Asgutu.aan	Village in the Woods	West side of Taylor Bay
155	Neixinté Seiyí	Area below the Blue-Green Claystone	Off Wimbledon Point
156	T'íx'aa X̱'aká (T'íx'aa)	Ice Point at the Mouth (Ice Point)	Taylor Bay
157	Táas' Daa Yádi	Child of Double-Headed Tide around It (Lemesurier Island)	Small island just above Lemesurier Island
158	Lakweishnáx̱ Táak	Bottom Interior of Lakweishnáx̱ (#158.1)	Murk Bay
158.1	Lakweishnáx̱	*	Horn Mountain peninsula or Torch Bay*
159	T'íx'aa X̱'akax'áat'	Island at Mouth of Ice Point	Taylor Island
160	L'ewtá	Head of [Glacial] Sand	Graves Harbor
161	Gux̱ X̱'aagák'u (X̱'aak Takaadé Wuduwaḵani Yé)	Slave's Ravine (Place Where the Argument Was Settled)	Valley behind Groundhog Bay
162	Táas' Daa	Double-Headed Tide around It (Lemesurier Island)	Lemesurier Island
163	Sdakweix̱ Lutú	[Man's name] Point	Point Adolphus
164	Eey X̱'é	Mouth of Tidal Rapids	North Inian Pass
165	Táas' Daa Noow	Táas' Daa (#162) Fort	Gallagher Cove, Lemesurier Island
166	Taan Teiyí	Sea Lion Haulout	Sea lion haulout in North Inian Pass
167	Tsaa X'aayí	Seal Point	East point of Pinta Cove

Map #	*Name*	*Translation*	*Location*
168	K̲aashag̲eeyí	Person's Head (the bluffs look like a head) Bay	West of Point Adolphus
169	Aangóonk'	Town's Little Portage	In Graves Harbor
170	Tsaa X'aayí Táak	Head of Seal Point Bay	Pinta Cove
171	K̲ashgootl Seiyí	Area below the Hip Hill	Inian Cove
172	Lug̲ei Yá	Face of the Confines of the Point	Inian Islands
173	Lakanak̲áa	Tell Them by Mouth	Graves Rocks (where X̲akúch' killed a giant octopus)
174	Lulxágu	Fireweed Sand Beach	Homeshore, Excursion Inlet
175	Naguk̲ Héen	Stream at the Eye Of (Flowing Stream)*	Dicks Arm
176	Dak̲áa X̲oo	Among the Sleeping Man* (spirit)	Inian Islands
177	Tsaa Tak̲di X̲'áak	Between Which Seals Are Harpooned	South Inian Pass ("The Laundry")
178	Naguk̲.wa.aan (Naguk̲.aan)	Town at the Face of Naguk̲ (see #175) (Naguk̲ Town)	Head of Dicks Arm
179	Ta.aan	Sleeping Town	Head of Dicks Arm (same as #178)
180	X'aak'ú T'eik Héen	River behind the Little Point	Stream east of Village Point along Homeshore
181	Kax'noowú	Female Grouse Fort	Ground Hog Bay
182	X̲'aak Takaadé Duk̲aan	They Fight Down to the Bottom of the Ravine	Homeshore, Ground Hog Bay (alternative to #161?)
183	Anax̲ Séet	Passage through the Land	Pass to creek inside Point Villaluenga
183.1	G̲aat Héeni	Sockeye River	Inside Point Villaluenga
184	Goosh T'ei Héen	Stream behind the Thumb	Ground Hog Bay
185	T'awak̲x'áat'i	Goose Island	Goose Island in Mud Bay
186	Anax̲ Yaa Ashk'akwji Yé	Passing through a Small Opening	Cape Spencer
187	Naguk̲ K'i	At the Base of Naguk̲ (see #175)	Point Villaluenga
188	Yaanash Kweix̲	*	Cape Spencer Area
189	Kunax̲sa.aan	Portage Town*	Flynn Cove
190	Naguk̲.yadaa	Shoreline around Naguk̲ (see #175)	Cape Spencer to Polka Peninsula
191	K̲ooshnáax̲'i	Tumbling Water Shelter	George Islands
192	Xákw Tlein	Huge Sandbar	Cove west of Point Adolphus
193	X̲'óot'k'	Little Rapids*	Elfin Cove
194	Yáxwch' Áayi	Sea Otter Lagoon	Gallagher Flats
195	L'aa T'un* X'áat'k'i	Little-Island Breasts*	The Sisters
196	Dak̲áanáx̲	Into Dak̲áa (see #176)	Idaho Inlet
197	L'ílgúk'	Little Penis	Three Hill Island
198	Kanax̲ Aan G̲ashú	Land Extends Across It	Three Hill Island
199	Ts'axwel X'áat'i X̲'akahéen	Creek at the Mouth of Crow Island	Halibut Creek (Port Frederick)
200	X̲'akahéen	Stream at the Mouth	Halibut Creek (alternate name)
201	X̲'akahéen Yax'áat'i	River Mouth Island	Halibut Island (Port Frederick)

Map #	*Name*	*Translation*	*Location*
202	Ts'axwel X'áat'i	Crow Island	Halibut Island (alternate name)
203	L'ix' Xágu	Broken [Rock] Sandbar	Port Althorp
204	Kóoshdaa G̲eeyí	Land Otter Bay	Halibut Creek Bay (Port Frederick)
205	Ts'axwel X'áat'i G̲eeyí	Crow Island Bay	Halibut Creek Bay (alternate name)
206	Kóoshdaa X'aak'ú	Land Otter Little Point	Outer Point Sophia
207	Shax̲oo Eejí	[Chookaneidí shaman's name] Reef	Mouth of Port Frederick
208	Tawéik'	Little Mountain Sheep	Table Rock, Cross Sound
209	Gáaxw X'aayí	Duck Point	Cannery Point in Port Frederick
210	Yées Kéini	New Cannery	Port Althorp Cannery site
211	Gaaw Áak'w	Drum Little Lake	Behind cannery
212	Yaana.eit Xágu	Wild Celery Sandbar	Rocky Island*
213	Gaaw	Drum	Cliff/tunnel by Hoonah
214	Dei L'e.aan	Peaceful Road Village	Hoonah (first name)
215	Gundzi Shakée (Gundzi Shaa)	Gúnts (spirit name) on Top (Gúnts Mountain)	Mountain at headwaters of creek
216	Gaaw T'ak̲ Aan	Village beside the Drum	Hoonah
217	Gundzi Héeni	Gúnts (spirit name) Creek	Creek by Mary Johnson's house
218	Xunaa (Xunniyaa)	Lee of the North Wind	Hoonah
219	Xutsdeiyí	Brown Bear Road	Snug Harbor area in Hoonah
220	Yayá	Steep Side of It	Cape Bingham, Soapstone Point
221	Lak̲oox̲ás'	Like a Toy Boat (Palisade Island)	Spasski Island
222	Yan Kashada Tináa	On Top of the Head Copper	False Point near Hoonah Harbor
223	G̲aat Héeni (G̲athéeni)	Sockeye River	Gartina Creek in Hoonah
224	Cháas' K'ix̲' Héen	Humpback Salmon Gaff Creek	Humpback Creek, Port Frederick
225	Lak̲oox̲ás' T'aak̲ Héen	Creek beside Lak̲oox̲ás' (#221)	Spasski Bay/Creek
226	K'udeis X̲'ayík	Inside the Mouth of K'udeis (#239)	Lisianski Inlet
227	Tsaa Áayi	Seal Lake	Soapstone Cove to Bingham Cove area
228	K̲aakdahéen	Surface Water* Creek	Hoktaheen Creek
229	Xutsg̲eeyí	Brown Bear Bay	Port Frederick, Snug Harbor near airport
230	Neeká	[Chookaneidí slave's name]	Neka Bay
231	Kus'eil'	[Chookaneidí slave's name]	Port Frederick
232	Sigugu Shaa	Mountain with Ears	Ear Mountain
233	Kéidladi Héeni	Seagull Creek	Seagull Creek in Port Frederick
234	X̲aayta.aan	Inside the Red Cedar Village	Surge Bay
235	Xutshéeni	Brown Bear River	Game Creek in Port Frederick
236	X'áask'	Little Waterfall	Waterfall near Midway Island in upper Port Frederick
237	T'aawák̲ X'aayí	Goose Point	Flats at the head of Tenakee Inlet
238	Kéet Góoni	Killer Whale Portage	Portage between Tenakee Inlet and Port Frederick

Map #	*Name*	*Translation*	*Location*
239	K'udeis	*	Lisianski Strait
240	K'udeis X̱'é	Inside Mouth of K'udeis (#239)	Pelican area
241	G̱uwakaan X'áat'i	Deer/Peace Island	Island at the head of Tenakee Inlet
242	S'eesdéi X'áat'	Pouting* Island	Island at the head of Tenakee Inlet
243	Kulasá G̱eeyí	Skinny Bay	Long Bay, Tenakee Inlet
244	Asáani*	Freshwater Bay*	Freshwater Bay
244.1	Asáank'i	Little Freshwater Bay* (Little Asáani* [#244])	Pavlof Harbor
245	Tlaguwu Héen	Ancient River	Indian River, Tenakee
246	Tsaa G̱eeyí	Seal Bay	Seal Bay, Tenakee Inlet
247	Át Ahan Yé	Place Where a Person Stands	Mountain above Porcupine Bay
248	Keidladí Héen	Seagull River	Creek at southeast point of Seal Bay
249	Tlaguwu Aan	Ancient Town	Tenakee Village
250	Tlaguwu Noow	Ancient Fort	Grave Island
251	T'einaageey	Bay on the Hindward Side	Tenakee Inlet
252	T'aay X̱'é	Hot Springs Mouth	Tenakee Hot Springs
253	Aawateeni Héen	Water Storming Off	Iyoukeen Cove/Peninsula
254	Shanyak'í	At the Base of the Mountain Face	Sonyakay Ridge
NM	Koohk keh kee an (Kooḵ Keikee.aan*)	In the Front of the Damp Ground Village*	Point Couverden area; nonstandard spelling from Emmons (n.d.)
NM	Nagootk'í	At the Base of Nagoot*	Glacier Bay area
NM	Tínxi Aaní (Tínx Kayaaní)	Bearberry Country	Above Canadian border on Tatshenshini River
NM	Wéinaa Té	White Stone	George Islands area

3. *Jilḵáat Ḵwáan and Jilḵoot Ḵwáan*

Jilḵáat (from the Tlingit/Eyak word for "cache") Ḵwáan and Jilḵoot (from the Tlingit name for the settlement at Chilkoot Lake, Lḵoot) Ḵwáan comprise the northeastern frontier of coastal Lingít Aaní. Numerous trails, nicknamed "grease trails" due to importance of eulachon grease in trade, coursed overland into what is now Interior Alaska, British Columbia, and southern Yukon Territory. Jilḵáat and Jilḵoot areas at one time were united, and they remain closely linked today through proximity, intermarriage, and other ties. Broadly speaking, the Jilḵáat controlled the Chilkat River Valley above Chilkat Inlet, while the Jilḵoot possessed the Chilkoot, Taiya (from the Tlingit Dayéi, "To Pack"), and Skagway river valleys, and Lynn Canal north of Berners Bay. The modern villages of Haines (Deishú, "End of the Trail"), Klukwan (from Tlákw.aan, "Eternal Village"), and Skagway (from Shg̱agwei, "Rugged/Wrinkled-Up [Water]") constitute the major settlements lying within these ḵwáan territories today.

We documented more than two hundred place names within Jilḵáat Ḵwáan and Jilḵoot Ḵwáan. Our project was carried out in conjunction with the Chilkat Indian Village, Chilkoot Indian Association, and the Skagway Traditional Council, with additional consultation from the Carcross/Tagish First Nation. Joe Hotch Sr., a Kaagwaantaan clan elder and fluent speaker of Tlingit, served as the local research coordinator for the project in Klukwan, while the late Pete Johnson, also a Kaagwaantaan and a fluent speaker, assisted in Haines. Additional research in Skagway was carried out with encouragement and support from Skagway Traditional Council President Lance Twitchell. Key contributors included: Austin Hammond, Anna Katzeek, David Katzeek, Albert Paddy, George Stevens, Margaret Stevens, Charlie Jimmie Sr., Evans Willard, Laura Hotch, Marsha Hotch, John Marks, Agnes Bellinger, Lillian Hammond, Paul Jackson, Marilyn Wilson, Paul Wilson, Dixie Johnson, Nora Marks Dauenhauer, David Andrews, Si Dennis Sr., Tom Jimmy, Tom Katzeek, Victor Hotch, Richard Dick, Ada Haskins, and many others who corroborated names, attended meetings, and contributed to the project in a variety of ways. Our task was made easier by the pioneering work of George Davidson, Frederica de Laguna, George Emmons, Edward J. Glave, Walter Goldschmidt and Theodore Haas, Aurel Krause, Jeff Leer, Kalervo Oberg, Ronald Olson, Louis Shotridge, John Swanton, and others who documented place names over the years (see also Cruikshank 1981, 1990a). The first phase of the project fieldwork and mapping was carried out by Martha Betts with support from the Alaska Department of Fish and Game, Division of Subsistence. Harold Martin and Thomas Thornton carried out additional fieldwork and Jeff Leer of the Alaska Native Language Center and Nora and Richard Dauenhauer and John Marks of the Sealaska Heritage Institute provided linguistic review.

Indigenous place names mark important settlements, pathways, and sites frequented by the aboriginal inhabitants of this area. Concise recognition of this fact is evidenced in a wayside exhibit recently placed in Skagway, entitled *Asaayíx' Ḵudziteey Haa Léelk'u Hás Aaní, This Land of Our Grandparents Has Tlingit Names*, co-designed for the federal government by the Skagway Traditional Council based on names collected for this project (see below).

In contrast to some areas of Southeast, where non-Native "discoverers" ignored, belittled, or replaced aboriginal names, here their value was appreciated. Early explorers and mapmakers who relied on local experts to guide them through the rugged Interior (*terra incognita* among Euro-Americans until the late nineteenth century) often recorded and translated Native names. Some, like Edward J. Glave, who explored the Interior via the upper Chilkat Valley in 1890, favored retaining the indigenous geographic nomenclature:

> Throughout my letter I have retained the native names of geographical points wherever I could learn them. In my opinion, this should always be studied. The Indian names of the mountains, lakes and rivers are natural land marks for

the traveler, whoever he may be; to destroy these by sub-
stituting words of a foreign tongue is to destroy the natural guides. You ask for some point and mention its native
name; your Indian guide will take you there. Ask for the
same place in your substituted English and you will not be
understood. Traveling in Alaska has already sufficient difficulties, and they should not be increased by changing all
the picturesque Indian names. Another very good reason
why these names should be preserved is that some tradition of tribal importance is always connected with them.
These people have no written language, but the retention
of their native names is an excellent medium through which
to learn their history. (Cruikshank 1991, 113)

There is much truth in this statement. Tlingit names for
Jilḵáat Ḵwáan and Jilḵoot Ḵwáan provide a detailed picture of the country's distinguishing geographic features,
and embody its rich social history. This is one reason
why the great Jilḵáat leader Kohklux insisted on detailing
the Native names for places when he helped geographer
George Davidson map the Interior in 1869. As Davidson
(1901a, 76) tells it, Kohklux took great care in the mapping
exercise, even though the Tlingit had no tradition of cartography, and the endeavor "cost him and his two wives two
or three days' labor with pencil and no rubber…It began
at Point Seduction, in Lynn Canal, with islands, streams
and lakes; and with mountains in profile." Davidson recorded the place names in his own orthography, some of
which we were able to decode and re-elicit from elders for
our study. We are fortunate that this remarkable artifact of
collaborative research has been preserved in the Bancroft
Library at the University of California, Berkeley, and can
be used by local tribes and First Nations as a source of aboriginal place names, historic trails, trade routes, and other
valuable information (see YHMA 1995; Thornton 2000a).

Some Important Named Sites

With abundant sources of food available from the major
rivers and valleys, the inhabitants of Jilḵáat and Jilḵoot territories did not have to venture far to obtain their food.
Thus, their villages were comparatively large and occupied
much of the year. Villages and camps along the major rivers were connected by a network of trails. Deishú (End
of the Trail, #143), now known as Haines, marked the
southern terminus of this trail system which stretched to
Klukwan and beyond along the bank of the Chilkat River,

and also linked to Lḵoot Village on the Chilkoot River.
Elders Mildred Sparks and Paul Phillips commented that
people often used this trail system "to travel between
Klukwan and Chilkoot Village, walking from Klukwan to
Deishú and then proceeding to Chilkoot by canoe — thus
eliminating the hazardous canoe trip around Seduction
Point" (Sackett 1979, 60). In explaining the meaning of
the Tlingit name for Seduction Point, Evans Willard and
Tom Jimmy (SENSC 1995–2002) made reference to these
hazards:

Ayík [part of the name for Seduction Point, #171] is, "you
gotta get ready." It's a very, very stormy place there, Ayiklutú;
you gotta be ready when you go around there, either wind,
north or south wind, and the tides are strong there, and you
always find…great big seas there, big, high waves (E.W.).

Yayiklutú, which is Seduction Point, and the story that
I heard that went along with this, was that when you go
across that point in a canoe, and the low tide is coming in,
it's like you hear voices, somebody inside a canoe. *Yayik* is
the word [referring to] canoes, it's derived from that, and
that's the story I heard about that (T.J.).

Tlákw.aan, (Eternal Village, #52). Known as Klukwan
today, this was the largest and oldest village in the ḵwáan,
located some twenty miles upriver from Lynn Canal. The
settlement reportedly had five hundred to six hundred
residents living in sixty-five community houses in 1881
(Krause 1956) and was the site of the famous Gaanaxteidí
Whale House, so vividly characterized by Emmons (1916).
The village was located far upriver for three reasons. First,
there are few productive salmon tributaries below the
village, while there are many above it. Second, the location provided protection from the fierce southeast winds
which batter Lynn Canal and a large, safe eddy for landing canoes. Third, it afforded convenient access to Interior
trade routes and to hunting grounds where mountain goat,
deer, and furbearers were taken. Klukwan remains the
"eternal" village today. Elder George Stevens (Thornton
2004b) relates how Tlingits first came to Tlákw.aan:

[A Tlingit leader came from Sheet'ká (Sitka) with his nephews, whom he instructed to survey the Chilkat River]. They
scouted that river from Deishú, which is now Haines…
kept going up this river…They look it [over], they scout
it. Finally they stopped at 19-Mile; they camped there. But
that evening…while they were eating, he was telling his
nephews, "Tomorrow I want you to look over that place
up here." That's Klukwan now. The next day they loaded

up their canoe, the young men, they poled up here; they were somewhere here [Kaatx'waaltú, #62]. They came back in the evening... One says, "Oh, they got everything there. Fish, porcupine signs; look up the mountain... mountain goats; you go right along beach, lots of bears, lots of fresh water coming down off the mountain." Next day they're somewhere along the bank here, river bank... "Ah ha," he says... He stooped down; he put up his arms and let the sand run from his hands... In Tlingit what he was saying, "It's ours." Then he walked to the riverbank, he scooped up handful of water. Also the whole valley he circled... He was saying, "[It's ours]."

Kaatx'waaltú (Rockslide, #62). Just below Tlákw.aan, also on the east bank of the Chilkat River, was the town of Kaatx'waaltú, named for the rocky lateral moraine at the foot of which it was built. This village was founded by residents of Yandeist'akyé, a village near the mouth of the Chilkat, who established a fishing camp here that later grew into a village. The village grew to a population of 125 (Petroff 1884) with eight houses, before it was destroyed by a mud slide in the 1890s (Emmons n.d.; Sackett 1979, 51).

Yandeist'akyé (Where Everything from Afar Drifts on Shore, #139). Located at the mouth of Chilkat River at the present site of Haines Airport, Yandeist'akyé village takes its name from the point on which it stands, which "turns the course of the river from above and obstructs the tide from below and so catches the drift from both directions" (Emmons n.d.). Formed by a glacial moraine, this bank also provides shelter from the southeast winds and ready access for boats. Between this village and Kaatx'waaltú lay an important eddy and point, called X'akw.áayi (Spawning Salmon Lake, #100), where salmon would collect after ascending into the fresh waters of Chilkat River and begin to change color (Emmons n.d.). Yandeist'akyé grew to be

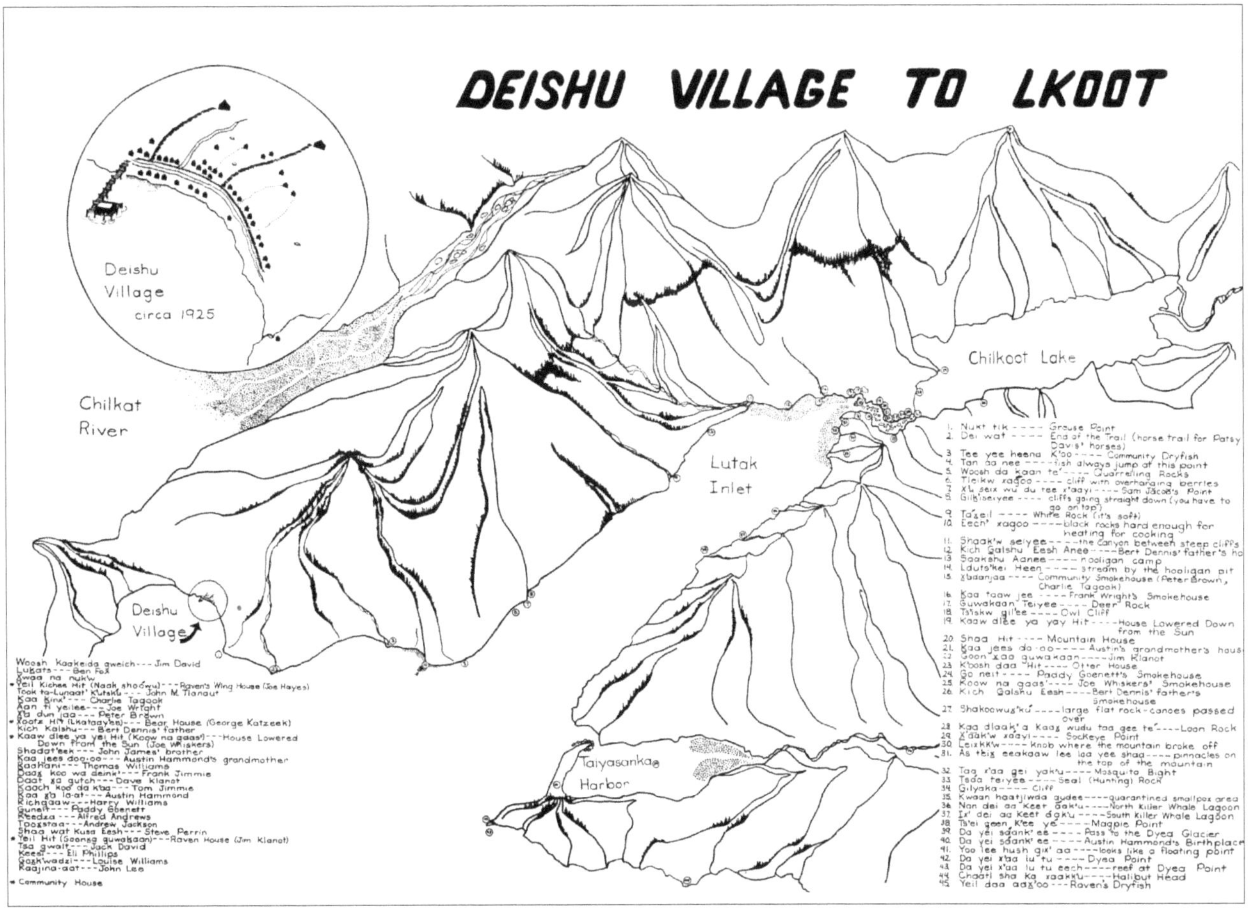

Map of Deishú Village and Lkoot Lake area prepared for "The Old Story of Chilkoot" ceremony in August 1980, led by Lukaax.ádi elder Austin Hammond (Daanaawáak). The map is based on names recorded from Daanaawáak by Jeff Leer. Courtesy of Haines ANB/ANS.

a very large settlement with 150–200 inhabitants and sixteen houses recorded in 1880 (Petroff 1884).

Geisán Aan (*Geisán Village or Land, #141*). The area embracing Yandeist'akyé is known as Geisán Aan. Geisán (#131) is the name of Mount Ripinski, located behind the village. Austin Hammond (n.d.) relates the following story about this place:

> While we were living at Yandeist'akyé, there was a war. We call that place "War Canoe Cove." My people didn't know warriors had come in canoes from the south. When they were cooking a big pot of food together, here they came. "Hoo-oo-oo," they were yelling and my people started running. We ran right up on top of Geisán. When they got on top, the shaman asked his attendant, "Where's your drum?"
>
> The young man said, "It's still down there."
>
> The shaman said, "You better go get it. I'll sit here."
>
> He sat with the blanket over his head, and he's still going to start singing, tapping the ground. By doing this he is going to keep the eyes closed of the ones who came in the war canoes, so they won't see him and he won't fall. The shaman said, "As soon as you get down there put your hand through the strap and start beating the drum. I'll take care of it from there."
>
> So the young man went down. All the enemy was there. He did just what the shaman told him. He put his arm through the strap and started beating the drum. The drum was about flying with him on top of all the willows. And the enemy didn't get a chance to get him. He kept running right up that cliff. That's how strong our shaman is. That's how some of our people were saved.
>
> We use that name because we were safe there, and because we belong to that place.

Geisán remains the sacred property of the Lukaax.ádi clan and is commemorated on regalia and other *at.óow*. There is an effort underway to restore a community house at the site of Yandeist'akyé.

Lkoot (*Storehouse,* or Place of Abundance of Food** [*Emmons n.d.*], *#84*). Situated on the Chilkoot River between Lutak (Lkoot T'áak, #112) Inlet and Chilkoot Lake (Lkoot Ka Áa, #71) this village was smaller than either Tlákw.aan or Yandeist'akyé and inhabited mainly by the Lukaax.ádi, who migrated north from the Stikine (Shtax'héen) River area. John Marks (interview) notes that the Lukaax.ádi took their present name from Duncan Canal (Lukaax) near Petersburg, and later moved north, where some settled at Excursion Inlet (Kuyeik') and took the name Kuyeik'ádi (People of Excursion Inlet), while others continued north to Lkoot. The Chilkoot River is a short but productive salmon river, fed by Chilkoot Lake, where prized sockeye salmon spawn. Large boulders in the lower river were owned and used as platforms for harvesting salmon with spears (Sackett 1979, 52). Some of these rocks were nicknamed "Raven's Luggage" [i.e., dry-fish bundle] (Yéil Daa Aaxoo, #90). Like Kaatx'waaltú, this village never grew large, possessing only eight houses and 120 inhabitants according to Petroff's 1880 census. In the post-contact era Lkoot was ravaged by disease, damaged by mudslides, and eventually abandoned, as people became consolidated in the larger settlement of Haines by the 1930s. When the road leading to Chilkoot Lake was built in the 1960s, some key landmarks associated with this village were damaged or destroyed including the Guwakaan Teiyí, or "Peace Rock" (#91), the remains of which were subsequently cobbled together and marked by a wayside exhibit.

Along with these four major villages, there were at least five smaller villages whose history prior to contact has been documented almost exclusively by oral tradition (Sackett 1979, 59). Among the more permanent of these were villages at Dyea at the base of the Chilkoot Trail and a village at Skagway River near the modern city of Skagway (James Lee in Goldschmidt and Haas 1998, 101).

Deishú (*End of the Trail, #143*). Described as an old "Chilkat Village" at Portage Cove, four miles east of Yandeist'akyé (Young 1915; Muir 1915), Deishú was not heavily populated until the establishment of the Presbyterian mission (Chilkoot Mission) there in 1880. The Presbyterians' decision to place the mission at a neutral site was a strategic attempt to escape the traditionalism of the village and also the appearance of favoring a single village. As the missionary, Mrs. Eugene Willard (1884, 47) remarked: "Each of these villages has its chief or chiefs and medicine men, each its distinct nobility, and each its own interests and jealousies of all the others." Renamed Haines by the Presbyterians, Deishú grew rapidly in population, largely at the expense of Lkoot and Yandeist'akyé villages.

Tan.aaní (*Fish Jumping Grounds, #128*). Located at Tanani Bay, this village, like Deishú, was situated in a bay with southern exposure and not along the main river. Joe Hotch (interview) says of this name: "[I]t's the place the fish jump . . . when they're jumping, we are supposed to say 'Ey Ho!'; you see a fish jump, 'Ey Ho,' [then] they know they're being appreciated so they keep jumping. And I guess our people say it so they can know which way it's going. Just keep saying 'Ey Ho,' and that's the way they want to be talked to; the fish want to be appreciated." Tanani Point was called Tan.aaní Lutú (Inside Point of the Fish Jumping Grounds, #135).

Kaltsex̲x̲'i Héen (Kicking River, #147). This village takes its name from the Kicking Horse River, and was said to have been located at the confluence of this tributary and the Chilkat River, across from nine-mile Haines Highway. It was reportedly devastated by an epidemic of smallpox, probably in 1836 (or perhaps in 1775), in which only one woman and her child survived. Sackett (1979, 59) recorded the following narrative from Jilk̲áat elder Mildred Sparks about this tragic event and the courageous survivors:

> Smallpox came along and wiped everybody out except one young woman and her child. Everybody was moving down from Klukwan to 7-mile and 9-mile [during the eulachon season in late May or early June], and they didn't see smoke coming from the houses. When they went through the houses, they found no one. Just that one woman and her child survived...
>
> The woman lived there with no transportation, no nothing; and she was courageous and she was brave. Even now I teach my children and grandchildren that the Chilkat are known to be courageous and brave...
>
> When they found her, she tried not to cry. She just grieved in her Indian way until she saw the people and heard the word *eesháan* which means "have pity." Eesháan, that broke her heart. All the days she spent without anybody she did not shed a tear. But that word broke her lips, so she cried.

Dayéi (To Pack, #28). This small village was located on the Taiya River at the present site of Dyea. According to Sealaska's (1975) survey and Sackett's (1979, 60) sources, the village was occupied year-round at one time, but by

Austin Hammond (Daanaawáak̲) wears the Sockeye Point Robe (Chilkat Blanket) (X̲'áakw X'aayí Naaxein), a sacred object (*at.óow*) of his clan at a 1981 ceremony near Chilkoot Lake in Haines, Alaska. Among other things the robe encapsulates important clan history and signifies title to the lands and waters around Chilkoot Lake, where freshwater (spawned-out) sockeye salmon (*x̲'áakw*) are harvested. Photo by Richard Dauenhauer.

the time of the gold rush and the founding of modern Dyea, it was used primarily as a fishing camp for salmon and eulachon and a staging area for trade expeditions to and from the Interior. Due to the lack of an overland trail from Lḵoot to Dayéi and the difficulties of marine travel in upper Lynn Canal (i.e., stiff winds and strong tides), key landmarks, rest stops, and points of refuge were named along the water route to aid navigation. For example, the point on Dalasuga Island opposite Seduction Point was called Yoo Lititgi X'aa, or "Undulating Point," a reference to its wave-like movements in particular weather conditions. As Joe Hotch (interview) explains:

> It's all cliff…[but] between there is sand, and when the north wind is blowing, the sand goes this way [south], and when the south wind is blowing, it goes this way [north], and we call it Yoo Litigi X'aa; it moves south when the north wind is blowing and it moves north when the south wind is blowing.

A similar bellwether, Yoo Lihashgi X'aa, or Floating Point, marks the entrance to Taiyasanka Harbor. According to Anna Katzeek (interview), "when the tide is up it looks like it floated, and when the tide goes down it looks like it separated, so they call it the Floating Point." Taiyasanka Harbor itself was called Dayeisáank'i (#111), a reference to its proximity to Taiya Inlet (also known as Dayéi). The bay offered safe harbor to canoes traveling north and signaled that Dayéi village was "just right over [there]…towards Skagway…The opposite side of Dayéi, that's what Dayeisáank'i [refers to]." Closer still to the village of Dayéi, in Taiya Inlet, lay another refuge place for inclement weather: Dayéi X̱'akax'áas (#116). As John Marks notes, "they had kind of a place where they had a stop off. If it was real bad weather you could spend the night there or whatever. Kind of like a little, dinky village." Above, Dyea itself was the home of Kanagoo, "the child of the North Wind."

Dyea was a permanent village at one time, if we understand "permanent" to mean regularly, but not necessarily constantly, occupied. Jack David (Goldschmidt and Haas 1998, 101) states:

> At Dyea there was a trail which went up to the Interior Indians who were met at Lutsis Aan [not mapped]…
>
> I remember also when the Tsimshians came to trade at Klukwan, which was a trade center for people from all over. The Tsimshians didn't go up the Dyea pass or beyond Klukwan.

> …There were also permanent villages at Dyea [and] at the mouth of the Skagway River.

Si Dennis Sr. (1998) elaborates on the nature of the settlements at Dyea and Skagway:

> Dyea was considered better than this [Skagway] valley because it had a lot less wind…My grandfather, Nahku, lived there practically all his life, and in fact the long bay that's between Dyea and Skagway is named for him on the charts. Five or six families lived out there year round, mainly for subsistence.

Nahku Bay may be a rare instance where a place is named after a person, as Si Dennis suggests, although Náx̱k'w also means "Little Harbor," an apt description of the locale (thus the name may originally derive from the place).

Skagway or Shg̱agwei (Rugged/Wrinkled-Up [Water], #34). The name of this famous gold rush city refers to the effect of the strong north wind on the waters of Lynn Canal and Taiya Inlet, which generates rugged seas and whitecaps or "wrinkled-up" waves. According to Herman Kitka Sr. of Sitka (see also Krause 1956), the story behind this name relates to a Tlingit warrior who became stuck trying to move up Taiya Inlet in the face of the stiff north wind. He spoke to the wind like a woman, and gave her the name Shg̱agwei. The North Wind responded by appearing to him as woman, and the two made love. Afterward, the wind calmed, leaving only small ripples on the water. These ripples are called Kanagoo, the children of Shg̱agwei, and they are said to run along the water "like steam" in the aftermath of a strong north wind. According to Richard Dick and other elders, the princess-like image of one of Shg̱agwei's daughters graces the contours of Face Mountain (Kanagoo Yahaayí, "Kanagoo's Image," #35), and continues to gaze upon Skagway.

The area between Chilkoot Inlet and Dyea, including the settlement and hunting and fishing grounds at Skagway, was controlled largely by the Lukaax̱.ádi clan until the beginning of the gold rush period in the 1890s, when the populations of Dyea and Skagway began to swell as points of departure for Klondike gold stampeders. The great Lukaax̱.ádi leader, L'unaat', fought and died to defend his clan's right to guide and supervise activities on the Chilkoot Trail (A Shakée, #11), which, under Tlingit law, the Lukaax̱.ádi owned, maintained, and insured against liability (Thornton 2004b).

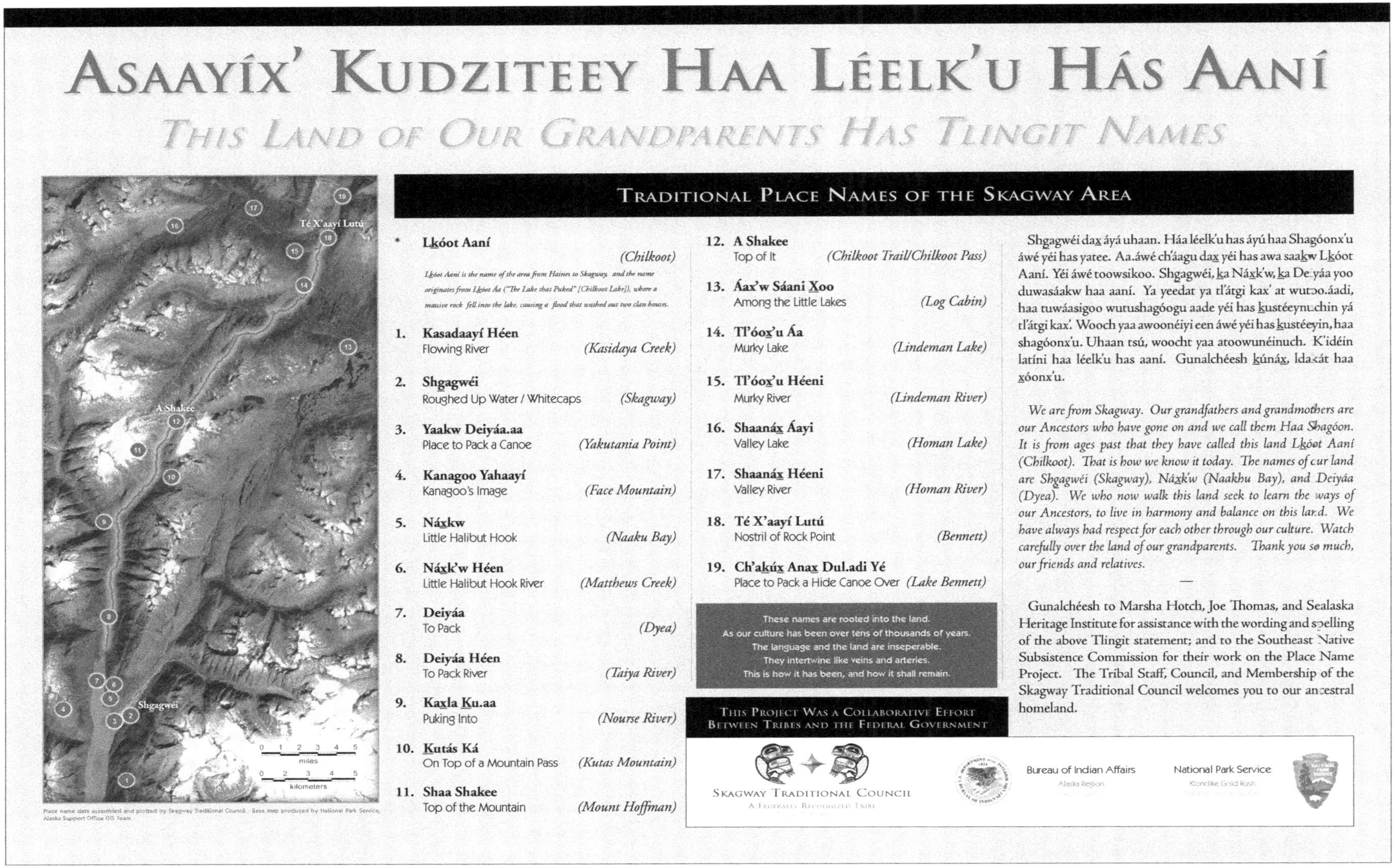

Asaayíx' Kudziteey Haa Léelk'u Hás Aaní, This Land of Our Grandparents Has Tlingit Names. Although nearly one million tourists a year visit Skagway (Shgagwei), few are aware of the rich nomenclature bestowed on the land by local Tlingit and Athabaskan peoples. This wayside exhibit, installed in Skagway, is an effort to reinscribe indigenous names on the land. It is a joint project of the Skagway Traditional Council, Bureau of Indian Affairs, and the National Park Service, and incorporates selected names from the Southeast Native Subsistence Commission place names project. Courtesy of the Bureau of Indian Affairs.

Final Thoughts

The Jilkáat and Jilkoot kwáan place names project reveals how Tlingits came to settle and name this rugged region, illuminating its contours, history, and culture with a richly-descriptive geographic nomenclature. Just as the early explorers like Davidson and Glave were appreciative of — even dependent upon — Native place names for orientation, we should continue to embrace indigenous names on the land. The geographic expertise of Kohklux, L'unáat', and other great Tlingit and Tagish men and women made this country meaningful, navigable, and habitable. Through the resonance of Native place names, we can continue to maintain a sense of their rich geographic worlds.

Today, the the Chilkat Indian Village, Chilkoot Indian Association, and Skagway Traditional Council are using results of the place names project to maintain tribe members' ties to the land through education, culture camps, and appropriate management of local natural and cultural resources, including Klondike Gold Rush National Historical Park and the Chilkoot Trail (see wayside exhibit, reproduced above). The results of the Southeast Native Subsistence Commission (SENSC) place names project are being used to revitalize the traditional meanings of important cultural landscapes like the Chilkoot and Chilkat trails, which we all enjoy today.

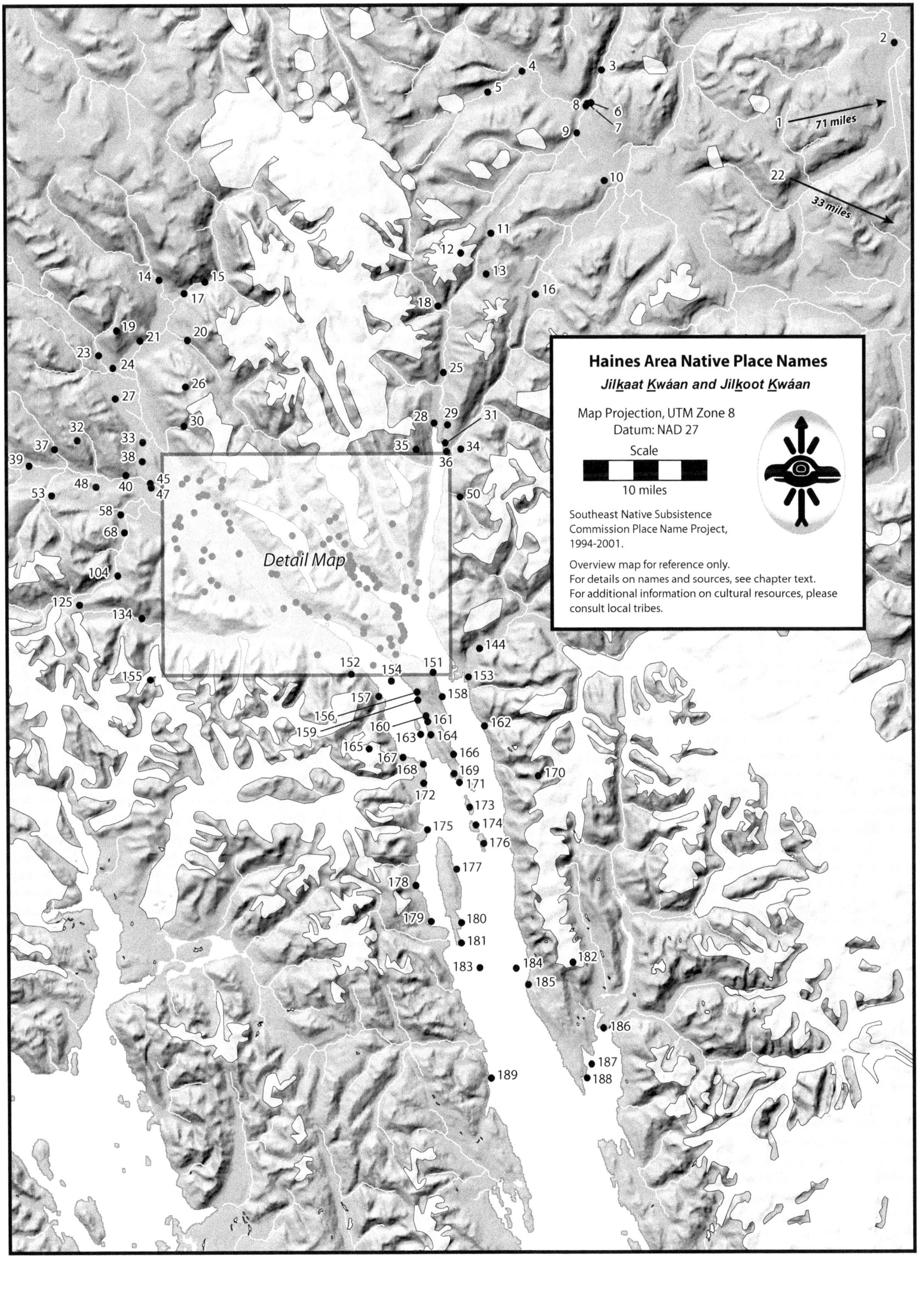

Haines Area Native Place Names

Jilḵaat Ḵwáan and Jilḵoot Ḵwáan

Map Projection, UTM Zone 8
Datum: NAD 27

Scale

10 miles

Southeast Native Subsistence
Commission Place Name Project,
1994-2001.

Overview map for reference only.
For details on names and sources, see chapter text.
For additional information on cultural resources, please
consult local tribes.

Detail Map

71 miles

33 miles

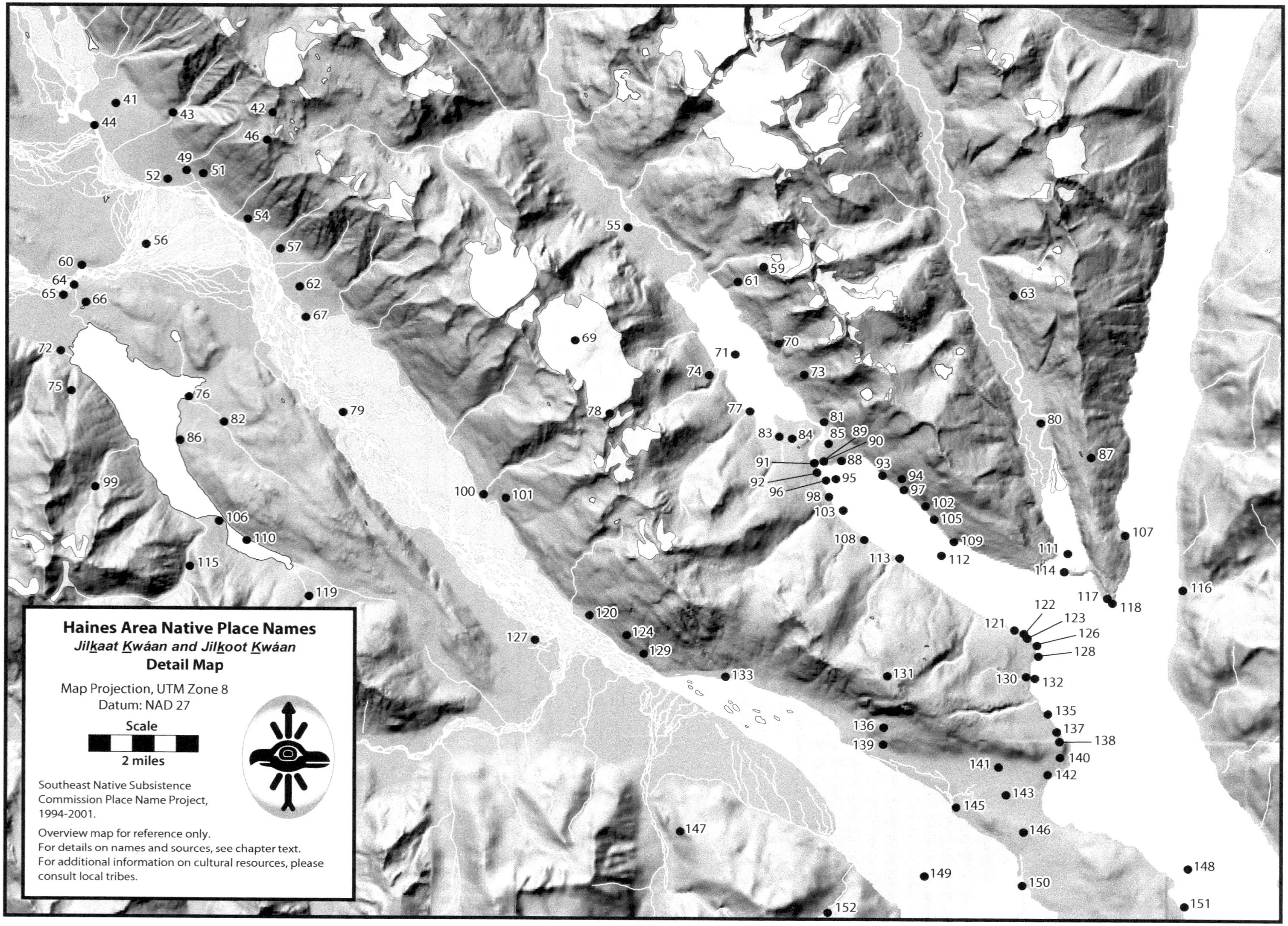

Haines Area Native Place Names
Jilkaat Kwáan and Jilkoot Kwáan
Detail Map
Map Projection, UTM Zone 8
Datum: NAD 27
Scale
2 miles
Southeast Native Subsistence Commission Place Name Project, 1994-2001.
Overview map for reference only.
For details on names and sources, see chapter text.
For additional information on cultural resources, please consult local tribes.
41
42
43
44
46
49
51
52
54
55
56
57
59
60
61
62
63
64
65
66
67
69
70
71
72
73
74
75
76
77
78
79
80
81
82
83
84
85
86
87
88
89
90
91
92
93
94
95
96
97
98
99
100
101
102
103
105
106
107
108
109
110
111
112
113
114
115
116
117
118
119
120
121
122
123
124
126
127
128
129
130
131
132
133
135
136
137
138
139
140
141
142
143
145
146
147
148
149
150
151
152

Jilk̲áat K̲wáan and Jilk̲oot K̲wáan Place Names

Asterisk indicates uncertain, unconfirmed, or partial; NM = not mapped.
Some names have more than one pronunciation or translation.

Map #	*Name*	*Translation*	*Location*
1	Deisleen	Stream Flows Out [of Lake] (from Athabaskan)	Teslin
2	T'ooch' Áayi	Black Lake*	Tutchi Lake
3	Ch'ak̲úx̲ Anax̲ Dul.áayi*	Pack a Skin Canoe Over to the Lake*	Outlet of Lake Bennett
4	Shaanáx̲ Héeni	Valley River	Homan River
5	Shaanáx̲ Áayi	Valley Lake	Homan Lake
6	Té X'aayí Lutú	Nostril of Rock Point	Bennett
7	Ch'ak̲úx̲ Anax̲ Dul.adi Yé	Place to Pack a Skin Canoe Over	Lake Bennett
8	L'óox̲'u Héeni	Murky River	Lindeman River
9	L'óox̲'u Áa	Murky Lake	Lindeman Lake
10	Áax'w Sáani X̲oo	Among the Little Lakes	Log Cabin
11	A Shakée	Top of It	Chilkoot Trail/Pass
12	Shaa Shakée	Top of the Mountain	Chilkoot Pass, Mount Hoffman
13	K̲utás Ká	On Top of the Mountain Pass	Kutas Mountain
14	T'ahéeni	King Salmon River	Tahini River
15	Koosawu Áa	Narrow Lake	Narrow lake formed by a gorge in upper Chilkat River
16	G̲éelák'w	Little Mountain Pass	Mountain pass used to access Dry Bay
17	X̲alak'ach' L'eedí	Porcupine Tail	Rock below gorge in upper Chilkat River
18	Kax̲la K̲u.aa*	Puking Into*	Nourse River
19	Xíxch'i Shaayí T'éik	Behind (or back of) Frog Mountain	South ridge of Frog Mountain, upper Chilkat
20	Xóots Héeni	Brown Bear River	Creek that divides upper Chilkoot and Chilkat rivers
21	X'aask'i.áa	Lake at the Base of the Waterfall	Upper Chilkat River
22	Áa Tlein	Big Lake	Atlin Lake
23	Yéil Héeni	Raven's Creek	Kelsall River
24	Chookan Áa	Grass Lake	Upper Chilkat River
25	Dayéi Héen	To Pack River	Taiya River
26	X̲'akashaanáx̲	Valley at the Mouth	Mountainside canyon in upper Chilkat Valley
27	Tsikhéeni	Roasting-Spit River	Small creek below Kelsall River
28	Dayéi	To Pack	Dyea
29	Náx̲k'u Héen	River of Náx̲k'w (#159)	Matthews Creek

Map #	*Name*	*Translation*	*Location*
30	Yax Kei Dlakwt Aan*	Land Where [Sheep*] Scratch Up the Side [with Hooves or Paws]	Goat Mountain, upper Chilkat River
31	Náxk'w	Little Harbor	Letnikof Cove
32	Sít'i Shaanáx	Glacier Valley	Little Boulder Creek
33	Xunt'i Áa	——* Lake	Mosquito Lake
34	Shgagwei	Rugged/Wrinkled-Up [Water]	Skagway
35	Kanagoo Yahaayí	Kanagoo's Image	Skagway
36	Yakwdeiyi Áa	Canoe Road Lagoon	Yakutania Point cove
37	Yakwyaax	Alongside Boat	Big Boulder Creek
38	Séet X'ayík	Entrance to the Strait	Moose Valley
39	L'ehéeni	——* River	Klehini River
40	Kaxwéix Kóogu	Cranberry Pit	On hillside at 28-mile Haines Highway
41	Gatx'ayeehéeni	Ready for Sockeye to Eat River*	Wells, across from the mouth of Klehini
42	Ch'ak'ilú	Beak of Small Eagle	Peak of mountain behind Klukwan
43	Dakshaanáx	Inland Valley	Behind Klukwan
44	X'akwhéenak'u	Little Spawning River	Above confluence of Klehini and Chilkat rivers
45	K'ideiyí Héeni	Path at the Base of It* River	Klehini River, ca. 27-mile Haines Highway
46	T'ukyík	In the Cradleboard	Dip or crutch below peak (Ch'ak'ilú, #42)
47	Gaay Kúdi	Eagle Nest	Across from 25-mile Haines Highway
48	Ayaan Héeni	Tutchone River	Herman Creek
49	Kei Daxakji Héen	River That Keeps Retreating Upward	Ravine behind Klukwan
50	Kasadaayi Héen	Flowing Creek	Below Skagway
51	Íxt'i Daakeidí	Shaman's Coffin	Hill behind Klukwan, 21-mile Haines Highway
52	Tlákw.aan	Eternal Village	Klukwan
53	Xalak'ach' Héeni	Porcupine River	Porcupine Creek
54	Tlaxaneis' (Tlaxanas') Noow	Kingfisher Fort	*
55	Goonk'	Little Spring	A spring-fed spawning area, north end of Chilkoot Lake
56	Gathéeni	Sockeye Stream	Mouth of Tsirku River, portion below Chilkat Lake outlet
57	Neixinté X'aak	Blue-Green Claystone Ravine	19 ½-mile Haines Highway
58	Eey X'é	Mouth of Rapids	Bend in upper Tsirku River
59	Jánwu Deiyí	Mountain Goat Trail	In canyon north of Chilkoot Lake
60	Tayayee	Lying in Wait for Rock	Bend in Tsirku River
61	Aasnoowta.aan	Town at the Back of Aasnoowú	Cove in north Chilkoot Lake
62	Kaatx'waaltú	Rockslide (Place Where the Landslide Comes Down)	19-mile Haines Highway

Map #	*Name*	*Translation*	*Location*
63	Dayeisáank'i Deiyí	Dayeisáank'i (#111) Trail	Pass to the Dyea Glacier
64	Yéil Teiyí	Raven Rock	Tsirku River, Chilkat Lake outlet
65	Aan Yanaade Héen	River Headed toward the Village/Land	Chilkat Lake tributary, northwest corner
66	Guchk'ihéeni	River at Base of Hill	Chilkat Lake outlet creek (not main drainage)
67	T'á Noow	King Salmon Fort	18-mile Haines Highway
68	Dzix̲kú	*	Tsirku River
69	Dak̲shaa	Inland (Mountain Interior)	Mountain range behind Klukwan
70	Daak Uwa.iyi Yé	Place Where Rocks Slid Out	East side of Chilkoot Lake
71	Lk̲oot Ka Áa	On Top of Lk̲oot (#84) Lake	Chilkoot Lake
72	Ch'áak' Héeni	Eagle River	Chilkat Lake tributary, northwest corner
73	Léik̲'wk'	Little Red Snapper	Chilkoot Lake
74	Goonák'w	Little Spring	On west side of Chilkoot Lake
75	G̲aatáa X̲'ayahéen	Creek at the Entrance of Trap[ping Grounds]	Tributary to Chilkat Lake
76	Kagit X'áat'i	Loon Island	Island group in Chilkat Lake
77	X̲'áakw X'aayí	[Spawned-Out] Sockeye Salmon Point	Chilkoot Lake
78	Cháatl Ist'eix̲í A Káa Wlilaayi Shaa	Mountain on Which a Halibut Fisher Melted	Mountain peak west of Chilkoot Lake
79	Jilk̲áat	Cache (from Eyak)	Chilkat River
80	Dayeisáank'i Héen	Dayeisáank'i (#111) River	Ferebee River
81	Shakuwúx̲'k'u	Little Wide-Head (large flat rock canoes passed over)	Chilkoot Lake
82	X'éitaa Héeni	Cutthroat Creek	Tributary to Chilkat Lake
83	Shakda.íshk'*	*	West side of Chilkat Lake
84	Lk̲oot	Storehouse* (Place of Abundance of Food*)	Village at Chilkoot Lake
85	Tsísk'u G̲íl'i	Owl Cliff	Between Lutak Inlet and Chilkoot Lake
86	Áa Ká	On the Lake	Chilkat Lake
87	K̲aas'eiltseen G̲íl'i	[Chookaneidí man's name] Cliff	East of Taiyasanka Harbor
88	T'áax'aa G̲eiyák'u	Mosquito's Little Bay	East side Lutak Inlet
89	Yéil Daa.áax̲u	Raven's [Dryfish] Bundle	Lower Chilkoot River (general name)
90	Yéil Daa Aaxoo	Raven's [Dryfish] Bundle	Chilkoot River, rocks below weir
91	G̲uwakaan (K̲uwakaan) Teiyí	Deer/Peace Rock	Lower Chilkoot River
92	Ldus'k'ihéen	Body of Water That Dries Up after Snow Is Gone*	North Lutak Inlet
93	Tsaa Teiyí	Seal Rock	East side Lutak Inlet
94	G̲íl'yaká	In Front of the Cliff	East side Lutak Inlet
95	Kéet Áak'u	Killer Whale Lagoon	Salt chuck on the west side of Lutak Inlet

Map #	*Name*	*Translation*	*Location*
96	Saak Shu Aaní	Eulachon Camp	North Lutak Inlet
97	Kwaan Haat Jiwdagoodí	Epidemic Came to Fight / Make War	East side Lutak Inlet
98	Kichgalshú Éesh Aaní	Kichgalshú's (man's name) Father's Land	North Lutak Inlet
99	Watkalch'áal'	[River] Having Willows at Its Mouth	Tributary to Chilkat Lake
100	X'akw.áayi	Spawning Salmon Lake	13- to 14-mile Haines Highway
101	Cheech Gíl'k'i	Porpoise Little Cliff	Cliff near 13-mile Haines Highway
102	Nánde Aa Kéet Áak'u	North Killer Whale Lagoon	East side Lutak Inlet
103	Shaak'w Seiyí	Area below [and Sheltered by] Little Mountain	North Lutak Inlet
104	Gíl' X'áak	Between Cliffs	Tsirku River
105	Íxde Aa Kéet Áak'u	Further down (south) Killer Whale Lagoon	East side Lutak Inlet
106	Aanwán	Edge of Village/Land	Chilkat Lake, southwest shore
107	Cháatl Shakaxaakwk'ú	Cut-Off Skull of Halibut	West shore of Taiya Inlet, around from Taiya Point
108	Éech' Xágu	[Igneous] Rock Beach	West Lutak Inlet
109	Ts'eigeenk'i Yé	Magpie Place	East Lutak Inlet
110	Áa Yuwaa Héeni	Belly Portion of a Lake River	South Chilkat Lake
111	Dayeisáank'i	Dayéi (see #28) Little Cove	Taiyasanka Harbor
112	Lkoot T'áak	Back Side of Lkoot (#84)	Lutak Inlet
113	Taxéil	White Rock (it's soft)	West Lutak Inlet
114	Yoo Lihashgi X'aa	Point That [Looks like It] Floats Up and Down	Point south of Taiyasanka Harbor
115	X'akwhéeni	Spawning Salmon Creek	Tributary to Chilkat Lake
116	Dayéi X'akax'áas	Waterfall at the Mouth of Dayéi (see #111)	Mouth of a creek on east side of Taiya Inlet
117	Dayéi X'aa Lutú Eech	Reef inside Dayéi (see #111) Point (nostril)	Reef at Dyea Point
118	Dayéi X'aa Lutú	Inside Dayéi (see #111) Point (nostril)	Dyea Point
119	Shakkwásk'i	Little Chamber Pot at the Head*	Tributary to Chilkat Lake
120	Áanák'w	Little Village	9 ½- to 10-mile Haines Highway
121	Gíl'k'i Seiyí	Area at Base of Little Cliff	Chilkat River, about 9-mile Haines Highway
122	X'usyeex.wudutee Aaní	[Sam Jacob's Tlingit name] Land	Outside Lutak Inlet
123	Tléikw Xágu	Berry Sand Beach	North of Tanani Point
124	Gíl'k'i Seiyí	Area at Base of Little Cliff	Lutak Inlet
125	Kéet Séedak'u	Killerwhale Little Strait	Pass from upper Tsirku River to Takhin River
126	Wooshdakanté	Quarreling Rocks	North of Tanani Point
127	Áanák'w Noowú	Áanák'w (#120) Fort	North of Kicking Horse and Chilkat rivers confluence

Map #	*Name*	*Translation*	*Location*
128	Tan.aaní	Fish Jumping Grounds	Tanani Point, mouth of Lutak Inlet
129	Saak Aaní	Eulachon Grounds	9-mile Haines Highway
130	Téeyi Héenak'u	[Community] Soaked Dryfish Creek	Tanani Bay
131	Geisán	Top of Bay	Mount Ripinski
132	Tan.aaní Geiyí	Tan.aaní (#128) Bay	Tanani Bay
133	Dúk X'aayí	Cottonwood Point	7-mile Haines Highway
134	Dakhéen	Inland River	Takhin River
135	Tan.aaní Lutú	Inside Point of the Fish Jumping Grounds	Tanani Point
136	Jánwu Gíl'i	Mountain Goat Cliff/Bluff	Above Yandeist'akyé (#139), 4-mile Haines Highway
137	Dei Wát	Mouth of the Trail	Horse trail for Patsy Davis's horses
138	Núkdík' Shakée	Above Núkdík' (#142)	Hill above Grouse Point
139	Yandeist'akyé	Where Everything from Afar Drifts on Shore	4-mile Haines Highway
140	Núkdík' Lutú	Inside Núkdík' (#142) Point (nostril)	Nukdik Point
141	Geisán Aan	Geisán (#131) Land	Area around Mount Ripinski (Geisán)
142	Núkdík'	Little Grouse	Shoreline north of Haines
143	Deishú	End of the Trail	Haines
144	Wulix'áasi Héen	Cascading River (River That Has Waterfall[s])	Katzehin River
145	Kaach Kulnux'ák'w*	*	Jones Point
146	Agóon	The Isthmus of It	The isthmus from Haines to Jones Point
147	Kaltsexx'i Héen	Kicking River	Kicking Horse River
148	Ketlgaxyé	Place Where Dog Cries	Battery Point
149	Jilkáat Wát	Mouth of the Jilkáat (#79)	Head of Chilkat Inlet
150	Laxách' T'áak	Back of Laxách' (#154)	Mainland shore east of Pyramid Island
151	Kuxdeinú	Whirlpool/Eddy	Cove below Battery Point
152	X'asdahéen	Waterfall Creek	Haska Creek
153	Wulix'áasi Héen Wát (X'asdahéen)	Mouth of Wulix'áasi Héen (#144) (Waterfall Creek)	Mouth of Katzehin River
154	Laxách'	*	Pyramid Island
155	Dakhéen Shaa	Inland River Mountains	Takhinsha Range
156	Gagaan Gooní	Sun Spring	North of Letnikof Cove
157	Ldeiniyé	*	Pyramid Harbor
158	Yéil Háatl'i	Raven Excrement	Rocky shore south of Battery Point
159	Náxk'w	Little Harbor	Nahku Bay, near Skagway
160	Léix'w Noow	Ochre Fort	Mattson's Cove, south of Letnikof Cove
161	Tlekwxágu	Berry Sand Beach	From spit at Mattson's Cove south to Twin Coves
162	Xíxch' Kanduwataayi Yé	Place Where Frogs Drift in Bunches	Drainage south of the Katzehin River

Map #	*Name*	*Translation*	*Location*
163	Lanéesi	*	Rocks at south end of Kochu / Alexander Island
164	Si.áat'i Goon	Cold Spring	Inside Mattson's Cove
165	Lkoodaséits'k	[Giant's name]	Rainbow Glacier
166	Goon Héeni	Springs River	Shore between Battery Point and Seduction Point
167	Náanax̱.á Jigei	Northern Crook of Arm	North of Glacier Point
168	Sít' X'aayí	Glacier Point	Glacier Point
169	Yoo Lititgi X'aa	Undulating Point (as if rocked by waves)	High Water Island (Dalasuga Island on USGS map)
170	Yéil Áx' Sh Wulg̱eig̱i Yé	Place Where Raven Swung	Head of a mountain canyon, mainland west of Anyaka Island
171	Ayiklutú	Point inside of It*	Seduction Point
172	Éexnax̱.á Jigei	Southern Crook of Arm	South of Glacier Point
173	Aanyakax'áat'i	Island in Front of the Village	Anyaka Island
174	Ligooshi X'áat'	Island with a Thumb (or dorsal fin)	Shigosi Island
175	Yaana.eit Xágu	Wild Celery Spit (or sandbeach/ sandbar)	Spit on mainland
176	Kadagoon	That Which Has Springs	North cove on Kataguni Island
177	S'alwán	*	Sullivan Island
178	S'alwán T'áak	Back Side of S'alwán (#177)	The mainland west of Sullivan Island
179	Cháas' Héeni	Humpback Salmon River	Mainland west of Sullivan Island
180	Shakóox̱' T'áak	Back of Wild Celery Umbrel	Sullivan Island
181	Shakóox̱' T'áak Lutú	Back of Wild Celery Umbrel Point	South Sullivan Island peninsula
182	Ḵáak'w X̱án	By the Little Man	Kakuhan Range
183	Jilḵatká	On Top of Jilḵáat (#79)	Chilkat side of Lynn Canal
184	Lḵootká	On Top of Lḵoot (#84)	Chilkoot side of Lynn Canal
185	Ḵáak'w X̱anseiyí	Area Below by the Little Man	Point Sherman
186	Dax̱anáak L'éiw Shuká	Dax̱anáak (#187) Sandy End	Head of Berners Bay
187	Dax̱anáak	Between Two Points*	Berners Bay
188	Ax̱'aká (Dax̱anaak X̱'aká)	The Mouth/Estuary (Mouth of Dax̱anáak [#187])	Mouth of Berners Bay (also name of Teslin Village)
189	Lḵoot Saayee	The Crook of the Knee of Lḵoot (#84*)	William Henry Bay
NM	Daas'aadiyáash	Snare Platform*	Dezadeash Lake
NM	Kóoshdaa Xágu	Land Otter Sandbar	Marsh Lake
NM	Ḵaa Dlaak' A Kaax̱ Wudutaagi Té	Rock Off Which a Man's Sister Was Speared (or pushed with a pole or spear)	Chilkoot Lake area
NM	Ḵáa Shoowú	Half a Person	*
NM	Leix'u* (Léix̱'u*)	——* (Red Ochre*)	Interior*
NM	Lux̱.aaní	Whitefish Lake	Kluane Lake

Map #	*Name*	*Translation*	*Location*
NM	L'ukshú	End of the Coho Salmon	Klukshu, Yukon Territory
NM	Nadashaa Héeni	Water Flowing from Mountain	Carcross, Yukon Territory
NM	Nánde Héeni Yei Kéich Yé	Place Where He/She/It/One Sits in the Water Facing North	Three Guardsmen, Yukon Territory
NM	Taagish Áayi	Taagish Lake	Tagish Lake, Yukon Territory
NM	Ta Héena*	——* River	Yukon River
NM	Tsuxx'aayí	Fence* Point	*
NM	Waneik'axoo	Flooded Over with It	Swanson Harbor, Icy Strait

4. *Áak'w K̲wáan and T'aak̲ú K̲wáan*

Áak'w K̲wáan and T'aak̲ú K̲wáan comprise a good part of what is today the City and Borough of Juneau. While Juneau is built on Gold Creek, which Tlingits named Dzantik'i Héeni (Flounder at the Base of the Creek,* #115), the original winter settlement of the Áak'w people was at Auke Recreation Area and, even earlier, at Indian Cove. The oldest dated archeological material drawn from sites at Auke Nu (fort site; Áak'w Noow, #93), Auke Cape (X'unáx̲i, #95), and Montana Creek (Kax̲digoowu Héen, #81) suggests a human presence in the area dating back at least seven hundred to nine hundred years. Due to its cultural significance, Auke Cape was recently found to be eligible for inclusion in the National Register of Historic Places as a traditional cultural property, the first such designation in Southeast Alaska (Thornton 1997c). Beyond the Auke Bay area, the collective territory of Áak'w K̲wáan extends to Point Bishop to the south, Berners Bay to the north, and Douglas Island and the northern tip of Admiralty Island to the west.

The origins of the T'aak̲ú K̲wáan are more difficult to pinpoint based on archeological evidence, mainly due to the fact that the Taku watershed's dynamic glacial and riverine landscape has destroyed many traces of early habitation. T'aak̲ú K̲wáan boundaries extend up the Taku River into present-day Canada, southeast to Port Snettisham, and west to Admiralty Island's Young Bay, Seymour Canal, and Gambier Bay. Certain areas, however, seem to have been used by both k̲wáans (Goldschmidt and Haas 1998).

We documented more than 150 place names within Áak'w K̲wáan and T'aak̲ú K̲wáan areas. Our project was carried out in conjunction with the Tlingit and Haida Indians of the City and Borough of Juneau and the Douglas Indian Association. Nora Marks Dauenhauer served as the local research coordinator for the project. Other key contributors include: Forrest DeWitt Sr., Marion Ezzre, Charlie Johnson, George Jim, Phillip Joseph, Cecilia Kunz, Emma Marks, John Marks, Rosa Miller, Elizabeth Nyman and Jeff Leer, and many others. We also recognize the contributions of past researchers, including Nora and Richard Dauenhauer, Frederica de Laguna, George Emmons, Walter Goldschmidt and Theodore Haas, Madonna Moss, Ronald Olson, and John Swanton. Nora Marks Dauenhauer and John Marks of the Sealaska Heritage Institute provided linguistic review.

Áak'w K̲wáan

Áak'w K̲wáan is centered in Auke Bay north of Juneau and takes its name from Auke Lake (Áak'w, "Little Lake," #86), which drains into the bay and supports sockeye salmon and other key resources. A thorough Tlingit history of this k̲wáan is yet to be written, although ethnogeographical information is available in Emmons (n.d.), Goldschmidt and Haas (1998), Beverly Keithahn (n.d.), and Phillip Joseph (1967). Major changes occurred here during the gold rush era, when Juneau and Douglas became destinations for gold seekers and hubs in the developing commercial mining industry.

Áak'w was one of the smaller k̲wáans in terms of area and resources and, unlike most of the other mainland settlements, possessed no major trade route to the Interior. As a consequence the area traditionally supported a smaller population in comparison to other k̲wáans such as those at Chilkat (Jilk̲áat) and Stikine (Shtax'héen) rivers. Major clans included the L'eeneidí, G̲aanax̲.ádi, and L'uknax̲.ádi on the Raven side and Wooshkeetaan on the Eagle/Wolf side.

Important places within this territory include:

Berners Bay (*Dax̲anáak*, #46). Known as "biggest berrying picking place for the Juneau people," Berners Bay was also home to several settlements, located at the head of the bay on the Lace and Berners rivers (Goldschmidt and Haas 1998). Emmons (n.d.) recorded a village here called Dax̲anáak, apparently carrying the same name as the bay itself. Another consultant said the upper village was called K̲utak.aan* (Goldschmidt and Haas 1998; see #41). Both rivers were rich in salmon and their uplands yielded mountain goat, deer, and furbearers. The bay was owned by the Wooshkeetaan, whose rights were recognized by the Juneau Native corporation (Goldbelt, Inc.) when it selected lands there. Rights to these selected lands were later conveyed to the corporation in a traditional ceremony led by Wooshkeetaan elder George Jim.

Auke Bay (*Áak'w Tá, #94*). At the Auke Recreation Area just west of the present boat harbor at Auke Bay lies the historic village of the Áak'w K̲wáan. In Tlingit the settlement was known as the "Town That Moved" (Aanchgaltsóow, #92) due to its relocation from its original site at Indian Cove. The single best source for this history is Phillip Joseph, an Áak'w K̲wáan elder, who began recording the history of his people in the 1960s and published "The History of Aukquwon [Áak'w K̲wáan]" in 1967 in the journal *New Alaskan*. According to Joseph, prior to settling in Juneau the Yax̲teitaan (Dipper People) were living at Stikine River near present-day Wrangell. They decided to move because of a quarrel with another group in the village. Journeying north up the coast of Admiralty Island, they stopped at Young Bay before ultimately settling at Auke Bay and Indian Cove. Remarkable in its chronology of events and level of geographical detail, Joseph's narrative is worth quoting at length:

> The people started off towards the North. This was a rough trip for some people with women and children. It took them weeks. They finally came to Stephens Passage. They explored every island and bay. The only place they didn't explore was the Taku Inlet and Gastineau Channel. They went outside Douglas Island, then they came to Youngs [*sic*] Bay.
>
> Here they discovered lots of seal. They came inside a big hole just above the high water mark. It had a small entrance at the high tide through which the seal comes into the inlet. The seal go after fish in the creek. Then the natives go out to the entrance in small canoes. They line up their canoes across the entrance and use paddles for plungers until the tide goes out. After the tide goes out behind the flats then the seals come down to get out to sea. That is when they use clubs to kill all the seals they need.
>
> The people wanted to stay there but the Chief refused and told them to go on. He told them if they didn't find another place to suit them, they can always go back... They came by Outer Point and came to Auk Bay. The Chief then told his people where they would make their new settlement.
>
> They landed in Fairhaven [Indian Cove] and started building. They put up big houses, huts, and smokehouses. At the same time most of the people explored the whole bay. They soon find Auk Lake. And they find out the creek [that] runs from the lake is a good sockeye creek. They also find out the herring spawns in the spring. There were all kinds of berries, game, and shellfish food.
>
> The name "Auquwon" comes from the lake. In Thlinget, lake means "auk" and "quwon" means the people. That's how the people who go there were named Aukquwon.
>
> The name of Auk Bay in Thlinget is "Auk-ta" [see #94]. Then one day the Chief told some of the men and his nephews to go back and up Taku Inlet. When they left they went behind the Island south of Auk Bay and they saw a channel leading through a bar, where the airport now stands. They went through this channel and came out at what is now called Gastineau Channel.
>
> They saw ducks of all kinds, many animals like bears and mountain goats. This place suited them and they went right back to report to the Chief. He came and looked the place over. He told his people they will make their settlement in Auk Village to live in winter time. After so many years they start building again for their main village.
>
> They built their Dipper House at Fairhaven. They worked for years, then they moved to Auk Village. Why the Chief took pains to find a village site was that they needed a sandy beach because they use canoes and also had to have a shelter like a boat harbor...
>
> The Auquwon claimed the lands from Berner's Bay down to Point Bishop...
>
> After the Dipper House was moved to Juneau it has been rebuilt four times. So the Auk Village should be four hundred years old. The Auk people landed in Auk Bay around 1564. (P. Joseph 1967, 8–9)

According to elder Marion Ezrre, Áak'w people used to move from Auke Village to Indian Point in the spring for herring, spring king salmon, halibut, and other resources, and then would move to Auke Creek to harvest sockeye. After the sockeye moved up river into the lake system in late summer, people would move to the Mendenhall Glacier/River sockeye run. She observes, "At that time the glacier used to be much closer to the lake."

Auke Cape (*X'unáx̲i, #95*). The story of Yeesk̲aanáalx̲, a famous Áak'w L'eineidí (dog salmon) clan leader, is localized at Indian Point at Auke Cape. Bessie Visaya (1972), Cecilia Kunz (1997), and Forrest DeWitt Sr. (1985) all recorded versions of this story. Part of the story is also recounted in Swanton (1909, 58ff.). Rosa Miller also tells a version of the story similar to her mother's (Bessie Visaya's) written account but with additional geographic details.

Most versions place the key event in the story, where the Áak'w leader (originally known as K̲uwudak̲aa) meets, challenges, and ultimately defeats his Yakutat rival through a display of wealth — thus earning the name Yeesk̲aanáalx̲ (Newly Rich Man) — at Indian Point on Auke Cape. The conflict was precipitated by the Yakutat leader's failure to pay a courtesy visit to the Áak'w leader when he passed through the latter's territory on a trip down to the Taku River. On the return trip, a messenger was sent to intercept the Yakutat group and invite them ashore at X'unáx̲i for a feast at which the Áak'w leader proceeded to insult the Yakutat leader by burning the ornate prow of the latter's canoe.

The Yakutat chief left in anger, returning to X'unáx̲i the following spring to remonstrate. A quarrel erupted and soon the Yakutat leader started throwing copper shields (*tináa*) — preeminent symbols of wealth among the Tlingit — into the water to show his superior status. The Áak'w chief responded in kind by bringing out his own coppers and disposing of them in the water. The Áak'w also brought forth a young woman who imitated her crest, the dog salmon, in a spawning dance, except that instead of laying eggs, she dropped valuable things like copper bracelets and abalone shells to symbolize the superior wealth of the Áak'w. Soon the Yakutat leader ran out of coppers, so instead substituted large pieces of spruce bark. However, although they weighted the spruce bark pieces with rocks so they would sink like the coppers, somehow one refloated and their ruse was exposed. Victorious, the Áak'w people then sang an insulting song, prompting the Yakutat group to give up in shame. From this event, K̲uwudak̲aa earned his new title, Yeesk̲aanáalx̲ (Newly Rich Man).

The story is important not only because it took place at Indian Point, but also because it was a major event in Áak'w L'eineidí clan history. In characteristic Tlingit fashion, the prestigious name that the Áak'w leader earns, Yeesk̲aanáalx̲, encapsulates the event itself, serving as mnemonic for the narrative and a symbol of the clan's triumph. The L'eineidí victory established them as a force to be reckoned with — not only a major clan but as gatekeepers for

The Tlingit fish trap pictured in the glass case, known as Kax̲dig̲oowu Héen Sháli ([Montana Creek] Fish Trap), was named for the site of its discovery, Montana Creek (Kax̲dig̲oowu Héen, #81). The five-hundred- to seven-hundred-year-old trap was found in 1989 when part of it became exposed in an eroding section of the creek's bank. Archeologists Jon Loring, Robert Betts, and Greg Chaney, along with a host of volunteers, worked diligently to remove the fragile cylindrical structure with minimal damage. Remarkably the hemlock wood and spruce root components of the trap had avoided decomposition by virtue of being entombed in a bed of wet, iron-rich and oxygen-poor soil. Removal of the trap necessitated keeping the wood and lashings wet with spray bottles and moistened gauze, as exposure to the air would otherwise cause immediate deterioration. The water-logged trap was then placed in a chemical bath of polyethylene glycol to stabilize and preserve the structural integrity of the organic materials. Somewhat flattened, the trap now resides in its own exhibit in the Juneau-Douglas City Museum, with a beautiful replica of its original form, crafted by Steve Henrikson and Janice Criswell, hanging above. Photo by Steve Henrikson.

the area. Finally, and perhaps most importantly, the story is significant because it is yet another expression, perhaps the very first recorded, of L'eineidí asserting their proprietary rights and the greater Auke Bay area as their territory which they were prepared to maintain and defend against those who would trespass without permission. This is the main reason why the story was presented in 1997 at a public hearing concerning a proposed fisheries laboratory and administrative facility to be built by the federal government on the site.

Gold Creek (*Dzantik'i Héeni, #115*). This creek was noted not only for its supply of flounder, which gathered at its mouth to feed on the remains of spawned-out salmon and were harvested in quantity by local Tlingits each fall, but also as the "biggest salmon creek of all, with dog salmon, humpies [pink], and cohos, and with steelhead after the freeze" (Goldschmidt and Haas 1998, 39). The Áak'w had a settlement here which became their main village after the gold rush began in the late nineteenth century. The name Dzantik'i Héeni came to be applied to the whole city of Juneau which grew up around Gold Creek. More recently, the name was chosen to grace the new Juneau middle school, located in Lemon Creek Valley (Shaanáx̱ or Shaanáx̱ Tlein, #88).

T'aaḵú Ḵwáan

The T'aaḵú Ḵwáan was, at the advent of European contact, centered at the mouth of Taku River. However, during the gold rush era, most residents removed to Douglas and Juneau. With the exception of Douglas, no settlement sites remain in this ḵwáan. The Taku was an important migration route and trade corridor to the Interior. Several clans made their way to the coast along the Taku, according to the oral histories. These early migrants settled in other areas, however, and the T'aaḵú Ḵwáan developed only after other parts of the coast were settled (Emmons n.d.). As late arrivals to the coast, the T'aaḵú maintained close connections to their Interior relatives, especially at Atlin (Áa Tlein, #8) in British Columbia. Important clans in this ḵwáan include Yanyeidí, Tsaateeneidí, and S'eet'ḵweidí in the Eagle/Wolf moiety and G̱aanax̱.ádi, Ishkeetaan (Ishkahittaan), Kooḵhittaan, and Tooḵa.ádi (Emmons n.d.) in the Raven moiety. A study of the Yanyeidí clan and their oral history in the Taku River area has recently been completed by Nyman and Leer (1993); otherwise ethnogeographical information on the T'aaḵú Ḵwáan is scant (Emmons n.d.; R. Olson 1967; McClellan 1975; Goldschmidt and Haas 1998). Their territory extended from the southeast coast of Douglas Island and Dupont Creek to the north to Port Snettisham on Stephens Passage. They also claimed the fringe of Admiralty Island from Point Arden to Point Hugh. Like the Jilḵáat Ḵwáan, the T'aaḵú territory extended very far inland due to trade connections with the Interior via the Taku River.

Some important named sites in this ḵwáan include:

Taku River (*T'aaḵú, #121*). This is likely a contraction of the longer phrase, T'aawáḵ G̱alaḵú, which may have originally referred specifically to Taku Inlet (Nyman and Leer 1993). According to Emmons (n.d.), the glaciers there once extended much farther toward the mouth of the river, creating large shallow lagoons near the shore where geese gathered in great numbers. The contraction of the name suggests that it is an old one. Interestingly, there is a folk etymology among some coastal Tlingit that the name is derived from *t'á* (king salmon) and *ḵú* (cove), a more direct and perhaps more salient gloss of the term from the coastal perspective, given that the Taku was valued more for its salmon than its waterfowl.

The Taku was also an important artery to the Interior, a highway of trade and travel. The earliest settlements in the ḵwáan were located there, including numerous villages and camps. These are described by a member of the ḵwáan as follows:

> Before the boundary was established, the Taku village was on the Canadian side, but later, it was moved to the mouth of the river. Taku Village was called [Asgutugíl'i] [#48]. There was another village above this one on the river called [Taaltsux̱éi] [#45, or perhaps L'éiw Aan, #65]. There was a third village still further up called [S'iknoow] [Black Bear Fort, #51]. This was a place where there were a lot of bears . . . I went with my mother up the river to get muskrat, mink, beaver, wolverine, and fox. I remember we went a long way up and I had a hard time getting there. There were smokehouses up the river, and the Indians caught fish there. When I was at the village called [S'iknoow] there were four smokehouses, but no tribal houses. At the mouth of the Taku River they used to have community houses, but these are all rotted away. There were three houses which belonged to the G̱aanax̱.ádi clan and two houses that belonged to the Yanyeidí. The former of these are Ravens, and the latter are Eagles. The Yanyeidí people claim the river, and the others just came in there because they were married in or related. (Goldschmidt and Haas 1998, 41–42)

Another village was located at the mouth of the river near Point Bishop, called T'aak̲ú X̲'aka.aan (#132). This settlement is reported to have flourished prior to the gold rush but was all but abandoned as residents moved to Juneau seeking economic opportunities. Interestingly, however, the village was rebuilt and resettled around 1888 when members of the S'iknax̲.ádi (or Sik'nax̲.ádi) clan, disillusioned with their lifestyle in the mining economy of Juneau, led a movement back to their old dwelling place (Emmons n.d.; Goldschmidt and Haas 1998).

Because the river and its tributaries were productive and yielded salmon from June through November, it was not necessary to maintain remote fishing grounds. As elder Jenny Klaney put it, "They could get all the fish they wanted so they lived right there" (in Goldschmidt and Haas 1998, 42). Fishing camps were established along the Taku, however, after the permanent settlements upriver were abandoned and residents removed to Juneau and Douglas. Similarly, trapping territories were staked out by individual families during the fur trade era.

Taku Harbor (S'iknax̲s'aank'í, #141). Taku Harbor was the site of another important T'aak̲ú village, and was named for its proximity to Limestone Inlet (S'iknáx̲ [or Sik'náx̲*], #142) from which the S'iknax̲.ádi clan derives its name (though the original site was up Stikine River; see the Shtax'héen K̲wáan chapter). The village was first reported by Vancouver in the late eighteenth century and became a vibrant center for trade when the Hudson Bay Company established a post there in the mid-nineteenth century. Later the village was depopulated as a result of the Juneau gold rush but was resettled when a commercial salmon cannery was established in Taku Harbor and Natives found employment there. Nearby, at Moose Creek, residents would gather in the spring to net eulachon and render the oil (Goldschmidt and Haas 1998, 43).

Port Snettisham (Sit'k̲ú, #144). Swanton (1908, 399) suggests this name refers to a variety of whale called *s'eet'*, and it is from this place that the S'eet'k̲weidí take their name. Other sources suggest, however, that the Sit'k̲weidí clan originates from here and that their name derives from Snettisham's location "among the glaciers." Interestingly, the same name applies to nearby Holkham Bay, suggesting perhaps that the two bays may have once been a single glacial landscape. After reaching the coast via the Stikine River, the Sit'k̲weidí are believed to have migrated north to Snettisham and settled on its southern shore at the head of a shallow bight under a glacier (*sít'*) (Emmons n.d.). Another segment of this group settled at Holkam Bay

The following poem by Andrew Hope III, a member of the Sik'nax̲.ádi clan (note: he uses alternative spellings of the clan and place names), was composed in 1993 and references his clan's ties to Limestone Inlet (#142) and Taku Harbor (#141). The Sik'nax̲.ádi are most closely associated with the Wrangell area which is where they are said to have emerged and ultimately settled after migrating from the Interior via the Stikine River (see Shtax'héen K̲wáan chapter) and traveling as far north as Taku River. Part of their history is linked to Limestone Inlet (Sik'náx̲,* #142), where they reportedly stopped to collect whetstone before heading south to Taku Harbor (Sik'náx̲ Aan G̲eey,* #141) and, finally, Wrangell.

Sik'náx̲ Aan G̲eey

I dreamt I lived
In a small
Protected cove
A peaceful place
Standing on the beach
Skipping rocks over calm water
At sunrise
On a clear
Early summer day

I traveled to
Sik'náx̲ Aan G̲eey
Grindstone Bay
Taku Harbor
For the first time
On a bright, clear
Early summer day in 1992

Grindstone rocks
Stand like monuments
At the bay entrance
My clan name
Sik'nax̲.ádi
Came from this place

Walking with those spirits
Dancing with those spirits
Grindstone Bay
The place I dream about
Grindstone Bay
The place I dream about

and founded the S'awdáan Ḵwáan. Ronald Olson (1967, 31) suggests that the Sit'ḵweidí were also ancestors to the Kayáashkiditaan of Wrangell, and that Sit'ḵweidí "may be one of the really ancient names and ancient clans, for at Wrangell the entire assemblage of Wolf moiety clans may be addressed as [Sit'ḵweidí]." According to ḵwáan members interviewed by Goldschmidt and Haas (1998, 43), there were villages at Whiting River and Port Snettisham, and camps at Mallard Cove, Sweetheart Creek, and inside Point Anmer. Mrs. Annie Rasmussen named the three camps in Snettisham as Tłaksidak* (#146), Seenáa (#138), and Tcatshini (Ḡathéeni, #136), but did not specify their exact locations. The latter is likely connected to the main sockeye stream, which was especially esteemed.

Young Bay (Tsaa T'ei Héen, #134). This area, important to both Áak'w and T'aaḵú ḵwáan history, was originally inhabited by a group known as the Tsaat'ineidí, who took their name from Young Bay, where they originally settled before moving to Auke Bay and Taku River. Young Bay is probably the settlement that Vancouver observed in 1794. Emmons locates it in a shallow bight on the northern shore of Admiralty Island. The Young Bay location is supported by Vancouver's geographic description of the bay itself — shallow — and by his record of another village across from this one on Douglas Island, undoubtedly at Point Hilda, which is directly opposite Young Bay. Seal would collect in the bay on floating icebergs dispensed by Taku Glacier, thus inspiring the name "Behind the Seals Creek." The area is still used by Juneau seal hunters. The bay also provided easy access to the west side of Admiralty Island via a short portage to Hawk Inlet (Weineidei, #137). This area also was used for hunting, fishing, and trapping, as was Funter Bay to the north.

Oliver Inlet (Deishú Áak'u, #139) / Seymour Canal (Kanaḵ'aa, #143). A short portage connected Oliver Inlet to Seymour Canal, which flanks the eastern shore of Admiralty Island. Emmons (n.d.) reports a village in this vicinity, but more recent land claims testimony (Goldschmidt and Haas 1998) suggests that the area was used primarily as a camp by the L'eeneidí, who dried dog salmon and trapped furbearers there. The area was also favorable for deer hunting and marine invertebrate and berry harvesting.

Gambier Bay (Ldaḵéex', #149). This area was claimed jointly by the T'aaḵú and Ḵéex' (Kake) people, as descendants of the families who dwelled there eventually settled in both communities. The bay was used mainly for hunting deer and drying salmon and also for trapping furbearers and harvesting seals and marine invertebrates. A small village was located near the cannery site and another settlement was reported between this site and the north arm of the bay (Goldschmidt and Haas 1998). In recent years the area has been utilized more by Kake Tlingits because it is closer to their village than to Juneau. One of the last great Tlingit shamans, Gambier Bay Jim, was a steward of this place, and took his English name from it.

Final Thoughts

The Áak'w Ḵwáan and T'aaḵú Ḵwáan place names project illustrates the plethora of Tlingit connections to Alaska's capital city area. Some of these names, like Auke Bay, remain a part of the cartography, and others, like Dzantik'i Héeni have made a resurgence into popular consciousness. Unfortunately, much of the rich, indigenous geography has been obscured by the dominance of English, and the decline of Tlingit-speaking populations in the area. The project has provided points of contact between Áak'w Ḵwáan, T'aaḵú Ḵwáan, and surrounding communities to preserve what remains of Native place names in the area and their cultural associations.

Today, the Juneau and Douglas Tlingit tribes are using the results of the place names project to maintain members' ties to the land through education and appropriate management of the natural and cultural resources tied to named sites. Native corporations (Thornton 2007) based in Juneau, such as Sealaska and Goldbelt, also are joining in this effort.

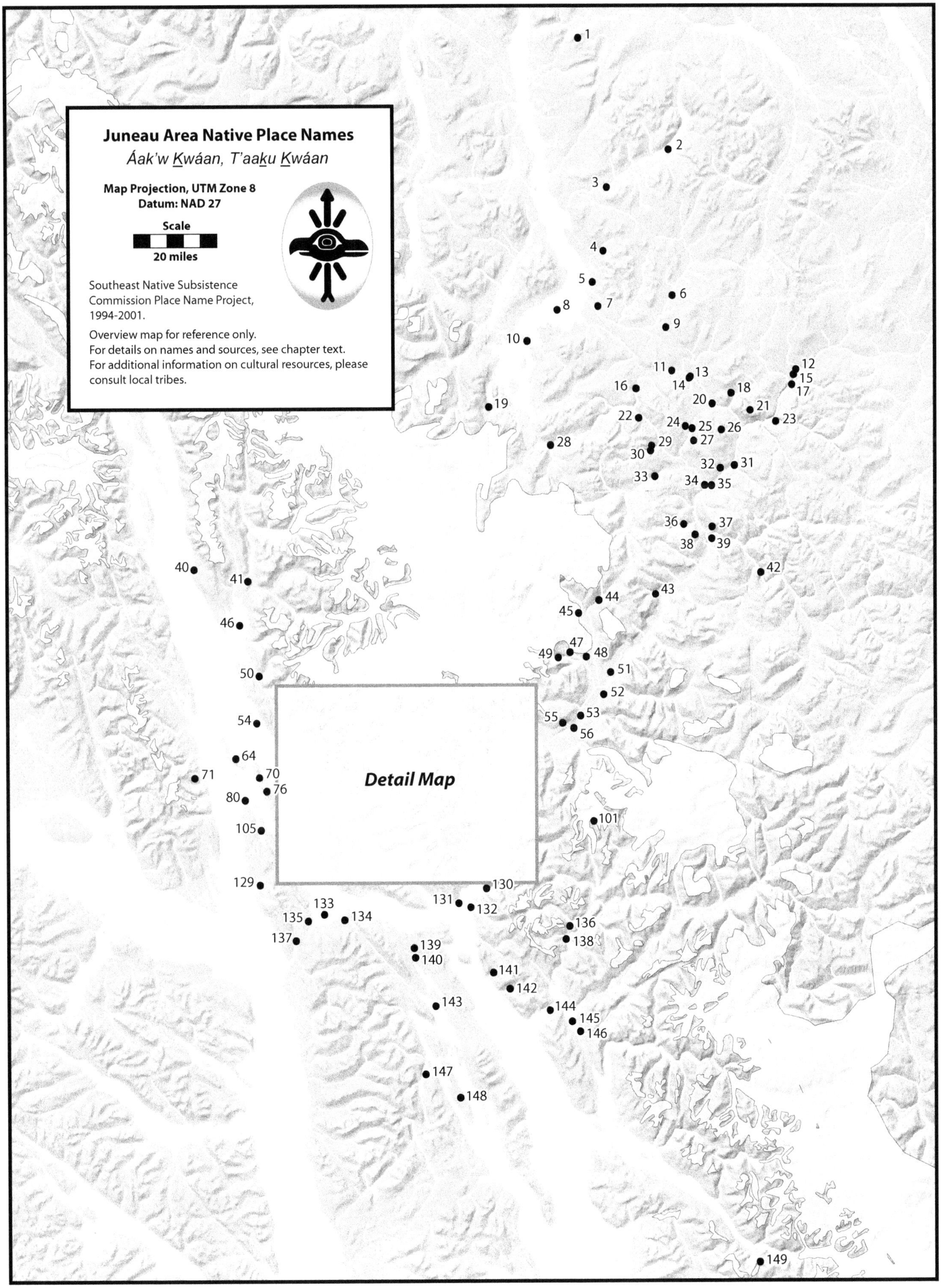

Juneau Area Native Place Names
Áak'w Kwáan, T'aaku Kwáan
Map Projection, UTM Zone 8
Datum: NAD 27
Scale
20 miles
Southeast Native Subsistence Commission Place Name Project, 1994-2001.
Overview map for reference only.
For details on names and sources, see chapter text.
For additional information on cultural resources, please consult local tribes.
Detail Map
1
2
3
4
5
6
7
8
9
10
11
12
13
14
15
16
17
18
19
20
21
22
23
24
25
26
27
28
29
30
31
32
33
34
35
36
37
38
39
40
41
42
43
44
45
46
47
48
49
50
51
52
53
54
55
56
64
70
71
76
80
101
105
129
130
131
132
133
134
135
136
137
138
139
140
141
142
143
144
145
146
147
148
149

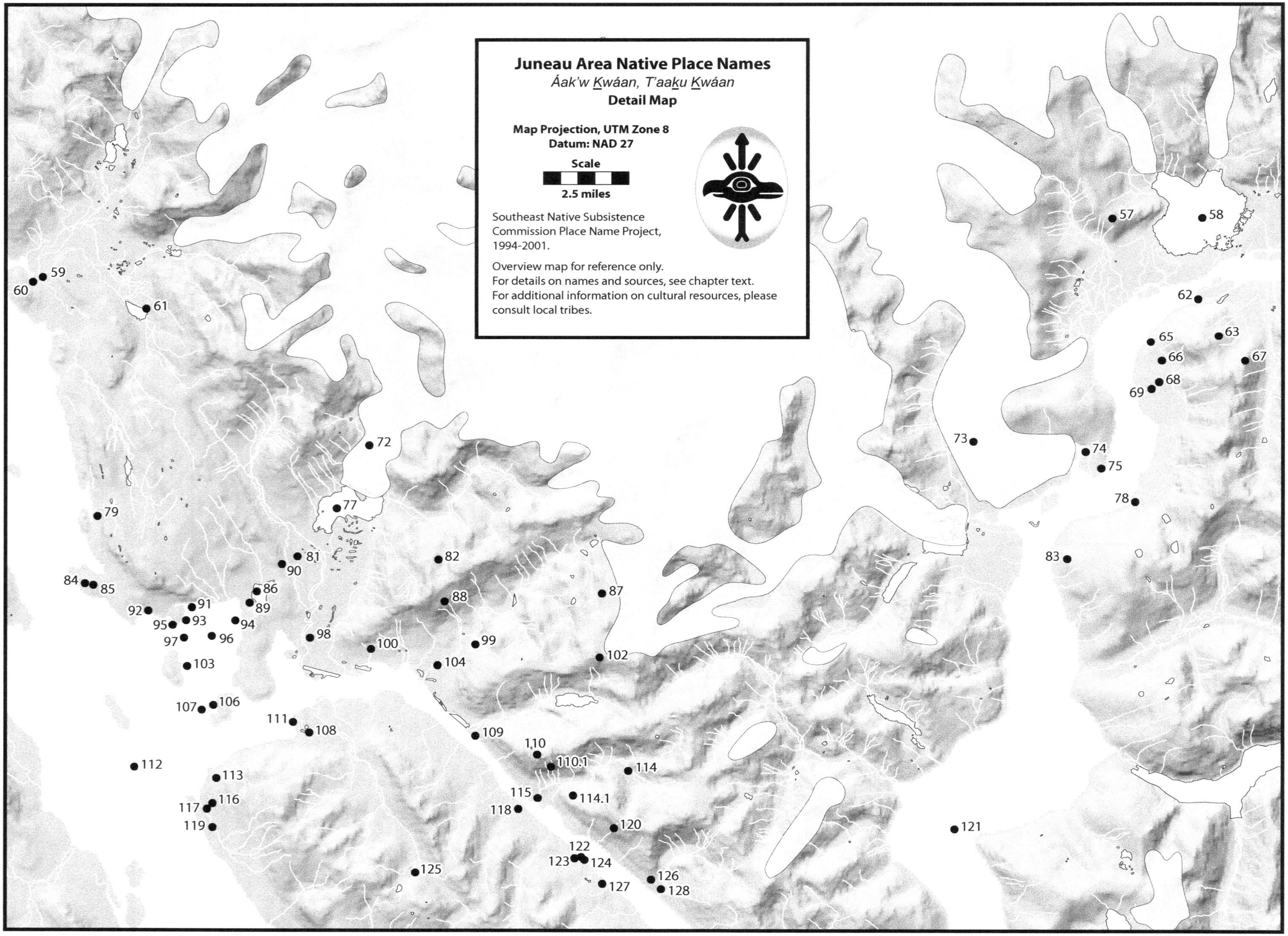

Juneau Area Native Place Names
Áak'w Ḵwáan, T'aaḵu Ḵwáan
Detail Map

Map Projection, UTM Zone 8
Datum: NAD 27

Scale

2.5 miles

Southeast Native Subsistence
Commission Place Name Project,
1994–2001.

Overview map for reference only.
For details on names and sources, see chapter text.
For additional information on cultural resources, please
consult local tribes.

Áak'w K̲wáan and T'aak̲ú K̲wáan Place Names

Asterisk indicates uncertain, unconfirmed, or partial; NM = not mapped.
Some names have more than one pronunciation or translation.

Map #	*Name*	*Translation*	*Location*
1	At Ch'éeni Shaa	[Sheep's] Bow Mountain	Upper Taku River (Carter Mountain)
2	Koosawu Áa	Narrow Lake	Surprise Lake
3	Koosawu Héen	Narrow Creek	Pine Creek
4	Inhéeni	Flint Creek	McKee Creek
5	Yaawat'aayi Héen G̲eeyí	Warm Water Bay	Warm Bay
6	Watsíx Héeni	Caribou River	O'Donnel River
7	Yat'aayi Héen	Hot Springs	Hot Springs
8	Áa Tlein	Big Lake	Atlin Lake
9	Dashdané Áayi	Suckerfish Lake	Dixie Lake
10	S'eek X'áat'i	Black Bear Island	Griffith Island
11	G̲at.áayi Shú	End of Sockeye Salmon Lake	End of Kuthai Lake
12	Neixinté	Blue-Green Claystone (Flint)	Near Nakina Village*
13	G̲at.áayi	Sockeye Salmon Lake	Kuthai Lake
14	Chookán Tlein	Great Grassland	Silver Salmon River
15	Naak'ina.áa	Naak'ina Village	Nakina Village area
16	Ts'eitina Héeni	Ts'eitina Creek (the first word is Athabaskan)	Gold Bottom Creek
17	Tatlenx'ix̲oo	Bestrewn with Big Rocks	Nakina Village site
18	Sinwaa Yádi	Little Limestone Outcropping	Upper Taku River
19	A Shuyee	The Foot of [the Glacier]	Head of Llewellyn Inlet
20	G̲athéeni	Sockeye Creek	Silver Salmon River
21	Sinwaa [Tlein]	[Big] Limestone Outcropping	White Quartz Mountain
22	L'óox̲'u Héen	Silty River	Sloko River
23	Tatlenx'ix̲oo Héeni (S'iknoowóo Héeni)	Tatlenx'ix̲oo (#17) River	Upper Nakina River
24	X̲'aak Tlein Héeni	Big Ravine Creek	Upper Taku River
25	X̲'aak Tlein	Big Ravine	Upper Taku River
26	T'ooch' Shakée	Peak of Charcoal [Mountain]	Upper Taku River
27	T'ooch' Héeni	Charcoal Creek	Fourth of July Creek
28	L'óox̲'u Áa	Silty Lake	Sloko Lake
29	Séik̲'u Té	Vermilion Rock	Sloko River area
30	Séik̲'u Té Héeni	Séik̲'u Té (#29) Creek	Sloko River tributary
31	Naak'ina.áa Héeni	Naak'ina.áa Creek	Lower Nakina River
32	T'ooch' Yayá	Side of Charcoal [Mountain]	Upper Taku River

Map #	*Name*	*Translation*	*Location*
33	Naak'ina.áakw*	Little Naak'ina Lake	Nakonake River
34	Woosh Keekanax̲ Kukwantaayi.áan*	Opposite Each Other Village (facing each other on opposite banks)*	Taku River near headwaters
35	T'eix̲ X̲'a.eetí	Fishhook Site	Upper Taku River
36	K'wálx̲i Héeni	Fern Creek	McGavin Creek
37	Yayuwaa	Interstice	Luwa Mountain ridge
38	Kax̲noowk'ú Tuk̲ká	Rise Adjacent to Kax̲noowk'ú (#39)	Abutment above Kax̲noowk'ú
39	Kax̲noowk'ú	Ancient Settlement	Upper Taku River
40	Aan Sakweis's'í*	Village ——*	Berners Bay area
41	K̲utak.aan*	——* Village	Mouth of Lace River, Berners Bay
42	Héen Tlein	Big River	Inklen River
43	Shaanax̲héeni	Valley River	Upper Taku River
44	Yayéinaa Héeni	Whetstone Creek	Shazah Creek
45	Taaltsux̲éi	In Front of Big Flat Basket*	Tulsequah River
46	Dax̲anáak	Between Two Points*	Berners Bay
47	Shaanáx̲ Tlein Héeni	Big Valley Creek	Wilms Creek (Canyon Creek)
48	Asgutug̲íl'i	Rocky Outcropping in Wooded Area	Near Polaris Mine
49	Shaanáx̲ Tlein	Big Valley	Wilms Creek Valley
50	Ch'eet' Taayí	Murrelet Fat*	Cowee Creek, Echo Cove
51	S'iknoow	Black Bear Fort	Above Tulsequah
52	K̲anaguk* Yík	Inside ——*	Upper Taku River
53	Aanx̲'atinyé	Place Where the Opening (mouth) of the Land Lies	Canyon Island
54	Taan X'áat'i	Sea Lion Island	Benjamin Island
55	Shaa Tlein	Big Mountain	Kluchman Mountain
56	Naahéeni	Tribe* Creek	Taku River, secondary channel
57	Lkoodaséits'k Shaayí	Lkoodaséits'k's (#67) Head	Taku River
58	Sít' Áayi	Glacier Lake	Twin Glacier Lake
59	Asx̲'ée	Twisted Tree (Dam)*	Eagle River
60	Eeyák'w	Small Rapids	Eagle River Landing
61	K̲aa Shaa Teiwalgi*	Person's Head Rock Hole*	Herbert Creek
62	T'aak̲ú Téix̲'i	Heart of the T'aak̲ú (#121)	Upper Taku River
63	Lkoodaséits'k Leikachóox̲'u	Lkoodaséits'k's (#67) Windpipe	Taku River waterfall
64	Naayádi	Child of the Clan	Lincoln Island
65	L'éiw Aan	Sand Village	Taku River*
66	Kax̲tóok	Cave*	Cave by Taku Lodge
67	Lkoodaséits'k	[Giant's name]	Taku River mountain
68	Kax̲tóok X̲'ayee	Area below Kax̲tóok (#66)	Area below Kax̲tóok
69	T'aawák̲ Éix̲'i	Goose Slough	Taku River

Map #	*Name*	*Translation*	*Location*
70	Kichx̱aak' Tuḵyee	Wing Island* Bottom End	Shelter Island fort
71	Jánwu Téix̱'i	Mountain Goat Heart	Mount Golub, Chilkat Peninsula
72	Sít'	Glacier	Mendenhall Glacier
73	T'aaḵú Ḵwáan Sít'i	T'aaḵú (#121) People's Glacier	Taku Glacier
74	Sít' Ḵunaa G̱eeyí	Glacier-Bidding Bay	Taku Glacier cove
75	Sít' X'aayí	Glacier Point	Swede Point
76	Kichx̱aak'	Wing Island*	Shelter Island
77	Sit'.áa	Glacier Lake	Mendenhall Lake
78	Yakwdeiyí	Canoe Path	Across from Taku Glacier
79	Wóoshde X̱'al.at Yé	Place Where the Open Sides Face Each Other*	Tee Harbor
80	Xutsnoowú Lutú	Brown Bear Fort Point (nose)	Point Retreat
81	Kax̱digoowu Héen	Going Back Clear Water	Montana Creek
82	Tleix̱satanjín	Hand at Rest	Heintzleman Ridge
83	Yanyeidi X'aayí	Yanyeidí Point	Taku Point
84	Nex̱'w X'aayí	Cloudberry Point*	Lena Point
85	Yéilch Awataayi Yé	Raven ——* Place	Lena Point shaman site
86	Áak'w	Little Lake	Auke Lake
87	Sít'	Glacier	Lemon Creek Glacier
88	Shaanáx̱ (Shaanáx̱ Tlein)	Valley (Big Valley)	(Lower) Lemon Creek Valley (Shaanáx̱ may reference upper valley)
89	G̱athéeni	Sockeye Creek	Auke Creek
90	Áak'w Táak	Inland from Little Lake	Mendenhall Valley
91	Ḵaalaká	Inside of Human Mouth	Ferry terminal
92	Aanchg̱altsóow	Town That Moved	Auke Bay village (modern Auke Rec. Area)
93	Áak'w Noow	Little Lake Fort	Fairhaven
94	Áak'w Tá	Back of Little Lake [Bay]	Auke Bay
95	X'unáx̱i	Camping Place*	Auke Cape
96	Yax̱té	Dipper	Auke Lake/Bay
97	Sawdáat X'áat'i	Soldier Island	Off Auke Cape
98	Kax̱digoowu Héen Dei	Going Back Clear Water Trail	Trail to Montana Creek
99	Sit'ḵú Héen	Glacier Area Creek	Lemon Creek
100	T'áa Shuyee	Board Squared at the End	Mendenhall Valley
101	Sít' T'ak Aaní	Land with Glaciers Above	Sittakanay River area
102	Katlaax̱ Jíni (Tlax̱ Satán Jín)	Hand of Moldy Head (Idle Hands)	Blackerby Ridge* ("hand" refers to ridge system)
103	Shaa X'áat'i	Mountain Island	Island at end of Fritz Cove
104	Eix̱'gul'héen	Creek at the End of the Slough	Lemon Creek or stream just north of Lemon Creek (Switzer Creek according to Nora Dauenhauer)

Map #	Name	Translation	Location
105	Yaxwch'i Ḵaadí Táak	Sea Otter Slide Back of [Bay]	Barlow Cove
106	Kadigooni X'áat'	Island That Has Spring Water	Auke Bay
107	Yaana.éit X'áat'i	Wild Celery Island	Auke Bay
108	Aangooxa Yé	Beside the Slaves of the Town Place	Fish Creek
109	Til'héeni	Dog Salmon Creek	Salmon Creek
110	Katlaax (Shaa Tlaax)	Moldy Top (Moldy Mountain)	Mount Juneau (top)
110.1	Yadaa.at Kalé	Beautifully Adorned Face	Mount Juneau (face)
111	Aangooxa Yé X'áat' T'aak	Beside Aangooxa Yé (#108) Island	Island at Fish Creek
112	L'awkalagé	Shiny Beach	Portland Island
113	Shikaagi Noow	Thick-Walled (of logs)* Fort	Outer Point
114	It'ji Shaanáx	Sparkling Valley	Perseverance Valley
114.1	Dzánti	Flounder	Hill above Gold Creek (Capitol Hill)
115	Dzantik'i Héeni (Dzanti K'ihéeni)	Flounder at the Base of the Creek* (Creek at the Base of Dzánti [#114.1])	Juneau (Gold Creek)
116	Deishú Áak'w	Little Lagoon at the End of the Trail	Douglas Island, Outer Point cove
117	Kanáxs'*	*	West side of Douglas Island, Peterson Creek*
118	Kaawa.ée Héenak'u	Kaawa.ée's (man's name) Little Creek	Kowee Creek, near Juneau-Douglas Bridge
119	Ḵaalahéenak'u*	Inside a Person's Mouth Creek*	Peterson Creek
120	Wooshkeenax Deiyí	Trails above Each Other	On Mount Roberts
121	T'aaḵú	Flood of Geese	Taku River
122	Shgóonaa Héenak'u	Schooner's Little Creek	Lawson Creek village
123	Deishú	End of the Trail	Lawson Creek village
124	Sayéik*	Spirit Helper*	Douglas
125	X'áat' T'áak	Beside the Island	Douglas (Mayflower Island*)
126	Chas'héeni	Humpback Salmon Creek	Sheep Creek
127	Anax Yaa Andagan Yé	Where the Sun Rays Hit First	Douglas Boat Harbor
128	Ḵoosh	Oozing Sore	Thane
129	Shakanáxk'w	Dead Trees on Mountain*	Funter Bay
130	Was'as'éi	[Giant's name]	Dorothy Peak*
131	Keishixjix'aa	Runs-Up Point	Bishop Point
132	T'aaḵú X'aka.aan	Town at the Mouth of T'aaḵú (#121) [Inlet]	Taku River
133	Kanak'aa Sít'[i]	Skinny* Glacier	Young Glacier
134	Tsaa T'ei Héen	Behind the Seals Creek	Young Bay creek
135	Weineidei Aan (Weineideiyan)*	Alkali Deposit* Village	In Young Bay
136	Ǥathéeni	Sockeye Creek	Snettisham
137	Weineidei	Alkali Deposit* Trail	Hawk Inlet
138	Seenáa	*	Camp in Snettisham

Map #	*Name*	*Translation*	*Location*
139	Deishú Áak'u	Little Lake at the End of the Trail	Oliver Inlet, Admiralty Island
140	Deishú Áak'u Aan	Camp on Deishú Áak'u (#139)	Camp on Oliver Inlet, Admiralty Island
141	S'iknax̲s'aank'í (Sik'náx̲ Aan G̲eey*)	Little One below S'iknáx̲ (#142) (Sik'náx̲ Town Bay)	Taku Harbor
142	S'iknáx̲ (Sik'náx̲*)	Black Bear Community* (Grindstone/Whetstone*)	Limestone Inlet
143	Kanak̲'aa	Skinny*	Seymour Canal
144	Sit'k̲ú	Glacier Area	Port Snettisham
145	Sít' G̲eeyí	Glacier Bay	Gilbert Bay
146	Tłaksidak*	——* (from Goldschmidt and Haas 1998, 43)	Sweetheart Creek*
147	Chichnáx̲	Porpoise Harbor*	Windfall Harbor
148	Kichx'aa Yík*	Inside the Wing* Point	Island in Seymour Canal
149	Ldak̲éex̲'	*	Gambier Bay
NM	G̲eiwk'óo (G̲eiwk'ú)	*	Upper Seymour Canal*

5. *Sheet'ká K̲wáan*

The Sheet'ká (Ocean Side of Shee [Baranof Island], #372) K̲wáan, now centered in Sitka, takes its name from the community's geography. Sitka in fact is derived from the Tlingit place name Sheet'ká, consisting of Shee (the name for Baranof Island) and *ká* (a locative suffix meaning "outside of"). Thus, Sheet'ká K̲wáan can be translated as "Baranof Island Outer Coast Inhabitants." All of the major settlements were on the ocean side of the island. There are two derivations of the term "Shee," one suggesting that it refers to the limb of a tree (Emmons n.d.) and the other to the legendary "Volcano Woman" of Mount Edgecumbe, named Shee, who appeared to the first settlers of the region as a great white figure (Herman Kitka Sr., interview). Although the story of Shee may be considered *tlaagú* (mythical) by most, until recently it was not uncommon for local Tlingits visiting Kruzof Island to leave a token offering for Volcano Woman to insure safety and good luck.

Sheet'ká K̲wáan is distinguished by its long and intimate contact with Europeans. Sitka was the hub of Russian activities in Southeast Alaska beginning in 1802 and remained the unofficial capital of the territory through the early American period. Sheet'ká K̲wáan included the west coasts of Baranof and Chichagof islands and the smaller islands offshore. The principal Raven clans consisted of the Kiks.ádi, L'uknax̲.ádi, X'at'ka.aayí, T'ak̲deintaan, K̲oosk'eidí, and Watineidí. Major Eagle/Wolf clans included the Kaagwaantaan and K̲óokhittaan, Chookaneidí, Wooshkeetaan, and X̲'ax'ahittaan.

In conjunction with Sitka Tribe of Alaska, we documented more than five hundred place names in Sheet'ká territory, along with information about their cultural associations. This project represents the culmination of work by many individuals and groups. Foremost, we want to thank the elders, past and present, without whose contributions this project would have been impossible, especially the late Charlie Joseph Sr., Mark Jacobs Jr., and Herman Kitka Sr., each of whom spent many hours recording ethnogeographic nomenclature and details. We also wish to thank members of the Sitka tribal government for their support and assistance with all phases of the research, as well as the Sitka Native Education Program, and the many others who corroborated names, attended meetings, and contributed to the project in a variety of important ways. Ethel Makinen and Vida Davis served as local research coordinators for the project, working closely with Robi Craig and Roby Littlefield of Sitka Tribe of Alaska. Thomas F. Thornton carried out additional field research, working especially with Herman Kitka Sr. Documentary material on Native geographic names from John G. Brady (n.d.), Frederica de Laguna (1960, 1972), George Emmons (1991, n.d.), Walter Goldschmidt and Theodore Haas (1998), Ronald Olson (1967), Louis Shotridge (n.d.), John Swanton (1908, 1909), and other sources provided a foundation on which to build. Jeff Leer of the Alaska Native Language Center and Nora and Richard Dauenhauer of the Sealaska Heritage Institute provided linguistic consultation and review.

Some Important Named Sites

Kruzof Island (L'úx Yadaa, "Around the Face of L'úx [Mt. Edgecumbe]," #242). Kruzof Island was named for its central feature, Mount Edgecumbe. The island is important not only because of its legendary volcano but for its role in the settlement of Sitka. As Kaagwaantaan elder Herman Kitka Sr. relates (Thornton 1998):

> Seeking evergreen trees suitable for building houses, a canoe party went north from Tongass along the outside coast. Ice flows still blocked the inside passages, and the land they found was thick with grass and alder, but no evergreens for timber. Soon, large smoke plumes twenty miles to the northwest became visible. The party made camp and sent a canoe to investigate the sources of the smoke. As they approached Sitka Sound, the scouting party saw a moun-

tain upon an island, spouting fire and smoke, the one they call L'úx [#228], "Blinking Top," Mount Edgecumbe. They named it that on account of that volcano. And the prevailing winds were coming from the northwest, blowing the smoke toward Sitka. That's how come there were no trees there. They decided to circle the island [Kruzof Island] and on the north side, at Sinitsin Cove [#195], they found there was no smoke and there was plenty of big spruce for making houses. So they started to cut and split the trees when a woman appeared to them dressed in white. She demanded that they leave her island in peace. The medicine man, dressed for battle, was sent to meet the volcano woman, who called herself Shee. As they spoke she noticed the jewelry of the Tlingit women. Shee agreed that in return for earrings, bracelets, and other gifts, the Tlingit could remain on her island. Later, they settled on the main island, Baranof Island, which was named Shee, after the Volcano Woman. In the Tlingit language "at'iká" means "on the outside" and so the people called the new village Shee At'iká, people living on the outside of Shee island. Today we call it Sitka.

And that is why the old people, when they are using that island for deer hunting and subsistence, would leave a small offering for Shee. They were thanking that volcano woman for the things they got from there.

Mount Edgecumbe's volcanic activity is also evident in the scientific record. For example, the geomorphology of the Indian River delta reveals thick tephra (volcanic ash) deposition dating to about ten thousand years ago and another thin layer laid down some four thousand years ago (Chaney, Betts, and Longenbaugh 1995, 15). Charcoal remains embedded in the tephra suggest that fire destroyed old-growth trees in the vicinity of modern Sitka. Again, this is consistent with the Native oral history in which pioneer settlers found only "grass and alder." Hence they bypassed Sitka in favor of the well-forested areas on the north end of Kruzof Island, especially Kalinin Bay (Naxiskéet, #204) and its "child," Sinitsin Cove (Naxiskéet Yádi, #195). The volcano's activities also have left prodigious amounts of pumice on Kruzof's outer shores, especially the area around Beaver Point (Géxkw Yaká, #224) which takes its name from this "floating stone." Just below this area, another precious stone, *neixinté* (see #229 and #231), or blue-green "jade" claystone (e.g., celadonite), which fills the veins of basalt and other rock, was used by Tlingits for blue-green paint.

Mount Edgecumbe (L'úx, #228) is an important landmark for Sitka Tlingits. Its name means "blinking," a reference to its historic volcanic activity. The smaller hills to the right of it are known as L'úx Yátx'i (Children of L'úx, #227), providing an example of a common kinship metaphor that is used to interpret relationships between landscape features. Photo by Tom Thornton.

Indian River (Kaasdahéen, #400). The lower Indian River is now the site of Sitka National Historical Park, one of the oldest parks in the state. On the weekend of April 26, 1996, the Tlingit clans of Sitka hosted guests from throughout Southeast Alaska, to dedicate the first Sitka Tlingit pole to be erected in the park (non-local poles had occupied the grounds for nearly a century). Thirty-five feet of magnificently carved cedar, the pole honors the five clans that first settled the area. Though classic in its form and style, the pole represented a departure from tradition in its content because it embraced both the Raven and Eagle/Wolf moieties (opposite sides) rather than sketching the history of a single clan. Local elders chose to recognize all the major clans that built houses in Sitka. The pole was given a Tlingit name, which translates into English as "Indian River Historical Pole," and its erection and dedication were marked by a solemn ceremony, led by the Kiks.ádi hosts upon their traditional lands at Sitka National Historical Park. Both the pole itself and the dedication ceremony serve as testimony to the central role of Indian River in Sitka Tlingit social history.

Tlingit place names are often opaque and need to be interpreted or "unpacked" to be understood. Claims to specific places almost invariably are based on stories or legends that explain the name. The story behind the name for Indian River exemplifies this pattern. Kiks.ádi leader Al Perkins intepreted the story of the frog crest through narrative and dance during the raising of the Indian River Historical Pole. A similar version of the story was recounted by Herman Kitka Sr., who heard it from Alex Andrew's father, a Kiks.ádi man known in English as "Sport" Johnson (because he is said to have "dressed rather flashy"). His synopsis, translated from the Tlingit, is this:

> There used to be three smokehouses beside the river [Indian River] where the Kiks.ádi stayed. Coming in from the bay [Jamestown Bay] with the tide they saw a little dugout canoe coming up the river with people in it. And from the three smokehouses that were alongside the river the Kiks.ádi came out. One of them hollered, "I wonder who you are and where are you from." And one of the persons who stood up in the canoe, one of them stood up in the small canoe, and said, "We are moving from Sockeye River [Ḵathéeni, #422] in Frog Bay [Xíxch'i Ḵeeyí, a.k.a. Silver Bay, #410] to our river, Ḵaasdahéen." And as soon as the person said this, it went down into the water. And what floated up in its place was a boom log on which three frogs were sitting. Because of this vision, the Kiks.ádi people to this day still call this place Ḵaasdahéen [Man's* Stream], the name that the frog people gave it. (pers. comm. 1998)

This version of the naming of Indian River is more detailed than others (e.g., R. Olson 1967) in its description of the sacred geography. We learn that the frog people originate from the sockeye stream at the head of Silver Bay, that Silver Bay itself was originally named for the frogs, and that the Kiks.ádi were already established at Indian River when they encountered the frog people. Mr. Kitka's version also stresses the fact that the vision of the frog people is itself sacred. Because the Kiks.ádi experienced this extraordinary vision, they have a special claim to Indian River; and the name itself, having been given by the frog people, is sacred. The Kiks.ádi also claim the frog as their central clan crest.

Nakwasina Sound (Daxéit, #295). This is a key subsistence site for the Kiks.ádi. It is the setting for the famous Aak'wtaatseen ("Alive in the Eddy," the name of the main character, which is still used by the Kiks.ádi clan today), or "Salmon Boy," story and also where the Kiks.ádi hero, Ḵaax'achgóok, returns after his long journey out to sea. The Aak'wtaatseen story, as told by Deikeenáak'w to ethnographer John R. Swanton (1909, 301–10) in 1904 is especially rich in geographic detail. Subsequent to this project, Tom Thornton had the opportunity to review Deikeenáak'w's text with elders of the Sitka tribe (Littlefield et al. 2003), and found that seventeen place names are either mentioned or alluded to in the text (Thornton 2008; see also figure 1 in the introduction). For example, there is de-

The Indian River Historical Pole at Sitka National Historical Park was raised and dedicated in the spring of 1996. The carved wooden frog in center of the pole is the central crest of the Kiks.ádi clan, and encapsulates the history of Indian River (Ḵaasdahéen, #400), where the Kiks.ádi came to settle after encountering the frog people along the river. Photo by Tom Thornton.

tailed description from a salmon's perspective of Xukxu Séet (Going Dry Strait, #187; referenced only as "Séet" in Swanton's version), a place "which gives scars to whichever one happens to get caught in it" as the salmon migrate back to their natal stream, Daxéit Héeni (#286). Thus, the Salmon Boy story not only highlights Tlingit perceptions of the landscape but also those of the salmon, who often see the world differently. Tlingit traditionally regarded salmon as non-human persons, possessing a social organization and other cultural attributes like their own. For this reason salmon were handled carefully and with respect. Disrespectful behavior, such as "playing with" or insulting fish, could result in reprisals by the salmon people, as in the Salmon Boy story where Aak'wtaatseen insults the moldy salmon offered by his mother and is subsequently carried off by the salmon tribe in what appears to him as a canoe. Living among the salmon people as he matures, Aak'wtaatseen comes to learn their customs and worldview — their migration from Daxéit to their ocean feeding grounds and return journey into Sitka Sound, where they "camp" and spawn. Aak'wtaatseen not only learns how the salmon get their markings, but also why the coho always return last to Sitka Sound (they broke their canoe), what salmon call humans (seal children's dog salmon), their rivalry with herring (over which is most important to humans), and so on. Eventually, Aak'wtaatseen returns to Daxéit, and is caught by his parents, who reckon his true identity by the familiar copper necklace that still encircles the salmon boy's neck. Ultimately, Aak'wtaatseen is converted back into human form and becomes a powerful shaman and a teacher of the ways of the salmon tribe, his many deeds and eventful life being further reflected in names on the land, such as Xijaa.éix'i (#290), the lagoon where the shaman beat his drum.

Other parts of Baranof Island (Shee, #424). The name for this large island served as a central reference in a constellation of orientational names for different parts of it, including Sitka itself (Sheet'ká, #372). The bottom of the island (Wooden Island, #571) was called Shee Sáank', while the lower ocean side of the island up to Warm Springs Bay was called Shee Lunáak (#569), and the lower inside was termed Shee T'éik (#553). The upper inside of the island to Peril Strait was known as Shee Yá (#173), whereas the upper ocean side of the island, where Chichagof Island lay, was called Shee Kaaḵ (#26). Following this logic of regionalization, additional names are constructed within the subregions, such as Shee Kaaḵ T'áak ("Head of Shee Kaaḵ," head of Hoonah Sound, #18) and Shee Lunáak Ḡathéeni

("Over the Nose [point] of Shee Sockeye Creek," Redfish Bay, #563). Redfish Bay was an important, early settlement according to oral histories from Kake and Sitka. Its antiquity is supported by recent archeological investigations, including the unearthing of a Tlingit-style woven basket, dating to approximately 5000 BP. Other important bays and settlements on lower Baranof included Whale Bay (see #538, #543, #545), Necker Bay (Dagák' Ḡeeyí, #529), Crawfish and West Crawfish Inlet (Kanat'ákw T'áak, #504, and Lax'áas, #502). Redoubt Bay (Ḵunaa, #457), and Silver Bay (Kageet [Ḡageit'], #426). As in Redfish Bay, many key settlements in these areas were associated with sockeye salmon rivers. Unique among these is Necker Bay, which Tlingits named for its "little sockeye" (*dagák'*), a species they distinguish with a separate term from full-size sockeye (*gaat*), and which is unique to Sheet'ká Ḵwáan and now found exclusively in Necker Bay. At one time, these little sockeye were also found at Suloia Bay (#145) and a Green Lake creek (#411). The latter is named for the fact that the little sockeye there, finding their path upstream blocked by a weir, became insulted and left, never to return. A Tlingit proverb stems from this event, *Tlel dagák' aax aawateeni yík* (Don't leave insulted like those little sockeyes). This proverb was sometimes invoked by

Kaagwaantaan elder Charlie Joseph Sr. Courtesy of Sitka Tribe of Alaska and Sitka Native Education Program.

Sheet'ká hosts at memorial parties to insure their guests would feel welcome and wish to return, rather than leave insulted like the little sockeyes of Dagák' Aax̱ Aawateeni Héen (Thornton 2008, 173).

Above Sitka, along with Nakwasina Sound, Katlian Bay (Tl'ayaak̲', #314) was an important watershed, and settlements and camps were found in Saint John Baptist Bay (Jilk̲óok', #174), Fish Bay (K̲uwís'k', #163), Rodman Bay (Dagalk̲ú, #66), Saook Bay (Sa.ook̲, #75) and Hanus Bay (G̲áchkw Yayuwaa, #80).

Chichagof Island. The southeastern portion of Chichagof Island was known as Shee Kaak̲ (#26, the name for Hoonah Sound), while the southwestern portion was de-

fined by the tall mountain on Khaz Peninsula, known as Seilk̲ (#113). Khaz Bay and Slocum Arm feature a number of important settlements and subsistence sites including Seilgak̲oowú.aan (#120) and Ch'ux̲ Aan (#121) on the peninsula itself, and Ford Arm (Wanas'áx̲', #112) in Slocum Arm (X̲aas T'éik G̲eeyí, #116), which housed a fish cannery. Above Khaz Peninsula, western Chichagof Island also included a number of important settlements and subsistence and trapping camps. Among these were Ogden Passage (Dóol Aaní, #11), named for its plentiful game, Klag Bay (Chaas' G̲eeyí, #13), known for its large sockeye salmon run, Herbert Graves Island (Kun.aan, #7), Black Bay (Kun.aan Seiyí T'áak, #5), and Porcupine/Islas

---

Sitka Tribe of Alaska:
Building on Names Shared by Charlie Joseph Sr.

In 1975, Kaagwaantaan elder Charlie Joseph Sr. (K̲aal.átk'; 1895–1986) began working with the newly formed Alaska Native Brotherhood Education Program, today known as the Sitka Native Education Program. "Isabella Brady was the director of the program and she got us interested in recording place names around Sitka. We would pack up and travel around in the program's van as Charlie pointed out various locations and told us their names in Tlingit," explains Ethel Makinen, a fluent Tlingit speaker, the daughter of Charlie, and the *naa tláa* (clan mother) of the Sitka L'uknax̱.ádi.

This experience sparked an interest in Charlie Joseph, Isabella Brady, and the program's cultural instructors to record all the Tlingit names that Mr. Joseph could recall onto maps and audiotapes. "We were just learning how to spell our language, so this was difficult! Charlie was very patient with us and was always willing to share his knowledge with us so that we could pass it on to the children," adds Vida Davis, a fluent Tlingit speaker of Inupiaq heritage.

While pointing out named places around Sitka or on project maps, Charlie identified old Tlingit villages, campsites, shorelines, islands, bays, etc. Often, Charlie was able to add which clans and individuals used these areas for putting up food and trapping or would break into a Tlingit song or traditional story, all captured and preserved by the Sitka Native Education Program.

And Charlie would tell jokes—there is much laughter captured on the tapes of the project as well. In the end, Mr. Joseph shared nearly four hundred traditional Tlingit names for geographic features within Sheet'ká Kwáan territory!

In 1993 and again in 1998, the Sitka Tribe of Alaska (STA) supported resumption of the project by local elders. Ethel, Herman Kitka Sr., and Mark Jacobs Jr. spent the summer of 1998 reviewing the placement of all the names on seven new nautical charts. When either of the gentlemen conducting this peer review would add a new name or definition or history of a name these additions would be noted and credit given in the project booklet being compiled. After Ethel and Vida had carefully gone over the recordings made by Mr. Joseph in light of additions made by Herman and Mark, the maps were brought out at a Sitka Tribal Cultural Committee meeting on October 29, 1998. Since this time, these charts have been proudly displayed at the tribe's offices.

Finally, in 1999 Sitka Tribe partnered with the Southeast Native Subsistence Commission to collect additional place names and their cultural associations in a database and to map the total name set using GIS (geographic information systems). Ethel Makinen and Vida Davis served as local research coordinators for this project with assistance from STA staff. This phase of the project also brought in information from other sources, including Herman Kitka's previous work with Thomas Thornton (1997b). More than one hundred new names were added to Charlie Joseph's, and a host of others confirmed and interpreted.

(Watkas'aaẋ, #2). In Peril Strait and Sergius Narrows, all of the major bays on the Chichagof side had Tlingit names and subsistence camps, including Deep Bay (L'ugunáẋ, #153; see "Deep Ties to Deep Bay" below), Ushk Bay (Áshgu Tlein, #39), and Patterson Bay (Ǧeey Tlein, #22).

Sitka Sound area islands. Most islands in Sitka Sound had names and many were used for harvesting and drying fish or rendering herring oil during the spring. Halleck Island (Kasdaẋéiẋ, #273) was the site of a winter village, called Kasdaẋéiẋ Aan (Kasdaẋéiẋ [Halleck Island] Village, #300). According to Herman Kitka Sr. (Thornton 1995),

> That was a big winter village. There were quite a few families that used to live there. Most of them were children of the Coho clan and the Kiks.ádi clan, and all the children were married and their families had no place up in there [by Peril Strait], so they built a village; they called it [Kasdaẋéiẋ Aan]. And that's the only place [in the Sitka area] the Eagle clan can rightfully claim as their own.
>
> Before white people or Western people came among us, the people were fishing herring and cooking them for herring oil, when a large brown bear came and wrecked the village. He came because he smelled that herring cooking. He tore down all the community houses they had—this was a winter village, you know, the closest one to Peril Strait. And my grandfather had one quarter of that skin and we used to measure it; it was 6 foot by 7 foot—and that was only one quarter. They had a lot of beadwork on it; Daisy Peters' family had it. It was tanned so good it felt like cloth. When they used to pack it, they would fold it with yellow cedar boughs. When grandfather opened it up it had an eagle emblem in beads in the center. The skin was divided, a quarter for each of the four different clans that was at that site— Kaagwaantaan, Kiks.ádi, Coho [L'uknaẋ.ádi], Chookaneidí. After that brown bear tore down all those community houses, they moved to the cove at Halibut Point [#350].

Another important island was Middle Island (Táan or Táan Daa, #339), reportedly named for the salmon that jump there before moving in toward shore. Low Island (Shandák'w, #248) was a favored site for hunting seals with clubs and spears.

Using Place Names Today

Sitka Tribe of Alaska (STA) continues to build upon the place name work begun in the early 1970s through the Sitka Native Education Program (SNEP) and supplemented by the Southeast Native Subsistence Commission project. Today, Sitka's Tlingit place name maps can be accessed by visiting the STA website (http://sitkatribe.org). View the maps and click on a place name to hear the name spoken in Tlingit by Vida Davis. Demonstrating the proper pronunciation was very important to both Ethel and Vida. Exciting work in the area of technology and Sitka's Tlingit place names project was initiated by educator Chohla Dick. A teacher at Mt. Edgecumbe High School, Alaska's only tribal boarding school, Ms. Dick works with her students to use multimedia applications to build computer skills and their place-based knowledge.

Place-based knowledge is also practiced at the Blatchley Middle School through Tlingit place name boat tours that have been coordinated by teachers (originally Patricia Dick) for a number of years. Through these journeys, Tlingit leaders and traditional culture bearers bring the names to life for students as they tour the Sitka Sound area. In addition, the staff and Tlingit elders at SNEP continue to use these names in their daily cultural instruction for youth who range in age from pre-school to high school.

Place-based education also flourishes at Dog Point Fish Camp (see #319, #320), where Roby and John Littlefield run camps that immerse kids and elders in Tlingit language, culture, and geography in order to strengthen their minds, bodies, and spirits.

Today Sitka's Tlingit place maps are used by trainers to assist educators to develop strategies to integrate place-based knowledge into their classrooms. At STA, Tlingit names are often used in project proposals and in correspondence sent to state and federal governmental agencies, while the GIS maps hanging at the Resources Protection Department are used to perpetuate the Tlingit culture and to protect traditional resources. Tlingit geographical names have also become a component of STA's Tribal Enterprise Department's annual pre-tourism training program. Guides at Sitka Tribal Tours use Native place names to demonstrate the antiquity and the sustained vibrancy of Tlingit culture to the two hundred fifty thousand annual summer visitors to the shores of the Sheet'ká Ḵwáan.

Deep Ties to Deep Bay (L'ugunáx̱)

Subsistence is ultimately a relationship with places that provide the resources upon which life depends. The following geographic text by Herman Kitka Sr. (1998) outlines the network of places, paths, people, and projects that defined his training in the Tlingit seasonal round of his family, which revolved around two foci: the winter village at Sitka and his family's seasonal settlement at Deep Bay. As with the conventional Tlingit calendar, his year begins in the late spring, when his family moves from the winter village to fish camp.

My family was very lucky in selecting Deep Bay for their customary and traditional subsistence use. Deep Bay was called L'ugunáx̱ [#153]. My family moved to Deep Bay in May after the herring roe harvest in Sitka Sound [#455].

Black seaweed and ribbon seaweed was picked from the beaches in Salisbury Sound [#168], which was only about three or four miles from Deep Bay. The teaching was done by an uncle in each [matrilineal] clan. The uncles taught the young people the names of the places, months, and what tide to pick the seaweed. The next lesson was how to go about drying the seaweed to preserve it for use year round.

The taking of our customary, traditional food supply was taught by uncles through all families of Southeast Alaska.

With seaweed all taken care of, the next undertaking was to fish for halibut for drying. Bait for the halibut hooks has to be gotten. Uncle took us to Rapids Island [#157] at low tide. We learned to look for octopus dens at low tide's edge. We learned from Uncle how to catch the octopus with a gaff hook.

Next our uncle split the young group into two groups. One group was told to cut down alder wood for the smokehouses; the other group was shown how to bait the hooks. Uncle took us into the narrows outside of Deep Bay [#149]. Uncle showed us the halibut fish hole, which he called *éet* in Tlingit. Next we learned how to line up the halibut *éet* or fish holes by lining up two points on the beach. Today I still use this halibut *éet* line-up to catch my subsistence halibut for drying at Deep Bay.

With enough halibut caught and drying in the smokehouses to satisfy all the families in Deep Bay, halibut fishing stopped. Uncle noticed how we enjoyed the fishing; he told us that to fish for the halibut for fun we would be wasting our food supply — to do so would offend the Holy Spirit and cause us to lose our blessing and go hungry.

Back to winter homes in Sitka [#372] to store our subsistence foods for next winter use.

In my lifetime a change in living took place — going to canneries for summer work and seine fishing. All our families moved to Ford Arm [#112] cannery, which was first called Cape Edwards Packing Company, later renamed Deep Sea Salmon Company.

All the older men went seine fishing for salmon for two months. The women all worked in the cannery.

After the fishing season closed, the families all moved back to Sitka again.

The families again got camping equipment and collected to go to fish camp at Deep Bay; also jars for canning berries were taken, along with fishing gear for catching late summer dog and coho salmon for drying.

Uncle again told his trainees, "we can only take enough salmon for all the needs of each family in Deep Bay." Smokehouses were loaded with the fires being attended by our elders.

Next Uncle took all available persons berry picking. The berry picking places were out in the straits outside of Deep Bay among all the islands. Each island had a Tlingit name [e.g., #157], so we can remember where to get the blueberries in the future when we get old enough to go on our own.

The next project was to go seal hunting. Only the older boys were taken. I was lucky to be one of the seal hunters. We were taught how to shoot. The seal hunting areas

Herman Kitka Sr., Martha Kitka, and Richard Dalton Sr. taking a break from picking berries at Point Carolus (see Xunaa Ḵáawu #140), Glacier Bay, 1996. Photo by Tom Thornton.

were outside Deep Bay on certain islands, reefs, and narrow passes between the islands [e.g., #145 or #148]. After a lot of misses by each hunter, we finally learned the proper way to shoot at the seals in the water.

Uncle showed us how to skin the seals, save the fat, meat and skins.

We learned how to make stretchers using green, small alder poles. Seal skins were dried for winter projects in Sitka.

The fat and some meat were saved from young seals for smoking. Fat was rendered out and put in containers. Seal hunting stopped when all families in Deep Bay had enough for use through the year.

Next project — Uncle showed us how to make deer calls. A deer hunting party was selected, three persons to each party. Uncle took the hunting party up the mountain on the west side of Deep Bay — half way up in a basin on the mountain. Uncle told us to spread out and keep very quiet while he blew his deer call — one a little, long call, the next very short. He called in three deer while he was showing us how to use the deer call.

The three deer were shot by the hunters selected to do the shooting.

We got all three deer. Then Uncle showed us how to clean and fix the deer for packing back to camp. Two hunters in each group of three were selected to each pack a deer apiece back to camp, one person in each group had to be a look-out for safety reasons in bear country, and to take turns in packing the deer back to camp. All the hunters were successful that day. Deer were all skinned and cut for smoking and hung up in the smokehouses. After three days of smoking, the deer meat was taken down and cut into small chunks for cooking in pots. After cooking, the deer meat was put on racks again up in the smokehouses and then dipped in seal oil and packed in containers and covered with seal oil. This type of preserving smoked deer meat kept without spoiling through the winter to be eaten as "cold cuts." All fish, meat, and berries preserved, the families again moved back to Sitka, our winter homes.

The next project — the older men prepared for the winter trapping season that would start in December and January.

My grandfolks, my dad, and uncles went to Emmons Island [#36] at the entrance of Hoonah Sound [#34], just ten miles north of Deep Bay. Each family from Sitka also had their own trapping areas.

Some of our subsistence foods were gotten from our winter homes at Sitka. Gathering of clams and fishing for bottom fish, rockfish, flounders, halibut, crabs, and shrimp were done from our winter homes at Sitka.

Before the [commercial] herring sac roe fishery, the Sitka Tlingits used to engage in herring roe fishing from small rowboats. The herring caught in small rowboats was used for making herring oil. Herring roe was taken and dried in trees among the islands around Sitka. All the small islands have Tlingit names and were used together with all other families in the Sitka area [e.g., #455].

This herring was done the last week in March and the first two weeks in April, mostly under Uncles' directions to each family group.

All this teaching was done where our customary, traditional subsistence food supply was gotten. This teaching was what made each Tlingit a good citizen in each community. The young people learned to respect the land they live on. They also learned to take only what each family needed to make it throughout the year. We need to keep on teaching our children our subsistence lifestyle and our culture and religion. Without this teaching our Tlingit cultures will be lost forever.

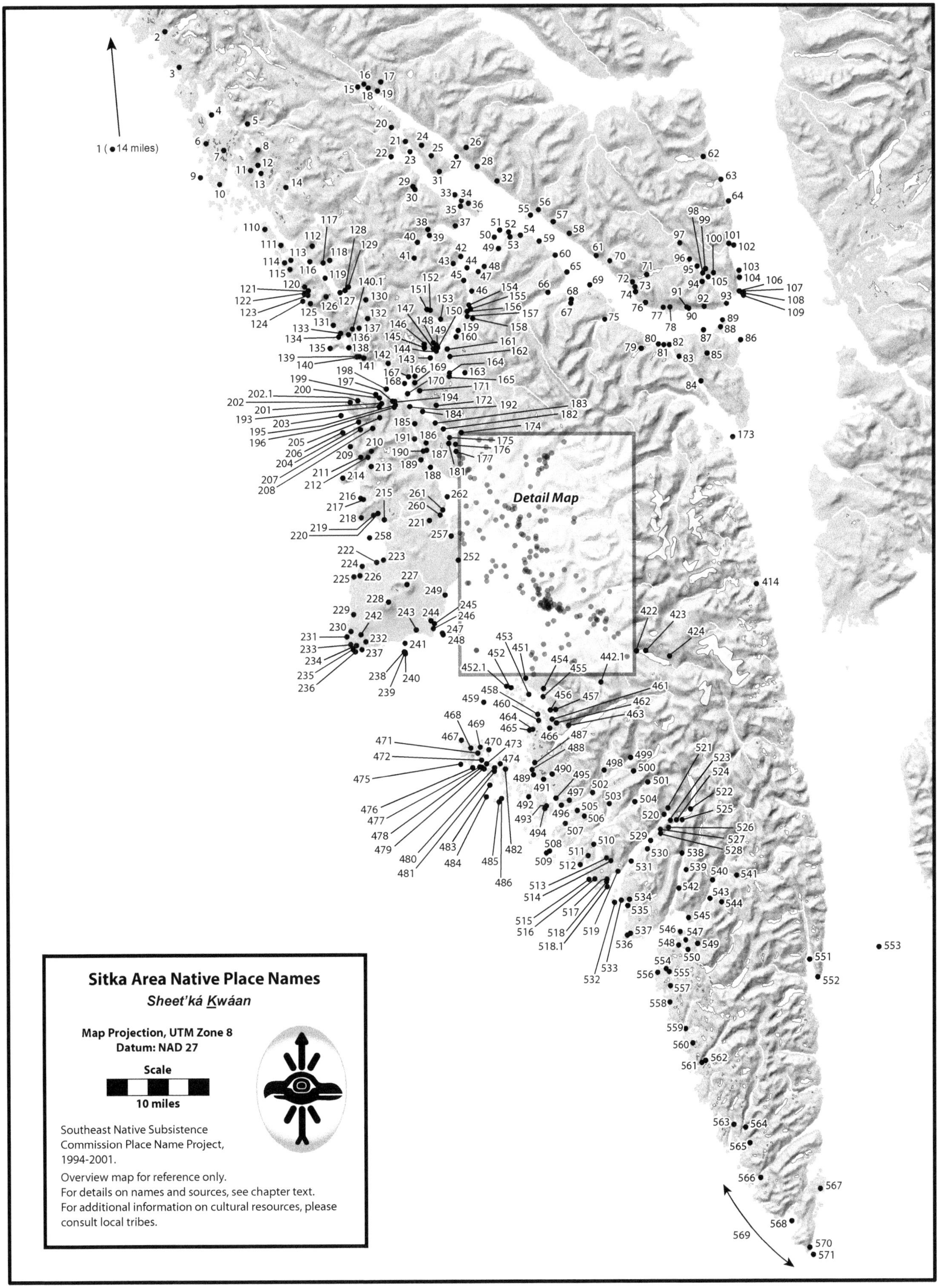
1 (● 14 miles)
Detail Map
Sitka Area Native Place Names
Sheet'ká Kwáan
Map Projection, UTM Zone 8
Datum: NAD 27
Scale
10 miles
Southeast Native Subsistence Commission Place Name Project, 1994-2001.
Overview map for reference only.
For details on names and sources, see chapter text.
For additional information on cultural resources, please consult local tribes.

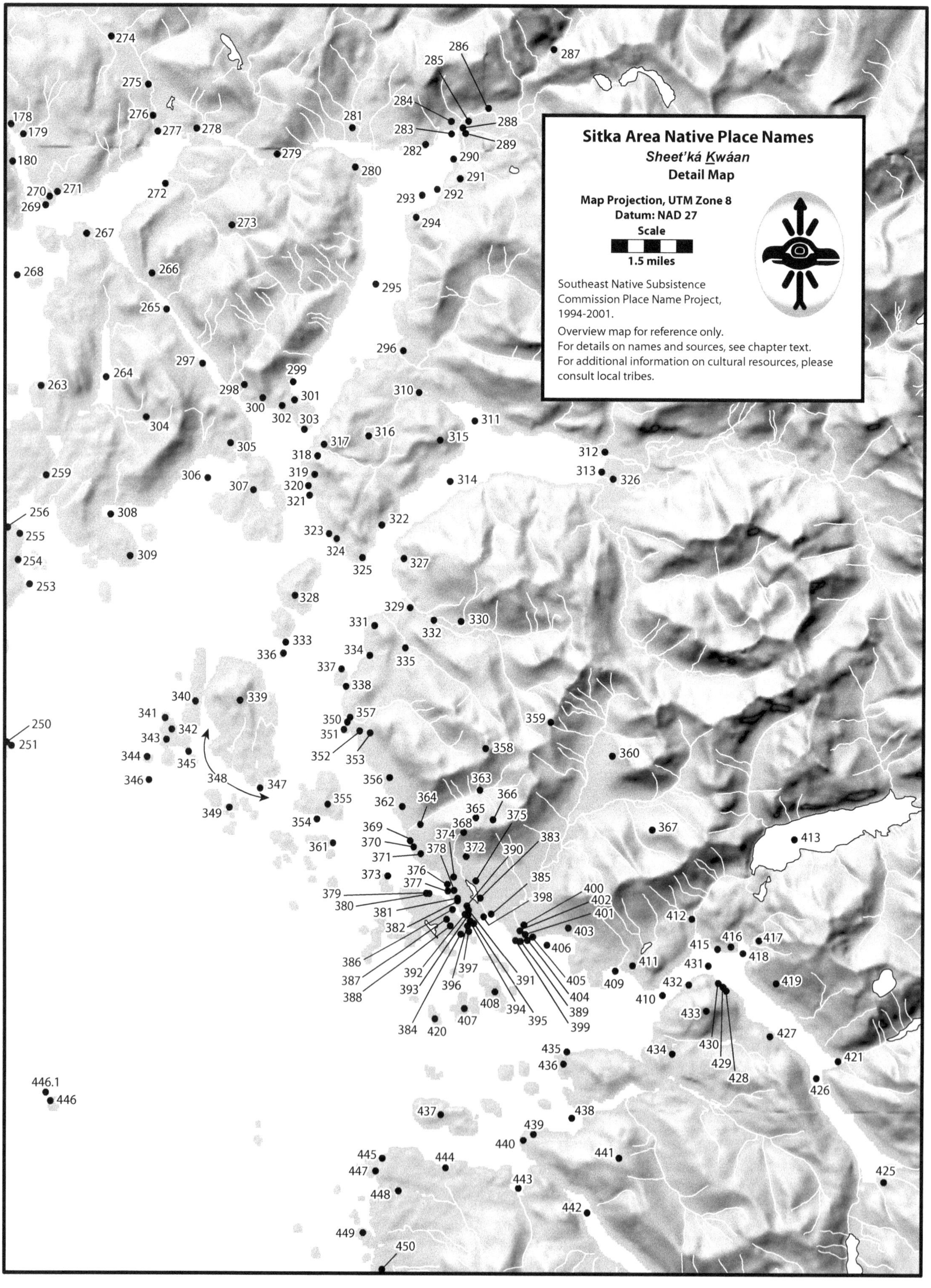
Sitka Area Native Place Names
Sheet'ká Kwáan
Detail Map
Map Projection, UTM Zone 8
Datum: NAD 27
Scale
1.5 miles
Southeast Native Subsistence
Commission Place Name Project,
1994-2001.
Overview map for reference only.
For details on names and sources, see chapter text.
For additional information on cultural resources, please
consult local tribes.

Sheet'ká Ḵwáan Place Names

Asterisk indicates uncertain, unconfirmed, or partial; NM = not mapped. Some names have more than one pronunciation or translation.

Map #	*Name*	*Translation*	*Location*
1	Wankatéix̱'	Heart on the Edge	Surge Bay
2	Watkas'aax̱	Groundhog on the Mouth [of Stream]	Porcupine Island / Islas Bay
3	S'aachx̱aan	*	Sea Level Slough
4	Kun.aan Seiyí	In the Shelter of Kun.aan (village, #7)	Portlock Harbor
5	Kun.aan Seiyí T'áak	Beside Kun.aan Seiyí (#4)	Black Bay
6	Katas G̱athéení*	——* Sockeye Creek	Elkugu Cove* (possibly in Necker Bay)
7	Kun.aan	Hunting Camp	Settlement in Portlock Harbor
8	Dóol	Bountiful Game	Doolth Mountain, Klag Bay
9	Taan Aaní	Sea Lion Country	White Sisters (rookery)
10	T'aawáḵ Séedi	Goose Pass	Tawak Passage
11	Dóol Aaní	Bountiful Game Country	Doolth Peninsula
12	G̱aat Héeni	Sockeye Creek	Klag Bay sockeye stream
13	Chaas' G̱eeyí	Humpback Salmon Bay	Klag Bay
14	X̱aat.ai Seiyí	Fish Resting Place	Pass between Sister Lake and Lake Anna
15	Shaanáx̱ Héeni	Valley Creek	River, Hoonah Sound
16	Tayeidí X'áat'i	Firecracker Seaweed Island	Island, Hoonah Sound
17	Kooshdaaḵáa Héeni	Land Otter Man Stream	Creek at head of Hoonah Sound
18	Shee Kaaḵ T'áak	Head of Shee Kaaḵ (#26)	Head of North Arm, Hoonah Sound
19	Kooshdaaḵáa X'áat'i	Land Otter Man Island	Island at head of Hoonah Sound
20	Sakwdakaxkíx̱'w	*	Hoonah Sound
21	Tsaa Anax̱ Yóo Kuwa.atgi Yé	Place Where the Seals Hop Across	Seal pass between Moser Island and Chichagof Island
22	G̱eey Tlein	Big Bay	Patterson Bay, Hoonah Sound
23	Katlaax̱ Góon	Katlaax̱ (#24) Portage	South Arm Hoonah Sound
24	Katlaax̱	Covered with Mold	Moser Island
25	G̱eey Tlénx' Yayuwaa X'áat'	Island between the Big Bays	Moser Island (early name)
26	Shee Kaaḵ	Above* Shee (#424)	Hoonah Sound / southeastern Chichagof Island
27	Shee Kaaḵ Yík	Inside Shee Kaaḵ (#26)	North Arm, Hoonah Sound
28	Shaaḵ Hít	Driftwood House	Campsite at "Log Cabin Narrows," Hoonah Sound
29	S'aḵhéeni	Bone Creek	River in Peril Strait
30	Yanshóok' áa yéi téeyin	Used to be a little camp (proper name uncertain)	Campsite, Peril Strait

Map #	*Name*	*Translation*	*Location*
31	Yéil Áx̱ji Éesh	Father of Raven Hearer	Trapping camp
32	Wattatéen	Rock Sitting at the Mouth	Creek in Hoonah Sound
33	Néengi Yátx'i	Néengi's (#36) Children	Vixen Islands
34	Néengi L'eedí	Tail of Néengi (#36)	Camp on sandy Emmons Island spit
35	Néengi T'aak Séet	Strait Back Inland of Néengi (#36)	Emmons Island passage
36	Néengi (Néengi Dáa)	[Woman's name] (Néengi Shoreline)	Emmons Island
37	Áshgu X̱'aku.aan (Áshkw X̱'aku.aan)	Settlement at the Mouth of Áshgu (#39) (Settlement at the Mouth of Áshkw)	Ushk Bay village
38	Atx'aan hítx'i áa yéi téeyin	Used to be smokehouses there (proper name uncertain)	Campsite, Ushk Bay
39	Áshgu Tlein (Áshgu)	Big ——* (——*)	Ushk Bay
40	Áshgu Tlein Aan*	Big Áshgu (#39) Village	Ushk Bay village
41	Áshgu Tlein T'aak Héen	Creek Back of Áshgu Tlein (#39)	Creek in Ushk Bay
42	Áshgu Yayuwaaká	Áshgu (#39) Shoreline (or land-sea interface)	Ushk Bay shoreline
43	Áshgu Yádi	Child of Áshgu (#39)	Poison Cove
44	S'áaw Noowú	Dungeness Crab Fort	Povorotni Island
45	Watkadliwuwu Héen	Creek Whose Mouth Is Whitish (foamy)	River, Peril Strait
46	Eey Ká	On the Tidal Rapids	Peril Strait area
47	S'áaw Noowú T'aak Héen	Creek inside S'áaw Noowú (#44)	River inside Povorotni Island
48	L'éiw Shuká Eech	Sand on End Reef	Shoreline, lower Deadman Reach
49	At Seiyí Tlein	Sheltered Shoreline	Deadman Reach
50	Tsaa Kanoow	Fort on Top of Seals	Hoggatt Island
51	Kaltlag̱anís Yátx'i	Children of Kaltlag̱anís (#52)	Elovoi/Krugloi islands
52	Kaltlag̱anís	[Island] Covered with Saplings	Ostoia Island
53	Kaltlag̱anís T'aak Héen	Creek Back of Kaltlag̱anís (#52)	River, Deadman Reach
54	Ḵaa Ts'akool Noowk'	Man ——* Little Fort	Nesmeni Cove
55	Kasnú	Get It to Sit Properly*	Broad Island
56	Kasnú T'aak Héen	River behind Kasnú (#55)	River, Hoonah Sound
57	Yáxwch'i Góon	Sea Otter Portage	Peril Strait (or portage to Sister Lake on western Chichagof Island)*
58	Watkals'íx'g̱aa	[Stream] with Moss at the Mouth	River, Hoonah Sound
59	Nax̱gushl'éi Yádi	——*'s Child	River, Peril Strait
60	Nax̱gushl'éi Tlein	——* Flats	River at Peschami Point
61	X̱'aalx̱'éi X'áat'i	Dwarf Maple Island	False Island
62	Ḵákwk'w (Ḵák'w)	Little Basket	Basket Bay
63	X̱'eik.wás'	*	Little Basket Bay
64	Tayeenáx̱ G̱adá	Underwater Stream Comes through a Cave*	River, Chatham Strait
65	Dáadzi X'aayí	Firestone Point	Point Elizabeth

Map #	*Name*	*Translation*	*Location*
66	Dagalkú	Inland Flood	Rodman Bay
67	Dagalkú X'aka.aan	Village at the Mouth of Dagalkú (#66)	Village at Appleton Cove (island)
68	Dagalkú Sáank'i	Dagalkú (#66) Little One	Appleton Cove
69	Yook Eejí	Cormorant Reef	Rodman Bay reef
70	Lék'waa* Héen	Red Ochre Stone* Creek	River, Peril Strait
71	Sit'kú Gathéeni Shak.áa	Lake at the Head of Sit'kú (#105) Sockeye Creek	Sitkoh Lake
72	Ch'áagu Aan	Old Village	Village, Peril Strait
73	Anax L'ukduyaa Yé	Where They Pack Cohos	Peril Strait to Sitkoh Creek trail
74	Deishu.aan	End of the Trail Village	Village at end of trail
75	Sa.ook	*	Saook Bay
76	Gaaw	Drum	Point, Peril Strait
77	Tlaganís Aan	Sapling Camp	Camp, Peril Strait
78	Kaa Sháa Teiwahayi Yé	Place Where the Rock Fell on the Man's Head	Village at Todd, Peril Strait
79	Gáchkw Yayuwaa Gathéeni	Gáchkw (#85) Shoreline Sockeye Stream	Hanus Bay creek
80	Gáchkw (Gáchgu) Yayuwaa	Gáchkw (#85) Shoreline	Hanus Bay, shoreline inside Catherine Island
81	Gáchkw (Gáchgu) Yayuwaa X'áat'	Gáchkw (#85) Shoreline Island	Dead Tree Island
82	Gáchkw (Gáchgu) Noowú	Gáchkw (#85) Fort (Kiks.ádi name)	Fort on Dead Tree Island
83	Gáchgu Góon	Gáchkw (#85) Portage	Portage Arm
84	Gáchgu Geeyí	Gáchkw (#85) Bay	Portage Arm (all)
85	Gáchkw	*	Catherine Island
86	Cháatl X'aayí Noow	Halibut Point Fort	Point Thatcher
87	X'ax'noowú	Crabapple Fort	Hanus Bay / Catherine Island* (or Point Hayes)
88	Kaanáx Adagaan	Light Shining over It (person's name)	Traders Island
89	Naagas'ei X'áatx'i	Fox Islands	Fairway Islands
90	Tlakwsatán X'aa	Long Branched Trees Always Lying There Point	Lindenberg Head
91	T'aa Toowú Aan*	Village with a Mind for Hot Springs*	Village, Peril Strait
92	Té Káas'k'	Little Rock Cleft	Rock in Peril Strait
93	Chaatlk'aanoow	Fort on Top* of the Halibut	Point Craven
94	Laxaagu Héenk'*	Sandbar* Little Creek	Creek on south shore of Sitkoh Bay
95	Gathéeni	Sockeye Creek	River at Chatham cannery
96	Yéil Katóok	Raven's Cave	Cave near Sitkoh Creek
97	Atahéen	Creek at the Head	River, Sitkoh Bay
98	Tinaa Gooní (Yéil Gooní)	Copper Shield Spring (Raven's Spring)	Spring near Sitkoh Bay cannery
99	Keishísh X'aayí	Beach Alder Point	Point, Sitkoh Bay

Map #	Name	Translation	Location
100	Yáxwch'i Áak'u	Sea Otter Lagoon	Cove, Sitkoh Bay
101	Ḵákw Héen	Basket Creek	River, Basket Bay
102	Ḵákw X'áat'i	Basket Island	White Rock
103	Déili	Harbor	Harbor from south winds
104	Xunniyaa	Shelter from the North Wind	Harbor, Chatham Strait
105	Sit'ḵú	Glacier Area	Sitkoh Bay
106	S'igeidi Noow	Beaver Fort	Fort, Point Hayes
107	Geesh X̱oo	Among the Bull Kelp	Morris Reef kelp patch
108	Noow áa yéi téeyin	There was a fort there (proper name uncertain)	Fort, Sitkoh Bay
109	Cháatl Séedi	Halibut Passage	Morris Reef halibut bank and pass
110	X'aal X'éi X'áat'i	——* Mouth Island	Ramp Island
111	Woosh Keekanax̱ Sa.áan (Akaanáx̱ Gadulnaa Aan)	All Tied Together Islands (You Can Move between Three Camps)	Outside of Slocum Arm
112	Wanas'áx' (Wana'ták')	Edge of the Cambium (Edge Inland*)	Takeena Peninsula, Ford Arm to Sister Lake
113	Seilḵ	Land of Plenty*	Chichagof Island (whole) and tall mountain inside Point Slocum
114	Eech X̱águ (Seilḵ Eech X̱águ)	Reef Sandbar (Seilḵ [#113] Reef Sandbar)	Rocks/sandbar off Khaz Peninsula
115	X̱aas Yá	Face of X̱aas (#137)	Khaz Peninsula
116	X̱aas T'éik Geey	Bay behind X̱aas (#137)	Slocum Arm
117	Yanashkwéix' Aan	Yanashkwéix' (#118) Village	Waterfall Cove village
118	Yanashkwéix'	[So Many Fish (humpback salmon)] Carrying the Water*	Waterfall Cove
119	X'áas T'ei Héenak'w	Little Creek behind the Waterfall	Slocum Arm*
120	Seilgaḵoowú.aan	Village in Seilgaḵoowú (#126)	Slocum Arm village
121	Ch'ux̱ Aan	Ch'ux̱ Village	Settlement, Khaz Peninsula
122	Seilgaḵoowú Héen	Creek at Seilgaḵoowú (#126)	Creek above Point Slocum
123	Yeilkíji Yakwdeiyí	Raven's Wings Boat Road	Passage through rollers, Chichagof Island
124	Yeilkíji Séet	Raven's Wings Strait	Passage into Yeilkíji Yakwdeiyí
125	Tlaganís X'aayí	Sapling Point	Point Slocum
126	Seilgaḵoowú	Going into Cove on Seilḵ (#113)	Mountain range between Klag Bay and Black Bay
127	X̱aas T'éik Geeyí	Bay behind X̱aas (#137)	Slocum Arm (Takheen Peninsula / Sister Lake*)
128	X̱aas T'ei X̱'éex'w	X̱aas (#137) ——*	Island Cove, Slocum Arm*
129	Ḵax̱héeni	Sawbill (Merganser) Creek	River, Slocum Arm
130	Tlagoowú Héen	Ancient Creek	River, east shore of Slocum Arm
131	Ḵaajitan Yé	Ḵaajitan's (man's name) Place	Campsite, Khaz Peninsula
132	X'áat' T'eik Héen	Creek behind the Island	River at Cobol / Island Cove

Map #	*Name*	*Translation*	*Location*
133	T'áx̱gu Yádi X̱'ei	T'áx̱kw's (#135) Child's Mouth	Lake Leo cove
134	T'áx̱gu Séet	T'áx̱kw's (#135) Channel	Pass behind Klokachef Island
135	T'áx̱kw	*	Klokachef Island
136	T'áx̱gu Yádi Héen	T'áx̱kw's (#135) Child's Water	Leo's Anchorage
137	X̱aas	*	Khaz Peninsula
138	T'áx̱kw T'aak Héen	Stream inside T'áx̱kw (#135)	Stream, inside Klokachef Island
139	Eech Xágu X'aayí (Shindíngi X'aa)	Rocky Sandbar Point (Shindíngi [#140.1] Point)	Point Leo
140	Eech Xágu (Shindíngi Xágu Tlein)	Rocky Sandbar (Shindíngi [#140.1] Big Sandbar)	Shoreline, Point Leo
140.1	Shindíngi [Áa]	——* [Lake]	Lake Leo
141	Shindíngi Xágu Yádi	Shindíngi (#140.1) Sandbar Child	Small sandbar
142	Lax'áas	Waterfall	Filipino Cove
143	Tatóok X'aa	Cave Point	Suloia Point
144	Yaakw Yátx'i Séet	Small Canoes' Pass	Pass at entrance to Peril Strait
145	Tsaa G̱eeyák'w	Little Seal Bay	Suloia Bay
146	Kuts'een G̱íl'i	Rat Cliff	Cave above Suloia Bay in Peril Strait
147	Nánde Aa Shee Kaaḵ	Northern One [Narrows] to Shee Kaaḵ (#26)	Sergius Narrows
148	Tsaa Héenák'u	Seal Streamlet	Streamlet at Suloia Bay
149	Cháatl Éedi	Halibut Hole	Halibut hole below Deep Bay in Peril Strait
150	Haatx̱ Ishḵaaḵ	Whirlpool (literally, "Keeps Perching in the Tide")	Rapids Island area, Sergius Narrows
151	L'ugunáx̱ Héen	L'ugunáx̱ (#153) River	Deep Bay river
152	L'ugunáx̱ Aan	L'ugunáx̱ (#153) Settlement	Deep Bay village
153	L'ugunáx̱ (L'uganáx̱)	Coho Clan Community	Deep Bay
154	Teil X'áatx'i (X'áat'ak'u)	Pitch Islands (Little Islands)	Islands near Rapids Point, Peril Strait
155	Lgéex̱'i*	*	Peril Strait*
156	Haat X'aayí	Whirlpool Point	Rapids Point
157	Haatx̱ Ishḵaaḵ X'áat'i	Whirlpool Island	Rapids Island, Sergius Narrows
158	Téil X'áat'i T'aak Héen	Creek behind the Pitch Island	Range Creek
159	Nax̱iskéidlát A Keeká	Across from Nax̱iskéidlát (#160)	Baby Bear Bay
160	Nax̱iskéidlát	*	Bear Bay
161	Ch'áal' G̱eeyí	Willow Bay	Schulze Cove
162	Ch'áal' G̱eeyí Aan	Willow Bay Village	Schulze Cove village
163	Ḵuwís'k'	[Fish] Coming into a Cove*	Fish Bay
164	Ḵuwís'k' Aan	Ḵuwís'k' (#163) Village	West side of Haley Anchorage
165	Ḵútl'gu Noowú	Mud Fort	Haley Point
166	Tuḵ Xágu	Needlefish Sandbar	Sandbar in Kakul Narrows

Map #	*Name*	*Translation*	*Location*
167	Íxde Aa Shee Kaak̲	Southern One [Narrows] to Shee Kaak̲ (#26)	Kakul Narrows
168	Eey X̲'é	Mouth of the Tidal Current	Salisbury Sound
169	Neixinté Seiyí	Area below the Blue-Green Claystone	Shoreline/cliff
170	Daalas'úx'	*	Scraggy Island
171	K̲alt'ás'gi Yá	*	Shoreline
172	K̲alt'ás'k Wan Héen	——* Creek	River, Saint John Baptist Bay
173	Shee Yá	Face of Shee (#424)	Kelp Bay area
174	Jilk̲óok' (Kalt'as'g̲eeyí)	——* (Rough Water Bay)	Saint John Baptist Bay
175	L'eedí Noow	Tail Fort	Neva Strait, Highwater Island
176	Ltooch Héen	Roasting Creek	River in Neva Strait
177	Nánde Aa Séet	Farther Away [from the Village] Strait	Neva Strait
178	Ltooch Héen Tlein	Big Roasting Creek	River and flats in Neva Strait
179	Ltooch Héeni	Roasting Creek	River in Neva Strait
180	Eey X̲'éidáx̲ Aa Séet	Tidal Current at the Mouth Strait	Whitestone Narrows
181	Ltooch X'áat'i	Roasting Island	Neva Strait, Highwater Island
182	Wóoshdáx̲ Kanax̲sa.aan	——* Village	Village, Sukoi Inlet
183	X̲'alyéis' G̲eeyák'w	Blackened Mouth* Little Bay	Gilmer Cove
184	X̲aa Tatóogu	Warrior's Cave	Cave, north Kruzof Island
185	Xukx̲u Séet X̲'aká	Mouth of Xukx̲u Séet (#187)	Sukoi Inlet
186	Téel' Héenak'u	Dog Salmon Little Creek	Creek at Sukoi Inlet
187	Xukx̲u Séet	Going Dry Strait	Pass between Krestof Sound and Sukoi Inlet
188	Kaawtootan* Yé	——* Place	Upper Krestof Sound*
189	Ch'aak'i Héeni	Eagles' River	Creek, east Kruzof Island*
190	G̲uwakaan Xágu	Deer Sandbar	Sandbar, Krestof side of Sukoi Inlet
191	Wat.lax'áak	River Mouth Teeming with Pectoral Fins	River, Sukoi Inlet
192	Xukx̲u Séet X̲'aka.aan	Village at the Mouth of Xukx̲u Séet (#187)	Campsite at Sukoi Point
193	Nax̲isk̲éet Nánde Aa	Nax̲isk̲éet (#204) Further Up Lagoon/Lake	Lagoon/lake at the head of Kalinin Bay
194	Koot'ex̲' Aank'átsk'u	Petroglyph Hamlet	Sinitsin Cove village
195	Nax̲isk̲éet Yádi	Child of Nax̲isk̲éet (#204)	Sinitsin Cove
196	Keel X'áat'x'i T'aak Héen	Creek at the Head of Keel X'áat'x'i (#197)	River at the head of Sinitsin Cove
197	Keel X'áat'x'i	——* Islands	Sinitsin Cove islands
198	X̲'ananóok	*	Sinitsin Island
199	Eech Xágu X'aayí	Reef Point	Submerged rock
200	Nax̲isk̲éet Tlein	Big Nax̲isk̲éet (#204)	Mouth of Kalinin Bay

Map #	*Name*	*Translation*	*Location*
201	Nax̲isk̲éet Aan (Koot'cx̲'.aan)	Nax̲isk̲éet (#204) Village (Petroglyph Village)	Kalinin Bay village
201.1	Nax̲isk̲éet Íxdei Aa	Nax̲isk̲éet (#204) Closer [to the Mouth] Lake	Lake Surprise
202	Léik̲'u X'aa	Red Snapper Point	Cape Georgiana
203	Deikeelatín Eejí (Ch'áak' Eejí)	Watching Outside Reef (Eagle Reef)	Eagle Rock
204	Nax̲isk̲éet	Bay System with Flooding Tides*	Head of Kalinin Bay
205	Kool T'aak Aan	Village/Land inside Kool (#206)	Kruzof Island, Sealion Cove
206	Kool (Kool X'áat'x'i)	Navel (Navel Islands)	Sealion Islands
207	Kool T'aak Héen	Creek Inland of Kool (#206)	Sealion Cove creek
208	Xeitl Ji.eetí	Thunderbird Scratch Marks	Ravines on mountainside, north Kruzof Island
209	Shalax̲'wách'	*	Twin Point
210	L'úx Áak'u	L'úx's (#228) Little Lake	Lake above Gilmer Bay
211	Wandei.éink'	*	Trollers' anchorage in Gilmer Bay
212	Agoon Áak'u	Portage to a Little Lake	Head of Gilmer Bay
213	G̲álwáat* (G̲alyáak*)	*	Gilmer Bay area
214	Shalax̲'éishx'w	Steller's Jay Crest	Point Amelia
215	L'éiwx̲ Nasdaa	Flowing against the Sand	Creek at Cuvacan Cove or Port Mary*
216	Kéidladi Eejí	Seagull Reef	Reef, outer Kruzof Island
217	Kéidladi Héeni	Seagull Creek	River, outer Kruzof Island
218	L'éiwx̲ Nasdaa Héen (G̲eey L'óot' G̲eeyák'w)	River That Flows against the Sand Creek (Bay's Tongue Cove)	Port Mary watershed
219	Goon Yádi	Little Spring Water	Goleta Cove
220	Goon Tlein	Big Spring Water	Port Mary spring
221	X̲'aan Goojí	Fire Hill	Little mountain near Port Krestof
222	L'éiw Tlein	Big Sand Beach	Beach in lower Shelikof Bay
223	Kalgáxwk'u Aaní	Floating Pumice Village	Shelikof Bay area
224	Géxkw Yaká (Géxkw Deiyí)	In Front of Pumice on It (Pumice Road)	Beaver Point shoreline
225	Géxgu Aan X'aa	Pumice Village Point	Beaver Point
226	Géxgu Aan	Pumice Village	Village at cove by Beaver Point
227	L'úx Yátx'i	Children of L'úx (#228)	Crater Ridge (Camel's Back Mountain)
228	L'úx	Blinking (lit., "Opening of the Eyes")	Mount Edgecumbe (volcano)
229	Neixinté Yat'ak̲.aan	Village beside Blue-Green Claystone Cliff	Settlement, outer Kruzof Island
230	L'úx T'ika Héen*	Creek outside L'úx (#228)	Neva Bay, Kruzof Island
231	Neixinté X̲'áak	Between Blue-Green Claystone	Engano Point
232	Shaak̲ X'aa T'áak	Behind Shaak̲ X'aa (#237)	Peak back of Aleutkina Bay
233	Kaa X̲'oosk'i X̲'aa	[Shaped like a] Person's Foot Up (resting) Point	Cape Edgecumbe, Trubitsin Point area

Map #	*Name*	*Translation*	*Location*
234	Yakwkalaseig<u>á</u>kw	Canoe Rest Cove	Cape Edgecumbe, <u>K</u>aa<u>x</u>'achgóok rest stop
235	Yakwkalaseig<u>á</u>kw Seiyí*	In the Shelter of Canoe Rest Cove	Cape Edgecumbe, <u>K</u>aa<u>x</u>'achgóok rest stop area
236	Yakwkalaseig<u>á</u>kw X'aa	Canoe Rest Cove Point	Point on left side of navigation marker, approaching Cape Edgecumbe
237	Shaa<u>k</u> X'aa	Driftwood Point	Sitka Point
238	Kanas<u>x</u>'éey	Island of Stunted Spruce	Saint Lazaria Island
239	K'asgax Ka<u>x</u>'wáal'	——* Bird Down	Saint Lazaria Island lake*
240	Kanasx'éey Noowú	Kanasx'éey (#238) Fort	Fort on Saint Lazaria Island
241	Kanas<u>x</u>'éey Séet	Kanas<u>x</u>'éey (#238) Strait	Pass between Saint Lazaria and Kruzof islands
242	L'úx Yadaa	Around the Face of L'úx (#228)	Area around Mount Edgecumbe (Beaver Point to Saint Lazaria Island)
243	Kanas<u>x</u>'éey Séet T'aak Héen*	Creek inside Kanas<u>x</u>'éey (#238)*	Creek below Shoals Point, Kruzof Island
244	Shandák'w (Tsandák'u) T'aak Héen	Creek inside Shandák'w (#248)	Inside Low Island (or in No Thorofare / Camp Coogan bays)*
245	Linnoowú	Tide Flat Fort	Tide flat on Kruzof Island
246	Shandák'w T'áak Aan	Village inside Shandák'w (#248)	Campsite, Shoals Point, Kruzof Island
247	Shandák'w X'aayí	Shandák'w (#248) Point	Point at Low Island
248	Shandák'w	Seal Clubbing Area	Low Island
249	Watkasaté	Stream with Rock at the Mouth	Freds Creek reef
250	Laa<u>x</u>di X'aa Áak'u	——* Point Lagoon	Cove at Inner Point
251	Laa<u>x</u>di X'aa	——* Point	Inner Point
252	Wátná<u>x</u> Tanaashuwu Héen	River with Rocks Standing along the Mouth	River, Kruzof Island
253	Ya<u>x</u>latit Noow	Drifting Ashore Fort	Kamenoi Point, Kruzof Island
254	<u>X</u>'anas Xágu	Lava Rocks	Kruzof Island*
255	<u>X</u>'ussa.aan*	Foot Path Village*	Point Brown
256	L'úx <u>X</u>'ashagik.aan	*	Village, Kruzof Island*
257	Shaak'w Seiyí	In the Shelter of Little Mountain	Shoreline of Port Krestof*
258	Kalgáxwk'u <u>G</u>eeyí	Floating Pumice Bay	Shelikof Bay
259	Nánde Sawátk'	[Flow] with a Small Mouth Facing North*	East Channel
260	Kalts'éi<u>x</u>	*	Port Krestof
261	Deishú Aan	End of the Trail Village	Mud Bay
262	Teey X'áat'xi	Yellow Cedar Bark Little Islands	Islands, Krestof Sound
263	Teey X'áat'i	Yellow Cedar Bark Island	Brady Island
264	L'úx Áa	L'úx (#228) Lake	DeGroff Bay (or lake on Saint Lazaria Island)*
265	Aan Niyaadé Aa Séet	Strait above the Village	Olga Strait

Map #	*Name*	*Translation*	*Location*
266	Yaadé Naadaayi Héen	River Flowing against the [Incoming] Tide	River on Halleck Island, Creek Point
267	L'úx Ka X'aa*	Point beyond L'úx (#228)	Olga Point
268	L'úx Ka Áa	Lagoon beyond L'úx (#228)	Krestof Sound
269	L'úx Yalatín X'aa	L'úx Yalatín (#270) Point	Neva Point
270	L'úx Yalatín	Looking toward L'úx (#228)	Old Girl Scout camp, Neva Strait
271	L'úx Áa Shayík.aan	Village inside L'úx Áa (#264)	Village at Neva Point
272	Xuts.héenak'u	Brown Bear Little Creek	Halleck Island creek
273	Kasdaxéix (Gasdaxéix)	Walking to Where You Rest*	Halleck Island
274	Jilkóok' T'aak Héen	Creek at Back inside Jilkóok' (#174)	Creek, Saint Johns Baptist Bay
275	S'awgeeyí T'aak Héeni	Creek Inland of Dungeness Crab Bay	Lake above Gilmer Bay
276	Íxde Aa S'aaw Héeni	Further down Creek from Dungeness Crab Bay	Creek in Nakwasina Passage near Neva Point
277	S'awgeeyí	Dungeness Crab Bay	Bay in Nakwasina Passage
278	Ch'áak' Saxa Héen	Eagle Eating River	Creek, Nakwasina Passage
279	Ch'áak' Saxa Séet	Eagle Eating Strait	Nakwasina Passage
280	Watta.aan (Daxéit T'eik Aan)	Town Back of the River Mouth (Town behind Daxéit [#295])	Allan Point
281	Yayuwaa Héen	Creek between Shorelines	River, Nakwasina Sound
282	Xíxch'i X'aayí	Frog Point	Point, Nakwasina Sound
283	X'as'tuhéen	Creek inside the Jaw (saliva)	Mouth of Nakwasina River
284	Taan Eejí T'áak	Back of Sea Lion Reef	Fish camp, Nakwasina Sound
285	Goonk'	Little Spring	Spring by Nakwasina River*
286	Daxéit Héeni (Kei.is.axji Héen)	Daxéit (#295) River (Noisy River)	Nakwasina River
287	Kei.is.axji Héen	Noisy Waterfall	Nakwasina River
288	Kaa Toowú Sigóowu Héen (Kaa Tú Kaxsake Héen)	Amusement Creek (——* Creek)	Creek, Nakwasina Sound
289	Xoodeexk'	*	Stream in Nakwasina Sound
290	Xijaa.éix'i	Beating Time for Shaman Lagoon	Nakwasina Sound
291	Íxde S'aa	Further Down Smokehouses*	Camp, Nakwasina Sound
292	Taan Xaanás' Eejí	Sea Lion Raft Reef	Reef in Nakwasina Sound
293	Kéidladi Eejí	Seagull Reef	Reef in Nakwasina Sound
294	Yoo Luklihashgi X'aa	Floating Point	Point, Nakwasina Sound
295	Daxéit	Fallen Stunned (winded)	Nakwasina Sound
296	Gat Yéekk'* (Galyáak* Héeni)	——* (——* Creek)	Lisa Creek
297	Haandé Aa Séet	Nearer Strait	Olga Strait (lower portion?)
298	Teey Héeni	Yellow Cedar Bark Creek	River, Halleck Island
299	Wóoshx Kadutit Geesh	Bull Kelp Pushed Together by Waves	Kelp bed, entrance to Nakwasina Sound
300	Kasdaxéix Aan	Kasdaxéix (#273) Village	Beehive village, Halleck Island
301	Yéilch Wóoshdáx Wulixidi Yé	Pass Where Raven Broke Through	Beehive Island

Map #	*Name*	*Translation*	*Location*
302	Yux Aa Kaanáx̱ At Yadugook̲	The Point It [the Spear] Was Thrown Across	Halleck Island
303	Kasdax̱éix̱ Aan X'aayí	Kasdax̱éix̱ (#273) Village Point	Halleck Island, Krugloi Point
304	Shaak'w Seiyí Ká	Shelter of the Little Mountain	Krestof Island
305	Shaak'w Seiyí G̲eeyák'w	Little Bay in the Shelter of Little Mountain	Krestof Island little bay
306	Shaak'w Seiyí G̲eey	Bay in the Shelter of Little Mountain	Krestof Island bay
307	Woosáani X̱oo	Among the Harpoons	Siginaka Islands
308	Shaak'w Seiyí G̲eeyák'u	Bay in the Shelter of Little Mountain	Promisula Bay
309	Anax̱ Yaalit X'aa*	——* Point	Kresta Point
310	Goon Tá	Portage	Creek Between Cedar Cove and Nakwasina Sound
311	Tl'ayaak̲' Sáank'i	At the Base of Tl'ayaak̲' (#314)	Cedar Cove
312	Tl'ayaak̲'a T'aak Héeni	River Back of Tl'ayaak̲' (#314)	Katlian River
313	Suk̲kahéen	Creek on the Grass	River, Katlian Bay
314	Tl'ayaak̲'	*	Katlian Bay
315	Tl'ayaak̲' Shaa*	Tl'ayaak̲' (#314) Mountain	Katlian Bay
316	Daxéit Ká	On Daxéit (#295)	Lisianski Peninsula
317	S'a.aan* Noow	——* Fort	Village/fort at entrance to Nakwasina Passage
318	Wat.la.aan Héenák'w	Village at the Mouth* Little Creek	River, Lisianski Peninsula
319	Kals'éix̱ T'ika Noow	Fort outside of ——*	Dog Point fish camp
320	Wáashdánk'	Little *Washington* (trading vessel)	Dog Point cove
321	Kaanax̱té	Between the Rocks*	Campsite, Lisianski Peninsula
322	Tl'ayaak̲' Yayuwaa	Tl'ayaak̲' (#314) Shoreline	Katlian Bay shoreline
323	Gidák̲w G̲íl'k'i	Gidák̲w's (Aleut sharpshooter's) Little Cliff	Cliff on southwestern Lisianski Peninsula
324	Nex̱'x'aak'ú	Little Granite Point	Blinker Point, Lisianski Peninsula
325	K̲ulashat X'aa	Point That Grabs People	Lisianski Point (or Gavanski Island point)*
326	Taaka* Héen	——* Creek	Big flats, Katlian Bay
327	Táax'aa G̲eeyí	Mosquito Bay	Mosquito Cove
328	Éil Daakahíx'i	Salt Storage Houses	Big/Little Gavanski islands
329	G̲ájaa Héen Wat	Mouth of G̲ájaa Stream (#332)	Mouth of Starrigavan Creek
330	G̲ájaa Héen Sháak	Head of G̲ájaa Stream (#332)	Valley behind Starrigavan Bay
331	Wat.lach'éix̱'k'i (Wat.lach'éix̱'i)	River with a Little Middle Finger at the Mouth (The Sun Never Shines in It)	Harbor Point area
332	G̲ájaa Héen	——* Stream	Starrigavan Creek
333	Éil Daakahíx'i Yádi*	Salt Storage Houses Child*	Little Gavanski Island
334	S'oow Tu.aan	——* Village	Cove, below Harbor Point
335	Chíx̱'i Héen	Always in the Shade Creek	Stream near Starrigavan Creek

Map #	*Name*	*Translation*	*Location*
336	Xóots Té	Brown Bear Rock	South of Little Gavanski Island
337	Kanat'á Xoo	Among the Blueberries	Old Sitka Rocks
338	Shaan Ooxk'ú	Little Old Person's Tooth	Island off Harbor Point*
339	Táan Daa (Táan)	Around Táan (Jumping Fish)	Middle Island
340	Ts'axweil X'áat'ak'u	Little Crow Island	Crow Island
341	Galxákwdi X'aayí	Galxákwdi (#343) Point	Gagarin Island point
342	Yakáa Ta.aan	Village Back of ——*	Village, Gargarin Island
343	Galxákwdi	*	Gagarin Island
344	Yakáa Tanoow	——* Head of Fort	Bieli Rocks
345	Galxákwdi Al'óon Aaní	Galxákwdi (#343) [Fur Seal] Hunting Grounds	Gagarin Island area
346	Cháatl Éedi	Halibut Hole	Bieli Rocks / Kasiana Islands area*
347	Táan Daa Tukyee Geeyák'u	Little Bay at the Outlet of Táan Daa (#339)	South end of Middle Island
348	Táan Yadaa	Around the Side of Táan (#339)	Shoreline around Middle Island
349	Néesh Sheeyí X'áat'	——* Branch Island	Chaichei Island
350	Wootsaagáa X'áat'i T'áak (Cháatl Xáayí)	Behind Cane Island (Halibut's Point)	Halibut Point
351	Wootsaagáa X'áat'i	Cane Island	Island, off Halibut Point
352	X'eis'awaa Héeni	Ptarmigan* Creek	Granite Creek
353	X'eis'awaa Héen Wat	Ptarmigan* Creek Mouth	Creek flowing from The Sisters mountains
354	Kall'óox' Yaté Daa (Kaltsalná Daa)	Surrounding the [Balancing] Rock on the Side of Kall'óox' (an island) ([Name of a balancing rock]* Around)	Area around Kasiana Islands
355	Kall'óox' Yaté (Kaltsalná)	[Balancing] Rock on the Side of Kall'óox' (an island) ([Name of a balancing rock]*)	Kasiana Islands
356	Lul.aaní	Fireweed Country	Sitka waterfront area (or Port Mary)*
357	Chil Xágu	Gravel Sandbar	Harbor Mountain valley creek bed*
358	Taxgu	*	Harbor Mountain
359	Sheet'ká X'áat'i	Area on Ocean Side of Shee (#424)	Sitka Sound area
360	K'isáani Yawdihayi Yé	Place of —— ——*	Between The Sisters mountains
361	Lx'áadushteen (X'áat'wusteen)	[Fish] Can't See between Them (Saw It Was an Island)	Apple Islands (or Crow Island / Middle Island pass)
362	Kadaleich Xágu	——* Sandbar	Sandy Beach
363	S'us' Héeni Sháak	Head of Harlequin Duck Creek	Section of Cascade Creek
364	S'us' Héeni	Harlequin Duck Creek	Cascade Creek
365	Tsísk'u Goojí	Owl Hill	Gavan Hill
366	Tsísk'u Goojí Aaní	Owl Hill Land	Area around Gavan Hill
367	Kanéisdi Shaa	Cross Mountain	Arrowhead (Mount Verstovia)

Map #	Name	Translation	Location
368	Tsísk'u Ḵaadí	Owl Slide	Gavan Hill slide
369	Taxgu Neech	Taxgu (#358) Beach	Beach below Harbor Mountain
370	Xágu Neech	Sandbar Beach	Near Watsons Point
371	Shitx'aa Lutú	Inside the Point (nose) of Shee (#424)	Watsons Point
372	Sheet'ká	Ocean Side of Shee (#424)	City of Sitka
373	Tatóok X'áat'ak'u (Kát Gaawtán)	Cave Islet (Drum Lying on It)	Battery Island
374	Ḵéet Gooshi Héen	Killer Whale Dorsal Fin Creek	River at Thomson Harbor
375	X'wáat' Héen Áak'u	Trout Water Little Lake	Swan Lake
376	Ḵéet Gooshi Geey	Killer Whale Dorsal Fin Bay	Thomson Harbor
377	X'aagú	Base of the Point	Point at Thomson Harbor
378	X'aagú Yadaa	Face of the Base of the Point	Governor Brady's house site area
379	Ḵulagaaw Xágu (Ḵulagaaw Xágu Yádi)	War Sandbar (Little War/Trouble Sandbar)	Sandbar on Japonski Island
380	Ḵulagaaw Xágu Tlein	Big War/Trouble Sandbar	Sandbar on Japonski Island
381	K'aan Héeni	Dolphin Creek	South side of Jamestown Bay, Thimbleberry Lake
382	S'aach Aaní	Fern Country	Sitka Indian village
383	Gáat Héeni (X'wáat' Héenak'u)	Sockeye Stream (Dolly Varden Little Creek)	Swan Lake Stream (and tributary*)
384	Yak'wkashaneixí	Boat Harbor*	Japonski Island
385	Keitlyátx'i Héeni	Puppies Creek	Stream in downtown Sitka
386	Anax Chookan Nalishoowu Yé	Area Where the Grass Grows Tall	Cliff near Sitka
387	Aya.áak'w	Little Lake in Front	Sealing Cove
388	X'us' Noowú	Crabapple Fort	Charcoal/Alice islands
389	Ḵaasdahéen Yadaa	Around the Face of Ḵaasdahéen (#400)	Indian River Peninsula ("Lover's Lane")
390	Aan X'áak Héeni	Spring between the Town	Spring near downtown Sitka
391	Ḵaa Tl'óogu Héen	Liver Creek	Creek in downtown Sitka
392	Yaaw Teiyí	Herring Rock	Herring spawning rock by Sitka
393	Kunageiyák'w Tá	Back of Little Cove	Cove in front of town
394	Noow Tlein	Big Fort	Castle Hill
395	Aanshukká Goon Héeni	Spring-at-the-Front-of-Town River	Spring by ANB Hall
396	Noow Sateiyi Yík	Fort ——* Inside	Shoreline of Castle Hill
397	Xaas X'áat'i	Buffalo Island	Aleutki Island
398	Sanóon X'aak'ú	Salted Fish Point	Point at Thomson Harbor (Russian saltery)
399	Íxt'i X'aayí	Shaman's Point	Point by Sitka National Historical Park
400	Ḵaasdahéen	Man's* Stream	Indian River
401	Shis'g'i Noow Ta.eetí	Green Tree Fort Clearing	Clearing, Sitka National Historical Park
402	Shis'g'i Noow	Green Tree Fort	Fort at Sitka National Historical Park

Map #	Name	Translation	Location
403	Shaa Seiyi Aan	Land beneath the Mountain	Jamestown Bay village
404	Ḵaasdahéen Sháak	Head of Ḵaasdahéen (#400)	Mouth of Indian River
405	K'aan Áak'u	Dolphin Lagoon	Jamestown Bay
406	Ts'axweil X'áat'i	Crow Island	Cannon Island
407	Kax' Atgagáan Yádi*	Child of Kax' Atgagáan (#408)	Galankin Islands (smaller one)
408	Kax' Atgagáan	*	Galankin Islands (largest)
409	K'aan Áak'u	Dolphin Cove	Cedar Cove (or Jamestown Bay)*
410	Xíxch'i Ḡeeyí	Frog Bay	Silver Bay (early name)
411	Dagák' Aax Aawateeni Héen	Little Sockeye Going Away [Insulted] Creek	Green Lake creek
412	Gijuk Héen	Golden Eagle Creek	Sawmill Creek
413	Gijuk Héen Yik.áayi (Gijuk Héen Shaak Áayi)	Lake inside Gijuk Héen (#412) (Lake at the Head of Gijuk Héen)	Blue Lake
414	Shee T'éik T'aay X'é	Below Shee (#424) Hot Springs	Warm Springs Bay
415	Kageet X'aká Yayuwaa	Shoreline at Mouth of Kageet (#426)	Mouth of Silver Bay, above Herring Cove
416	Ḵóokk'u X'aa	Little Box Point	Herring Cove point
417	Ḵóokk' Ta Héen	Creek at the Bottom of Little Box	Blue Lake
418	Yaaw Kookk'	Little Herring Fish Hole	Herring Cove
419	Ḵaa Káa Daak Uwadayi Yé	Place Where [the Land] Slid Down over the People	Slide in Silver Bay*
420	Yáayyák'w	Little Whale (name of Tsimshian warrior, slain)	Whale Island, Middle Channel
421	Shaanáx Héeni	Valley River (flows underground)	Green Lake river
422	Gathéeni	Sockeye Stream	Silver Bay, Green Lake creek
423	Kageet Tá	Back of Kageet (#426)	Green Lake
424	Shee	[Volcano Woman's name]	Baranof Island
425	Ḵóokk'	Little Box	Head of Silver Bay
426	Kageet (Ḡageit')	Loon (*)	Silver Bay
427	Xaachgú	*	No Thorofare / Camp Coogan bays
428	Ch'áak' Xágu (Ch'ak Lixákk'u)	Eagle Sandbar	Shoreline below Sugarloaf Mountain
429	Kuts'een Gíl'i	Rat Cliff	Silver Bay cliff
430	Kuts'een Katóogu	Rat Cave	Silver Bay cave
431	Kageet X'aká	Mouth of Kageet (#426)	Mouth of Silver Bay
432	Tuwool	Hole Inside	Silver Bay cave* (possibly same as #430)
433	Tawool Sháa	Hole inside Mountain	Sugarloaf Mountain
434	Kageet X'ananook	Loon Sits	Silver Bay
435	Kageet X'aa	Kageet (#426) Point	Silver Point
436	Sxinoowú Séet	——* Strait	Aleutkina / Leesoffskaia bays
437	Yaaw X'áat'i	Herring Island	Long Island

Map #	Name	Translation	Location
438	T'ooch' Aaní	Charcoal Country	Aleutkina / Leesoffskaia bays
439	Ḡatlgeeyí (Ḡatlgeeyák'w)	Bracket Fungus Bay (Little Bracket Fungus Bay)	Small bay below Aleutkina Bay
440	Aawateeni X'aa	Storming Off [Angry] Point	Cape Burunof point
441	Aawateeni Shaa (Aawateeniḵáa)	Storming Off [Angry] Mountain (Man Storming Off [Angry])	Mount Kinkaid
442	Cháash T'ák'w* Yá Ḡeey	——* Bay	Deep Inlet
442.1	Ts'axweil Héeni	Crow Creek	Creek at the head of Deep Inlet
443	Ts'axwel Héenak'u	Crow's Little Creek	Sandy Cove
444	Téel' Héenak'u Ḡeey (Ax Gadus.éeẕk')	Dog Salmon Little Creek Bay (——*)	Samsing Cove
445	Gall'óoẕu Séet	Looking Milky Strait	Cape Burunof, entrance to Redoubt Bay, pass behind island* (alternative to #460?)
446	Kool Daa X'áat'i	Around the Navel Island	Vitskari Island
446.1	Eey X'e.aa Kool (Kool Daa Eejí)	Tideflows Navel Mouth (Around the Navel Reef)	Vitskari Rocks area
447	Kawjixidi X'aa	Point with Petroglyphs on It	Cape Burunof
448	Kawjixidi X'aa Ḡeeyák'w	Little Bay of Painted Point	Three Entrance Bay
449	Kadaláax	Moldy*	Island, entrance to Redoubt Bay
450	T'aawáḵ Nax̱yík	Canada Goose High Tide Passage	Cape Burunof marshes/cove
451	Ts'een Waaḵḵ'í	*	Povorotni Point
452	Ḵaatl'éx (Ḵaatl'éx Goon)	——* (——* Spring)	Kita Island
452.1	K'wát' X'áat'ax'u Sáani	Little Islands with Bird Eggs	Two islands at the mouth of Necker Bay
453	Shaan Oox̱k'ú	Old Person's Tooth	Small island in front of Sitka
454	Leix̱ Héen	——* Creek	Kizuchia Creek
455	Shee At'iká	In the Shelter of Sheet'ká (#372)	Islands outside of Baranof Island
456	Ḵ'atx̱aan Áak'u (X̱ákw Ḡeeyák'u)	Little Cove (Pebble Beach Cove)	Redoubt Bay
457	Ḵunaa	Sending [into a Cave]	Redoubt Bay
458	Chijóok'	*	Cove, Redoubt Bay
459	Kangeeyí	Porpoise Bay	Kidney Cove
460	Gall'óoẕu Séet	Looking Milky Strait	Islet Passage, Redoubt Bay* (alternative to #445?)
461	Ḵunaa Sáank'i	At the Bottom of Ḵunaa (#457)	Cove, Redoubt Bay
462	Ḵunaa Shak.áayi	Lake at the Head of Ḵunaa (#457)	Redoubt Lake
463	Nalgáx̱ni	*	Kanga Bay
464	X'át'gu Noow	Dogfish Fort	Island outside Kanga Bay
465	Ḵunaa X'aká	Mouth of Ḵunaa (#457)	Mouth of Redoubt Bay
466	X'át'gu Noow Séet	Dogfish Fort Pass	Pass by Kanga Bay
467	Wasís Yádi	Wasís (#468) Child	Little Biorka Island

Map #	*Name*	*Translation*	*Location*
468	Wasís	*	Biorka Island
469	Wasís Geeyí	Wasís (#468) Bay	Symonds Bay
470	Jaanák	*	Wrangell Island
471	Shaak Geeyí	Driftwood Bay	Bay on southern Biorka Island
472	Xóots Ooxk'ú	Brown Bear Teeth*	Reef near Biorka Island
473	Kanakwás X'áak	Between Kanakwás (see #480)	Biorka Channel
474	Tatóok	Cave	Maid Island
475	Kadataan	Sea Lion Haulout	Kaiuchali Island
476	Yook Woolí	Cormorant Hole	Terbilon Island
477	Gooch Gúgu	Wolf Ear	Reef near Biorka Island
478	Kanakwás Noow Yax'áak	Channel between Kanakwás (see #480) Fort	Biorka Channel*
479	Kanakwás Taan Eejí	Kanakwás (see #480) Sea Lion Reef	Jacob Rock
480	Kanakwás Daa	Around the Chamber Pot (a concave rock)	Sea lion rock below Wrangell Island
481	Kanakwás X'áak Aan	Village at Kanakwás X'áak (#473)	Village site on Tava Island
482	Kutlayáat'	One Side Straight	Legma Island
483	K'ákw	Fish Hawk*	Golovni Island
484	Tsaa Keigú	Seal Lung	Jacob Rock area*
485	Gasyáagi	*	Rogers Island
486	Gasyáagi Yádi	Gasyáagi's (#485) Child	Nameless Island
487	Shee At'iká T'aay X'é	Shee At'iká (#455) Hot Springs Mouth	Goddard Hot Springs
488	Tl'axwan Áak'u	——* Little Lake	Hot Springs Bay
489	T'aay X'é Séedák'u	Little Hot Springs Narrows	Dorothy Narrows, entrance to West Crawfish Inlet
490	Takuwóox'	*	Big Bay
491	Takuwóox' X'aka.aan	Village at the mouth of Takuwóox' (#490)	South entrance of Big Bay
492	L'éex'i	Breakage	Golf Island
493	Naakw Séedi	Devilfish Pass	Walker Channel
494	Kataw.áak'u	——* Little Lagoon	Rakof Islands in front of West Crawfish Inlet
495	Kadak'w.aan	——* Village	Village in West Crawfish Inlet
496	Kóox Dakdatís X'aa	Kóox Dakdatís (see #497) Point	President Bay point
497	Kóox Dakdatís Geeyák'w	Wild Rice Back Up Inside* Little Bay	President Bay
498	Ch'a.aan	Just a Village	Arm of West Crawfish Inlet
499	S'awgeeyí	Dungeness Crab Bay	Crab Bay
500	Chíl Wan Héen	River by the Side of a Cache	Shamrock Bay
501	Kanat'ákw Yík	Inside ——*	Head of Crawfish Inlet
502	Lax'áas	Waterfall	West Crawfish Inlet

Map #	*Name*	*Translation*	*Location*
503	Kashdax'aldi Séet	——* Pass	Cedar Pass
504	Kanat'ákw T'áak (Kak'asdi Dzoow*)	Back of ——* (——*)	Crawfish Inlet
505	Wat.la.aan (Wat.aan)	Village at the Mouth*	Cove, West Crawfish Inlet
506	Kuyékk'	*	Cove, Lodge Island
507	Kataw Áa	——* Lake (saltwater)	Rakof Islands harbor
508	Kag̲anú* Yádi	——* Child	Reef by Biali Rock
509	Kag̲anú*	*	Biali Rock
510	Gwal X'áat'i	——* Island	Beauchamp Island
511	Kil'gax̲* X'aa G̲eeyák'w	Kil'gax̲* X'aa (#512) Little Bay	Cove, Beauchamp Island
512	Kil'gax̲* X'aa	——* Point	Beauchamp Island point
513	Yakwkashaanáx̲ G̲eeyí	Valley on the Canoe Bay	Jamboree Bay
514	Yakwkashaanáx̲	Valley on the Canoe	Slide in Jamboree Bay
515	Yeil Néig̲ani	Raven's Fish Trap	Slate Islets
516	Yeil Néig̲ani Séet	Yeil Néig̲ani (#515) Pass	Pass between Slate Islets and Yamani Island
517	Kalas'aach Séet	Kalas'aach (#518) Strait	Yamani Cove
518	Kalas'aach	Island with Bracket Fern	Yamani Island
518.1	Kalas'aach Aaní	Kalas'aach (#518) Village	Yamani Island village
519	Yeilk̲óogu	Raven's Box Cave	Necker Bay cliff formation
520	Naak̲w G̲íl'i	Devilfish Cliff	Cliff, Necker Bay
521	Wat.lateetk'	Sandbar at the Mouth of Stream	Cove, Necker Bay
522	Dagák' Áayi (Dagák' Héeni Sháak)	Little Sockeye Lake (Head of the Little Sockeye River)	Benzeman Lake and falls
523	Nánde Aa Dagák' Séedi	Further up Dagák' Séedi (#528)	Northern Secluded Bay passage
524	Dagák' Héeni	Little Sockeye Creek	River to Benzeman Lake
525	Ch'a Luká	*	Campsite, Necker Bay
526	Dagák' Áak'u	Little Sockeye Lagoon	Secluded Bay
527	T'adishaayi X'áat'i	——* Head Island	Island, Necker Bay
528	Dagák' Séedi	Little Sockeye Pass	Secluded Bay passage
529	Dagák' G̲eeyí	Little Sockeye Bay	Necker Bay
530	Nánde X̲'atán Áa	Northern ——* Harbor	Toy Harbor
531	Té Luká	Tip of the Rock	Necker Bay, cliffs
532	K'wát' X'áat'x'i	Egg Islands	Guibert Islets
533	Léigu X'aa	——* Point	Point, Necker Bay
534	K'wát' X'áat'x'i T'aak Héen	River inside K'wát' X'áat'x'i (#532)	River in cove inside Guibert Islets
535	K'wát' X'áat'x'i T'aak Áak'w	Little Lake inside K'wát' X'áat'x'i (#532)	Cove inside Guibert Islets
536	Naltóosh	*	Island at North Cape
537	Naltóosh Séet	Naltóosh (#536) [Island] Pass	Pass at North Cape
538	Chas' Héenak'u	Humpback Salmon Little Creek	River/campsite, Whale Bay

Map #	Name	Translation	Location
539	Tsaa X'aak'ú	Seal Little Point	Point, Whale Bay
540	Tl'aak'wách' Héeni	——* Creek	River, Whale Bay
541	Deigaashoowu Héen	Creek with Trail Running Down*	River, Whale Bay
542	Wanas'áx'	*	Small Arm passage
543	Geey Tlein	Big Bay	Great Arm
544	X'eikwás'	Chamber Pot* Mouth	River, Whale Bay
545	Geey Tlein X'akax'aa	Point in Front of the Big Bay	Kakovo Island/Point, Whale Bay
546	Íxt'	Shaman	Krishka Island
547	Íxt' Yat'ak Aan	Village beside the Shaman	Village in Kritoi Basin
548	L'ook Kágu (Kuchgé*)	Coho Basket (Carved Pool*)	Port Banks
549	Kél't' X'ayakóok	Looks like a Box*	Rakovoi Bay or Kritoi Basin*
550	Kuchgé* X'áas	Waterfall of Kuchgé (#548)	Campsite, Port Banks
551	Shee Yat'ák Geey	Bay on Inside of Shee (#424)	Patterson Bay, east Baranof Island
552	Shee Yat'ák Geey X'aayí	Shee Yat'ák Geey (#551) Point	Patterson Point, east Baranof Island
553	Shee T'éik	Inland Side of Shee (#424)	Warm Springs Bay area (northeast Chichagof Island)
554	Nal'áy*	*	Lower Baranof Island, Cape Ommaney to Whale Bay
555	K'éetx	*	Island, Still Harbor
556	K'éetx X'aak'ú Áak'w	K'éetx (#555) Little Point's Little Lake	Lake/lagoon, Still Harbor
557	Káa Xeil Kanasgoo	Foam Washes Over	Point Lauder*
558	Kasxáay*	*	Campsite/cove, Close Bay
559	Teet Lasaa Áak'w	Waves Little Lake	Sandy Bay*
560	Sakanak*	*	Snipe Bay area
561	Kagakú*	*	Snipe Bay
562	Yéil X'éeni	Raven's Screen (or mural)	Cliff formation, Snipe Bay
563	Shee Lunáak Gathéeni	Over the Nose (point) of Shee (#424) Sockeye Creek	Redfish Bay
564	Kagakú* (tlein)	——* (big)	Big Branch Bay
565	Kat'ulnax Sak'eik'*	*	Little Branch Bay
566	Kadaséix Geeyí	Breathing Bay	Puffin Bay
567	Shee Yat'ak.aan	Village beside Shee (#424)	Port Alexander
568	Yan Yoo Jikakgi Geeyí	Floating Up and Down* Bay	Larch Bay
569	Shee Lunáak	Over the Nose (point) of Shee (#424)	Cape Ommaney area
570	Shee Lutú	Nose (point) of Shee (#424)	Cape Ommaney
571	Shee Sáank'	Little [Island] at the End of Shee (#424)	Wooden Island
NM	Katsaa Geeyí	——* Bay	Jamboree Bay area
NM	Kunaa Shaa	Kunaa (#457) Mountain	Mountain behind Redoubt Lake*
NM	Naax Séedi	——* Strait	*

Map #	*Name*	*Translation*	*Location*
NM	Nánde X̲'atánk	North-Facing Entrance	Necker Bay
NM	Óos'ki Kwás'	*	*
NM	Sekanú	*	Hoonah Sound*
NM	Shaaw X'áat'i	Gumboot [Chiton] Island	Sitkoh Bay Islet
NM	Shaltláax̲	Rock with Lichen on Top	Small island near Biorka Island
NM	Sx̲inoowú Séet T'eik Aaní	Village behind Sx̲inoowú Strait (#436)	Aleutkina / Leesoffskaia bays
NM	Tlaganís Luká	Sapling Point	Below Nakwasina River
NM	Wat Aan Áayi	Lagoon at the Village Mouth	Salmon tribes' name for waters off Allan Point, Nakwasina Sound
NM	Yaakw Kalaseigákw (Aan Kalaseik*)	——* (Village ——*)	Cove, West Crawfish Inlet
NM	Yées' Eeyí	Large-Mussel Rapids	*

6. *Xutsnoowú K̲wáan*

The Xutsnoowú (Brown Bear Fort, #291) K̲wáan, now centered in Angoon (Aangóon, "Isthmus Town," #106) reportedly takes its name from the abundance of brown bear found on Admiralty Island. While the name Xutsnoowú has come to stand for all of Admiralty Island, it refers particularly to the western shore between Funter Bay and Point Gardner (Emmons n.d.) and may originally have been applied to the village at Chaik Bay. Aangóon territory also was known as Xoodzí (Charred Remains, #107) K̲wáan or Xudzídaa (Xoodzí Daa) (see Jacobs 2000). There was little contact with the k̲wáan during the early historic period, and throughout this century Angoon has been regarded as one of the more "traditional" Tlingit villages. The community has been the subject of an intensive archeological and ethnological study by Frederica de Laguna (1960) and others (see Moss 2004). Major clans on the Raven side include the Deisheetaan, K̲ak'weidí, Aanx̲'aakhittaan and L'eeneidí, and on the Eagle/Wolf side, the Teik̲weidí, Dak̲l'aweidí, and Wooshkeetaan. Xutsnoowú territory straddled Chatham Strait, stretching from below Hawk Inlet to Eliza Harbor on the east side of Admiralty Island and from Tenakee Inlet to Patterson Bay on the west side of Chatham Strait, including a portion of Peril Strait between Baranof and Chichagof islands.

We documented more than 285 place names in Aangóon territory, along with extensive information about their cultural associations. Garfield George served as the local research coordinator for the project. Matthew Kookesh of the Alaska Department of Fish and Game, Division of Subsistence, and Thomas Thornton carried out additional field research. Written source material on Native geographic names from Frederica de Laguna (1960), Brenda Campen (n.d.), George Emmons (n.d.), Viola Garfield (1945, 1947), Lydia George (n.d.), Constance Naish and Gillian Story (n.d.), and John Swanton (1908, 1909) provided a solid foundation on which to build. Jeff Leer of the Alaska Native Language Center and elder Lydia George provided linguistic advice, consultation and review. Martha Betts of Vanguard Research assembled the first draft maps, Matt Ganley executed the final GIS versions, and Thornton compiled the final database with assistance from Hans Chester and Jason Nelson. Finally, and most respectfully, we want to thank the elders who were interviewed for this project, including Lydia George, Matthew Fred Sr., George Jim, Billy John, Robert Duncan, Peter McCluskey, Peter Jack, and the many others who corroborated names, attended meetings, and contributed to the project in other important ways.

An excellent and elaborate concordance for named sites, archeology, and oral history was compiled by Frederica de Laguna in her monograph, *The Story of a Tlingit Community: A Problem in the Relationship between Archeological, Ethnological, and Historical Methods* (1960). Readers are directed to that publication for more detailed information on key cultural sites. Our project documented a significant number of additional names, especially in those areas not formally surveyed by Professor de Laguna.

Some Important Named Sites

Kootznoowoo Inlet (Eey Tlein, "Big Tidal Currents," #69). The protected waters of Kootznoowoo (from Xutsnoowú) Inlet provided shelter and abundant resources for Aangóon people. The inlet is separated from Chatham Strait by a long isthmus which opens to the northwest and penetrates deep into Admiralty Island, affording shelter and access to numerous productive salmon streams, shellfish beds, and terrestrial hunting and gathering areas in the interior of the island. Several villages were reported in the vicinity of Angoon, where the people stayed before moving to the modern settlement (e.g., Daax̲aatkanadaa, #73), along with numerous forts and campsites (de Laguna 1960; Moss and Erlandson 1992; Goldschmidt and Haas 1998). Aangóon was founded by the ancestors of the Deisheetaan (from Deishú-hít-taan, meaning "End of the Trail House

People"), who settled there after following a beaver to the isthmus. The clan's name is derived from the fact that they established a village at the end of the beaver's trail (de Laguna 1960, 131–33).

Hood Bay (Tsaagwáa, "Harbor-Seal Ice Flows," #163).* During the so-called "Little Ice Age," and perhaps before, icebergs from Glacier Bay and elsewhere choked northern Chatham Strait and would collect in Hood Bay, where harbor seals (*tsaa*) hauled out on them, thus inspiring the name. The name refers especially to the south arm of the bay. The Tsaagweidí, a branch of the Dakl'aweidí now located in Kake (Kéex'), took their name from this place, when they settled here after migrating from Stikine (Shtax'héen) River. The bay was the site of at least one famous village (Tanchwusxeek, "[Fish] Jumped and Kept Them Awake," #177), a fort (K'óox Noowú, "Marten Fort," #180), and several petroglyphs. Another landmark is Hood Bay Mountain (Tsaagwáa Shaanák'u, "Tsaagwáa's Old Woman," #158), at the top of which people are said to have taken refuge during the Flood. The rope that they used to anchor their raft can still been seen there, but "it is now so old that if touched it turns to ashes" (de Laguna 1960, 52).

Freshwater Bay / Pavlof Harbor (Asáank'i, #23). Pavlof Harbor, the site of a sockeye stream within Freshwater Bay, housed a winter village (Taakw.aaní, #19), reportedly established by the Wooshkeetaan after they separated from the Kaagwaantaan at Grouse Fort (Kax'noowú; see Xunaa Káawu #181) in Icy Strait. This branch of the Wooshkeetaan later became centered in Aangóon but continued to return to the area to fish and hunt at least until the end of the nineteenth century (Garfield 1947, 452; Emmons n.d.).

Chaik (Chayéek, #202) / Whitewater Bay (Naach'uhéen, #244). These bays were settled by the ancestors of the Aanx'aakhittaan and Deisheetaan, the Gaanax.ádi, who reportedly dwelled here before Aangóon was founded. The first permanent settlement was said to be inside Village Point, and it was here that the name Xutsnoowú may have first been applied. Another name, Yéil Gaawk'ú, (Raven's Little Drum, #189) was later associated with this site, or perhaps one farther inside the point below a fort called Jigayaa Noow (#186) on a rocky outcropping. The main village, Neltushkin (Naltóoshgán, #239), was abandoned when the group moved to Aangóon and then later reoccupied after a feud prompted the Aanx'aakhittaan to resettle there. Table Mountain (L'úx Yadaa, #250), just south of the bay, was identified as another Flood refuge site that was not to be "fooled around" with, as this would bring rain or fog (de Laguna 1960, 57, 131). As one elder told de Laguna:

Yéil Katóogu – Tinaa Gooní X'éen
"Raven's Cave – Copper Shield Spring Screen"

The wall crest or heraldic screen shown here, known as Yéil Katóogu – Tinaa Gooní X'éen, is both a Tlingit map of important Deisheetaan sites in Sitkoh Bay and a legal title to those sacred sites. It is also an important symbol of identity, like a family coat-of-arms or a national flag. Only Deishú Hít people use this crest. Yéil Katóogu, or "Raven's Cave" (#66), is located above Sitkoh Creek (Gathéeni, "Sockeye Stream," #72). Tinaa Gooní, or "Copper Shield Spring" (#75), lies near the old Tlingit village, which later became the site of the Chatham fish cannery. Deisheetaan elders know and cherish the history behind these places and Angoon residents continue to use the area for hunting, fishing, and gathering. At a 2011 memorial party in Angoon a new screen was brought out and dedicated, featuring these three sacred places in Deisheetaan clan history.

Deishú Hít leaders, regalia, and artifacts inside Deishú Hít, ca. 1965. From left to right: Jim Paul, Jimmy Johnson, and Robert Zuboff. Photo courtesy of Lydia George and Deishú Hít.

There was a Flood, when all the people had to go to the tops of the mountains. They built walls of rocks around the tops, like nests. Some people had dogs. The bears came up after them. Those that didn't have dogs to chase the bears were all killed, but those that had dogs were saved.

I have been on top of one of the mountains, above Chaik Bay. I saw the rope there at the top, all turned to ashes. (1960, 131)

Wilson Cove (Katákw, #254), an appendage of Whitewater Bay, was associated with a now extinct group called the Katákweidí, who took their name from the place.

Basket Bay (*Ḵák'w, "Little Basket,"* #42). A major sockeye system, this small bay was home to the Ḵak'weidí (Basket Bay People). The bay's name may refer to the basket-like grotto (Ḵak'w Áak'u, #39) along the salmon creek, where salmon would collect and were harvested, and where seals could be clubbed. The original village, situated at the mouth of the creek, was said to have been destroyed by a pet beaver who became angry at the village leader and turned the whole settlement upside down, singing as he worked (de Laguna 1960, 62, 137; Zuboff in Dauenhauer and Dauenhauer 1987, 63–71).

Sitkoh Bay (*Sit'ḵú, #100*). Another major sockeye system, this bay was home to perhaps the earliest settlement in Chatham Strait north of Peril Strait. The name is said to be derived from the fact that glacial icebergs from Icy and northern Chatham straits would collect there centuries ago (see Sitkoh Bay box). The strategic importance of this bay is evidenced not only by the abundance of productive resources to be found there but also by its optimal location at the intersection of Chatham and Peril straits. Thus we find fort sites at both entrance points (de Laguna 1960, 64–67), and trails leading over the mountains via Sitkoh Lake (Áa, #98) to northeast Peril Strait, where other villages, camps, and forts were found. Sitkoh Bay was an important site of the Gaanax.ádi clan before it was ceded to the Deisheetaan (de Laguna 1960, 64; Garfield 1947, 64, 67). Ancestors of the Teiḵweidí clan also resided in this area at one time, possibly at Point Craven or Todd (de Laguna 1960, 64, 67–68). Perhaps it was they who named the fort on Point Hayes, Xutsnoowú (Brown Bear Fort, #132), the same name that was applied to Admiralty Island. The area between Todd and Sitkoh Bay also provided temporary refuge for the Kiks.ádi upon their withdrawal from Sitka after battling the Russians there in 1804, and the fort site they built there has recently been identified and commemorated (Hope 2000). Sitkoh Bay remains an important sockeye salmon fishery for Angoon and Sitka residents (Thornton, Schroeder, and Bosworth 1990).

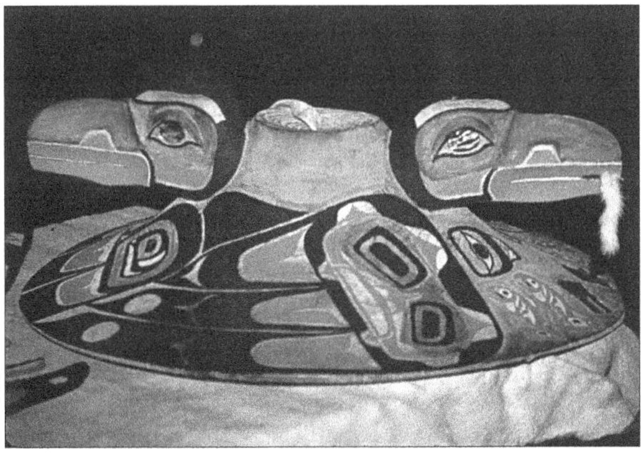

Yéil Katóogu S'áaxw (Raven Cave Hat) is another representation of Yéil Katóogu. The two ravens at the top of the hat frame the opening of the cave. The two salmon on the lower right side of the hat represent the sockeye salmon of Gathéeni (Sitkoh Creek), a precious source of food. Farther to the right are two inlaid copper shields, which symbolize Tinaa Gooní, a freshwater spring and setting for important events in Deisheetaan history. Photo by Scott Foster.

Yéil Katóogu X'óow (Raven Cave Blanket). This is yet another depiction of Raven's Cave, this time as a painting on a moose hide. Typically acquired from the Interior through trade, moose hides were highly valued. Deisheetaan elder and clan mother (*naa tláa*) Lydia George (right) explains the meaning of the designs. Like the wall crest and the hat, this blanket also features a representation of Tinaa Gooní. Photo by Scott Foster.

Hanus Bay (*G̲áchgu, #161*). It is not clear whether the Tlingit name for Hanus Bay refers to the whole bay and the former fishing camp at the outlet to Lake Eva, or just the latter. A settlement at Lake Eva, another sockeye system, has been excavated recently and yielded evidence of human occupation dating back well over five thousand years. In addition to fishing, archeological remains suggest that this site has been an important processing camp for berries (see Arndt, Sackett, and Ketz 1987). The camp was used until historic times by members of the Teik̲weidí clan, which had settlements on Dead Tree Island (G̲áchgu X̲'ayanéekw, #160) and at Todd (K̲aa Sháa Teiwahayi Yé, #150) on the opposite side of Peril Strait.

Kelp Bay (*Gishgeeyí, #221*). This large bay was the site of several substantial seasonal fishing and hunting camps at Portage Arm, Crow Island, and Pond Island. It was claimed by the Deisheetaan but was also used historically by other clans. This important subsistence area was used for salmon and halibut fishing; deer, bear, mountain goat, and seal hunting; and also for gathering shellfish, marine plants, octopus, berries, and yellow cedar bark. In 1946 (Goldschmidt and Haas 1998, 149), Deisheetaan elder Billy Jones spoke eloquently about his ties to this place and the deleterious effects of non-Native encroachments, especially white settlers and commercial fish traps.

> My family [Deisheetaan] claims Kelp Bay. It used to belong to my uncles. I had a home there until the whites tore it down, and I had two houses on Crow Island. I built them when I was a young man. My uncles before me had smokehouses which they also used for dwelling places. In my cabin, there were stove and furniture, and one year when I went down there, they told me that the place belonged to the United States government. They were white men who were in my cabin, and, being an Indian, I believed them and never went back. This was about the time the Killisnoo plant closed. This was an area that was open to all the members of the Deisheetaan clan. At the head of Middle Arm and South Arm of Kelp Bay there were streams which were very good for fish. We went up there and camped and smoked fish. Fish don't come up there any more like they used to. I think it is because the traps have been fishing that area out. It is still possible to see the places in that area where the Native people gathered the bark off the yellow cedar trees, which they used for shelter. At Kelp Bay, we get dog salmon, humpies [pink salmon], halibut, seal, blueberries, wild currants, mink, land otter, clams, horse clams, mussels, black and ribbon seaweed, and devilfish. In my youth, the Native people went from place to place to put up food that they got in each place, but in late years, we have been discouraged from doing that by the fact that the streams are fished out by the fish traps, and by the whites who have told us that we were not supposed to go to certain areas. In the old days, we went to Kelp Bay in March and would stay there all summer and smoke fish and gather food for winter use. About fall, we would come back to Angoon and harvest our potatoes. I still frequently go to Kelp Bay to get such foods as I can. The white houses are still there, but nobody lives in them anymore. Other people go to Kelp Bay to trap. Now we let any of the Angoon people go there. But the fish traps there keep it from being worthwhile to go there to dry fish.

Gut Bay (*Gatgeey #286*). This bay marks the southern extent of Aangóon territory, although areas farther south were apparently jointly held with K̲ée̲x̲' people. Gut Bay is noteworthy because of its association with Raven. At a place near the entrance, called Yéil G̲eiwú (Raven's Fishnet, #285), is an imprint of Raven's ancient fishing net, which can still be seen to this day in the rocky slope. Like many other outstanding sites in Xutsnoowú K̲wáan, this place is a productive sockeye fishery and is still used for subsistence fishing by people from Angoon and Kake.

Final Thoughts

The Xutsnoowú K̲wáan place names project reveals the wealth of profound cultural and historical ties that Tlingits have to this important central southeastern region. Place names figured importantly in the Aangóon tribe's push for a just land claims settlement, and they remain an important tool for understanding the natural and cultural history of the region. Today, Angoon and other area schools are using the results of the place names project to maintain individual and collective ties to the land through the multimedia *Angoon Cultural Atlas* (see Sitkoh Bay box), education, language and culture camps. In addition, the tribe works with the U.S. Forest Service, Admiralty Island National Monument, and other agencies to appropriately manage the local natural and cultural resources that are associated with these named sites. In traditional Tlingit resource management, this is not only a sovereignty objective, but a cultural imperative. As the late Mary Willis (see Thornton 2000b) put it, "If you don't know your history... and the places you belong to, it can come back to hurt you."

Sit'k̲ú / Sitkoh Bay

Sitkoh Bay is an excellent example of how Tlingit place names serve as linguistic artifacts on the land, providing important clues about the natural and social history of a particular landscape. The map and text below are adapted from the *Angoon Cultural Atlas*, produced in conjunction with the Angoon Community Association in 1998, with support from SENSC's Southeast Alaska Native Place Names Project (funded by a National Park Service grant) and the Alaska Rural Systemic Initiative (funded by a National Science Foundation grant). It is accessible through the Alaska Native Knowledge Network (http://www.ankn.uaf.edu), which maintains the multimedia website as a resource for educators. The place names are linked to sound files recorded by Deisheetaan elder Lydia George, and to important Deishú Hít (a Deisheetaan house group) leaders, artifacts, and regalia, documented by Lydia's son, Jimmy George. Examining the indigenous names one is struck first by their density in comparison to the English name set (part of which is derived from the Tlingit). Second, a clear maritime and riverine orientation is evident in the Tlingit identification of important bays, streams, and points along the coastline, whereas many upland features are left unnamed. Third, the Tlingit toponyms contain numerous cultural references to important foods, such as sockeye salmon, icons, such as Raven (who was also active here), settlements (e.g., villages and forts), and events, such the exchange of a copper shield, or *tináa*, near Tinaa Gooní (also carved in petroglyph near Sitkoh Creek; see Garfield 1947, 441; de Laguna 1960, 75). The name Sit'k̲ú also begs important questions about the bay's natural history. For example: Why is Sitkoh Bay named for glaciers when there are none in its vicinity today? Deisheetaan oral history of the "Little Ice Age," combined with scientific evidence of the region's past, helps answer this question.

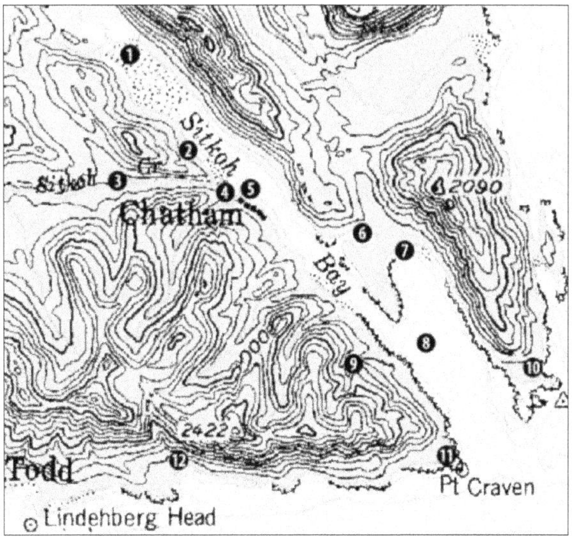

1. Atahéen, Creek at the Head of the Bay
2. Yéil Katóogu, Raven's Cave
3. G̲athéeni, Sockeye Stream
4. Tinaa Gooní, Copper Shield Spring
5. L.awdagaan, No Sunshine
6. Yáxwch'i Áak'u, Sea Otter Little Lake (lagoon)
7. Xakwgeeyí, Sandy Bay Beach
8. Sit'k̲ú, Glacier Area
9. Lukahéen, Creek at the Point (nose)
10. Shux̲'noowk'ú, Robin's Little Fort
11. Keishísh X'aak'ú, Beach Alder Little Point
12. Chaatlk'aanoow, Fort on Top* of the Halibut

Tlingit traditional knowledge and Western science each provide important details about Sitkoh Bay. Deisheetaan clan history tells how the name Sit'k̲ú was derived from the presence of glacial ice in Sitkoh Bay and Chatham Strait many years ago. Although we don't find glaciers there today, geomorphological studies suggest that a large valley glacier carved-out Sitkoh Bay during the late Wisconsin Ice Age (25,000–10,000 years ago). Glacial ice probably also clogged the waters of Chatham Strait during the so-called Little Ice Age (700–225 years ago). The oldest Deisheetaan stories about Sitkoh Bay begin with the phrase *aan galak̲ú*, meaning "at the time of the Flood," perhaps corresponding to the warming of the glaciers and consequent rise in water levels (and flooding) that occurred at the end of the Wisconsin Ice Age. Thus, Sit'k̲ú is both a very old name and a very descriptive one.

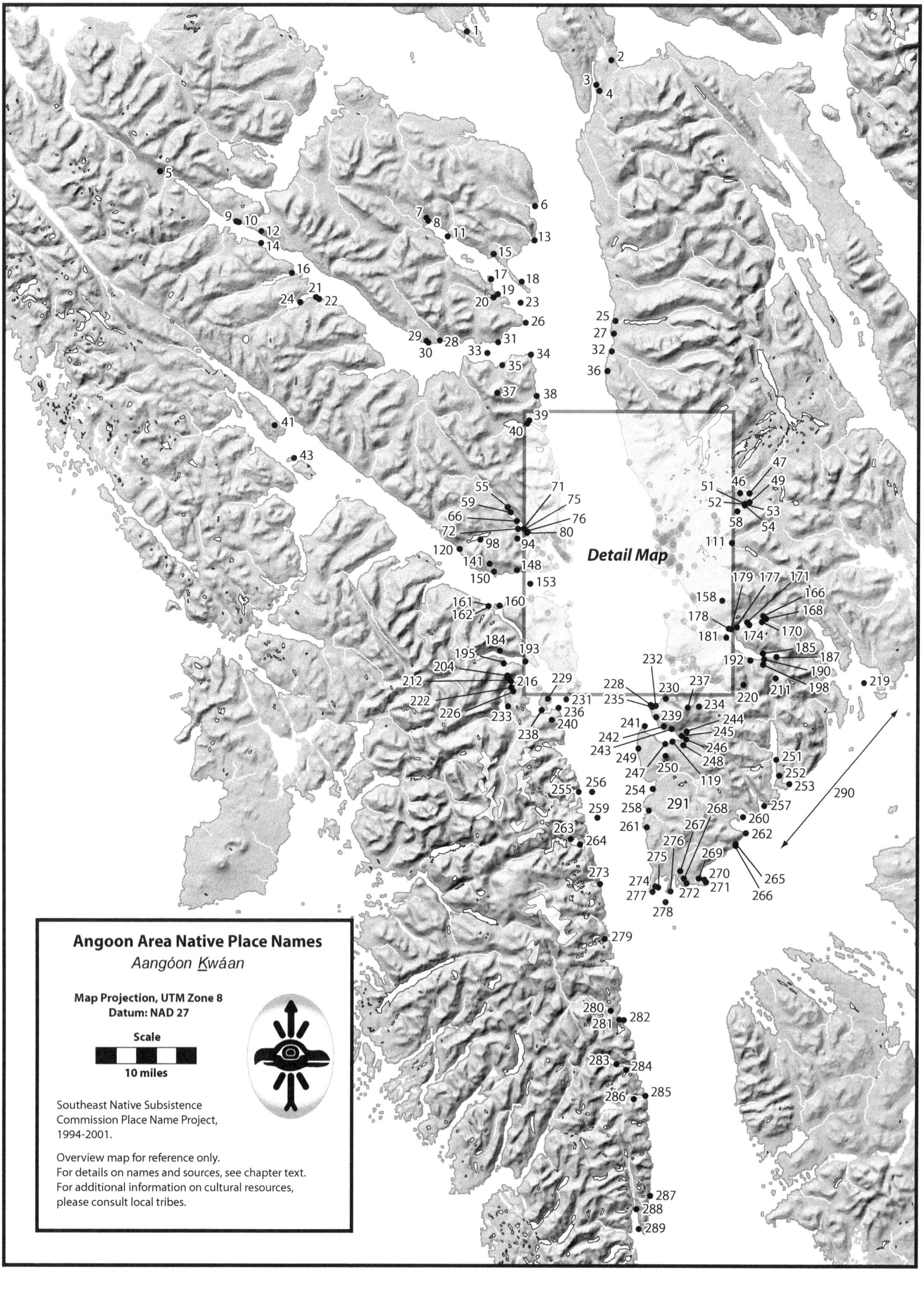
Detail Map
Angoon Area Native Place Names
Aangóon Kwáan
Map Projection, UTM Zone 8
Datum: NAD 27
Scale
10 miles
Southeast Native Subsistence Commission Place Name Project, 1994-2001.
Overview map for reference only.
For details on names and sources, see chapter text.
For additional information on cultural resources, please consult local tribes.

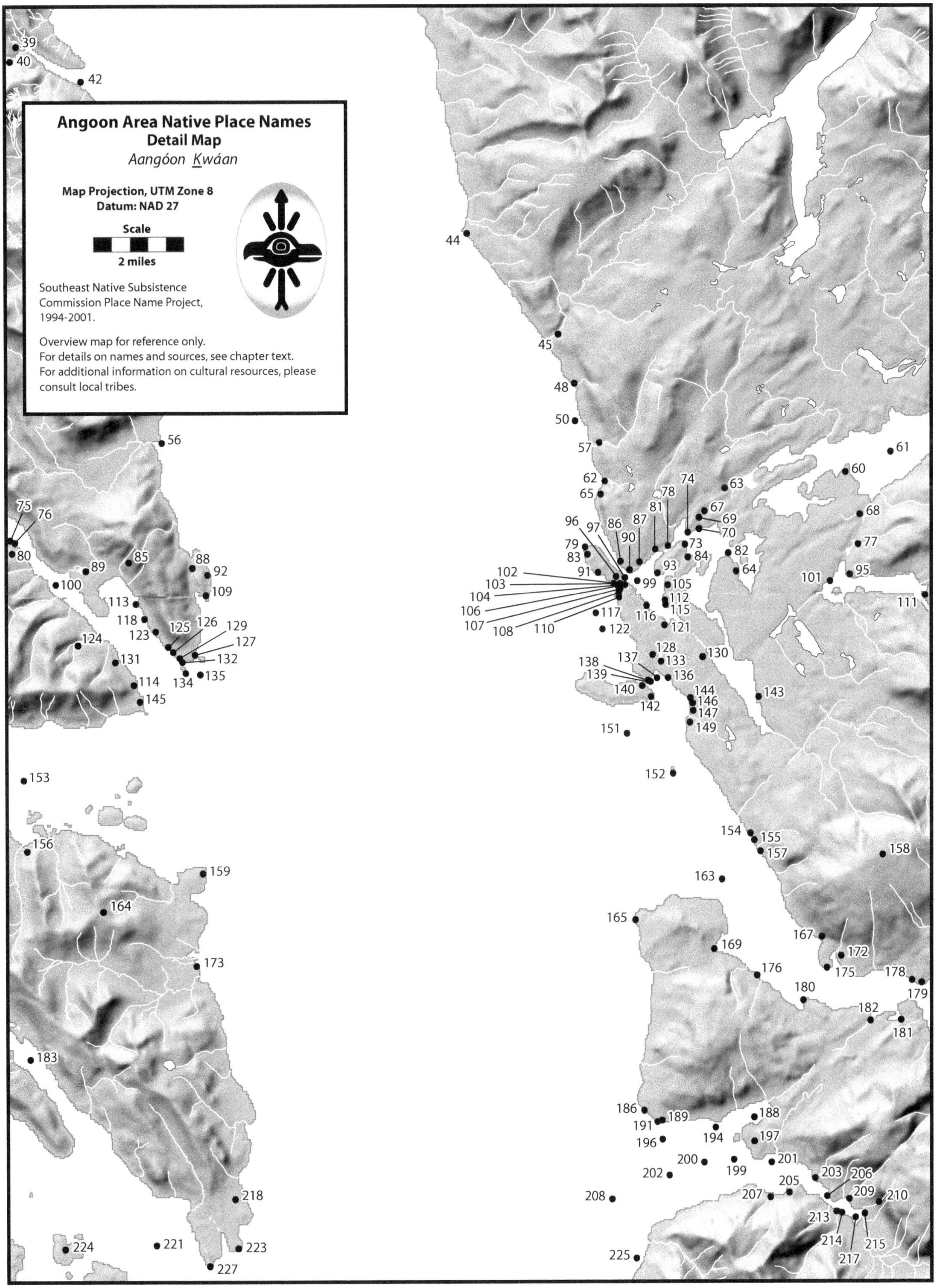

Angoon Area Native Place Names
Detail Map
Aangóon Kwáan
Map Projection, UTM Zone 8
Datum: NAD 27
Scale
2 miles
Southeast Native Subsistence Commission Place Name Project, 1994-2001.
Overview map for reference only.
For details on names and sources, see chapter text.
For additional information on cultural resources, please consult local tribes.

Xutsnoowú K̲wáan Place Names

Asterisk indicates uncertain, unconfirmed, or partial; NM = not mapped.
Some names have more than one pronunciation or translation.

Map #	Name	Translation	Location
1	Wanyeik'ax̲oo	Near among the Edge Place*	Swanson Harbor
2	Weineidei Góon	Alkali Deposit* Trail Portage	Hawk Inlet to Young Bay portage
3	Weineidei	Alkali Deposit* Trail	Hawk Inlet
4	Táax'aa Héeni	Mosquito Creek	Hawk Inlet
5	T'aawák̲ X'aayí	Goose Point	Flats at the head of Tenakee Inlet
6	Yayikhéen	Creek of Noise (of something unseen)	False Bay, Iyouktug Creek
7	Lax'áask'i	Little Falls	Head of Freshwater Bay
8	L'ookx̲nasdaa	Water Flowing around Coho	Salt chuck in Favorite Bay (or/also Hood Bay)
9	G̲uwakaan X'áat'i	Peace (Deer) Island	Island in Tenakee Inlet
10	S'eesde* X'áat'	Pouting* Island	Island at the head of Tenakee Inlet
11	Tsaa Eejí	Seal Reef	Seal Creek
12	Kéet Góoni	Killer Whale Portage	North Tenakee Inlet
13	G̲íl' Seiyí	In the Shadow of the Cliff	North of Iyoukeen Cove, Chatham Strait
14	Ketlyádi Héeni	Puppy Creek	Tenakee Inlet, Long Bay
15	Wanaté	Rock on the Side	North shore bight across Cedar Island
16	Takwsawu G̲eey	Bay with a Narrow Head/Back	Long Bay
17	Teinsanée*	Little One Behind*	Freshwater Bay, Cedar Island
18	Neenáx̲ Lunáa	——* Point (nose)	Iyoukeen Peninsula, North Passage Point
19	Taakw.aaní	Winter Village	Pavlof Harbor
20	Tax'áas	Rock Waterfall	Pavlof River (a sockeye stream)
21	Sít' Tux'aayí	Point inside the Glacier	Peninsula, Seal Bay
22	Tsaa Seiyí Sáank'i	Little Freshwater Bay below Tsaa Seiyí (#24)	Small Seal Bay
23	Asáank'i	Little Freshwater Bay*	Freshwater Bay / Pavlof Harbor
24	Tsaa Seiyí	Below (or in the shadow of) the Seals	Seal Bay
25	Shuchx'aak'ú	Little Point of Bathing	Point at Florence Lake outlet
26	Tax'áas X'áat'i Noow	Fort at the Island of Tax'áas (#20)	East Point
27	Watkaskíx̲ni	——* Mouth	Fishery Point
28	Tlaaguwu Héen	Ancient Creek	Indian River at Tenakee
29	T'aay X̲'é	Hot Springs Mouth	Tenakee Hot Springs
30	Tlaaguwu Aan	Ancient Village (Legendary Village)	Tenakee village (at hot springs)

Map #	Name	Translation	Location
31	Dzeitk'	Little Ladder	Tenakee Inlet
32	Na<u>x</u>k'uhéen	Little Harbor* Creek	Fishery Creek
33	T'einaageey	Hindward Side Bay	Tenakee Inlet
34	S'oow X'aayí	Greenstone Point	Entrance to Tenakee Inlet
35	Shak'wláa<u>x</u> Seiyí	Below (or in the shadow of) Shaak'w Láa<u>x</u> (#37)	Trap Bay, Tenakee Inlet
36	Kaya<u>x</u>lax'áas	Water Falls on the Face of It	Near Fishery Creek
37	Shaak'w Láa<u>x</u>	Little Mountain with Dead Trees	South of Trap Bay, Tenakee
38	Chas'héeni	Humpback Salmon Stream	North side of Basket Bay
39	<u>K</u>ak'w Áak'u	<u>K</u>ák'w (#42) Little Lake	Basket Bay grotto
40	Kóo<u>k</u>	Pit	Lake or creek to Kook Lake
41	Katlaa<u>x</u>	Moldy	Moser Island
42	<u>K</u>ák'w	Little Basket*	Basket Bay
43	Kakalwál	Lots of Holes on It	Vixen Island
44	Xoonyí<u>k</u> <u>X</u>oo X'aayí	Point amid the Valley of the North Wind	Parker Point
45	Watkasaté	Stream with Rock at the Mouth	Thayer Creek
46	Xunyei.áak'u	Xunyéi (#58) Lagoon	Salt Lake
47	Tsaagwáa <u>G</u>eeyí	Harbor-Seal Ice Flows* Bay	Mitchell Bay
48	Tu<u>k</u>tayee	Below the Anus (outlet of lake)	Thayer Creek area
49	Yéil Eeyí	Raven's Tidal Current	The Falls, Mitchell Bay
50	Tliséet	——* Pass	North of Danger Point Reef
51	Yéil Goo<u>x</u>ú	Raven's Slave	Mitchell Bay, near Kluchman Rock
52	Nás'giná<u>x</u> <u>K</u>áa	Three Men	Mitchell Bay, Kluchman Rock
53	Yéil <u>X</u>'anaa<u>x</u>gwál'	Raven's Mooring	Mitchell Bay
54	Keitl	Dog	Mitchell Bay
55	L'ukhéenak'u	Coho Salmon Little Creek	Small creek near the head of Sitkoh Bay
56	Kagu<u>k</u>kahéen	Half-Smoked Salmon Egg Creek	White Rock
57	X'áask'	Little Waterfall	Waterfall at creek northeast Danger Point Reef
58	Xunyéi	North Wind Tidal Current	Mitchell Bay / Salt Lake
59	Atahéen	Creek at the Head of the Bay (Up the Bay Creek)	Humpback salmon creek at the head of Sitkoh Bay
60	——* Noow	——* Fort	Steamboat Point
61	Xóots Kaháagu X'áat'	Brown Bear Roe Island	Target Island, Kootznoowoo Inlet
62	Katóok <u>X</u>'ayee	Area below the Mouth of the Cave	Kootznahoo Head
63	Nánde <u>X</u>'atánk	Its Mouth Faces North	Kootznahoo Inlet mouth
64	Kéet Kwásk'i <u>X</u>oo	Among the Killer Whales Little Chamber Pot	Rock formations at Peehand rapids, Kootznahoo Inlet
65	K'uxdzeitk'í	Marten's Small Ladder	Opposite Danger Point

Map #	*Name*	*Translation*	*Location*
66	Yéil Katóogu	Raven's Cave	Sitkoh Bay
67	Yéil Chaadí	Raven's Section above Tail	Stillwater Channel
68	Kanaay (Kéini*) Aaní	——* (Cannery*) Town	Lighter Creek area
69	Eey Tlein	Big Tidal Currents	Kootznahoo Inlet, esp. Stillwater Rapids
70	Sháa Eeyí [Áak'u]	Ladies' Tidal Rapids [Lagoon]	Above Pillsbury Point, Kootznahoo Inlet
71	Ishkahít	House on Top of the Fish Hole	Mouth of Sitkoh Creek
72	G̱athéeni	Sockeye Stream	Sitkoh Creek, Sitkoh Bay
73	Daax̱aatkanadaa	Where the Tide Flows Around [the Island]	Island opposite Pillsbury Point
74	Yáay Shanoowú	Whale's Head Fort	Cabin Point
75	Tinaa Gooní	Copper Shield Spring	Sitkoh Bay near cannery
76	Sít'tu.aan	Village inside the Glacier	Sitkoh Bay
77	Kanalḵú	Water Floods over a Reef	Kanalku Bay
78	G̱ánji Táayi	Tobacco Patch	Kootznoowoo Inlet
79	Xutsnoowú Lutú	Brown Bear Fort Point (nose)	Danger Point
80	L.awdagaan	No Sunshine	Sitkoh Creek village
81	Ḵeex̱itu.aan	Town inside ——*	Stillwater homestead
82	T'ookká	On the Cradleboard	Peehand Bay, lagoons between Mitchell and Favorite bays
83	X'aa Yadaa Noow	Fort around the Face of the Point	Danger Point peninsula
84	X'áax' Eeyí	Crabapple Tide Rapids	Peehand rapids, south of Pillsbury Point
85	Ḵaadí	Rockslide	Above Florence Bay
86	Eey Tlein	Big Tidal Rapids	North of Turn Point
87	Shaax̱haawastani* Aan	Gray Currant Leaves* Village	Angoon area*
88	Nánde X̱'atan Aa Ts'áḵli X'aa G̱eeyák'u	Northward-Facing Black Paint Point Little Bay	Near Peninsular Point
89	Yáxwch'i Áak'u	Sea Otter Lagoon	Tidal flat north of Florence Bay in Sitkoh Bay
90	Yát Haat Wudá	Current Going on Both Sides	Turn Point
91	Ch'ak'noowú	Eagle Fort	Near Danger Point cemetery
92	Ts'áḵli X'aa (Laḵli X'aa)	Black Paint Point (Bentwood Box* Point)	Peninsular Point
93	L'ook Aaní	Coho Village	Channel Point
94	L'óox̱'u Héenk'i	Silty Little Creek	Creek in Sitkoh Bay
95	Kanalḵú Aan	Kanalḵú (#77) Village	North Kanalku Bay
96	Yandeix̱ánk'	Back Close to Shore	Inside Angoon Village
97	Yax̱lahásh	Keeps Trying to Drift Ashore	Village Rock
98	Áa	Lake	Sitkoh Lake

Map #	Name	Translation	Location
99	Xeel	Foam	Rose Rock near Stillwater Anchorage
100	Sit'ḵú	Glacier Area	Sitkoh Bay
101	Té* Hít	Stone* House	Stone Island
102	Té X̱'éel'	Slippery Stone	Angoon west canoe launch
103	Yéil S'igeidí Noow	Raven-Beaver Fort	Angoon ANB Hall
104	Xuts.eeyí	Brown Bear Rapids	South of Turn Point
105	Aandaayaagú	Rowboat	Stillwater Anchorage
106	Aangóon	Isthmus Town	Angoon
107	Xoodzí [Daa]	Charred Remains [Around]	Angoon area
107.1	Ḡaanax̱sháa Noowú	Ḡaanax̱.ádi Women's Fort	Point, now a graveyard
108	Ts'eigeení X̱'aak'ú	Magpie's Little Point	Point near Angoon
109	Íxde X̱'atan Aa Ts'áḵli X'aa Ḡeeyák'u	Southward-Facing Black Paint Point Little Bay	South of Peninsular Point
110	Yéik Kahídi	House on [the Grave of] the Helper Spirit [of a Shaman]	East of Keenesnoow Rocks
111	Ḵátlx̱'	Inside the Pot*	Upper Kanalku Bay area (and Kanalku Lake?)
112	Ḵéex̱'shu.aan	Village at the End of ——*	Sullivan Point
113	Chál X̱'ayee	Below Opening of Cache	Florence Bay
114	X̱áaw Tayee Goon (X̱awtayee Goon)	Spring under the Log	Sitkoh Bay, above Point Hayes (alternative to #126)
115	Taakw.aaní Shú	End of Winter Village	Favorite Bay, near Sullivan Point
116	X̱'anax̱.ayei	Through the Middle	Point opposite Sullivan Point
117	X'áat'k'	Little Island	Kenasnow Rocks area
118	Xakwgeeyí	Sandy Beach Bay	Florence Bay
119	Chichx̱'as'gutuhéen	River in the Jaw of the Porpoise	Whitewater Bay
120	Anax̱ L'ukduyaa Yé	Where You Pack Coho Over to the Other Side	Peril Strait, northwest of Todd
121	Ḵeix̱itu.aan	Village inside the Brush	Garnes Point area
122	Hitx̱'áak	Between the Houses	Kootznahoo Roads, Kenasnow Rocks
123	Tlakw X̱'áak*	Giant Halibut Between*	Florence Bay
124	Lukahéen	Creek at the Point (nose)	Sitkoh Bay
125	Shux̱'noowk'ú	Robin's Little Fort	Point Hayes
126	X̱awtayee Goon	Spring under the Log	Sitkoh Bay, opposite Halibut Fort (alternative to #114)
127	Ts'axwelnoowú	Crow's Fort	Point Hayes (Chatham Strait)
128	S'igeidí Deiyí	Beaver Trail	Main road of Angoon
129	Tangeeyí	Sea Lion Bay	Sitkoh Bay, below Point Hayes
130	Féeshwaan Aaní	Fisherman's Town	Favorite Bay
131	Keishísh X'aak'ú	Beach Alder Little Point	Sitkoh Bay
132	Xutsnoowú	Brown Bear Fort	Point Hayes

Map #	*Name*	*Translation*	*Location*
133	Kadus.áak'w	Little Lake on It	North Killisnoo Harbor
134	X'us'noowú	Crabapple Fort	Point Hayes, Sitkoh Bay
135	Yáthaatwudá	Current Flows against the Face of It	Chatham Strait, Sitkoh Bay area
136	Tlaaguwu Noow	Ancient Fort	Across from Killisnoo
137	Kadas' X'ayík	Sound of Hailstones Hitting the Ground*	North Killisnoo Harbor
138	Chatlkoowú	Halibut Tail	Mainland north of Killisnoo Island
139	Yéil K'wádli	Raven's Cooking Pot	Killisnoo Harbor
140	Wooch Géide Tliséet*	Getting So Fat It's Coming Together	Channel north of Killisnoo Island
141	Adawutlhéeni	Battle Creek	Todd Cannery, Peril Strait
142	Kanasnoow	Windbreak Fort	Killisnoo
143	Wankageey	Bay on the Edge	Favorite Bay
144	Keitanji Aan	Village Where It Continually Lifts Up	Across from Killisnoo
145	Chaatlk'aanoow	Fort on Top* of the Halibut	Point Craven, Sitkoh Bay area
146	Dákde Yakatan Aas	Tree Leaning Out	Killisnoo Harbor
147	Daasakwt'aagaanoow	Fort of the Village alongside Daasákw	Shore in Killisnoo Harbor
148	Adawóotl Xágu	Battle Sandbar	North Peril Strait
149	Tsax'adaadzaayí Aan	Seal's Mustache Land	Killisnoo northwest base
150	Kaa Sháa Teiwahayi Yé	Place Where the Rock Fell on the Man's Head	Village at Todd, Peril Strait
151	Ts'axweil Noowk'ú	Crow's Little Fort	Table Island
152	Daasaxákw	Sandbars around It	Sand Island
153	Shee Ká	On Top of Shee (Baranof Island)	Peril Strait
154	Néex' Xágu	Marble Sandbar	Hood Bay opposite Cabin Point
155	Sax'aayi Héen	Stream with a Point	Hood Bay entrance
156	Tuwooli Héeni	Water inside the Holes	Just inside Peril Strait
157	Gíl'k'i Yat'ak Aan	Village beside the Little Cliffs	Hood Bay
158	Tsaagwáa Shaanák'u	Tsaagwáa's (#163) Old Woman	Hood Bay
159	Kalagooch	Hilly on Top	Bay on Catherine Island
160	Gáchgu X'ayanéekw	Gáchgu's (#161) Hurting Words	Dead Tree Island
161	Gáchgu (Gáchkw, Kátsx'u*)	*	Hanus Bay / Catherine Island area
162	Gáchgu Héen	Gáchgu's (#161) Creek	Hanus River
163	Tsaagwáa	Harbor-Seal Ice Flows*	Hood Bay
164	Gáchgu Léin	Gáchgu's (#161) Flats	Hanus Bay / Catherine Island flats
165	Dliwuwu X'aa	Whitened Point (the color of face powder)	Distant Point
166	Sax'aayi Héen	Stream with a Point	Creek, North Arm Hood Bay (alternate location of #155)
167	Héende Ketlgichx'iyé	Place Where They Threw Dogs into the Water	Cliff, Hood Bay

Map #	*Name*	*Translation*	*Location*
168	X̲'ayáa	Close to the Mouth	Point, east of Killisnoo Island
169	Keishísh Aaní	Beach Alder Country	Hood Bay
170	L'ookx̲nasdaa	Water Flowing around Coho	North Arm Hood Bay
171	K̲eex̲itu.aan	Town inside ——*	North Arm Hood Bay
172	Tayx'aayí T'éik G̲eeyí	Bay behind Garden Point	Inside Cabin Point
173	Kala.aasák'w	Having a Small Tree	Catherine Island*
174	Lax'áas	Waterfall (Cascading Waterfall)	North Arm Hood Bay
175	Tayx'aayí	Garden Point	Cabin Point in Hood Bay
176	X'aageegí	Old Point	Point Hood Bay
177	Tanchwusx̲eek̲	[Fish] Jumped and Kept Them Awake	Killisnoo
178	X'aatudeidu.áx̲ch	Where You Hear Noise inside the Point	Junction of North and South arms, Hood Bay
179	Tsaagwáa Yalatín	Watching the Face of Tsaagwáa (#163)	Hood Bay
180	K'óox Noowú	Marten Fort	Hood Bay
181	Kis'.áak'u	Tide Little Lake	Hood Bay
182	L'ukhéenak'u	Coho Salmon Little Creek	Hood Bay
183	Úchgu Séet	——*'s Strait	Portage Passage
184	Tsísk'u K̲óox'u	Owl Palisades	Middle Arm
185	Yeis G̲eiyi Héen	Horse Clam Bay Water	Creek, South Arm Hood Bay
186	Jigayaa Noow	Village Point Fort	Village Point
187	Kayáash Ká	On the Platform	Mountain east of Hood Bay
188	Chayéek Sáank'i	Chayéek's (#202) Little One	Whole North Arm Chaik Bay
189	Yéil Gaawk'ú	Raven's Little Drum	Chaik Bay, Village Point
190	Kayáash K'i Héen	Creek at the Base of the Platform	End of South Arm Point
191	Ch'ak'noowú	Eagle Fort	South Arm Hood Bay
192	Tsaagwáa Héeni	Tsaagwáa (#163) Creek	South Arm Hood Bay
193	Tsísk'w	Owl	Middle Arm (Bay)
194	Ch'eex̲' Aaní	Thimbleberry Land	Chaik Bay
195	Tsísk'u Sáani	Owl Freshwater* Bay	Kelp Bay, Middle Arm
196	X̲áat G̲eeyí	Fish Bay	Chaik Bay*
197	Táakw Noowú	Winter Fort	Chaik Bay
198	Yíshx̲	Old Lady Cliff	Cliff, South Arm Hood Bay
199	Kawsigaani X'áat'	Burnt Island	South of Rocky Point
200	Chayéek Éedi	Chayéek (#202) Halibut Hole	Chaik Bay
201	Téel' Kwásk'i	Dog Salmon's Little Chamber Pot	Chaik Bay, small islands
202	Chayéek	Arm Goes Way Up Inside*	Chaik Bay
203	L'ukhéenak'u	Coho Salmon Little Creek	Chaik Bay, near tidal flat
204	Tlaguwushú	Ancient End*	Mountain, South Arm Kelp Bay
205	G̲uwakaan Xágu	Deer's Sand Beach	Chaik Bay

Map #	Name	Translation	Location
206	Ayadatíx'	Sand Island	Chaik Bay, tidal flat
207	Ts'áḵli Xákwk'u	Black Paint* Small Sandbar	South Chaik Bay
208	Chayéek X'ananúk	Sitting by Chayéek (#202)	Chaik Bay, islands at mouth
209	Chayéek Léin	Chayéek (#202) Flats	Chaik Bay, tidal flat
210	Tus'ḵaadí	Shark Landslide	East of Chaik Bay
211	Góon	Portage	Hood Bay to Eliza Harbor (trail/ portage)
212	Ḵaadí Shoowú	Half Slide	Kelp Bay, South Arm
213	Tsaa Yík	Inside the Seal	Chaik Bay
214	Ḵútl'gu Noowú	Mud Flats Fort	Chaik Bay
215	Noow Yayee Ísh	Fish Hole below the Face of the Fort	Chaik Bay
216	Tleiyaḵú Éek	Beach of Tleiyaḵú (#222)	South Arm (west shore point)
217	Téel' Kwásk'i	Dog Salmon's Little Chamber Pot	Tidal flat in Chaik Bay
218	Kanax.adagán	Light Shining Over	Catherine Island
219	Ḵéex' Ḵwáan Geeyí	Ḵéex' (Kake) People's Bay	Pybus Bay
220	Yáay Dix'ká	On the Back of a Whale	East of Chaik Bay
221	Gishgeeyí	Kelp Bay	Kelp Bay
222	Tleiyaḵú	*	South Arm Kelp Bay
223	Gooch Tuḵyee Geeyák'w	Little Bay on the Area below the Hill	Point Lull
224	Úchgu Yádi	Úchkw's Child	Pond Island
225	Xáat Téis'k'i	Little Fish Heart	Chaik Bay, small island
226	Yees Yayee	Stone-Ax Face*	Sandbar, South Arm bight
227	Shaayá	Mountain Face	Point Lull, Catherine Island
228	Káak'wtaan X'aa Lutú	Tip of Male Sea Lions' Point	Woody Point
229	Tiyx'áat'i	Yellow Cedar Bark Island	Pond Island, The Basin
230	Tuwooli Héen	River with a Hole Inside	South of Rocky Point
231	Yéikheenwu.aat	The Helper Spirits Have Gone into the Water	Kelp Bay
232	Woochyagíl'i	Cliffs Facing Each Other*	Cliff, north of Whitewater Bay
233	Kóoshdaa Áak'w	Land Otter Lagoon	South Arm Kelp Bay
234	Shalak'áts' Yádi	Sharp Head Baby	Mountain, south of Chaik Bay
235	Káak'wtaan X'aa	Male Sea Lions' Point	Woody Point
236	Kichx'anagaat Noow	Rainbow Fort	South Point, Kelp Bay
237	Shalak'áts'	Sharp Head	Mountain south of Chaik Bay
238	Wulis'ixi Aan	Stinking Village (Fermented Village)	Point, The Basin
239	Naltóoshgán	*	Village at Whitewater Bay
240	Yaawuljaḵk'i Shaa	Herring Hole* Mountain	Mount Cosmos, Kelp Bay
241	Ichlugei	In the Nose of the Reef*	Point Caution
242	T'ooch' X'áat'i	Black Point	Black Point

Map #	Name	Translation	Location
243	Ḵaa Shaayí X'aak'ú	Man's Head Little Point	North Whitewater Bay
244	Naach'uhéen	——* Creek	Whitewater Bay
245	Shan.ooxú	Old Lady's Teeth	Whitewater Bay
246	Deikeenaa Héeni	Haidas' Stream	Whitewater Bay
247	S'eek Xwáa	Black-Bear Young-Man	Rocky Point area, Whitewater Bay
248	Til'héeni	Dog Salmon Stream	Whitewater Bay
249	Ch'ak'gíl'i	Eagle Cliff	South Arm
250	L'úx Yadaa	Around the Face of L'úx (Blinking)	Table Mountain
251	Gúnx	Still Water* (shortcut/pass over mountain*)	Eliza Harbor
252	X'aak'w Aan	Town on a Small Point	Loon Point, Eliza Harbor
253	Tiyx'áat'i (Ḡaanax.ádi X'aka.aan)	Yellow Cedar Bark Island (Ḡaanax.ádi Village at the Mouth)	Liesnoi Island
254	Katákw	*	Wilson Cove
255	Tekáas'	Rock Split	Takatz Bay
256	Tekáas' Tiyx'áat'i	Tekáas' (#255) Yellow Cedar Bark Island	Island, Takatz Bay
257	Shaa Wool	Mountain Hole	Chapin Bay
258	Katakwsáank'i	——* Boiling Small One	Wilson Cove
259	Shee Yá	Face of Shee (Baranof Island)	Eastern Baranof Island shore
260	Takuwóox'	Wide-Bottomed	Herring Bay
261	Xaaxágu	War Party Sandbar	South of Wilson Cove
262	Kóoshdaa X'aak'ú	Land Otter Little Point	Brightman Point, Herring Bay
263	T'aay Ḡákw	Hot Springs Coming Out	Warm Springs
264	Yat'aayi Ḡeey	Warm Bay	Warm Springs Bay
265	Tsaa Héeni	Seal Creek	Southwest of Herring Bay
266	Ch'áak' Teiyí	Eagle Rock	Southwest of Herring Bay
267	Kuchx'ahéen	River at the Mouth of [Murder Cove] (River by the Ribbon Seaweed)	Tyee
268	Tawanyee Ḡeeyí	Right-Alongside Bay	Little bay east of Murder Cove
269	Xalnú Tukyee	Outlet of Xalnú (#271)	Behind Carroll Island
270	Xalnú Séet	Xalnú (#271) Pass	Pass behind Carroll Island
271	Xalnú	*	Carroll Island
272	Taan	Sea Lion	East of Walker Point
273	Tsaa X'aayí	Seal Point	Cascade Bay
274	Yéik Wán	Edge of the Shaman's Spirit	North of Point Gardner
275	Daaxixch'daak.uhú	Frogs Wading Up Around [It]	Surprise Harbor
276	Teet.lasaa	Breathing Sound of Waves	Bartlett Point
277	Xutsnoowú Tukyee	Outlet of Brown Bear Fort	Point Gardner
278	Teilnú	Pitchwood* Fort	Yasha Island
279	Léix'w.awashaa*	Red Snapper Married*	Nelson Bay

Map #	*Name*	*Translation*	*Location*
280	Jigúx	Have Slaves	Red Bluff Bay
281	Yéilch Áa Yoo Awsigani Yé	Place Where Raven Burned [the Land] Here and There	Entrance to Red Bluff Bay
282	X'éixdusaayí	Putting the Names in Your Mouth	Entrance to Red Bluff Bay
283	Deiyadaa Geeyí	Bay around the Side of the Trail	Hoggatt Bay
284	Watkasaté (Watkasatí*)	Stream with Rock at the Mouth (Poison Water*)	Hoggatt Bay, stream
285	Yéil Geiwú	Raven's Fishnet	Gut Bay
286	Gatgeey	Sockeye Salmon* Bay	Gut Bay
287	Tsaa Geey Yík	Inside Seal Bay	Lords Pocket, Patterson Bay
288	Geey Tlein	Big Bay	Patterson Bay
289	S'áxt'i Geeyí	Devil's Club Bay	Patterson Bay
290	Xutsnoowú T'éik	Inland Side of Xutsnoowú (#291)	East shore of Admiralty Island
291	Xutsnoowú	Brown Bear Fort	Admiralty Island
NM	Kakdahéen*	Accidental* Creek	Creek with many boulders in Tenakee Inlet
NM	L'úx Yátx'i	L'úx's (Table Mountain's; see #250) Children	Smaller mountains beside Table Mountain
NM	Téel' Noow	Dog Salmon Fort	Whitewater Bay
NM	X'us'k'i* Héen	Club [Dog Salmon] at the Base* Creek	Creek near Tenakee
NM	Yéikheen.áa	Spirit Water Lagoon	Lagoon in Middle Arm, Kelp Bay
NM	Yéik Shaa	Spirit Mountain	Yeek-Sha Mountain,* Seymour Canal
NM	Yuknoowú	Cormorant Fort	Island off Point Hayes, Sitkoh Bay*

7. K̲éex̲' K̲wáan, Kooyú K̲wáan, and S'awdáan K̲wáan

K̲éex̲' (Kake), Kooyú (Kuiu), and S'awdáan (Sumdum) k̲wáans comprise the heart of central Southeast Alaska. Today the modern village of Kake, from the Tlingit K̲éex̲', is the only major Native community lying within these traditional territories.

Speaking to land claims investigators in 1946 about the relationships between Kake Tlingits and their land, elder Fred Friday explained, "The Native people know all the points and rocks and every little area by name. If I told you all the names of all the places that I know it would fill many pages. These areas were used so much that we were familiar with every little place" (Goldschmidt and Haas 1998, 177).

Although Fred Friday passed away many years ago, we were able to map named sites he identified, and confirm them with contemporary Kake elders, including his descendants. Indeed, Kake residents have maintained their ethnogeographic knowledge to a remarkable degree. This is due in no small part to their continuing productive relationships with the land through commercial fishing and trapping and subsistence hunting, fishing, and gathering.

We documented more than three hundred place names within K̲éex̲', Kooyú, and S'awdáan k̲wáan territories. Our project was carried out in conjunction with the Organized Village of Kake, the local, federally-recognized tribe. Ruth Demmert, a knowledgeable elder and speaker, writer, and teacher of Tlingit, served as local research coordinator for the project. Other key contributors included: Gladys Aceveda, Doyle Abbot, Wesley Brown, George Davis, Vesta Dominicks and Walter Williams, Frank Gordon, Clarence Jackson, Johnny C. Jackson, Mike Jackson, Thomas Jackson Sr., Kelly James, Charles Johnson, Marvin Kadake, Harold Martin, Richard Newton, and many others. We also recognize the contributions of past researchers, including Constance Naish and Gillian Story, Frederica de Laguna, George Emmons, Viola Garfield, Walter Goldschmidt and Theodore Haas, Ronald Olson, Louis Shotridge, and John Swanton. The first phase of SENSC project fieldwork and mapping was carried out by Martha Betts of Vanguard Research with support from the Alaska Department of Fish and Game, Division of Subsistence. Harold Martin and Thomas Thornton carried out additional fieldwork and Thornton prepared the final database. Jeff Leer of the Alaska Native Language Center and Nora and Richard Dauenhauer of the Sealaska Heritage Institute provided linguistic review.

K̲éex̲' K̲wáan

K̲éex̲' K̲wáan is classified as southern Tlingit, although the territory extended north of Frederick Sound (the major divide between northern and southern Tlingit) to the south end of Admiralty Island. The origin of the name K̲éex̲', applied to the first village established in Keku Strait, is not altogether clear. According to Emmons (n.d.), it was derived from Geka ("To Blister," not mapped), the name of a creek on Kupreanof Island, where the sand on the shores would get in between children's toes, causing them to blister. But he adds, "Another explanation is that in walking along the sand and gravel beach [there], a noise was made like the sound of the word [K̲éex̲']." A third explanation recorded by Emmons is that the name is of mythological origin, given by the trickster-demiurge Raven, who likened the innumerable channels in Keku Passage to the lines on his hands and feet, and thus named the country. Two elders we interviewed linked the name to Rocky Pass, one suggesting that it relates to the pass "going dry" at low tide, and another to the way morning's first light shines through the pass to mark the opening of the day. Although its precise meaning may be obscure, K̲éex̲' is undoubtedly a very old name.

K̲éex̲' K̲wáan covers a multitude of islands and waterways, as well as a portion of the mainland. The k̲wáan is centered on northwest Kupreanof and northeastern Kuiu islands, but clan territories extended as far as Gambier

Bay on Admiralty Island to the north and Windham Bay on the mainland to the east. Some clans in K̲ée̲x̲' were closely related to those in the neighboring Kooyú (Kuiu), Xutsnoowú (Angoon), Hinyaa (Klawock), and Shtax'héen (Wrangell) k̲wáans. As a consequence, territorial boundaries are perhaps not as sharply defined, with many areas claimed jointly. Major clans on the Raven side included the K̲aach.ádi, Suk̲tineidí, Teeyineidí, Tanyeidí, and X̲'alchaneidí, and on the Eagle/Wolf side, the Shangukeidí, Was'ineidí, Tsaagweidí, Nees.ádi, and Wooshkeetaan. Census records dating back to 1838 document populations of up to six hundred, while the present population is just over seven hundred.

Some important sites within K̲ée̲x̲' territory include:

Hamilton Bay / Keku Strait (K̲ée̲x̲', #80). Vancouver reported eight fortified villages in the vicinity of Hamilton Bay in 1794, and in 1869, when Commander Richard W. Meade bombarded Kake on behalf of the U.S. government, the settlement had some twenty community houses (Emmons n.d.). The present community of Kake stands on the shores of Kupreanof Island just above Hamilton Bay. The original name of the settlement was said to be Ta.aan (Sleeping Town), but it later became known as "The Town Where No One Sleeps" (#147), in commemoration of a famous memorial party (potlatch) that took place there. As Charles Johnson (interview) relates the story:

> The hosts were two brothers, X̲atawu and K̲anaash, from the Was'ineidí clan. The host house was Táa̲x̲' Hít (Many-Tiered House). After their mother died, they invited their paternal uncles to a feast, and after the festivities had gone on continuously for several days, the clan leader of the guests announced that from now on this place will be known as "Town Where No One Sleeps." It is said that that the house had so many tiers that when the tide came in the central fire would float. [Similarly,] when the brothers brought their father to the entrance and he looked down they had to grab him to keep him from falling down; he was overcome by the unexpected depth of the house. That is as I have it.

K̲ée̲x̲' Luwoolk'í (Little Nostrils of K̲ée̲x̲', #121) was the location of the first Tlingit settlement in the Kake area, according to oral history. The beach was said to have been much larger prior to the big Flood which drove residents into the Interior. When they returned, they recognized their beloved village, but found that it was no longer ideal for permanent habitation. This historic site is commemorated in Tlingit oral literature, dance, and regalia. Photo by Norio Matsumoto.

The earliest settlement, K̲ée̲x̲', was across Keku Strait from the present village in the shadow of K̲ée̲x̲' Luwoolk'í (Little Nostrils of K̲ée̲x̲', #121), an apt description of the hole in the rock promontory that marks the site (see photo). Johnny C. Jackson's narrative (see "Returning Home" below) of his ancestors' epic journey back to Keku Strait after the Flood (in Tlingit tradition, a calamity similar to that in Genesis) drove them inland to what is today Canada, identifies this site as one his ancestors recognized and celebrated upon their return. Clarence Jackson (2003), a descendant, elaborates:

> And they came through Rocky Pass and they still didn't know for sure where they were, but they ended up in Keku Straits. And they knew they were looking for a cliff that came down to the water that had a hole in it that you could walk through... And they were looking for a large beach. In the stories, they said that we lived on a beach that was very large, and there was a rock where that cliff came down. And they called that rock "The Nose of Kake." And they called the hole "The Nose Hole." And in our ceremonial dances long ago, certain people could wear a nose ring in the dancing regalia. And that's where it came from. And I don't know how long it was before we came back to the Kake area but they discovered that beach and the cliff, perhaps hundreds of years had gone by, and they kept the story alive of where home was supposed to be. And so when they found it they reported it back to the family, and they went back to move there, and they discovered that the beach had washed away, perhaps the ice had gouged a deep place in front of the village site. And it wasn't a very suitable place to live any more.

Later the people became consolidated at the modern village of Kake. But K̲ée̲x̲' Luwoolk'í continued to be commemorated in dance and story. The Keku Strait area proved to be a bountiful place for food. As Clarence Jackson notes, when his ancestors returned from Canada, "they always said they were able to get everything they needed from the Kake area. And it's still the same to us today." Keku Strait was valued for its rich salmon runs, but also for productive halibut banks and concentrations of marine mammals, all of which are still harvested there. Keku Strait is also Raven's country, a place where the trickster-demiurge tried to recreate the Nass River. George Davis, interviewed in Juneau, sketched one of Raven's places, Yéil Gaachk'u Séet (Raven's Little Mat Pass, #91), on a scrap of paper, and was sure we would recognize the place when we saw it. Indeed we did (see photo).

Saginaw Bay (Skanáx, #133). Saginaw Bay is also a site of Raven's work, as evidenced by the story behind Yéil Kawóot (Raven Beads, #159; see "The Mystery of Yéil Kawóot" box). The high density of place names in the bay, including numerous fort and settlement sites on its shores and islands indicates that it was a thickly-settled, strategic locale. The meaning of the Tlingit name, Skanáx, may be related to the name of a village on the eastern shore which was said to be a disagreeable place to live due to the noise made by clams constantly squirting water on the beaches there (Emmons n.d.). The original people who lived there were known as the Skanax.eidí (People of Skanáx), but they later became the Tsaagweidí, after a portion migrated to Hood Bay (Tsaagwaa, #10) near Angoon. Later they returned to Kéex' territory but kept the Tsaagweidí clan name. Five out of the six clan houses at Saginaw Bay were destroyed by Commander Meade's USS *Saginaw* during the bombardment of Kake in 1869. This horrific incident (a reprisal for the murder of a white man) invests the English name for the bay with distinctly negative connotations for Kake Tlingits, and some would like to see it officially changed back to its original Tlingit name.

Security Bay (Kúchx'w, #175). Two stockaded settlements were evident here, along with several fishing camps, before the bombardment of 1869. After these were destroyed, a new, smaller settlement was established on the eastern shore. In the contemporary era, the area has been used by Kake people for hunting, fishing, gathering, and trapping. Especially prized is the fall run of dog salmon, the presence of which extends the fishing season long after other runs have ceased. These dog salmon are said to be of the highest quality for smoking and eating.

Little Pybus Bay (Káach, #40). It is from this bay that the Kaach.ádi (People of Little Pybus Bay) clan derived its name. After migrating from the Interior, the group is said to have made their first houses out of bark, mat, and brush gathered here, thus inspiring the name (Johnny Jackson 1971; Emmons n.d.). Later, segments of this clan moved to Kéex' and Shtax'héen areas. Kaach.ádi regalia maps and commemorates important cultural events and geographic sites associated with Little Pybus Bay. Today the bay is used primarily for subsistence by Kake residents.

Was'héeni (Louse Creek, #148). Emmons (n.d.) reports that this name commemorates an incident involving an old woman who resided at a creek in or below Hamilton Bay, though the name may also refer to Hamilton Bay itself. The woman was constantly scratching her back but unable to find relief. Finally, she took a sharpened stick with which she pierced her body, letting forth "myriads of water lice" which spewed into the stream and "ever afterwards in the spring of the year when the buds sprouted they swarmed in the water" here, thus giving the creek and the clan, Was'ineidí, their names.

Tunehean Creek (Tanahéen, "Jumping Fish Creek," #236). This was a celebrated coho, humpback, and dog salmon stream, from which the Tanyeidí clan is said to have ob-

Kake elder George Davis, now living in Juneau, initially could not recall the name of the island known as Yéil Gaachk'u Séet (Raven's Little Mat Pass, #91), yet he could see it in his mind. Later he remembered the name, spelled it out phonetically, and drew a sketch of the place, so we would know it when we saw it. Photo by Norio Matsumoto.

The Mystery of Yéil Kawóot (#151): Traditional Knowledge and Geological Science

Tlingit legend has it that Raven fashioned a necklace for his wife from the beautiful and uniquely symmetrical fossil shells he found at Yéil Kawóot. Retired biologist and student of Tlingit John Palmes explores the mystery from a geological perspective.

I'd been studying the Tlingit language for about five years, so when I saw Yéil Kawóot in a list of Tlingit place names I could translate it. "Raven Beads," was an intriguing name. What are Raven's beads? What did this place name mean?

The *Tlingit Noun Dictionary* by Naish and Story (1976, 35) translates *Yéil kawóodi* as petrified coral. This is actually not correct as a visit to the site has shown.

Harold Martin, a native of Kake and head of the Southeast Native Subsistence Commission place names project, marked the general location on a map. On August 17–18, 1997, I visited the site and searched Kuiu Island beaches from south of the old cannery, to the head of the bay. Yéil kawóodi were found in strand lines of wave sorted particles on the upper beach, particularly on points near the head of the bay. They were not plentiful anywhere, although the best spots may not have been found.

What are Yéil kawóodi? Using a standard invertebrate zoology textbook for reference, the beads were found to be segments of sea lily or crinoid stems and arms. Sea lilies are related to sea urchins and starfish, and though they survive in small numbers, they were once so prolific that their dead bodies formed thick limestone deposits. However, in nearly two days of searching no crinoids were found in the local bedrock, only loose pieces on the beach.

Most starfish relatives (echinoderms) have a five-part radial symmetry, so most starfish have five legs or multiples of five and sea urchins have a mouth with five teeth. However, the textbook (Barnes 1968) says that they are fossil species of sea lilies, the oldest and most primitive of today's echinoderms.

The central "hole" in several of the Raven's beads collected at Yéil Kawóot show a star-shaped pattern, but most do not. This could be because not all segments are from the same part of the animal, or this may indicate the age of the fossils. One of the beads shows small bumps that appear to be where small arms were attached (like bumps on a sea-urchin shell where the spines attach).

What do geological studies tell us about the presence of crinoid fossils in Southeast Alaska? There is a U.S. Geological Survey bulletin (1241-C; Muffler 1967) on northwest Kuiu Island which shows a large deposit of crinoid limestone comprising the larger and more westerly of the two islands on the east side of Cornwallis Point and underlying the northeast trending drainage on the east side of the point. This crinoid limestone is judged to be of Mississippian age (about 350 million years ago, when most of the world's coal was being made).

The Yéil Kawóot area is mapped as part of the Halleck Formation ("a heterogeneous sequence of siltstone, sandstone, limestone, conglomerate, and basaltic volcanic rock"). The Halleck Formation is of Permian age, about 100 million years younger than crinoid limestone on the east side of the point. It is possible that some of the earlier crinoid limestone is incorporated in the Halleck Formation or the beads at Yéil Kawóot may have been picked up and moved by glaciers [or Raven] from the east side of the point to the west side.

tained its name. At one time there was a settlement here, but it was so ravaged by smallpox that only one Tanyeidí woman remained with her sick children. According to Emmons (n.d.):

> A Souke tee nadi [Suk̲tineidí] woman begged her to drown her sick children, but she would not listen and when they were taken from her and killed, she wandered away in the woods lamenting their death. The spirit of the yellow-cedar [*teey yéik*] heard her and, feeling sorry for her, embraced her and from this union the family was reestablished, and survives today [as the Teeyineidí].

Davidson Bay creek (*Suk̲tuhéen, "Stream in the Short Grass," #161* [*alternate location same as #178*]). It is likely from this stream, on a flat in Keku Strait south of Hamilton Bay, that the Suk̲tineidí clan derives its name. Dog salmon were said to mass in the grassy water at the mouth of the stream, and the people gathered there to harvest them.

Port Camden (*L'áan Yík, #189*). According to Garfield (1945), this bay was owned by the Suk̲tineidí, who used the mountain at the head of the bay (Éinaasháa, not mapped) as a crest on a dance shirt. Like Security Bay, this place also was known for its fall salmon run.

Gambier Bay (*Ldak̲éex̲', #8*). Located on eastern Admiralty Island, this bay was claimed jointly by the T'aak̲ú (Taku) and K̲éex̲' people and served as a border zone between the two territories. A small village was located near the cannery site there, and another settlement was reported between this site and the north arm of the bay (Goldschmidt and Haas 1998). Gambier Bay Jim, a well-known shaman from Gambier Bay, took his English name from this place.

Kooyú K̲wáan

The Kooyú people are closely related to the K̲éex̲' and Hinyaa Tlingit, and their k̲wáan boundaries overlap with those of both groups. Emmons (n.d.) states that the name "Kuyu" derives from the word "stomach," a metaphorical association referring to the shape of Kuiu Island or some bay in which the people first settled. The name refers to Tebenkof Bay which is said to resemble a stomach or "cave-like opening" (Herman Kitka Sr., interview). Tebenkof Bay was the site of numerous settlements and forts. However, much of the population there was decimated by smallpox epidemics in the nineteenth century. According to one elder, "The survivors from this epidemic walked across the island to the other side [K̲éex̲' territory] and later most of them went to Klawock and McCartney [Macartney]. However, they had formerly been Kake people. That is how the Klawock people came to use this island and claim this area in later years" (Goldschmidt and Haas 1998, 178). Raven clans included the L'uknax̲.ádi and Kooyu.eidí and the major Eagle/Wolf clan was the Naasteidí. All of these groups are believed to have migrated from the west coast of Prince of Wales Island. Historical population estimates for Kooyú K̲wáan vary from a high of 262 in the 1860s to a low of just 60 in 1890 (de Laguna 1990, 205).

Tebenkof Bay (*Kuyú, #254*) / *Bay of Pillars* (*Gwaat'ahéen, #227*). Tebenkof Bay was the hub of the Kooyú territory. Elders suggest there may have been as many as a dozen settlements in the bay over time, as well as numerous camps and fort sites. The bay supported a significant year-round community and abounded with fish and wildlife resources, including hair seal and sea otter, the latter of which has made a strong comeback in recent years along the west coast of Kuiu Island. Some of the human habitation sites here have been investigated recently by Sealaska (1975), and by Maschner (1992, 280), who argues that the distribution of prehistoric settlements at Tebenkof Bay was a function of key environmental variables, especially cardinal exposure, beach quality, and island size. Bay of Pillars was also a large and important historic settlement site, the inhabitants of which were known as K'waat'aneidí from the Native name for the bay. According to Charles Johnson (interview), the last surviving members of this group were Fred Friday and his brother Billy. He notes, "That clan, along with the Tebenkof people known as the Kooyú K̲wáan, were a sub-branch of the Suk̲tineidí."

Port Beauclerc (*Shak̲óon, #271*). The Tlingit name for Port Beauclerc was applied to a settlement there as well. Emmons (n.d.) reported only forty-five members of the Kooyú K̲wáan all living at the village here in 1889. With the introduction of schools and commerce centers at Kake and Klawock, however, the last Kooyú residents moved to these modern communities, though they continued to use aboriginal areas for seasonal activities.

Port Alexander area (*Shee Lunáa, #281*). Very little is known about the aboriginal geography of these places, other than that they were early settlements of the Kooyu.eidí, perhaps the oldest Kooyú K̲wáan clan.

S'awdáan Kwáan

Relatively little is known about S'awdáan Kwáan, centered in Holkham Bay. Its inhabitants, predominantly Raven Gaanax.ádi and Eagle/Wolf Sit'kweidí and Yanyeidí, were closely related to those residing in T'aakú Kwáan. According to Emmons (n.d.), the first settlement in Holkham Bay was founded by a branch of the group that eventually settled at Snettisham and became the Sit'kweidí. The region never supported a high population and the main village, S'awdáan (#3), was largely abandoned after the founding of Juneau.

In 1889 Emmons reported five community houses and a population not exceeding fifty. Both the kwáan and village name stem from the name for Endicott Arm (Tsu Dun, "The Hunting Ground," according to Emmons, but more likely S'awdáan, "Dungeness Crab Grounds"; a third interpretation is that the first syllable refers to the greenish color of the water). The kwáan boundaries extended from below Point Anmer at Port Snettisham to approximately Point Windham. Unlike the T'aakú Kwáan, S'awdáan territory did not extend across Stephens Passage to Admiralty Island.

Holkham Bay (Sit'kú, "Glacier Area," #2). With its rich glacial fjords (Endicott and Tracy arms), this bay was the seat of S'awdáan territory. In addition to the village below Sumdum Glacier, Emmons noted a "stockaded village" on Sumdum Island in 1869. Elders also mentioned a third settlement on the south shore of Endicott Arm, possibly in Sanford Cove, where Sumdum mining camp was established. The area was considered to be an excellent hunting ground for seal, which haul out on the icebergs in great numbers. Alexander Stevens (Goldschmidt and Haas 1998, 119) stated in 1946: "Endicott Arm is mostly used for seal... Charlie Sumdum used to live up Endicott Arm. He died about 1931, and nobody lives up there now... This is not very good country, though there are a few mink, marten, and other animals to be trapped in that territory. There is a good sockeye stream at Fords Terror. It is a bad place to get to because the tide runs at nine knots." This statement suggests several factors, beyond the founding of Juneau, that contributed to the depopulation of the S'awdáan territory over time.

As elsewhere, settlements that became depopulated were not abandoned altogether. S'awdáan territory continued to be used for subsistence and commercial production, as well as for commemoration.

Final Thoughts

Kéex', Kooyú, and S'awdáan kwáan geographic names reveal the power of place and the resonance and resilience of indigenous names on the land. Despite modest elders' claims that much of their language and culture had been lost, the place names data we collected proved extraordinarily rich and vital. Native place names continue to radiate myriad links to historical and contemporary cultural identities and practices.

Today, the Organized Village of Kake is using the results of the place names project to maintain tribe members' ties to the land through education and appropriate management of the natural and cultural resources tied to named sites.

Returning Home: The Odyssey of the Kaach.ádi

Johnny C. Jackson (Gooch Éesh, "Wolf Father") was born Johnny Sumdum at Sumdum Bay in 1893. His mother was of the Raven Kaach.ádi clan, and his father a member of the Eagle/Wolf Sit'kweidí clan. Mr. Jackson lived most of his life in Kake and was renowned as a clan historian and storyteller until his death in 1985 (see Dauenhauer and Dauenhauer 1994 for a more extensive biography). In 1979 he related the geographic narrative excerpted, translated, and mapped here, which is remarkable for its tracing of clan migrations, and for the thirty-six Tlingit place names he unpacks in the context of his people's history.

Now this is what I shall tell. My grandfathers had all replaced each other — the leaders of Kaach.ádi clan... when we still lived in the Interior [Canada]. Then we moved here, from the time of the Flood... They didn't care for the Interior, where the Flood had left them, since our former homes were on the coast. So they set out to search. Freshwater flows out into the salt water. So they followed the river. We who now live in Kake, we came out from the Nass [Naas] River area.

"Let's look for our original homeland," they said. So after a meeting they did... [After traveling northwest,] they found their homelands there. So they build houses there again. Across from here [at Keku Islands] they built houses there; their village used to be known as

K̲éex̲' Luwoolk'í [1; see migration story map]. They recognized that place. From there they began searching, out to the point: L'axwein Aan [2], L'axwein Héen [3], and X'aaltunoow [4]. Those were the places where they used to live, before the big Flood. They recognized these places. And here, the present site of Kake, the name of this place is Ta.aan [5]. Ta.aan.

From there south they recognized where their grandfathers once lived. The river — L'axwein Aan, L'axwein Héen, and X'aaltunoow. They had lived there with their tribal children. Our children's fort was close to shore. They called that fort X'aaltunoow. And the one farther out was K̲aach.ádi Noowú [6]. This, too, they recognized.

From that place they set out to search for their land across the water [Frederick Sound]. They headed across, saying, "Our land used to be in that direction." When they arrived there, they recognized K̲áach [7]. The one closer on this side, the water[fall] runs down into the salt water... It was just as they had been told, K̲áach Héen [8], flowing into salt water, full of salmon. Even their old fort was there, a K̲aach.ádi fort site [9; see below].

From there they began searching again. Inside the bay, they recognized where they, their children, and grandparents used to gather, process, and dry their harvest. The one at the head of the bay and the one down further they recognized as places they used to live. It was named Sit'k̲ú [10]. The lower one, Xakwli'héen [11], was where it was at.

From there north — Yoowka Noow [12], in back there is also a large salmon river. They recognized K̲utis'noow [9] also in the bay. Then by chance they came across Dliwuwu X'aa [13], a place they had been told about and recognized. The bottom was all marble rock, so it was easy to recognize.

Continuing south they came upon a small bay overgrown with dwarf maple growing. So it was named X'als'eeigeiyak'w [14]. South there's a point of land, there is a trail on the other side. Then on this side, X̲'algihéen [11], Kudakak̲ Héen [15], and their village used to be named K̲udadak Aan [16]. These places I have named are the areas used and claimed by the K̲aach.ádi clan. They also claimed all the islands in front of the bay [Neek, 17].

Further north all the way up to Ldak̲éex̲' [18] is claimed by those people who are related to us, they are called G̲aanax̲.ádi. G̲aanax̲.ádi claim from there north on into the bay up to Kanak̲'aa [19]. They had many forts in there; they knew the sites of their own forts...

X̲akwhéen [20]. There they used to gather and render herring for oil; they also dried halibut there, and black seaweed and red ribbon seaweed, and dried meat there. That is why so many from here used to gather there in the spring and fall...

From there a marker can be seen — it's red. It crosses over to K̲udadak Aan. People still gather food from there. Since our grandfathers have all gone on, [it's] up to us now. Until recently, I used to go there until my health no longer permitted it. They use to get fish there and it was a good place for *lein eetí* [food from the tidal area] from the beaches there.

The territory of the Angoon people starts at the island, Lisnoi Island, at the entrance to Eliza Harbor... towards Point Gardner [Taan X'aayí, 21]. From there towards here was an area we [the K̲aach.ádi] owned.

G̲atgeeya [22]. At G̲atgeeya, there are things that date back to the time of the Flood. The mountain was sticking out of the water. At the top of the mountain there is something that dates back to the big Flood. During that big flood the people tied a rope there... There were no storms during that flood; that is why not all the people perished. Those people that had tied up to that mountain, after the Flood receded they were safe here... There is a river there named Was'héeni [23]. Was'ineidí and those across at X̲'alchanhéen [24], some of them survived too. However, everyone else perished.

There is much history related to the big Flood, which has been told right up the present. *That is why the place names are the names of the different clans.* From Kooyú [#25] this way, the Kooyú K̲wáan and the Naasteidí intermarried. In Keinyík [26], the name of their village there is called Xóots Noow [27]. From there, in this direction, are Kooyú K̲wáan place names. Kwaat'aa Héen [Bay of Pillars, 28] was jointly owned by the Kooyú K̲wáan and Shayá K̲wáan [Rowan Bay, 29], who are known as the Shangukeidí clan... Coming this way, K̲úchx'w [Security Bay, 30] was claimed by the Tanyeidí clan... The last caretaker of Security Bay before I moved here was Nawnuk [John Nannauck].

[Concerning Tsaagweidí history of Saginaw Bay] the clan originally inhabiting this place was known as the Skanax̲.eidí [People of Skanáx̲, 31]. Their original village was Chana.aan [32]. Their fort names were: Taakw.aani Noow [33]; from there up to the head of the bay was Watlax̲'aak Noow [33]; another is Yankatudutináa* [35]; and then there is Woogaani Noow [36].

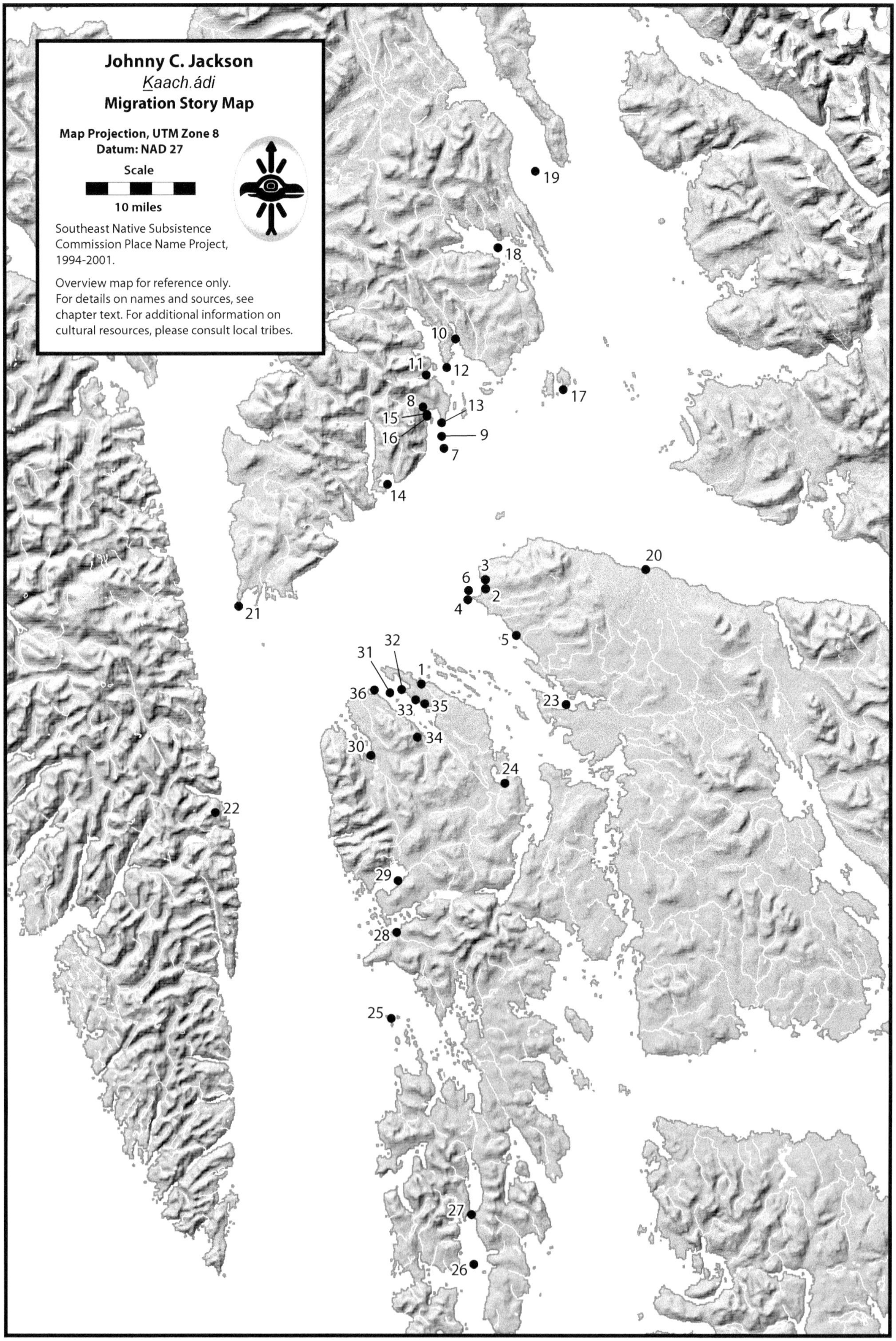

Johnny C. Jackson
Kaach.ádi
Migration Story Map
Map Projection, UTM Zone 8
Datum: NAD 27
Scale
10 miles
Southeast Native Subsistence Commission Place Name Project, 1994-2001.
Overview map for reference only. For details on names and sources, see chapter text. For additional information on cultural resources, please consult local tribes.
1
2
3
4
5
6
7
8
9
10
11
12
13
14
15
16
17
18
19
20
21
22
23
24
25
26
27
28
29
30
31
32
33
34
35
36

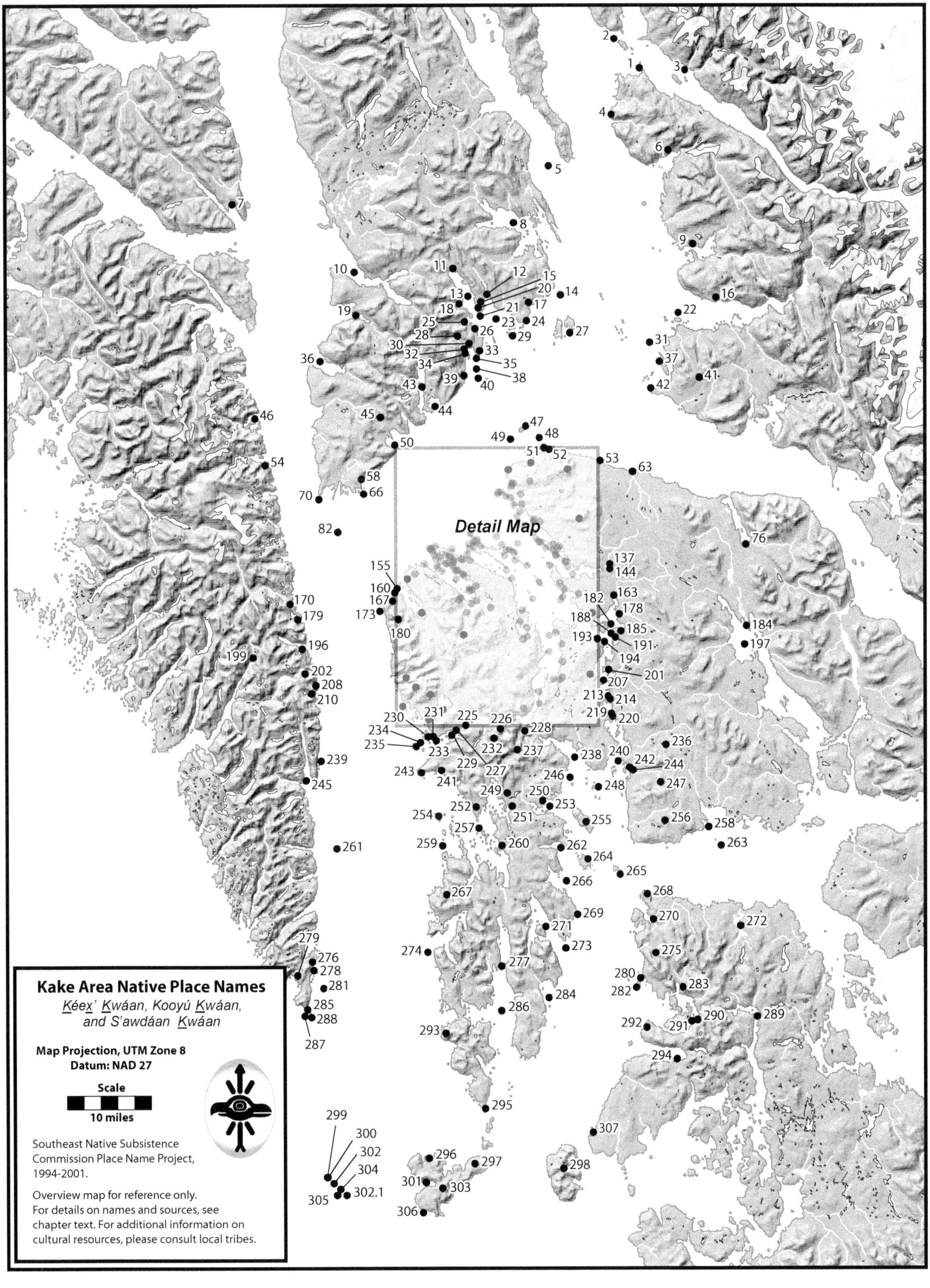

Kake Area Native Place Names

*Ḵéex' Ḵwáan, Kooyú Ḵwáan,
and S'awdáan Ḵwáan*

**Map Projection, UTM Zone 8
Datum: NAD 27**

Scale

10 miles

Southeast Native Subsistence
Commission Place Name Project,
1994-2001.

Overview map for reference only.
For details on names and sources, see
chapter text. For additional information on
cultural resources, please consult local tribes.

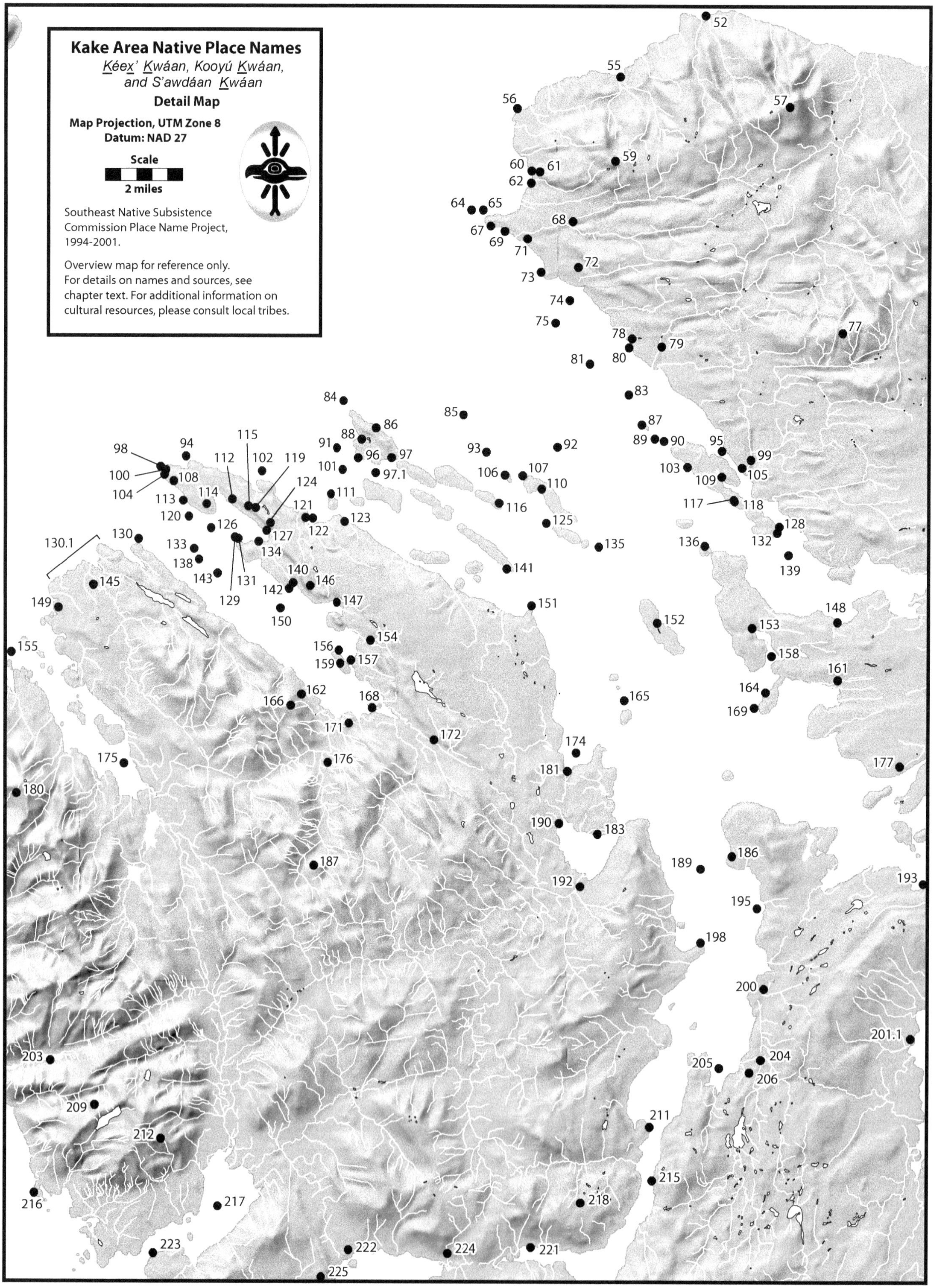
Kake Area Native Place Names
K̲éex' K̲wáan, Kooyú K̲wáan, and S'awdáan K̲wáan
Detail Map
Map Projection, UTM Zone 8
Datum: NAD 27
Scale
2 miles
Southeast Native Subsistence Commission Place Name Project, 1994-2001.
Overview map for reference only. For details on names and sources, see chapter text. For additional information on cultural resources, please consult local tribes.
52
55
56
57
59
60
61
62
64
65
67
68
69
71
72
73
74
75
77
78
79
80
81
83
84
85
86
87
88
89
90
91
92
93
94
95
96
97
97.1
98
99
100
101
102
103
104
105
106
107
108
109
110
111
112
113
114
115
116
117
118
119
120
121
122
123
124
125
126
127
128
129
130
130.1
131
132
133
134
135
136
138
139
140
141
142
143
145
146
147
148
149
150
151
152
153
154
155
156
157
158
159
161
162
164
165
166
168
169
171
172
174
175
176
177
180
181
183
186
187
189
190
192
193
195
198
200
201.1
203
204
205
206
209
211
212
215
216
217
218
221
222
223
224
225

Kéex' Kwáan, Kooyú Kwáan, and S'awdáan Kwáan Place Names

Asterisk indicates uncertain, unconfirmed, or partial; NM = not mapped.
Some names have more than one pronunciation or translation.

Map #	*Name*	*Translation*	*Location*
1	Kéet Noowú	Killer Whale Fort	Wood Spit at Endicott Arm
2	Sit'kú	Glacier Area	Holkam Bay, Endicott Arm, and Tracy Arm
3	S'awdáan	Dungeness Crab Grounds	Sumdum
4	Yadat'ook	Glancing at It	Cliff in Stephens Passage below entrance to Endicott Arm
5	Kanak'aa	Skinny*	Seymour Canal
6	S'iknaxsáani	Black Bear Community* Freshwater Bay	Windham Bay
7	Sit'kú	Glacier Area	Sitkoh Bay
8	Ldakéex'	*	Gambier Bay
9	Kashdán	Drops Down (entrance to salt lake)	Hobart Bay
10	Tsaagwáa	Harbor-Seal Ice Flows*	Hood Bay
11	Xáat Héen	Fish Creek	Pybus Bay
12	Sit'kú	Glacier Area	Pybus Bay
13	L'axséet	Dance* Pass	Pass in Pybus Bay
14	Neek Séet	Neek (#27) Pass/Strait	Pass inside The Brothers
15	Ch'aal' X'aka Xágu	Willow on Where It Was Sandbar	Henrys Arm area, Pybus Bay
16	Náx Tlein	Big Harbor	Port Houghton
17	Xutsnoowú T'éik	Inland Side of Brown Bear Fort (Admiralty Island)	Pybus Bay
18	Shkaxakwl'i Héen	Foaming Water	Donkey Bay, Pybus Bay
19	Chayéek	Arm Goes Way Up Inside*	Chaik Bay
20	Lux'aa	Nose Point	Pybus Bay area
21	Yoowka Noow	On the Stomach Fort	Pybus Bay area
22	Noow Tlein	Big Fort	Port Houghton, Crow Island
23	Noow K'iyeenaa	Sector in the Direction of the Rear of the Fort	Pybus Bay
24	X'aaksaxákw	Sandbar between Islands	Point Pybus
25	X'algihéen	Suds Creek	Pybus Bay
26	Tatóok X'ayee Aan	Cave at the Mouth of the Village	Iron Mike Cove in Pybus Bay
27	Neek	News (Rumor)	The Brothers
28	Káach Héen	Káach (#40) Creek	Creek at head of Little Pybus Bay
29	X'aaksaxákw [X'áat'i]	White Sand Between [Island]	Island at mouth of Little Pybus Bay

Map #	*Name*	*Translation*	*Location*
30	Daax̲anaheen	Fish Swimming alongside It	Rock off the mouth of creek (K̲áach Héen [#28]), head of Little Pybus Bay
31	S'é	Glacial Clay	Storm Island, Cape Fanshaw
32	K̲áach Kwásk'i	K̲áach (#40) Small Urine Pot	Small brook at head of Little Pybus Bay
33	G̲eey Ta Noow	Fort at the Head of the Bay	Island in Little Pybus Bay
34	K̲udadak Aan	Where People Come to [Visit] Village	Village at Little Pybus Bay
35	Dliwuwu X'aa	Whitish Point	Little Pybus Bay point
36	Naltóox̲ch'án	Round Hole at High-Water Mark*	Whitewater Bay, Admiralty Island
37	S'áx	Starfish	Whitney Island at Cape Fanshaw
38	K̲utis'noow	Looking-Out Fort	Little Pybus Bay, island at east entrance
39	K̲utis'héen	Looking-Out Creek	Creek at the mouth of Little Pybus Bay
40	K̲áach	*	Little Pybus Bay
41	Yakw Náx̲i	Canoe Harbor	Portage Farragut Bay to Port Houghton
42	Sax̲anx'aa	Love Point	Cape Fanshaw
43	Gúnx̲	Still Water* (shortcut/pass over mountain*)	Eliza Harbor
44	X̲'algéi G̲eiyák'u	Shining Entrance Little Bay	Woewodski Harbor
45	Shaak'w Wool	Hole in the Small Mountain	Chapin Bay and mountain behind
46	Tak̲as' G̲eey	Rock Crevice Bay	Takatz Bay
47	Kéin	*	Turnabout Island
48	Kéin Séet	Kéin (#47) Pass	Pass inside Turnabout Island
49	Kéin Yátx'i	Children of Kein (#47)	Rocks/islets by Turnabout Island
50	Takuwóox̲'	[Bay That Is] Wide at the Back/Head	Herring Bay
51	Haat X'aayí	Tide Point	Point near Kake
52	Woosh Kát Wat.il.át	Mouths of Streams Lie atop Each Other	Where two salmon streams converge at low tide, east of Pinta Point
53	Ch'ak'x'aayí	Eagle Point	North Kupreanof Island
54	T'aay X̲'é	Mouth of the Warm Springs	Warm Springs Bay
55	Cháatl Héeni	Halibut Creek	Sand beach inside Pinta Rocks
56	Cháatl Waak̲k'i X'aa	Halibut's Small Eye Point	Cape Bendel
57	L'axwein (Tl'axwein)	*	Turn Mountain
58	Xutsnoowú Tuk̲yee	Outlet of Brown Bear Fort	Tyee
59	Shaanák'w	Little Old Lady	Mountain near Kake (alternate location of #180)
60	L'axwein (Tl'axwein) Héen	L'axwein (#57) Creek	Above Point Macartney
61	Ligaaw Héen	Loud Waters	Above Point Macartney
62	L'axwein (Tl'axwein) Aan	L'axwein (#57) Village	Above Point Macartney
63	Xakwhéen	Sandbar Creek	Big Creek, north Kupreanof Island
64	K̲aach.ádi Noow	K̲aach.ádi Fort	Outer island off Point Macartney

Map #	*Name*	*Translation*	*Location*
65	X'átgu Noow	Shark Fort	Inner island off Point Macartney
66	Xalnú (X'alnú)	*	Carroll Island, off Admiralty Island
67	X'aaltunoow	Fort inside the Point	Point Macartney
68	Wat.ltaganís	Creek Mouth with Saplings	Stream north of Point White
69	Dei Gaashoowu Yé	Where the Trail Goes Down	Beach north of Point White
70	Taan X'aayí (Taan X'aa)	Sea Lion Point	Point Gardner
71	Dei Gaashoowu Aan	Village at the End of Dei Gaashoowu Yé (#69)	Near Point Macartney
72	Aan Luká	Village at the Point (nose)	Kake area
73	Deikinaa Xágu	Haida Sand Beach	Point White
74	Yook	Cormorant	Kake area
75	Teik Éedi	Bottomfish Hole of Teik (#86)	Between Payne Island and Point Macartney
76	Náaxdík'	Short Portage*	Portage Bay
77	Kéex'i Tlein	Big Kéex' (#80)	Mountain valley behind Kake
78	Wat.lateetk'	Sandbar at the Mouth of Stream	Small stream, north end of Kake
79	Gánák'w [Héen]	Small Firewood [Creek]	Gunnuk Creek
80	Kéex'	Going Dry*	Kake (originally Keku Islands)
81	Táax'aa Daax'áat'i	Island around the Mosquito	Mosquito Island
82	Teilnú	Pitchwood* Fort	Yasha Island
83	Aan Yakax'áat'i	The Island in Front of Town	Grave Island
84	Teik Lunáa	Around the Point (nose) of Teik (#86)	Keku Point
85	Deikéenáx Gasxíx	Dropped Way Out	Progressive Reef, Keku Islands
86	Teik	*	Payne Island
87	Woogaani Noow X'áat'	Burnt Fort Island	Burnt Island
88	Teik Tukyee	Bottom End of Teik (#86)	Payne Island, beach in west cove
89	Goox X'áat'ak'u	Slave Islet	Keku Strait island
90	Keitl X'áat'ak'u	Dog Islet	Keku Strait island
91	Yéil Gaachk'u Séet	Raven's Little Mat Pass	Flat-top rock in Keku Islands
92	Yéilch Wusxá	Raven Ate It (meat)	Keku Strait
93	Yéilch Wusxá	Raven Ate It (meat)	Keku Islands area (alternate location of #92)*
94	X'aayik Noow*	Inside the Point Fort*	Saginaw Bay*
95	L'axséet	Dance* Pass	Portage Bay, pass between Hamilton and Kupreanof islands
96	L'itkasatáxk'	——* Tail	Keku Islands area
97	Teik Séedak'u	Small Pass of Teik (#86)	Strait in Keku Islands
98	Goon Héen	Spring Water Creek	Saginaw Bay, east side of entrance
99	L'axséet Héen	Dance* Pass Creek	Sitkum Creek
100	Kéet Noowú	Killer Whale Fort	Saginaw Bay, Cornwallis Point

Map #	*Name*	*Translation*	*Location*
101	Yéil G̲áachk'	Raven's Little Mat	Keku Strait island
102	Shkawulhteetk' (Shkawushteetk')	Waves-Washing-Up Rock	Rock northeast of entrance to Saginaw Bay
103	L'áx̲	Dance	Hamilton Island
104	Skanáx̲ Lunáa	Around the Point (nose) of Skanáx̲ (#133)	Cornwallis Point
105	L'ax̲séet Héeni Wat Aan	L'ax̲séet Creek (#99) Mouth Village	Portage Bay / Sitkum Creek
106	Daalas'oox'	Milky around It	White Sand Island in Keku Islands
107	Shkas.áak'w	It (island) has a Lagoon [Lying] on It	North Keku Islands, Peggy Island
108	Skanáx̲ Tatóok*	Skanáx̲ (#133) Cave*	Cave at entrance to Saginaw Bay
109	L'ut'kasatá	Bite (flatten) Your Tongue*	Bay inside Hamilton Island
110	K̲óoshk' X'áat'i	Little Weeping Sore* (or man's name*) Island	Peggy Island
111	L'eetk'	Small Tail	Keku Point
112	Yaandayen Aan	Backpacking Village	Village at Halleck Harbor
113	K̲aa Káa Dagáat	Crumbling on People	North Halleck Harbor, crumbling cliff
114	Tatóok X̲'ayee Aan	Cave at the Mouth of the Village	North Halleck Harbor
115	Yoox̲ankoojeek (Yandayein Aan)	Curious about Pudenda (Packing Something Village)	Halleck Harbor
116	Tl'ik̲kasták̲k'	Little Poke*	Keku Islands*
117	Goonka.aan	Village on the Isthmus	Crow Bay, Hamilton Island
118	Gunax̲sa.aan	Isthmus ——*	Isthmus on Hamilton Island (first Teik̲weidí village)
119	K'óox Dzeitk'í	Marten's Little Ladder	Fossil Bluffs, Halleck Harbor
120	X̲'anax̲ Yaa Litch Yé	Place Where You Almost Slide Right Through	Home League Pass, Keku Islands
121	K̲éex̲' Luwoolk'í	Little Nostrils of K̲éex̲' (#122)	Opposite Halleck Harbor
122	K̲éex̲'	Going Dry*	Keku Islands village
123	Kóoshdaa Xágu	Land Otter Sand Beach	Beach on Northeast Kuiu Island
124	Xakwtú	Inside the Point (or sandbar)	Saginaw Bay, head
125	K̲óoshk' (a.k.a. #107)	Little Weeping Sore*	Keku Islands
126	Kalshíxwt (Shkas.áak'w)	[Sea Otter] Too Tired* (——* Lagoon)	Halleck Harbor
127	Skanáx̲ Noow	Skanáx̲ (#133) Fort	Saginaw Bay
128	L'áx̲ Tuk̲yee	Outlet of L'áx̲ (#103)	Southeast end of Hamilton Island
129	Chana.aan (Chun.aa)	——* Town (Smelly One)	Saginaw Bay
130	Woogaani Noow	Burned Fort	Saginaw Bay, mouth
131	Shalx̲'aak Noow	Between Hills Fort	Halleck Harbor
132	Yéil G̲eeyák'u	Raven Little Bay	Small cove on south Hamilton Island
133	Skanáx̲	Noisy Beach*	Saginaw Bay
134	Skanáx̲ Neejí	Skanáx̲ (#133) Beach	Southeast Halleck Harbor
135	Kals'íx'g̲aa	Moss on It	Three islands in the Keku Islands

Map #	*Name*	*Translation*	*Location*
136	T'akjaa X'aa	Exploding Rocks* Point	Point Hamilton
137	Lxáachduteen	The War Party Can't See It	Cathedral Falls Creek, above cliff
138	Yáay Eejí	Humpback Whale Reef	Rock in Saginaw Bay
139	Kóoshdaa Yaakw	Land Otter Canoes	Hamilton Bay
140	S'ikgeeyí	Black Bear Bay	East side of Saginaw Bay
141	Lax'nanook	Blue Heron Sits	Rock at south end of Narrow Island
142	Taakw.aani Noow	Winter Town Fort	East side of Saginaw Bay
143	Tsaa Eejí	Seal Reef	Reef off Sachem Island
144	Tawool	Hole in the Bottom	Fort at Cathedral Falls, Hamilton Bay
145	Gagaan Héeni	Sunshine Creek	Sunshine Creek, west of Saginaw Bay
146	Yankatudutináa*	Looking at the Shoreline*	Rocks in Saginaw Bay
147	Lxex'wxu.aan	Town Where No One Sleeps	Kake
148	Was'héeni	Louse (or triangular "green bug") Creek	Stream in south Hamilton Bay or Hamilton Bay itself*
149	Chadéink	Gray Berries Campsite	Cove south of Meade Point
150	Skanáx Aaní	Skanáx (#133) Country	Whole of Saginaw Bay and uplands
151	Léix'u Geeyák'w	Red Snapper Little Bay	Cove, northeast Kuiu Island
152	Keixeilnú	[——*] Surf Foam Fort*	Hound Island
153	Kóoshdaa Deiyí	Land Otter Trail	Dakaneek Bay, trail to salt lake
154	Kéet Lakahéen*	Dog* Creek	Below cannery in Saginaw Bay
155	Kanax.aangashú	Village That Extends Across	Christmas Island, Security Bay (or in Saginaw Bay)*
156	Yéil Kúdi	Raven's Nest	Head of Saginaw Bay
157	Yéil X'óowk'u	Raven's Little Blanket	Head of Saginaw Bay
158	Daakunéek'	Tidied Around*	Dakaneek Bay (including the salt lake)
159	Yéil Kawóot	Raven Beads	Beach on an island in Saginaw Bay
160	Aanyoo.átk X'áat'ak'w	Village between the Islands	Paralysis Point, Security Bay
161	Suktuhéen	Stream in the Short Grass	Davidson Bay creek or Big John Creek*
162	Tsaxwel X'áat'	Crow Island	Rock at head of Saginaw Bay
163	Was'xik.héen	Inside Was'héeni (#148)	River at head of Big John Bay
164	Yáay Lunáa	Humpback Whale Nose	Peninsula at northwest entrance to Davidson Bay
165	Yéilch Wusxá	Raven Ate It (meat)	Hare and Clark islands (see also #92, #93)
166	——* Noow	——* Fort	Saginaw Bay
167	S'ach.aaní	Fern Country	Cove east of Kingsmill Point
168	Wat.lax'aak Noow	Fort of Stream with a Ravine at the Mouth	Head of Saginaw Bay
169	Yáay	Whale	Salt Point, off Dakaneek Bay
170	Yéilch Awsigani Yé	Place That Raven Burned	Red Bluff Bay

Map #	*Name*	*Translation*	*Location*
171	Wat.lax̲'aak	Stream with a Ravine at the Mouth	Saginaw Creek
172	Naas Sháak	Head of the Naas (Nass River)	Straight Creek
173	Shaanák'w Seiyí	Area below Shaanák'w (#180)	Area around Kingsmill Point
174	X'wáts	Hard Club*	Gil Harbor
175	K̲úchx'w	Noisy*	Security Bay
176	Skanax̲héen	Skanáx̲ (#133) Creek	Saginaw Creek
177	Kaaguntéeyi	Can Go Way Inside (a harbor)	Entrance Island and cove
178	Ch'ayáa Héen	Ch'ayáa (#182) Creek	Big John Creek
179	Kátlx'*	*	Falls Lake
180	Shaanák'w	Little Old Lady	Kingsmill Mountain
181	Tayeidí G̲eeyák'w	Firecracker Seaweed Bay	Gil Harbor
182	Ch'ayáa	*	Big John Bay
183	X̲'aadéik'	*	Kadake Bay
184	Lukaax̲ (Lukaax̲ Héen)	In Haste (Off the Point* Stream)	Duncan Canal and estuary
185	Tóolk' T'eihéen	Creek behind Tóolk' (#188)	Creek on south side of Big John Bay
186	L'awx'aa	Sand Point	Sandy spit, mouth of Point Camden
187	Kooyú X'áat'	Cave-Like Entrance* Island	Kuiu Island
188	Tóolk'	Small Wooded Hill (or ridge)	Point in Big John Bay
189	L'áan Yík	Channel inside ——*	Port Camden
190	X̲'alchanhéen	Stinky Mouth Creek	Kadake Creek
191	Awdlisini X'áat'	Hidden Island	Islands in cove south of Big John Bay
192	Atahéen	Creek at the Back/Head [of the Bay]	Kadake Creek
193	Woosh Tayeex' Kalxwás'	They Hang [like Roots] under Each Other	Bench-terraced hillside, north entrance to Rocky Pass
194	Yakwxis'héen	Boat's Curved-Prow Creek	Rocky Pass, cove
195	S'ikháni	Black Bear Standing Up	Slough in Port Camden
196	Ldi.adi G̲eey	Empty Bay	Hoggatt Bay
197	X̲'akhanhéen	Stream That Stands In Between	Duncan Canal
198	Kals'oow X'aa	Point with Greenstone	Spit, west Point Camden
199	Shee	*	Baranof Island
200	Yéilch Yaawax̲ut'i X'aa T'éi	Raven Adzed [Three] Notches in a Rock Point	Small bay, east Port Camden
201	Yéik	Helper Spirit [of Shaman]	High Island, Rocky Pass
201.1	K̲áa Tlein Héeni (K̲aatléinu)	Big Man Creek (Person ——*)	Creek near High Island (Kuiu side), Rocky Pass*
202	G̲atgeey	Sockeye Bay	Gut Bay
203	G̲ákw	Slippery*	Washington Bay
204	Ldix̲'tahéen	Creek at the Back of Ldíx̲' (#206)	Creek off the small cove in Port Camden
205	Nék	*	Island in Port Camden

Map #	Name	Translation	Location
206	Ldíx̱'	Neck	Small cove in Port Camden
207	Ḵéex̱' Yík	Pass inside Ḵéex̱' (#80)	Rocky Pass
208	Katx'úl'	The Water Upwells in the Middle of the Bay [like a Whirlpool]	Arena Cove
209	G̱akwsáani	G̱ákw (#203) Freshwater Bay*	Stream, south of Washington Bay
210	Aani.a Nat*	——* Village	Below Gut Bay*
211	Kawjixitk'i Yé	Place with Little Paintings on It	Point Camden
212	Shánkw	Highest Peak	Highest peak north of Rowan Bay
213	Áa Kakook'aayi Yé	Place That Is Too Narrow	The Summit in Rocky Pass
214	Dzánti Áayi	Flounder Lake	Lagoon in Rocky Pass, near Summit Island
215	X̱'eikwás'	Chamber Pot* Mouth	Point Camden, stream comes down a cliff
216	Yéil Noowú	Raven's Fort	Point Sullivan
217	Shayá	Face of Mountain	Rowan Bay
218	Shaa Ḵwáani	Mountain Dwellers	Mountain inside of Port Camden
219	X̱óots Shaayí Té	Brown Bear Head Rock	Island in pass south of Summit Island
220	X'áat' Séet	Island Passage	Rocky Pass*
221	Keita.áak'w	Upwelling Little Lake	Shallow lake, Port Camden
222	Yan Wushinuwu X'áat'	Island Floating in the Refuge of the Shore	Bay of Pillars
223	Shánkw Séet	Pass below the Highest Peak	Pass at mouth of Rowan Bay
224	Chas'héenak'u	Humpback Salmon Little Creek	Creek north of salt lake, Bay of Pillars
225	Shis'ḵ Daakeidí	Island with a Group of Small Trees	Island in Bay of Pillars
226	Kalaḵú Áa	A Salt Lake, Always Surging (from tides)	Upper Bay of Pillars including lakes
227	Gwaat'ahéen	Trout Stream	Bay of Pillars and Kwatahein Creek
228	Yéil Héeni	Raven's Creek	Creek, head of Point Camden
229	Séetnáx̱ Tayeidí Geesh X̱oo X'áat'	Kelp in the Pass between the Island and the Mainland	Bay of Pillars
230	Gwaat'ahéen X'aká	At the Mouth (confluence) of Gwaat'ahéen (#227)	Island, mouth of Bay of Pillars
231	Kasg̱eeyí Séet	Artificial Bays Strait	Mouth of Bay of Pillars
232	Kalaḵú	Always Surging	Bay of Pillars, Kutlaku Lake area
233	Dakdachunséet	Pass Headed Out	Mouth of Bay of Pillars
234	Yaana.eit X'áat'ák'u	Wild Celery Small Island	Bay of Pillars, island
235	Daalateetk'	Little [Rock with] Waves Washing Up on It	Bay of Pillars, rock
236	Tanahéen	Jumping Fish Creek	Tunehean Creek
237	Éinaa Sháa	Drying-Rack Mountain	Mountain between Pillar Bay and Point Camden
238	L'ax̱'anḵú	Inside ——*	Three Mile Arm

Map #	Name	Translation	Location
239	Taaxyee* Aan	——* Village	Lords Pocket
240	Axaa X'aayí	Paddle Point	Rocky Pass, between Lovelace and Tunehean creeks
241	Kétldalxu Héen (Kichdaxuhéen)	Dog Doo Creek (——* Creek)	Small creek inside north entrance to Tebenkof Bay
242	Ḵóoshk'	Little Weeping Sore*	Keku Strait cove (duplicate of #125?)
243	Texanx'aa Lunáa	Around the Point by the Rock	Point Ellis and rock offshore
244	Yakwxis'héen (Yaakw Xées'i Héen)	Boat Prow Creek	Creek in Rocky Pass, above (or below*) Lovelace Creek
245	X'eixdasaa	Breathes Out [through] the Mouth	Mist Cove, Fawn Lake creek
246	K'uxeet Aa	Salt Lake Lagoon*	Seclusion Harbor
247	Watkalshéix'w	Red Alder at Mouth	Lovelace Creek
248	Katxaan Tan Daa	Fish Jumping Around by It	Monte Carlo Island
249	Aanlkwá	Village ——*	Alecks Creek, Tebenkof Bay
250	Daax'un.áa	Fourth Lagoon	No Name Bay
251	Goon	Spring (of water)	Village at mouth of Alecks Creek
252	Kalhin Aan	——* Water Village	Happy Cove, Tebenkof Bay
253	K'alsa*	Unnamed*	No Name Bay area
254	Kuyú	Inside of a Cave	Tebenkof Bay
255	L'áach	*	Conclusion Island
256	Ḵushnahéen	Unclean Creek*	Kushneahin Creek
257	Shéen	A Carved Wooden Bailer	Gap Point, Tebenkof Bay
258	Lukax.aan	Off the Point (nose) Village*	Totem Bay, village site
259	Kalshaayi Noow	Hilly Fort	Windfall Island, Tebenkof Bay
260	Daxun Áa	Lake Facing [Out of the Woods] (guarding, watching)	Narrow pass in Tebenkof Bay
261	Shee Yá	Face of Shee (Baranof Island)	Cape Ommaney to Peril Strait
262	Awljooch*	*	Alvin Bay, south Rocky Pass
263	S'éech X'anóok	*	Shingle Island, near Totem Bay
264	Shaxán	*	Sumner Island
265	Éisht'	*	Strait Island
266	Ḵaaseitáaw	Stealing Something*	Reid Bay
267	Tíxwt	Stamped His Feet (applauding)	Gedney Harbor
268	Xaaséedák'u	Small Pass through Which the War Party Goes [at High Tide]	Point Baker
269	Ḵaach X'aa Yadaa	On the Face of Ḵaach* Point	Boulder Point
270	Kél	*	Port Protection
271	Shakóon	Flicker Head*	Port Beauclerc, south Kuiu Island
272	L'ax'wgeeyí	Red Ochre Bay	Red Bay
273	Shakóon X'ananóok	Shakóon (#271) Mouth Rock*	Port Beauclerc

Map #	*Name*	*Translation*	*Location*
274	Saná	Voicing in There*	Port Malmesbury
275	Tatóok	Cave	Hole-in-the-Wall
276	L'áach Séet	——* Pass	Breakfast Rock Reef, Port Alexander
277	Xóots Noow	Brown Bear Fort	Affleck Canal, point at Bear Harbor
278	Tsaa Teix'í Séet Aan	Seal Rocks Pass Village	Breakfast Rock, Port Alexander
279	Yéil Yakwdeiyí	Raven's Canoe Trail	Beach at cove in Larch Bay
280	Alux̲'áak	——* Between	Barrier Island pass
281	Shee Lunáa	Nose (point) of Shee (Baranof Island)	Port Alexander area
282	Kanook	Something Sitting There*	Barrier Islands (both)
283	S'ux̲daa*	*	Calder Bay
284	Ts'ix'w (S'ix'w) G̲eeyák'w	Dish Little Bay	Louise Cove
285	Shee X'aa Lunáa	Around the Point of Shee	Cape Ommaney
286	Keinyík	Inside ——*	Affleck Canal
287	Shee Sáank' Séet	Pass at End of Shee (Baranof Island)	Pass between Wooden Island and Cape Ommaney
288	Shee Sáank'	Little [Island] at the End of Shee (Baranof Island)	Wooden Island
289	Kayéen Ká	On ——*	El Capitan Passage
290	Chax̲.áayi (Shakan*)	Grebelet Lake (——*)	Shakan and lake above
291	Shakan* X'úx Héen	——* through Water	Shakan Strait
292	Sheishóox̲	Rattle	Hamilton Island, Shakan Bay
293	S'eesaa	Wind Blew It Away	Table Bay
294	Eesh Yík (Kaxt*)	Inside a Fish Pool* (——*)	Shipley Bay
295	Áat Séet	Áat's (#303) Pass	Cape Decision pass
296	Áat K̲úx̲k	Áat's (#303) Reef	Coronation Island, harbor
297	Áat Daa (Aan Daa)	Áat (#303) Island (Surrounding the Village*)	Coronation Island
298	Náash	*	Warren Island
299	Deikinoow (Sdaalk' Kinaahàat*)	Far Out to Sea Fort (No Place to Anchor*)	Big Hazy Islet
300	K̲úx̲k (K̲úx̲k'*)	Flat Reef (man's name who always went for seagull eggs there)	Hazy Islands, east of Big Hazy Islet
301	Sdaalk' Kinaahàat* G̲eey	No Place to Anchor* Bay	Coronation Island bay
302	Taan Shaayí Séet*	Sea Lion Head Pass	Hazy Islands, easternmost pass
302.1	Taan Shaayí	Sea Lion Head	Southernmost of Hazy Islands
303	Áat	*	Coronation Island
304	Taan Shaayí X̲oo	Among the Sea Lion Head	Hazy Islands, easternmost islet
305	T'aaw Túlx'u	Feather Drill	Hazy Islands, southernmost islet
306	Yaandayéin	Packing Something Heavy*	Coronation Island, south end (or second largest of Hazy Islands)*
307	Náash Séet	Náash's (#298) Pass	Warren Channel, Cape Pole area

Map #	*Name*	*Translation*	*Location*
NM	Deikeenaa Xágu	Haidas' Sandbar	Point White area
NM	Éinaasháa	Fish Rack Mountain	Mountain at head of Port Camden
NM	Jigúk	*	Red Bluff Bay
NM	Káach.adagook'*	Beach Back of Káach* (#40*)	Bay of Pillars or Little Pybus Bay*
NM	L'achneech	——* Beach	Shoreline in Saginaw Bay
NM	L'akadaxach* Aan (Kaa Káa Dagáat Aan)	——* Village (Crumbling on People Village)	Saginaw Bay, entrance to Halleck Harbor
NM	Taan Kanoow	Fort on Top of the Sea Lions	Point Macartney area
NM	Tax'w Náx'w*	——* Passage*	Portage to Farragut Bay*
NM	Ts'axweil Noow	Crow Fort	Fort in Saginaw Bay
NM	Yakwxdují	They Think It's a Canoe	Petroglyph near Security Bay, exact location uncertain

8. *Shtax'héen K̲wáan*

Shtax'héen was the largest and perhaps most powerful southern Tlingit k̲wáan at the advent of historical contact. Their geographical position was analogous to the powerful northern Jilk̲áat (Chilkat) in that they controlled a major river, the Stikine (Shtax'héen, #83), which provided access and a profitable trade corridor to the Interior. Building this trade allowed the Shtax'héen K̲wáan to accumulate great wealth and prestige. The k̲wáan appears to have been formed at an early date by groups that migrated down the Stikine River, and their territory was among the largest of any group in Southeast Alaska in terms of population, geographic area, and coastline. The boundaries of the k̲wáan extended along the mainland from Farragut Bay in the north to the foot of the Cleveland Peninsula in the south and as far west as northeastern Prince of Wales Island and southeast Kupreanof Island. Thus, the Shtax'héen groups controlled not only the large mainland rivers but also the major inland marine waterways in central Southeast Alaska. The vast resources encompassed within this territory and its links to the Interior supported a comparatively high population of some 1,500 in 1840–41 (de Laguna 1990, 205). Although Shtax'héen people were tenacious and largely successful in defending their territory and trade from encroachments by the Russians and the Hudson Bay Company in the early nineteenth century, smallpox, measles, and tuberculosis epidemics, combined with the ill effects of the American military occupation and the Cassier mining boom in the 1870s, reduced the population to several hundred by 1890. Despite these assaults, the Shtax'héen K̲wáan has endured and today is centered in the communities of Wrangell and Petersburg. Clans on the Raven side included the Kiks.ádi, Teeyhíttaan, K̲aach.ádi, Kaasx̲'agweidí, and Taalk̲weidí, and on the Eagle/Wolf side, the Naanyaa.aayí, S'iknax̲.ádi, Kayáashkiditaan, X̲ook'eidí, and the X̲eel K̲wáan.

We documented more than 160 place names in this region. Our project was carried out in conjunction with the Wrangell Cooperative Association and the Petersburg Indian Association. This project represents the culmination of work by many individuals and groups. Richard Stokes served as the local research coordinator for the fieldwork. Other key contributors included: Herbert Bradley, George Davis, Forrest DeWitt Sr., Vesta Dominicks and Walter Williams, Frank Gordon, Clarence Jackson, Johnny C. Jackson, Martha Jaeger, Ethelyn Lopez, Richard Newton, and many others. We also recognize the contributions of past researchers and visitors to the region, including, William P. Blake (1868), Frederica de Laguna (1960, 1972), George Emmons (1911, 1991, n.d.), Viola Garfield (1945), Walter Goldschmidt and Theodore Haas (1998), Edward Keithahn (1945, 1966), Ronald Olson (1967), Chris Rabich-Campbell (1988), Louis Shotridge (n.d.), and John Swanton (1908, 1909). Harold Martin and Thomas Thornton carried out additional fieldwork on behalf of SENSC. Jeff Leer of the Alaska Native Language

Local research coordinator Richard Stokes (center) and representatives of the Southeast Native Subsistence Commission, Harold Martin (left) and Tom Thornton (right), meet to discuss Shtax'héen area place names with Richard Inkster (second from left) of the Tahltan First Nation at the Nation's headquarters in Telegraph Creek, B.C., October 1999. Photo by Jim Leslie.

Center, John Marks of the Sealaska Heritage Institute, and James Crippen provided linguistic review. Additional support was provided by the Tahltan Band of Telegraph Creek, B.C., the U.S. Forest Service, Alaska Waters, Inc., John Feller, and the Wrangell Museum.

Some Important Named Sites

Named places within the ḵwáan included many major bays, streams, and islands, where various clans settled and from which they took their names.

Eastern Passage / Blake Channel (Daḵséet, #78). Prior to settling at present day Wrangell, the early Shtax'héen villages had been situated on the mainland along this passage. According to Ronald Olson (1967, 32), the Naanyaa.aayí established the first village at Shumacher Bay (where the Wrangell Institute was later built) and called it Ḵeishangita.áan* (Alder Top* Village, #79). Later, the group moved to Choox'as Aan (Waterfall Town, #75), which stood five miles below the mouth of the Stikine River at Mill Creek and reminded them of their earlier home. Finally, the group moved to Shaaxhít.aan (Driftwood Town, #71), where the people, lacking proper tools, built houses out of driftwood. This town name also sometimes has been translated as "Willow Town" (Ch'aal'it.aan), but elder Charles DeWitt (James Crippen, pers. comm. 2007) is certain it is "driftwood" and not willow, having heard the story of its construction from his father, Forrest DeWitt Sr., and other Shtax'héen Ḵwáan elders. Reportedly, the people moved here because it offered more sun, shellfish, and game birds (R. Olson 1967, 49), though Emmons (n.d.), Edward Keithahn (1945), and elders we interviewed at Wrangell suggest it was partly the result of a feud. The other Shtax'héen clans followed and this site, also known as Old Wrangell, became the principal settlement of the ḵwáan beginning perhaps in the early eighteenth century until 1837, when the village of Wrangell was established.

Bradfield Canal / Anan Creek (An.áan, #91). Bradfield Canal boasted several settlements and camps, the most important of which was Anan Creek, from the Tlingit An.áan (Resting Village, #91). This creek supported excellent salmon fishing, with an especially large run of humpbacks, as well as an abundance of wildlife. Today the site is known among tourists for its brown and black bear populations which feast on the salmon and can be viewed from an observatory erected near Anan Creek falls. Not

far from here was a place called As.áat that was said to be a cliff "that produces magic." Shtax'héen Ḵwáan elder Herb Bradley (1990) relates how his first cousin Henry made a wish there that came true:

> It's a cliff, like this see…you have to go around…to get there. And they told Henry…Henry was about 16 or 18 maybe, "Now before you look you make a wish and you have to tell me before you look, all right?" "I wish that [I have] all girls" [Henry said]. [*narrator laughs*] And they claimed that these little midgets used to come out and play; now you just see their tracks. Nine girls [he had], no brothers…It works!

Tuḵutl'gu Aan (Mud inside the Village, #87) was another important settlement in Bradfield Canal, located at Marten River.

Wrangell (Ḵaachxan.áak'w, Little Lake Accessible to People, #72). According to Emmons (n.d.), the Tlingit name for this settlement was inspired by the "peculiar configuration of the shore" in the "lake-like" harbor here, which was said to resemble a man's hip. More likely, however, it comes from the Tlingit word for "accessible" (Jeff Leer, pers. comm.). A third possible explanation is that the place name is derived from a local man's name, Ḵaachxán (or Ḵaachxán). According to Charles and Margaret DeWitt (James Crippen, pers. comm. 2007), Ḵaachxán wanted to live away from other people, and so he built a house on the small island in the middle of what is now Wrangell Harbor, Shakes Island (from the Tlingit Sheiksh). His family gradually moved in with him and the bay became known for him. In the old days the mouth of the bay went dry (or almost dry) at low tide, so the bay appeared to be a lake separate from the salt water, which is why they called it *áak'w* (little lake or lagoon) rather than *geey* (or, locally, *geiy*, meaning "bay").

The Native community of Wrangell resettled here after the establishment of the Hudson's Bay trading post in 1840. Before Hudson's Bay Company, it was a Russian garrison, and, subsequent to the American occupation, it became the site of a U.S. military fort and the principal village for both Natives and non-Natives.

Helm Bay (Kíks, #135). Located on the southeastern side of the Cleveland Peninsula, Helm Bay was an early settlement site for the Kiks.ádi clan, and it may be from here that they derive their present name. However, other sources suggest the original "Kíks" from which the clan takes its name is in the vicinity of Nass River (R. Olson 1967, 31).

Port Stewart (*G̱aanáx̱*, #124). The G̱aanax̱.ádi and G̱aanax̱teidí clans derive their names from this bay, which was said to provide excellent shelter. Originally, the two groups lived as one in a single settlement but later split, with the G̱aanax̱teidí establishing a separate village near the head of the bay. When Vancouver's ships stopped here in 1784, these groups greeted him and exchanged gifts. Later the G̱aanax̱.ádi and G̱aanax̱teidí moved north to T'aaḵú (Taku) and Jilḵáat (Chilkat) country, among other places (see R. Olson 1967).

Stikine River (*Shtax'héen*, #83). According to Emmons (n.d.), the name of the river reportedly refers to the copious amounts of glacial mud brought down by the river or, alternatively, from the phrase "Tu tuck"(possibly *dutáx*, "to bite") which he interprets as "cold water that makes the teeth chatter." Tlingits typically interpret the name as "biting itself water." According to James Crippen (pers. comm. 2007), a descendant of Shtax'héen Ḵwáan, "The river's name seems to come from the idea of the circular motion of a dog trying to bite its own tail. This motion is found in the many whirlpools and eddies in the river, particularly near the mouth of the Stikine Grand Canyon." The river served as the main artery for food, travel, and trade, and, like the Jilḵáat and the Chilkat River, all the major Shtax'héen groups had fishing camps along it. The rich watershed of the Stikine also provided residents with all five species of salmon, eulachon, and other fish, wildlife, and plants; even valuable obsidian could be found upriver

Chief Shakes is not the name of a single Naanyaa.aayí leader but rather a lineage of leaders who inherited this title. The original Chief Shakes house was built by Ḵaachxán, who wanted to live away from other people, and thus built his house on the small island in the middle of what is now Wrangell Harbor, Shakes Island (from the Tlingit Sheiksh). His family gradually moved in with him and prospered, and the area became known for the Tlingit leader and his prominent house. The Taalḵunax̱k'u Shaa (#20) crest is displayed to the right of the door. Alaska State Library, Winter & Pond Photograph Collection, P87-0117.

at Mount Edziza. As an ancient migration and trade corridor, the Stikine figures in many clan oral histories and interactions with the Interior Taaltan Kwáan. The following Dakl'aweidí legend is one example:

> The legendary home of the clan was far up the Stikine, about a hundred and fifty miles. Their village, still occupied by a few of the clan, was called Takun [Dakl'éiw, #10]. In their migration they came down the river on a raft and reached a point where a glacier blocked the valley. Here they sent an elderly couple down on a raft to see if the tunnel under the glacier could be negotiated. They stood up a small tree with feathers tied to the tip to test the height of the passage. As the two set forth they sang a song. The passage was negotiated safely and the rest of the people followed. (R. Olson 1967, 32)

Landmarks of special significance on the Stikine were taken as crests, including a prominent mountain peak rising above the river's banks, Taalkunaxk'u Shaa (#20), and Tlon* (not mapped), an unusual rock located upriver.

It also may have been a place on the Stikine that inspired the Kayáashkiditaan name. According to Emmons (n.d.), the clan took its name from the site of their original house (Kayáash, #51) on Reindeer Island at the mouth of the Stikine River. According to Forrest DeWitt Sr. (James Crippen, pers. comm. 2007), the Kayáashkiditaan clan is named for their original house, Kayáashka Hít (Platform House). This house was composed of people who moved out of a Naanyaa.aayí house that had become so crowded residents were forced to sleep on boards laid across the rafters, a location normally reserved as a storage platform (like an attic). The Kayáashkiditaan claim Reindeer Island.

Etolin Island. Like Wrangell Island, Etolin Island also afforded protection and resources combined with easy access to the Stikine River. The Xook'eidí, or Snag Creek

---

The S'iknax.ádi (People of S'iknáx), like many Tlingit clans, take their name from a place on the land where they settled. The following excerpt is taken from tape recordings made in the 1970 and 1980s of L'eeneidí elder Forrest DeWitt Sr. (Héennak'w Taax'w), and transcribed from the Tlingit by James Crippen (Dzéiwsh), a descendant of Shtax'héen Kwáan. Mr. DeWitt locates S'iknáx near Telegraph Creek, British Columbia. Like several other clans, including the Dakl'aweidí, the group later migrated down the Stikine and settled in Southeast Alaska. The S'iknax.ádi became centered in the Wrangell area, although some segments of the clan later became associated with Limestone Inlet and Taku Harbor (see the T'aakú Kwáan section of chapter 4). Mr. DeWitt's narrative also shows how S'iknax.ádi symbolic property (at.óow), *such as personal names like Shaal.aaní, records the historical geography of the clan.*

There was a place
up in
Telegraph Creek
I guess it's hundred miles up from the salt water
in the river
I knew a ways
below,
call place S'iknáx.
And that's the town
before they moved down here.
Down salt water.
'Cause they move back an' fort' all the time
to salt water.
. . . . .
It's all sandy places,
sand, sandy place.
And then they used to have Indian trap there,
it run by water power, that's the way they made it
at that time.
They never used no gaff hook.
They running that
water wheel
and the wheel [tree'd*] right in the
right in the
bank
'n' there they'd get it.
See, they never used no gaff hook.
See, they got a name outta that,
they called Shaal.aaní.
Shaal.aaní.
Sháal means a fish trap
in Tlingit.
So which is my brother in law, the oldest one, that's his name.

People (Emmons n.d.; R. Olson 1967, 58; Swanton 1908), settled here at a place now called Olive Cove (X̱ook', #89), or possibly Kunk Creek. Similarly, the Tansiyageidí,* a small branch of the Kiks.ádi clan, took their name from their main salmon stream on the island, Tans* (#93), at McHenry Inlet (R. Olson n.d.). The Dak̲l'aweidí are also said to have once inhabited and utilized much of Etolin Island, where many petroglyphs bearing the image of their principal crest, the killer whale, are found.

Thomas Bay (*Taalk̲ú, #25*). The Taalk̲weidí take their name from this glacial bay, which is said by some to resemble a *táal*, or wide-mouthed basket, though the name is typically pronounced with a low tone, and thus may refer to something else. The Taalk̲weidí are said to be the only Wrangell clan that traces their origins in the Shtax'héen K̲wáan back to the Flood (R. Olson 1967, 57). According to their legend, the bay was carved by the powerful ice spirit Sít' Yéik (Glacier Spirit) in his "rush to embrace the salt water" (Emmons n.d.). The bay's entrance (Kax̲kuyéndu Áa, #25.1), however, was blocked by a mighty spirit, "Kohk-kah-on-to-ah" (Kax̲kuyéndu) who dwelt in a large underwater rock home and was guarded by many spirits. Many Tlingits lost their lives attempting to bypass these spirits and enter the bay, including the father of a family that lived at the bay's entrance. His sons trained hard to avenge their father's death and, following the advice of their grandmother, succeeded in negotiating past the nefarious spirits and their traps, penetrating the perilous entrance to the bay, and killing the monster, who was then transformed into a rock that can be seen to this day at the head of the bay (Emmons n.d.; Swanton 1908, 415). Thereafter, they became the Taalk̲weidí in honor of their purchase of the bay with their father's life, and established their village at Wood Point (Taalk̲ú Aan, #23). The monster-transformed-into-stone became one of their crests. The landmark mountain now called Devils Thumb (Taalk̲unax̲k'u Shaa, "Mountain at the Back of Taalk̲ú," #20) also became the crest of the Taalk̲weidí, as this is where they sought refuge when driven from Taalk̲ú by the great Flood. A segment of the Taalk̲weidí later moved to Duncan Canal, where they became Lukaax̲.ádi, again taking their name from their place of dwelling. In historic times, perhaps 150 years ago, a major avalanche is reported to have wiped out the village of Taalk̲ú Aan.

LeConte Bay (*Xeitl G̲eeyí, #35*). This name literally means "Thunder Bay" and derives from the cacophony of calving at LeConte Glacier (Xeitl Sít', #29) which reverberates within the bay. This bay also was inhabited by the Taalk̲weidí. The bay also supports large concentrations of marine mammals, especially hair seal, which local Tlingits still hunt there.

Petersburg (*Séet Ká, "On the Channel," #31*). The modern settlement, a major fishing community of some three thousand mainly non-Native residents, overshadows a long-abandoned village just across the channel, now labeled Kupreanof on USGS maps. Occupied by several Shtax'héen clans, the original settlement was known

---

How Cone Mountain and the Brown Bear became Sacred to the Naanyaa.aayí

This story is adapted from John R. Swanton's Tlingit Myths and Texts *(1909, 231), and was recorded from the Kaasx̲'agweidí leader K̲aadaashaan in Wrangell in 1904. It shows well how events and features anchored in particular landscapes become sacred elements of clan's heritage, or* shagóon.

At the time of the Flood the Naanyaa.aayí were climbing a mountain on the Stikine River, called Sêku'qłe-ca [Seikook̲léi* Shaa, #67], and a brown bear and a mountain goat went along with them. Whenever the people stopped, these two animals stopped also, and whenever they moved on the animals moved on. Finally they killed the bear and preserved its skin with the claws, teeth, and so forth, intact. They kept it for years after the Flood, and, as soon as it went to pieces, they replaced it with another, and that with still another up to the present time. This is why they claim the brown bear. During the times when this bear skin has been shown thousands of dollars worth of slaves and furs have been given away. Shakes [Sheiksh], head chiefs of this clan, would go up to a row of slaves and slap each one, upon which the slave would either have to be killed or sent home. This is why they gave great names to their children. They were very proud of owning this bear and did all kinds of things toward it. That is why all Alaska speaks of the Naanyaa.aayí as the chief ones owning the brown bear. Very many songs were composed concerning it, with words such as these, "Come here, you bear, the highest bear of all bears."

in Tlingit as Aansadaak'w (Village Before, #33; see R. Olson 1967, 31). Later, when steamships began to ply the Wrangell Narrows, the channel became known as Gánti Yaakw Séedi (Steamboat Pass, #36).

Brown Cove (*Kaasx̱'aa,* #26*). Located just north of Petersburg, this village was founded by the Kaasx̱'agweidí clan, who took their name from the place. In addition to the village, the bay is also said to house several petroglyphs, perhaps relating to the clan's history and identity.

Duncan Canal (*Lukaax̱, #34.1*). This canal and its famous salt marshes were used extensively for hunting and trapping. A fort site and a productive salmon stream (from which the bay probably takes its name) were also located within the canal. The Lukaax̱.ádi, the well-known Raven clan today associated with northern Southeast Alaska, trace their origins to this creek (cf. R. Olson 1967, 32; Emmons n.d.). However the site proved uninhabitable in winter because the navigable waters leading to and from the village would freeze over. Consequently, the Lukaax̱.ádi migrated north, first to Excursion Inlet and eventually to Chilkoot (Jilḵoot) and Dry Bay.

Chickamin River (*X̱eel, #106*). This river was named for the foam at its mouth, and is the birthplace of the X̱eel Ḵwáan or "Foam People." It was an important eulachon fishery and subsistence camp.

Salmon Bay (*Dagák' Diyé,* #84*). According to William Paul (n.d.) of the Teeyhíttaan clan, this bay on eastern Prince of Wales Island was among the first places settled in Shtax'héen territory, when the people, whom he identifies as Tsimshian, first migrated from Nass River. Mr. Paul narrates the story of how, after a dispute, one segment of the community departed this favored "place for sockeye" to settle permanently in Klawock, leaving the bay to the family of a prominent woman, known as "the Esteemed One." The name may refer to the same subspecies of "small sockeye" (*dagák'*) found in Necker Bay, south of Sitka.

Final Thoughts

The Shtax'héen area place names project reveals the deep historical ties that a wide range of Tlingit social groups have to Stikine River country. Today, the Wrangell and Peterburg Tlingit tribes are using the results of the place names project to maintain tribe members' ties to the land through education, language, and culture camps. Through cooperation with the Tahltan First Nation of the upper Stikine River and appropriate land management agencies, local tribes are seeking to assure respectful management of local natural and cultural resources that are defined by these named sites. As one elder put it, "We heard a lot of these names when we were younger; it's nice to see them brought back to life."

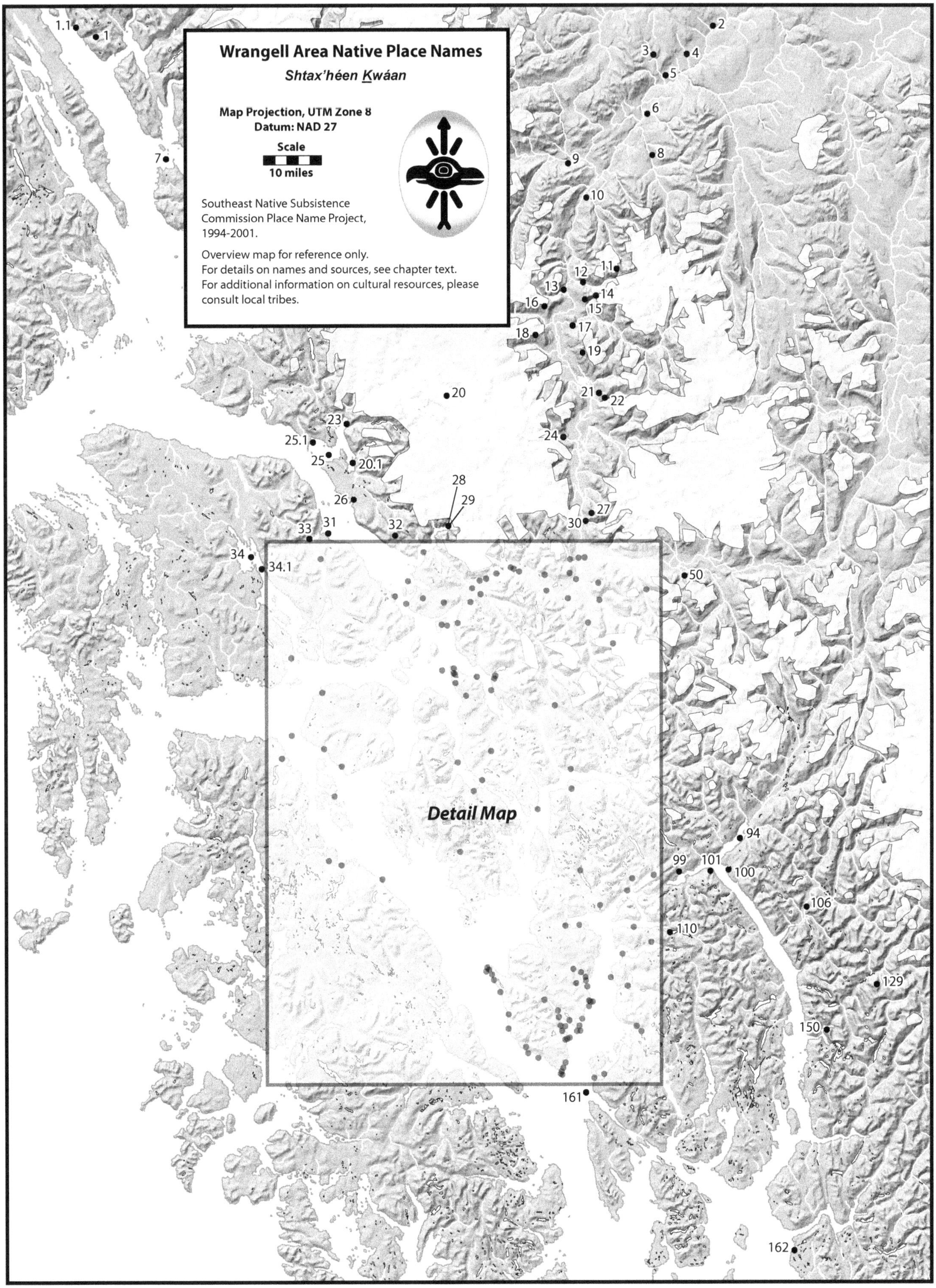

Wrangell Area Native Place Names
Shtax'héen Kwáan
Map Projection, UTM Zone 8
Datum: NAD 27
Scale
10 miles
Southeast Native Subsistence Commission Place Name Project, 1994-2001.
Overview map for reference only.
For details on names and sources, see chapter text.
For additional information on cultural resources, please consult local tribes.
Detail Map
1.1
1
2
3
4
5
6
7
8
9
10
11
12
13
14
15
16
17
18
19
20
20.1
21
22
23
24
25
25.1
26
27
28
29
30
31
32
33
34
34.1
50
94
99
100
101
106
110
129
150
161
162

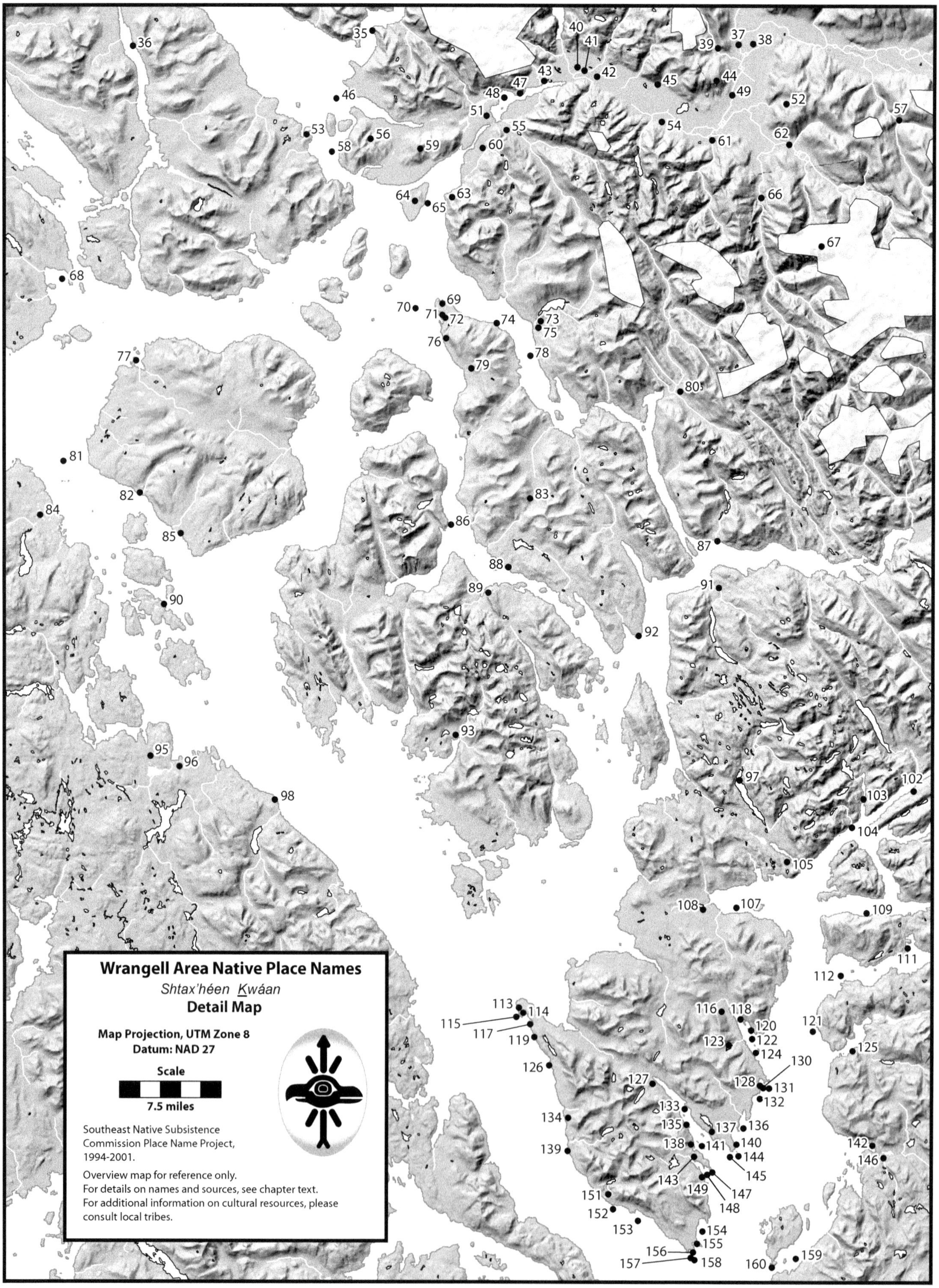

Wrangell Area Native Place Names
Shtax'héen Kwáan
Detail Map
Map Projection, UTM Zone 8
Datum: NAD 27
Scale
7.5 miles
Southeast Native Subsistence Commission Place Name Project, 1994-2001.
Overview map for reference only.
For details on names and sources, see chapter text.
For additional information on cultural resources, please consult local tribes.
35
36
37
38
39
40
41
42
43
44
45
46
47
48
49
51
52
53
54
55
56
57
58
59
60
61
62
63
64
65
66
67
68
69
70
71
72
73
74
75
76
77
78
79
80
81
82
83
84
85
86
87
88
89
90
91
92
93
95
96
97
98
102
103
104
105
107
108
109
111
112
113
114
115
116
117
118
119
120
121
122
123
124
125
126
127
128
130
131
132
133
134
135
136
137
138
139
140
141
142
143
144
145
146
147
148
149
151
152
153
154
155
156
157
158
159
160

Shtax'héen K̲wáan Place Names

Asterisk indicates uncertain, unconfirmed, or partial; NM = not mapped.
Some names have more than one pronunciation or translation.

Map #	*Name*	*Translation*	*Location*
1	S'iknáx̲	Black Bear Community*	Near Telegraph Creek, B.C. (see also Limestone Inlet, T'aak̲ú K̲wáan)
2	Tináa Goon(í)	Copper Shield Spring	Near Tahltan
3	Taal Shaa Héen	Bowl Mountain Stream	Stikine River, below Telegraph Creek
4	Tléik̲w Héen	Berry Creek	Telegraph Creek
5	G̲atyeil.ádi*	Sockeye Raven's Children*	Alkali Lake
6	Tukun*	*	Stikine River
7	Sit'k̲ú	Glacier Area	Holkham Bay
8	Yelhéenak'u	Raven's Little Creek	Yehinko Creek
9	Shulhéeni	River on the Edge	Chutine River
10	Dak̲l'éiw	Sandy Place Upriver/Inland	On Stikine River
11	Dák̲de Aan Shaa	Mountain behind the Village Trail	Dokdaon Mountain
12	Xixch'i Héen	Frogs' Creek	Stikine River
13	Lx'áas	Waterfall (Falling Water)	Deeker Creek
14	Shakayáanáx̲	Beyond the Prow	Cone Mountain range
15	Sak.aani T'áak*	Behind Eulachon Country*	Stikine River
16	Ka-ra-kai*	*	Pendant Glacier
17	Sx'athéeni (Skathéeni)	Sharp[ening] River	Scud River
18	Sti-né-nia*	*	"The Desert" area between Flood and Pendant glaciers
19	Taouk-ti-nia*	*	Mount Pereleshin
20	Taalk̲unax̲k'u Shaa	Mountain at the Back of Taalk̲ú (#25)	Devils Thumb Mountain
20.1	Taalk̲unáx̲k'w	Taalk̲ú's (#25) Little Harbor	Harbor in Thomas Bay
21	X̲aat Héenak'u	Spruce Root Little Creek	Stikine River tributary
22	X̲'anúk*	Hungry*	Saddle Mountain
23	Taalk̲ú Aan (Taalk̲uka.áan)	Taalk̲ú (#25) Village (Village on Taalk̲ú)	Wood Point, Thomas Bay
24	Klichatanoow*	*	Stikine River
25	Taalk̲ú	Within Wide-Mouthed Basket*	Thomas Bay
25.1	Kax̲kuyéndu Áa*	[Monster's name] Lagoon*	Mouth of Thomas Bay
26	Kaasx̲'aa* (K̲aach X'aa*)	——* (——* Point)	Brown Cove
27	Tiet-lia*	*	Warm Springs Mountain
28	Xídlaa [X'áat'i]	Herring Rake [Island]	Stikine River
29	Xeitl Sít'	Thunder Glacier	LeConte Glacier
30	K'ishukal.aan	——* Village	Stikine River

Map #	*Name*	*Translation*	*Location*
31	Séet Ká	On the Channel	Petersburg
32	Xeitl Shaa	Thunderbird Mountain	Thunder Mountain
33	Aansadaak'w	Village Before	Petersburg Creek, Kupreanof
34	X̲'alchán	Smelly Mouth	Head of Duncan Canal
34.1	Lukaax̲	In Haste (Off the Point)	Duncan Canal
35	Xeitl G̲eeyí	Thunder Bay	LeConte Bay
36	Gánti Yaakw Séedi	Steamboat Pass	Wrangell Narrows
37	Xakwdeiyí	Sandbar Trail	Stikine River
38	Tuk-i-snook*	*	Point near Iskut River
39	Tás'aa G̲il'i Héen	Pestle Cliff Creek	Stikine River
40	Soynai*	*	Shakes River
41	Tlákw.aan	Old Village	Sixteen miles up Stikine River
42	Xakwdeiyí	Sandbar Trail	Stikine River
43	Shaka.aan	Bow* Town	Mouth of Stikine River
44	Shaa G̲íl'i	Cliff Mountain	Elbow Mountain
45	Ka G̲íl'i Héen	Cliffs on Creek	Ketili Creek
46	Aan X'áat'	Village Island	Camp Island
47	Xakw.aan	Sandbar Village	Point on Stikine River
48	Haaw	Hemlock Branches	Lower Stikine River
49	Tás'aa G̲íl'i Yá	Pestle Cliff Face	Stikine River
50	Tsashathéeni*	Seal Head Creek*	Stikine River tributary
51	Kayáash	Platform	Reindeer Island
52	Lx'aasiyá (Lx'aasiyé)	Place Where There Are Waterfalls	Stikine River tributary
53	Kask̲l'éik*	*	Ideal Cove
54	Shak̲tuseiyí	The Shore below Drift Log	Stikine River
55	Tás'aa Yayik Aan	Village inside the Face of Pestle	Andrew Creek
56	Xákw X'áat'	Sandbar Island	Dry Island
56.1	Chayahéen	——* Water	North Arm, Stikine River mouth
57	Inhéeni	Flint Creek	Inhini River
58	Xákw Séet	Sandbar Strait	Dry Strait
59	Shantayee	Beneath Its Head	Mountain on Farm Island
59.1	Chaanteiyí*	Smelly Rock*	Farm Island
60	Naaxéin	Chilkat Blanket	Point on Cottonwood Island
60.1	Dak̲héen	Inland Water	South Channel, Stikine River mouth
61	Kekkikacié*	——* Creek	Stikine River tributary
62	Katéti*	*	Stikine River
63	Duk̲ Noowú	Cottonwood Fort	Near Wrangell
64	K̲ux̲nuk X'áat'i	Set Back Island	Sergief Island
65	Xakwnoowk'	Little Sandbar Fort	Rynda Island

Map #	Name	Translation	Location
66	S'ikhéeni	Black Bear River	Kikahe River
67	Seikooḵléi* (Setutle'h) Shaa	——* Mountain	Cone Mountain
68	Ḵaasheet	[Man's name*]	Kah Sheets Bay
69	Xakwnoowú	Sandbar Fort	Point Highfield
70	Taan X'áat'i	Sea Lion Island	Liesnoi Island
70.1	Aan Daa	Around the Village	Sokolof Island
71	Shaaxít.aan (Ch'aal'it.aan)*	Driftwood Town (Willow Town)	Old Wrangell
72	Ḵaachxan.áak'w (Ḵaachxan.áak'w*)	Little Lake Accessible to People (Ḵaachxán's [man's name] Little Lake*)	Wrangell
73	Tlagoo Héeni	Ancient Water	Virginia Lake
74	Yoowatsisgi X'aa	Floating Point	Mountain Point
75	Choox'as Aan	Waterfall Town	Mill Creek
76	Sxaantlaat*	[Shaman's name] Mother*	Cemetery Point
77	Shtax' Noow	Shtax' (#83) Fort	Zarembo Island
78	Daḵséet	Back Channel	Blake Channel
79	Ḵeishangita.áan*	Red Alder* Village	Wrangell Institute
80	Yeiyanḵú	Shoreward Place*	Aaron Creek
81	Taan Teiyí	Sea Lion Rock	Rookery Island
82	Té Aaní Gunat X̱'áak*	Town with Rocks at the Entrance*	Near Snow Passage
83	Shtax'héen	Water Biting Itself	Stikine River
84	Dagáḵ' Diyé*	Place of the Little Sockeye Salmon*	Salmon Bay
85	G̱athéeni Wat.aan* (K!athiniwáta'*)	Town at the Mouth of the Sockeye Stream* (Town at the Mouth of Big Shark*)	Village on Snow Passage
86	Kaatsḵu* Noow	——* Fort	Anita Bay
87	Tuḵutl'gu Aan	Mud inside the Village	Bradfield Canal, Marten Creek
88	Aanyádi Yakwdeiyí	Nobles' Canoe Landing	Old Wrangell
89	X̱ook'	*	Olive Cove, Etolin Island
90	X'áat' X̱oo	Among the Islands	Middle Islands
91	An.áan	Resting Village	Anan Creek
92	Yeinakatan* Noow	——* Fort	Southeast Cove
93	Tans*	Fish Jumping*	McHenry Inlet / Hatchery Lake
94	Joonáx̱	*	Burroughs Bay
95	Atahéen	Creek at the Head	Indian Creek
96	Tatxánk*	*	Lake Bay
97	Deishú Aan	End of the Trail Village	Lake MacDonald
98	Shis'gi Noow	Sapling Fort	Luck Point
99	Katnax̱* Séet	——* Channel	Anchor Pass
100	Shaayag̱eey	Face of the Mountain Bay	Fitzgibbon Cove

Map #	Name	Translation	Location
101	Tux'al.us'kw	Washing the Anus	Point Whaley
102	L'itt'aḵkanoow	*	Orchard Lake
103	Yeis Shakageey*	Bay at the Head of Yeis (#105)	Bailey Bay
104	Kuts'een Ḡíl'i	Rat Cliff	Bailey Bay
105	Yeis Ḡeeyí	Horse Clam Bay	Yes Bay
106	X̱eel (X̱eil)	Foam	Chickamin Rive
107	Wás'	Bush*	Spacious Bay
108	Was'tahéen	Creek at the Head of Wás'* (#107)	Wasta Creek
109	Ḵagit Áak'w	Little Dark Lake	End of Shrimp Bay
110	X'ul'jàa T'ika	*	Bell Arm
111	X̱akw Ḡèeyi	Sandbar Bay	North shore of Neets Bay
112	Guteenaxti*	*	Neets Bay
113	Chòonèit Xweis'	Arrow Smallest	Tip of Lemesurier Point
114	Shinséet	Bailer Pass	West side of Lemesurier Point
115	Sheen	Bailer	Misery Island
116	Ḡaanáx̱ Tahéen	Stream at the Head of Ḡaanáx̱ (#124)	Port Stewart
117	Wòosh X̱'adàa Yaa	Wagering Done on That Island	South of Lemesurier Point
118	Goosh	To Treat with Food	Port Stewart
119	Shinséet Héen	Bailer Pass Stream	Myers Chuck
120	Lax̱' Xagu	Crane Sand Beach	South Entrance
121	Lik'ats'i Noow	Sharp Fort	Bushy Point
122	Lees'*	Plenty of Water (Minus Tide)*	Port Stewart
123	Ḡaanáx̱ Áak'w	Ḡaanáx̱ (#124) Little Lake	Port Stewart Lake
124	Ḡaanáx̱	Sheltered Place*	Port Stewart
125	Ḵoonáx̱*	*	Traitors Cove
126	Ḡil'yé	Cliff Place	South of Lemesurier Point
127	Kiks Tahéen	Stream at the Head of Kíks (#135)	Helm Bay
128	Ḡaanáx̱ Noow	Ḡaanáx̱ (#124) Fort	Port Stewart
129	Gweka'h*	*	Adam Mountains
130	Lugán Noowú	Oystercatcher Fort	Point Francis
131	L'ux̱'shu X'àa	——* Point	Point Francis
132	Lax̱' Héeni	Crane Stream	Shore southwest of Point Francis
133	Nandesawat	[Inlet] With Mouth toward the North	Helm Bay, cove
134	Shachx̱'àan*	Women Drying [Fish]*	Near Ship Island
135	Kíks	*	Helm Bay
136	Daalgaasiyé	Place Tabooed All Around	Raymond Cove
137	Kiks.áa	Kíks (#135) Lake (or lagoon)	Helm Bay
138	Teyat'aḵkahéen*	Little Stream Run Down Rock*	Helm Bay
139	Tuwawóoli Héen	Stream with a Hole in It	Creek inside Ship Island

Map #	Name	Translation	Location
140	Daalgaasiye Yádi	Smaller Daalgaasiyé (#136)	Wadding Cove
141	Kikska X'áat'	Island on Kíks (#135)	Island in Helm Bay
142	Keet Noowú	Killer Whale Fort	Loring
143	Kiks Áak'w	Kíks (#135) Little Lagoon	Lagoon on the west shore of Helm Bay
144	Kal.àasak'w	Having Small Tree on It	Trunk Island
145	Kíks X'aa	Kíks (#135) Point	Helm Point
146	Naa.áa	Nation Lake	Naha Bay
147	Katgàawtan	Drum Lying on It	Island, Smugglers Cove
148	Guwakaan X'áat'i	Deer Island	Deer Island
148.1	Guwakaan X'aa	Deer Point	Kuakan Point, Deer Island
149	Ḵakwnáx'i*	Basket Stay*	Smugglers Cove
150	X̱eenáa	*	Rudyerd Bay
151	S'òow Héen	Green Stream	Above Niblack Point
152	S'èeḵ G̲èeyi	Smoke Bay	Inside Niblack Point
153	Shaltlax̱séet	Lichen-Covered-Rock-Island Pass	Below Niblack Point
154	Xakw Tóode Nadàa	Runs into Sand Beach	North Bond Bay
155	Wat.lax̱'àak	Having Ravine at the Mouth	West shore Bond Bay
156	Kóoshdàa Kóogu	Land Otter Pit	Near Caamano Point
157	Yakwseejan*	Canoe Safe*	Near Caamano Point
158	Kadax̱tgut*	*	Caamano Point
159	Lik'atsi*	Sharp Points*	Clover Island
160	Satá Yádi*	Smaller Child*	Pup Island
161	S'ix'gaanáx̱	Snail Rocks	Guard Islands
162	Asgutu.aan	Village in the Woods	Kah Shakes Cove
NM	As.áat	*	Bradfield Canal area cliff
NM	Déix̱ Sháak'u*	Two Little Women	Twin-peaked mountain
NM	Taal Aan	Wide-Mouthed Bowl* Village	Tahltan River
NM	Tlon*	*	Rock up Stikine River
NM	Toocha.aaní*	Fish Go Up Little Stream*	Mouth of Tahltaan River

9. Hinyaa Ḵwáan

Centered today in Klawock (Lawáak, #72), Hinyaa Ḵwáan encompasses several historical subdivisions. According to Emmons (n.d.) the Lawáak Ḵwáan is among the oldest divisions and areas of settlement of the Tlingit; indeed the original inhabitants may have preceded the Hinyaa Tlingit and been absorbed by them. Krause (1956) also maps the "Klawak" (but not the Taḵjik' Àan) as a separate subdivision. Hinyaa-Klawock also comprises a distinct dialect of Tlingit, often characterized as "sing-songy" by non-local Tlingits, especially those from the north. This "sing-songy" quality is reflected in the orthography by the contrast between high and low tones, both of which are marked, whereas in northern Tlingit only the high tone is stressed. Historically, Hinyaa Ḵwáan has been most closely associated with the Raven K'óoxeeneidí (a local branch of the Ganaax.ádi), Taakw.aaneidí, and Teeyneidí clans and Eagle/Wolf Ḵaax'oos.hittaan, Shangukeidí, and Lḵuweidí clans.

The Taḵjik' Àan subdivision of Hinyaa Ḵwáan refers to the collective areas of clans previously centered in Tuxekan (Taḵjik' Àan, #18), which was abandoned as a permanent village in the early twentieth century. Combined, the territory of the two ḵwáans extended from Point Baker in the north to the vicinity of Waterfall Cannery, south of the modern community of Craig. It also included the southwestern part of Kuiu Island. Raven clans based here included the Taakw.aaneidí, Teeyneidí, L'eeneidí, and Ganaax.ádi. The Eagle/Wolf moiety was composed of the Shangukeidí, Ḵaax'oos.hittaan, Teiḵweidí, and Naasteidí. The Naasteidí became prominent in the division following their migration from their southern Kuiu Island clan territory in the aftermath of the 1862 smallpox epidemic. Their oral tradition indicates that they had previously occupied the vicinity of Nossuk Bay prior to moving north to Kuiu Island (Steve Langdon, pers. comm.).

Our project was carried out in conjunction with the Klawock Cooperative Association and the Craig Community Association and the Organized Village of Saxman.

Steve Langdon served as the principal investigator and the local research coordinator was John Rowan. Key contributors included Fanny Brown, Florence Demmert, Eva Keta, Benny James, Clara Peratrovich, Theodore Roberts, Alicia Roberts, Elwood Thomas, and many others who corroborated names, attended meetings, and contributed to the project in important ways. We also benefited from the ethnogeographic work of other scholars, including George Emmons, Walter Goldschmidt and Theodore Haas, Ronald Olson, Wallace Olson (1989), Louis Shotridge, John Swanton, and others who documented indigenous place names over the years.

Some Important Named Sites

According to Emmons (n.d.), Hinyaa Ḵwáan takes its name from a contraction of the phrase "Hay-nuk-a koo-oo kwaan," meaning "People from the other side," which refers to the group's residence on the outer coast of Prince of Wales Island. Another origin for the name given by Emmons is linked to Raven, who was flying over the outside coast of Prince of Wales Island, when the sun shone upon his outstretched hand or foot, casting a "hand shadow" on the landscape, thus creating the rugged landscape of the outer coast with its many finger inlets, channels, and islands. Whatever its origins, the Native history of this area is deep, with archeological remains of fish weirs and other technologies dating back 350 to 2,300 years ago (Langdon 2006), and the earliest skeletal remains dating back approximately 9,000 years (Dixon 1999; Moss 2004).

Klawock Inlet area. The name Klawock is derived from Lawá, the Teiḵweidí man who discovered the site. It is said to be one of the earliest settlements in Southeast Alaska. Additional settlements in the vicinity included Yúxwch' Ka Àan (Village on Top of the Sea Otters, #84) and Shis'ḵ Àan (Young Spruce Village, #86), and others (cf. R. Olson 1967). Beyond being a rich salmon fishery, especially for sockeye, the area also was favored for its halibut banks, some of which are named, such as Cháatl Àani Lunáa (#105). Halibut banks often are referenced by coordinating the nearest landmarks, in this case a point of land, Cháatl Shàayi Lunáa (#94), on San Fernando Island.

On the Klawock River is a well-known fishing hole, Nakw Ishk' (#81). This site was an important spot for salmon fishing located below a set of falls at the outlet of Klawock Lake. Many generations of Klawock Tlingit have come to this location to "spear" (a southern Tlingit style of in-stream fishing) salmon for food. The term *ísh* refers to a deep hole in a stream where salmon rest and gather strength before continuing their ascent to spawning grounds (Langdon 2006).

Little Salt Lake (Tux̲'a.áak'w, #54). This is the site of one of the largest tidal fish weirs documented in Southeast Alaska, containing more than fifteen thousand wooden stakes. Steve Langdon has mapped many of the wood stake fish weirs and traps at this site. Radiocarbon dates from the wood stakes indicate that Little Salt Lake fish weirs and traps were constructed from twenty-three hundred to thirty-five hundred years ago. Over this period, a variety of weir and trap designs were used, leading Langdon to refer to the site as a Tlingit salmon fishing "R & D" (research and development) center, where fishermen developed and adapted a variety of fishing technologies best-suited to local fishing conditions. Nearby, at Gáal' Séet ("Clam Passage," NM), Langdon also has found evidence of "clam gardens" (Williams 2006), cultivated by trapping rich fill behind strategically constructed stone walls in order to enhance the size and productivity of choice clam beds.

Klawock elder Jim Martinez at Nakw Ishk' (#81), where he "speared" salmon as a boy. Photo by Steve Langdon.

Saint Philip Island (Shankw, #41.1). According to Ronald Olson (1967, 104) and Klawock elder Theodore Roberts, the Shangukeidí (People of Shankw) clan derives its name from this island name. However, they note that the original Shankw was in the vicinity of the mouth of Taku River, and when the Shangukeidí migrated to Hinyaa they brought the place name with them and applied it to Saint Philip Island, where they also established a village, Shankw Lkwa (#43). Northern Shangukeidí oral history suggests that the Shangukeidí were originally known as Dag̲isdinaa in Jilk̲áat (Chilkat) country, but part of the group changed their name after intermarrying with a Raven clan from Klawock, where some remained, while others returned to their native lands at Jilk̲áat K̲wáan and Jilk̲oot K̲wáan.

Hole-in-the-Wall (Nakw.itx̲òo, #55). Situated in the Maurelle Islands, this was an important settlement and subsistence landscape. Three habitation sites associated with this area were Làag̲ak Àan (#50), Kashak̲.àan (#56), and Kakux̲doowu* (#38), the latter reportedly being the setting of the famous G̲aanax̲.ádi story in which a young woman of the clan nursed a woodworm as her own child until it grew to monstrous proportions, threatened the community, and was killed by her relatives (Paul n.d.). This story and the Strong Man (Dukt'ootl') story are shared by the G̲aanax̲teidí and Taakw.aaneidí clans, suggesting a genealogical connection between the groups. Hole-in-the-Wall also appears in the migration story of the G̲aanax̲teidí of the Whale House of Klukwan; indeed, it is from this settlement that the clan set out on their northern migration. In addition to the settlements, there was a fort site in this vicinity, known as Kéitladi Nòow (Seagull Fort, #131). These and other sites in the Maurelle Islands continued to be used by Native fishermen as camps during the heyday of the commercial fishing era, and their remains can still be seen hidden among the islands by those who know what to look for, as Steve Langdon has shown in his recent work.

The Tak̲jik' Àan K̲wáan subdivision also includes a number of important sites. The antiquity of this k̲wáan is uncertain, but it is associated with the settlement of Tuxekan

(Tak̲jik' Àan, #18), which became an important village during the early historic period because of its strategic location for salmon and marine mammals. In the twentieth century the village was abandoned as a permanent settlement as people consolidated in Klawock and other communities with government schools and services.

*Ts'x'wa.aan** (#29) / *Taakw.aan* (#37). Prior to moving to Tak̲jik' Àan, many people lived at this village in Warm Chuck Inlet, where there was a well-known humpback salmon creek. It was here that four boys were drowned in a canoe after mistreating a frog. They were captured by the land otter people, triggering a war between the human villagers and the land otter tribe, which was settled only after a peace ceremony. This legend was carved on a Raven pole featured in Klawock Totem Park (Garfield and Forrest 1961, 105–9). While Ts'x'wa.aan is indeed associated with the Taakw.aaneidí, the more important settlement, abandoned probably after the smallpox of 1862, was at the mouth of the sockeye creek on the north shore. There were at least six houses there in mid-nineteenth century, and the village name, Taakw.aan, was carried from the Sanyaa K̲wáan settlement where the clan had previously dwelled (Steve Langdon, pers. comm. 2011).

This restored pole, now residing in Klawock, symbolizes the Teik̲weidí clan's possessory rights to the prized sockeye salmon stream at Deweyville-Sarkar (#14), which provided sustenance and wealth to the group. Photo by Steve Langdon.

Deweyville/Sarkar (*S'a.àa Ká*, #14). This productive sockeye system was an important fishing area. The largest historic village, Tak̲jik' Àan (#18), was located just below the entrance to Sarkar Cove. In the nineteenth century this settlement housed as many as nine hundred people. The Deweyville-Sarkar river system was celebrated for its productive salmon fishery. The slender sockeye here, called *s'a.aa* or *s'ak̲a* (boney?), are found only in a few rivers in Southeast Alaska, and may have been named for, or inspired the name, for this watershed. Today the area is still used by Natives of Craig, Klawock, and other communities to harvest sockeye salmon and other resources for subsistence.

Viola Garfield (n.d., 6; see also Garfield and Forrest 1961, 110–11) describes a totem pole at Klawock which symbolizes the Teik̲weidí (brown bear) clan's claim to a wealthy, sockeye salmon stream:

> The property, a salmon stream at Deweyville, on the western shore of Prince of Wales Island, is represented by the face at the lower end of the pole. Three salmon are entering the mouth of the stream. At the base is a basket trap . . . full of fish. At the top of the pole is a brown bear, which identifies the clan to which the owners of the stream belong. In his paws is a salmon, which further emphasizes the wealth of fish in the stream [and that it's a sockeye]. The man holding the wolf's tail symbolizes the house head, restraining his people who are members of the Wolf phratry. The story is, in brief, the stream at Deweyville belongs to the Sockeye Salmon House of the brown bear clan of the Wolf phratry. However, the Wolf people are generous and hold back so that others may come and share in their wealth, at their express invitation, of course.

Significantly, a topographical aspect of the salmon stream, its narrow mouth, is depicted in the pole.

Named sites reference other well-known stories, too, such as that of Dukt'ootl', the "Strongman," who is said to have engaged the sea lions at Tàan Àani Lunáa (#62.1; Steve Langdon, pers. comm. from Theodore Roberts). A full Tlingit version of the story, as told by Frank Johnson, can be found in *Haa Shuká, Our Ancestors: Tlingit Oral Narratives* (Dauenhauer and Dauenhauer 1987, 138–51).

Final Thoughts

The Hinyaa area place names project shows a plethora of settlement and use sites on Prince of Wales and surrounding islands.

Today, the Craig and Klawock tribes are using the results of the place names project to maintain tribe members' ties to the land through education, culture camps, and appropriate management of local natural and cultural resources. The Hinyaa place names map co-produced with the Southeast Native Subsistence Commission is prominently located in the classroom of Tlingit culture teacher (and local research coordinator) Jon Rowan, who uses it in his instruction of local pupils in the history and heritage of the Hinyaa Tlingit.

The Origin of Klawock

The following excerpt is from a history of Klawock collected by anthropologist Ronald L. Olson (1967, 103–5) from John Darrow of the G̲aanax̲.ádi clan in the early 1930s. It is an important ethnogeographic text, but also traces the relationships between Hinyaa K̲wáan clans and other communities. Olson's original orthography is maintained but a few stylistic inconsistencies and punctuation errors have been fixed. Olson's bracketed comments have been converted to parenthetical comments, while the editor's comments are in brackets.

There was (once) a man named Tlȧwa´h. He had a son named Tihge´t. Tihget's mother was Takuye´tl and his uncle (mother's brother) was Yetlcani´h (old raven). The uncle's wife was quite young while her husband, Yetlcanih [Yéil Shaani], was along in years. She took a fancy to Tihget, who was living in his uncle's house, as is customary. One day on the pretext of giving him some clothing and tobacco she asked him into her bedroom and began making love to him. Eventually he yielded. That same night she felt she was pregnant. Her husband was away at the time. He returned, and after some months he asked her how it was that her menses had stopped. Then she confessed to her affair. She was childless and she hoped her husband would give her to his nephew Tihget as a wife (a fairly common custom). But the husband was angry and threatened to kill Tihget, saying, "If I forgive him the next generation will do the same thing."

Tihget was blasé and said, "All right. Let him kill me. I didn't wish to sleep with her." The wife told her husband, "If you wish to kill me, all right. If you kill your nephew, I'll die with him. It is better if I and his child within me die with him." But he wished to kill only his nephew. The woman went to her husband's sister and told all, asking her to tell her husband, Tlawah, Tihget's father, so he could plan to save his son.

The next day Tlawah said to his wife, "We had better leave this country." They agreed to go to the north. She wanted to. (They were living at Kȧdŭkhuka´h on Kanaganut Island.)

Tihget no longer slept in the house but hid himself.

Tlawah called together all the Ganaxadi [G̲aanax̲.ádi] men who were married to Tekwedih [Teik̲weidí] women. He said he wanted to move away to prevent war between the two clans, and to save his son. He asked the Ganaxadi if they wanted to war on their own "children," the Tekwedih. They answered "no." They agreed to take their wives and children and to go away themselves.

Near Ketchikan is a humpback salmon creek called Ana´n [An.áan; see Shtax'héen K̲wáan chapter], owned by the Tekwedih. Tlawah went where the Ganaxadi had fishing camps, while Yetlcanih and his group went to Anan. Later he went to the Ganaxadi camp because his wife was soon to have her child and he came to kill his nephew. It was night and high tide. Tlawah and his group secretly packed their things in canoes and hid them. In the morning it was foggy and they started out, singing a song called "kȧtna´wustakihcĭ´n" (moving away our clan).

Then Yetlcanih called all the remaining people together on the beach and wept. He was sorry for what he had done. Tlawah and his group sang "akanitlkukȧtl´n" (my land nevermore I'll see) as they went. Tihget stood in the bow of the canoe and faced out to sea, for he didn't wish to see his uncle. As the tide came in, the current took the canoe to the north. They didn't paddle. But Yetlcanih stood at the beach and let the tide reach to his waist. He was going to allow himself to drown because his wife was the cause of his losing his nephew and his father's people. But his brothers-in-law came out, took him in and talked to him, and "made him feel good."

Tlawah's party paddled to Kasaan Bay that same day. They hid there. The next day after breakfast Tlawah asked his clansmen and brothers-in-law what was the best thing to do. They advised not to stay on the beach but to follow up the stream Gunȧxhehĭn [G̲unak Héen, #104] ("going ashore creek," Harris River) where no one would find them. They decided to go up the stream and find a place to live. The next morning they hid their canoes far back in the woods. They took only small packs, food, and blankets. Everyone except babies carried packs. They found a place behind Yesgahinogaca [Yèis G̲èiyi Héen Shàa, #102]. There they camped, and stayed one day. At daybreak the next morning Tlawah climbed the mountain to look around. He saw the straits and channels to the west. He saw Klawak [Klawock] Lake and decided to go down to see if it was a bay or a lake. He went down Clay Creek and saw many sockeye salmon. At the shore of the lake he tested the water. He found a good animal trail. (This is the one now used by the Forest Service.) Then he went back to camp, told the people what he had seen, and advised that they go down to the lake. They reached the lake the next morning by sunrise. He told them to catch and smoke only a few fish and to roast a few.

The next day Tlawah and his men made a raft of red cedar. They left four limbs standing up. They pointed the ends of the logs and built a small platform on the raft. They made a double-bladed paddle. The next morning Tlawah went down the lake. He wanted to find the outlet, where the fish came from. At the middle of the lake on the north side he found a stream which he named Kàtlce′k! (alder) [Kàlshex̲'w Héeni, "Creek with (Lots of) Red Alder," #78], where there were many sockeye spawning. There he ate salmon berries, roasted some fish, and rested. Then he went on down to the foot of the lake where he found the animal trail by the river (the present trail). The stream was full of humpback and dog salmon. On the island just above the present weir he saw a large spruce. Under the

Tuxekan, or Tak̲jik' Àan in Tlingit, was an important Tlingit settlement which boomed during the early historic era, due to its proximity to productive fishing grounds. In the twentieth century, consolidation of schooling and services led Natives to move their permanent residences to communties like Craig and Klawock. Alaska State Library, Case & Draper Photograph Collection, W. H. (William Howard) Case, P39-0686.

tree it was like a house. He decided to bring the people there. The limbs were huge and hung down to the ground. Even heavy rain did not penetrate underneath. Then he went down to the mouth of the creek, tested the water, and found it salt. Tlawah walked on down the present village site. He heard a sound like the roar of gusty wind. It was the animals — hair seal, sea otter, and fur seal — on the reef. He walked on . . . (an omission here in the manuscript is indicated by ellipses) . . . six small houses and one large house. In the large one were held the feasts and ceremonies. This was built and owned by the Ganaxadi and Tekwedih in common. The south side of the big house was the Ganaxadi's place; the north side belonged to the Tekwedih.

The palisade was called Asnu'h [Àas Nòow, not mapped] (tree fort or tree wall). The Tekwedih side was called Xutshit [Xoots Hít] (Bear House), the Ganaxadi side was called Yăghĭt [Yaay Hít] (Whale House). Five times this palisade was rebuilt until the time of JD's grandmother. The fifth was of spruce. The first had been of young spruce. Whenever the logs became rotten it was rebuilt. JD's mother was a small girl when they started to build the sixth, which was of red cedar. The communal house was also of red cedar. This stood until about 1830. The rotting logs can still be seen.

In this town the Ganaxadi men and their Tekwedih wives occupied one side, the Tekwedih men and their Ganaxadi wives the other. Young couples slept on the house platforms, the old people on the floor. In the six houses lived old and young. The big house was for the overflow. This communal house was "two big trees long."

In the middle of the stream just below the island is a big flat rock with a point sticking up like a killer whale's fin. It is called Tlàwaguci [Làawa Gooshí, NM] (*guci* [*gooshí*], "fin"). When a Tekwedih died the clan went there and set this stone so the fin stood up. Then the Ganaxadi would get excited, knowing there would be a big potlatch. The Ganaxadi did not raise the stone as a signal, for it did not belong to them. But a Ganaxadi man whose wife was giving a feast would have it set up.

About the time of the fourth set of houses, the sea otter, fur seal, and sea lion started to leave this district. Up to that time the people of the village had no canoes. Now they built some. They cut a big red cedar. The Tekwedih started to build one and the Ganaxadi started a second. One was built at the site of the present town hall, where charcoal may still be seen. (By this time there were also houses at the present site of Klawak [Klawock].) A fire was built on top of the logs, the charcoal scraped off with rough stones. Afterward the outside was also shaped with fire. This is called *wŭddutsganàyă'k* (fire-shaped canoe). Then they made other canoes of various sizes. With these they hunted sea otter and other creatures. Just below the island village a salmon weir was built.

There were three Ganaxadi brothers who were famous sea-otter hunters. They were hunting at a place called Ayuktahklen [Ayakwta Tlèn, #120] in Port San Antonio on Baker Island. There came a big trading schooner with a Hawaiian crew. The men thought the ship's boat was an *akutsti'yàt* (water monster) with long legs, and they ran ashore. They tried to run away but were caught. They called the white people K!ekàddĭhkwani [Kéidladi K̲wáani] (seagull people) because of their "white" color. The Hawaiians looked like dark ducks (*yuk* [*yook̲*, "cormorant"]), so were called Yŭk!kwani [Yook̲ K̲wáani]. It was thought the rice of the strangers was worms or maggots. The captain of the boat gave them a warm bath, but they thought he was going to cook them. But the captain washed their hair. He gave them white men's clothes. Then the natives skinned the ten sea otter and five fur seal they had shot. The captain asked them if they ate sea otter and seal. The natives showed them how to draw blood out of seal meat with salt water and how to use stones for cooking. The captain showed them how to use iron pots and gave each of the three men one. Then they traded blankets and clothes for the furs. The captain gave them one gun each, and a keg of powder flints, and bullets. He also gave them hardtack, molasses, rice, and some calico.

They wondered how they would take it all home in their canoes, but the captain let them have three boats. He taught them how to use guns. When a gun was fired they all fell down, for they had never heard a gun. But they put cotton in their ears. Finally the men took guns with a half load of powder. They thought the firing hammer "fought" with the flint. They succeeded in killing a duck. They practiced for several days. By means of sign language the captain told them they could kill all sorts of game with a gun. Finally they started hunting fur seal. They killed a swimming buck. This meat the captain salted. The Tlingit cooked the liver and heart with stones inside the stomach. This made a feast. Then the captain gave them more pots.

The next day the captain and his men took them home with boats with sails. The eldest brother guided them to Klawak. They sailed to the mouth of the creek. The eldest cried "hu+" as a signal to the village. Everyone ran down to see. No one knew the brothers in their new clothes. Their hair had been cut by the captain, who took the hair home with him. The eldest told them the whites were "sea-gull people," the Kanakas "black-duck people." "Ship" was the first word the Tlingit learned. They called the ship's boats "ship gatsguh [k'áts'k'u]" (little ships). Their trade goods were taken to the communal house. The captain and the others stayed one night. The eldest brother proceeded to demonstrate the gun. When he fired, everyone fell down. The next day the captain left, but gave them a boat for the canoe left aboard the ship. The captain agreed to return in twelve months (the following July). He gave them a box of tools. Arrangements were made for trading a year later. The following spring the whole village went out to get furs to trade. The next year the ship returned. By now, everyone had guns, steel tools, and so on. On the fourth visit the ship anchored off the east coast of San Fernando Island.

After this the Tongass (Tantakwan [Taant'a Kwáan]) and Klawak people began seeing each other. The Tekwedih of Klawak went to visit in a big canoe. Some of the Tantakwan came to Klawak and built houses on either side of the lower falls, the Tekwedih on the north side of the creek, the Ganaxadi on the south side. There was called a big meeting in the communal house at Asnu [Àas Nòow]. There was talk of going back to Ketchikan. But the Ganaxadi refused, saying that they had been driven away but that the Tekwedih had not, so the Tekwedih should return.

The Tekwedih loaded their canoes and as they drifted out on the tide they sang a song. Then one got up and made a speech, giving the whole country to the Ganaxadi, because their "father" Tlawah had found it. So the town came to be called Tlâwa'k [Lawáak] (Klawak). Up to this time the Ganaxadi had held the south side of the creek, the Tekwedih the north side. So all the Tekwedih except those married to Ganaxadi and some of the old people moved away to the country of the Tantakwan (Port Tongass). Some of the Tekwedih who were left here joined with the Cangukedih [Shangukeidí] who lived on Canku [Shankw, #41.1] (St. Philip Island) and they intermarried with the Ganaxadi. The Tinedih [Teeyneidí] clan also lived to the north, around Kosciusko Island. The Tagwanedih [Taakw.aaneidí] clan held Heceta Island. To the north of the Tinedih was the country of the Tittlhĭttan [Teeyhíttaan*] or Klinedih [L'eeneidí].

After the Tekwedih went back to the Tantakwan the whole ceremonial house belonged to the Ganaxadi and the name was changed to Gauhĭt [Yaaw Hít*] (Herring House[*]). The small houses had no names. The bay on the south side just above the present village was called Ganaxadi Anyákuta'h (Ganaxadi real bay)[G̱àanax̱.adi Àan Yakat.àa, "Sitting in Front of G̱àanax̱.adi Land," #82]. After the Tekwedih went south the Ganaxadi married the Cangukedih and the Kakushittan [Ḵaax̱'oos.hittaan], that is, the people to the north.

The Tagwanedih clan of Heceta Island originally came from near Prince Rupert and are named from a place called Takua'n [Taakw.aan, "Winter Village," #37].

After the Tekwedih went south the Ganaxadi multiplied and prospered.

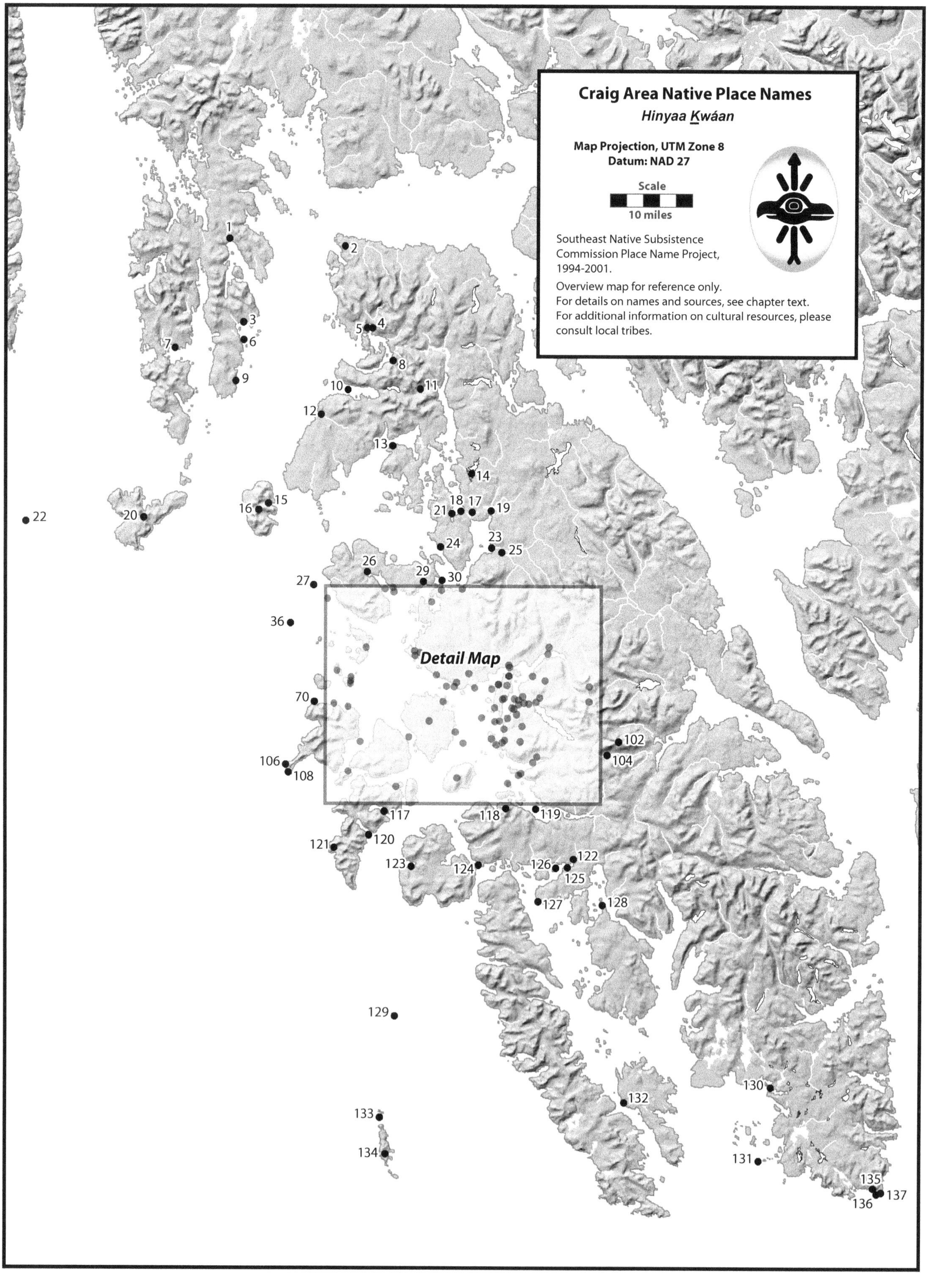
Craig Area Native Place Names
Hinyaa Kwáan
Map Projection, UTM Zone 8
Datum: NAD 27
Scale
10 miles
Southeast Native Subsistence Commission Place Name Project, 1994-2001.
Overview map for reference only.
For details on names and sources, see chapter text.
For additional information on cultural resources, please consult local tribes.
Detail Map
1
2
3
4
5
6
7
8
9
10
11
12
13
14
15
16
17
18
19
20
21
22
23
24
25
26
27
29
30
36
70
102
104
106
108
117
118
119
120
121
122
123
124
125
126
127
128
129
130
131
132
133
134
135
136
137

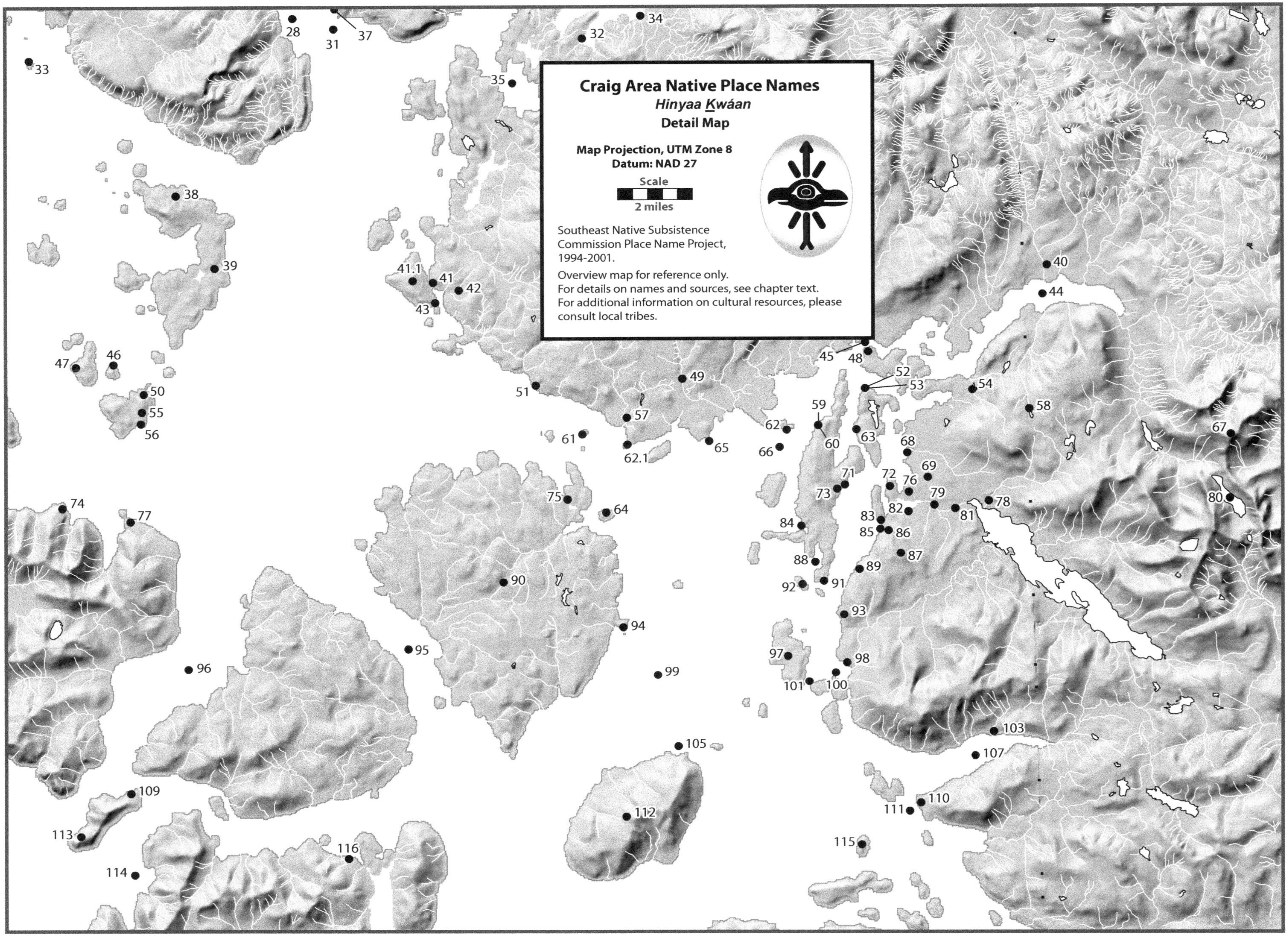

Craig Area Native Place Names
Hinyaa Kwáan
Detail Map
Map Projection, UTM Zone 8
Datum: NAD 27
Scale
2 miles
Southeast Native Subsistence Commission Place Name Project, 1994-2001.
Overview map for reference only.
For details on names and sources, see chapter text.
For additional information on cultural resources, please consult local tribes.
28
31
37
34
32
33
35
38
39
41.1
41
42
43
40
44
47
46
50
55
56
51
49
57
61
62.1
65
45
48
52
53
54
58
59
60
62
66
63
67
68
69
71
72
76
73
79
78
80
82
81
83
85
86
84
87
88
89
92
91
74
77
75
64
90
93
94
95
96
97
98
99
101
100
103
105
107
109
110
111
112
113
115
116
114

Hinyaa Ḵwáan Place Names

Asterisk indicates uncertain, unconfirmed, or partial; NM = not mapped.
Some names have more than one pronunciation or translation.

Map #	Name	Translation	Location
1	Shunàask'i	Little End-Intestines	Village in Port Beauclerc
2	X'àa Séedak'w (Xaaséedák'u)	Little Channel by the Point (Small Pass through Which the War Party Goes [at High Tide])	Point Baker
3	T'eek*	*	Kuiu Island Bay, southeast
4	Suḵ Dàa	Dry Around	Calder Bay
5	Neix'* Héen	Marble* Creek	Marble Creek and settlement at Calder
6	Chaat'adi*	Sea Lion Flippers*	Kuiu Island rocks
7	S'eek Ḡèeyi	Black Bear Bay	Kell Bay; Suknu garden site, Affleck Canal
8	Shix'áan	——* Village	Shakan Bay and village site
9	Til' Ḡèeyi	Dog Salmon*	Southeast Kuiu Island, Louise Cove area
10	Kàax't'*	*	Shipley Bay
11	Naḵw Àani	Devilfish Land	Devilfish Bay
12	Cháatl Ḵóok	Halibut Storage*	Kosciusko Island, south of Shipley Bay
13	Tuḵhéen	Needlefish Creek	Tokeen
14	S'a.àa Ká	Lake in a Lake*	Sarkar Lake, Deweyville
15	Cháatl Wàaḵ	Halibut Eye	Warren Island fish camp in northeast cove
16	Náash Dàa	——* Island	Warren Island
17	Jinḵu Ḡeey	Wrist (or cuff) Bay	Jinhi Bay
18	Taḵjik' Àan	Little ——* Village	Tuxekan
19	Nàakigèey	Upstream (northward)	Naukati Bay
20	Áan (Áat) Dàa	——* Island	Coronation Island
21	Jinḵu Aan	Wrist (or cuff) Village	Jinhi Bay village
22	Dèikinòow	Far Out to Sea Fort	Hazy Islands (Big Hazy Islet)
23	Chas'héeni	Humpback Salmon Creek	Near Staney Creek*
24	Xàa Héen	War Party Creek	Tuxekan Island, Karheen
25	Sdéini Héeni	Sdéini's (man's name) Creek	Staney Creek
26	S'ik.héeni	Black Bear Creek	Creek where cannery was located in Warm Chuck (head of Warm Chuck)
27	K'watl' [X'áat']	Bird Eggs [Island]	Cape Lynch, small offshore island
28	Yakw Te	Ship Rock	Small island in Warm Chuck Inlet

Map #	*Name*	*Translation*	*Location*
29	Ts'x'wa.aan*	*	Taakw.aaneidí village and garden, east Warm Chuck Inlet
30	Tanawaak̲* Séedi	——* Strait	Tonowek Narrows
31	Yat'àayi Héen	Warm Water	Warm Chuck Inlet
32	Kagukkahéen*	——* Creek	Kaguk Cove
33	Kala.àasak'w Dàa	Forested with Small Trees	Emerald Island
34	Shahéen	Head Creek	Shaheen Creek
35	Náasak*	*	Nossuk Bay
36	Àan Sha X'àa	Village Head Point*	Timbered Island*
37	Taakw.aan	Winter Village	Village by sockeye stream in Warm Chuck Inlet
38	Kakux̲doowu*	On the Point Dwellers*	Anguilla Island
39	T'àawak̲ Séedi	Goose Passage	Launch Passage between Esquibel and Anguilla islands (Maurelle Islands)
40	Àashat Héeni	Steelhead Creek	Stream north of Picnic Bay
41	Shankw Séet	Shankw (#41.1) Pass	Channel inside Saint Philip Island
41.1	Shankw	*	Saint Philip Island
42	Tàk̲akw	*	Stream on Prince of Wales Island, opposite Saint Philip Island
43	Shankw Lkwa	Shankw (#41.1) Little Point	Village on Saint Philip Island
44	Kax'wàaka*	*	Big Salt Lake
45	Yikdawáa	*	Dog salmon stream just inside Big Salt Lake on north shore
46	Daa Gíl' Daa*	Island with Cliffs around It*	Small island in Maurelle Islands, north of Hole-in-the-Wall
47	Dàaw Hit	Kelp House (a fort site)	West end of Sonora Island
48	Dlèit Ka.utsk'u	White Stone Fort	At rapids entry, Big Salt Lake
49	Ts'ak̲l Héen	——* Creek	Creek east of Eleven Mile Creek
50	Làag̲ak Àan	Marine Grass (or seaweed*) Village	Grassy beach, northeast of Hole-in-the-Wall fish camp
51	Tatuknèech	Along Shoreline of Caves	Eleven Mile Beach, north shore opposite Rosary Islands
52	Yòo Yakatnukgu X'àak'w	Little Shifting Point	North Sandy Point, Peratrovich Island
53	Yòo Yakatnukgu X'àa	Shifting Point ("moves" according to wind direction)	North Sandy Point, Peratrovich Island
54	Tux̲'a.áak'w	Little Anus Lake	Little Salt Lake
55	Nakw.itx̲òo	Place Among [the People*]	Hole-in-the-Wall, San Lorenzo Island
56	Kashak̲.àan	——* Village	Sandy beach, south end of Hole-in-the-Wall fish camp
57	Gut'ak T'àak Héen	Creek behind ——*	Eleven Mile Creek
58	G̲aks Héen	——* Creek	Main creek to the east in Little Salt Lake

Map #	Name	Translation	Location
59	Xixch' Gèeyi	Frog Bay	Northwest Wadleigh Island, where the cliffs are
60	Xixch'	Frog	Northwest Wadleigh Island, where the cliffs are
61	Ḵóok X̱òo	Amidst the Box [Islands]	Rosary Islands
62	Shahéen Áak'w*	Head Waters of the Little Lagoon*	Shinaku Inlet
62.1	Tàan Àani Lunáa	Sea Lion Point (nose)	Rocky point at south end of Eleven Mile Beach
63	Ḵàashàasx̱áaw X'áat'ak'u	Dragonfly Islet	West side of Peratrovich Island
64	Gut'ak X̱òo	Among ——*	Cruz Islands
65	Tàan Àani	Sea Lion Land	Timbered Island
66	Shayanaḵu	Coming Down the Mountain	Shinaku Inlet and Creek
67	Yadayéil Shàa	Mountain with Raven on Its Face (Black Bear Mountain*)	Highest peak at the head of Big Salt Lake
68	Yèil Héenak'u	Raven's Little Creek	Bennetts Creek, north of Klawock
69	——* Áak'w	[Man's name (Robert Peratrovich's Tlingit name)] Lake	Klawock, small lake east of village
70	Kéitlhadi Tèiyi	Seagull Rock	Cape Ulitka, Noyes Island
71	Ḵàwut Xakwk'u	Bead Little Sand Beach	First beach above Flounder Bay
72	Lawáak	(Named after Lawá, the man who founded Klawock)	Klawock
73	Dzanti Gèeyak'w	Flounder Little Bay	Small shallow bay on east side of Wadleigh Island, just opposite Klawock Island
74	Sèegáaxwk'	*	Steamboat Point, Noyes Island
75	Naklakw*	*	Cruz Pass on San Fernando Island across Eleven Mile Creek
76	Suḵhéeni	Grass Creek	Grassy divide between Klawock Lagoon and bay to north
77	Sèegáaxwk' Àan	Sèegáaxwk' (#74) Village	Haida camp on Noyes Island
78	Ḵàlshex̱'w Héeni	Creek with [Lots of] Red Alder	Sockeye creek one-half mile from outlet of Klawock Lake
79	Was'x'àantléigu X'áat'i	Salmonberry Island	Island in lower Klawock River
80	Tòolch'an Áayi	Round Lake	Black Bear Lake
81	Nakw Ishk'	Little Fishing Hole of Nakw	Deep hole for fishing below second falls on Klawock River
82	G̱àanax̱.adi Àan Yakat.àa	Sitting in Front of G̱àanax̱.adi Land	South part of Klawock Lagoon
83	Séedak'w	Small Passage	Canoe Pass, between Klawock Island and Prince of Wales Island
84	Yúxwch' Ka Àan	Village on Top of the Sea Otters	South point of Wadleigh Island, village/ camping site
85	Kaxdaa* X'áat'i	Walk-Around* Island	Island/peninsula that forms the main part of Klawock Village
86	Shis'ḵ Àan	Young Spruce Village	Opposite side of lagoon from Klawock

Map #	Name	Translation	Location
87	Nadáakw Shàa	Table Mountain	Klawock, mountain to south
88	Ḵutl'k'w G̲èeyak'w	Little Mud Bay	Small bay on southwest Wadleigh Island, across from Clam Island
89	T'òoch' L'éiw Xagu	Black Sand Beach	Beach between X̲'ex̲yat.s.àak'w (#93) and Craig
90	X'áandàa	*	San Fernando Island
91	Ḵàa Shàak'u Lunáa	Small Human Head Point (nose)	Entrance Point, Wadleigh Island
92	Kastax't Dàa	Pieces Bitten Off (i.e., sound of herring eggs being consumed) Around	Clam Island
93	X̲'ex̲yat.s.àak'w	Little [Place Where] One Turns One's Face to the Mouth of It (Kiss Water)	Freshwater runoff from cliff on Klawock Inlet between Craig and Klawock
94	Cháatl Shàayi Lunáa	Halibut Head Point (nose)	Fern Point on San Fernando Island
95	Dakx̲'áak	Interior Divide	Portillo Channel
96	Dèikix̲'áak	Exterior Divide	Saint Nicholas Channel
97	Sháan Dàa	Around ——*	Fish Egg Island
98	Dèi Shu Àan	End of the Road Village	Village at sandy beach by Canoe Pass, Crab Bay area*
99	Cháatl Nadáakw	Halibut Table	Halibut bank between Fish Egg and San Fernando islands
100	Tsàa Èeji*	Seal Reef*	Crab Bay, north side of Craig
101	Sháan Séet	——* Strait (or pass)	Channel by Fish Egg Island (also applied to Craig)
102	Yèis G̲èiyi Héen Shàa	Horse Clam Nectar Mountain	Harris Peak
103	K'óox Héenak'u	Marten's Little Creek	Stream on north shore of Port Saint Nicholas, approximately three-quarters way in
104	G̲unak Héen	Creek on G̲unak (Going Ashore Creek*)	Harris River
105	Cháatl Àani Lunáa	Halibut Country Point (nose)	Halibut bank between Fish Egg and San Fernando islands
106	Tàan Téix̲'i	Sea Lion Heart	Cape Addington, Shaft Rock
107	Sèenax̲éi	Close to Light	Port Saint Nicholas
108	Dòol Shàayi	Shark Head	Point inside Cape Addington
109	Sáank'w	Little ——*	Cone Island, spring camp
110	Shòogu X'àa	First as You Travel [South]* Point (White Clam Shells* Point)	Point Miraballes
111	Ligàasi Àan	Taboo Village	Small island south of Rancheria Island
112	Sáan Dàa	Around ——*	San Juan Bautista Island
113	Yúxwch' Àayí*	Sea Otter Lagoon	Cove facing Siketi Sound, west Baker Island
114	S'igeidi Lunáa*	Beaver Point (nose)	Siketi Point, Cone Island
115	Dàalagil' Dàa	Around [Island] with Cliffs around It	Toti Island
116	Xakw Àan	Empty Clam Shell Village	Village site, northeast Baker Island

Map #	Name	Translation	Location
117	Ayakwta	Big Boat Harbor Inside	Port Asuncion, Baker Island
118	Yàade Ḵàatuḵdutèen	A Human Butt Is Visible on the Face (of the mountain)	Mountain on east side of Port Caldera, Trocadero Bay
119	Naẋ Tlèn	Big Harbor	Trocadero Bay
120	Ayakwta Tlèn	Boat Harbor Inside	Port San Antonio, Baker Island
121	Cháanwàan Shàayi	Chinaman's Head	Cape Chirikof (Granite Point), island in Chirikof Bay
122	Yaskugu Àan	Village of ——*	Soda Bay, on Hydaburg side
123	Ẋantàyik	Inside the Crotch	Port Santa Cruz, Suemez Island
124	Yúxwch' Ka Àan	Village on Top of the Sea Otters	Village/camp at southeast end of Suemez Island
125	Yaskugu Ya	Face (of cliff) of ——*	Cliff area in Soda Bay, near entry*
126	Yaskugu G̲èey	Bay of ——*	Soda Bay
127	Cháatl Lunáa	Halibut Nose	Halibut Nose
128	Suḵw Àan	Grassy Village*	Sukkwan Island, northern end
129	G̲òoch Te	Wolf Rock	Wolf Rock
130	Lenḵu.àan	Tidal Flat Area Village	Klinkwan
131	Kéitladi Nòow	Seagull Fort	Outer Barrier Islands area from Egg Rock to Seagull Island
132	Katg̲àawtan	Drum on Both Sides	Howkan
133	Dèikèelunáak	Way Out to Sea Lower Point (nose)	Lowrie Island, Forrester Island Wilderness*
134	Kaal.àasak'w Dàa	Island Forested with Small Trees	Forrester Island
135	Dziska* Shàayi	Monkey* Head	Rock formation on mountain above Cape Chacon
136	Tàan Àani Yadàa	Around the Face (side) of Sea Lion Country	Cape Chacon
137	Ẋóots	Brown Bear	Cape Chacon, west side
NM	Àas Nòow	Tree Fort	Klawock Area
NM	Gáal' Séet	Clam Passage	Salt Lake area of Klawock
NM	Katg̲àawtan Àani	Drum on Both Sides Country	Howkan Tlingit and Haida villages and their environs
NM	Làawa Gooshí	Lower End* Dorsal Fin	Klawock area

10. *Taant'a K̲wáan and Sanyaa K̲wáan*

If Tlingit origins lie near Nass River, as oral histories suggest, then one would expect to find a high concentration of Tlingit names in that vicinity. Indeed, while Nass River (Naas, not mapped) is Tsimshian country today, Tlingit names can still be found there, and the highest density of Tlingit names is found just north of there in Sanyaa K̲wáan and Taant'a K̲wáan. In 1922 anthropologist Thomas T. Waterman (1922a) interviewed four local Tlingits—Joe Baronovitch, Thomas Johnson, James B. Williams, and Pete Williams—and documented more than 856 indigenous geographic names in these southern Tlingit territories, which he mapped on nautical charts. This remarkable data set served as a baseline for our own research seventy-five years later. Significantly, the name set also includes numerous toponyms from the Kasaan and Metlakatla areas, where we were unable to conduct interviews for this project, as well as other neighboring k̲wáan territories.

Esther Shea (d. 2004), a Teik̲weidí clan leader and Tlingit language instructor, served as our local research coordinator, and reviewed the entire Waterman name list. She worked with Tongass-speaking elder Emma Williams and linguist Jeff Leer (who had earlier worked with Frank and Emma Williams, the last speakers of the Tongass dialect of Tlingit) to clarify pronunciations, spellings, and translations, and with anthropologist Priscilla Schulte and U.S. Forest Service staff to verify locations, record new names, and document important cultural associations (see "This Was Not Wilderness—This Was Our Home" box).

Note that names in the Tongass and Sanyaa dialects sound different, and may be challenging for those familiar only with northern Tlingit. The Tongass dialect includes a four way contrast between short, long, glottalized, and fading vowels (see Williams and Williams 1978). This is represented in the orthography by the use of contrasting high and low tone marks, whereas northern Tlingit marks only the high tone.

Our project was carried out in conjunction with the Ketchikan Indian Corporation and the Organized Village of Saxman. Besides Esther Shea and Emma Williams, other contributors included Martha Cosello, Elizabeth Denny, Martha Denny, Willard Jones, and William Kushnick, and many others who provided logistical support for the project. In addition to Thomas Waterman's pioneering investigation, we also benefited from the ethnogeographic work of other scholars, including George Emmons, Walter Goldschmidt and Theodore Haas, Jeff Leer, Dan Monteith, Ronald Olson, Louis Shotridge, John Swanton, and others who documented indigenous place names over the years. Matt Ganley prepared the GIS maps and Thomas Thornton prepared the final database with assistance from Irene Dundas.

Taant'a K̲wáan

Although originating on the mainland coast, the Tongass, or Taant'a, K̲wáan adopted their current name from their subsequent home on Prince of Wales Island (Tàan, "Sea Lion," #922). The name was applied due to the prevalence of sea lions along the western shores of the island and at Forrester Island, Southeast Alaska's largest sea lion rookery. The group was largely displaced from Prince of Wales Island, however, by the K'áyk'aanii (Kaigani) Haida, who colonized the southern portion of the island in the past two centuries. As a result, the Tongass Tribe, as they are also known, began moving eastward, first to Annette Island (now Tsimshian territory), where they established villages at Port Chester and Tamgas Bay (Ch'èix̲' Àani, "Thimbleberry Village," #679), and then to Tongass Island (Taagwas',* #930) in Portland Canal, where they settled at Kadúk̲x̲uka (Place on the Cottonwoods, #931), and finally to Ketchikan (Kichx̲áan, #396) on Revillagigedo Island, where they are centered today (Emmons n.d.). That they are one of the oldest and most important groups is evidenced by the fact that many of the northern k̲wáans have clans and migration histories stemming from Taant'a

K̲wáan. Unfortunately, despite the recent discovery of nine-thousand-year-old human remains (Dixon 1999), little is known about their early history and development on Prince of Wales Island, although the many Tlingit place names for habitation sites and other landmarks there attest to their presence.

The G̲aanax̲.ádi clan was the main group under the Raven moiety, while the Eagle/Wolf side included the Dak̲l'aweidí and the Teik̲weidí. The latter were believed to have migrated from the Nass River area, at a rocky island called Teik̲ (not mapped). Emmons (n.d.) interpreted their name to mean "Brown Bear Rock House People."

The extent of the contemporary Taant'a K̲wáan is somewhat ambiguous due to their own relocations and shifting territoriality among their neighbors: the Sanyaa and Shtax'héen Tlingit, Annette Island Tsimshian, K̲'áyk̲'aanii Haida, and the Tsetsaut in Portland Canal (Dangeli 1996). But their territory includes the southwestern Revilla-

"This Was Not Wilderness — This Was Our Home": Reflections on Work with Esther Shea
by Priscilla Schulte

Esther Shea, a Tlingit elder and leader of the Taant'a K̲wáan Teik̲weidí shared much of her love of the land and sea in her work with the Southeast Alaska Native Place Names Project. Much of her homeland is designated as wilderness within the Misty Fjords National Monument and Tongass National Forest, a point that she found ironic, since to her it was home and the home of her people. Esther Shea's happiest days were living with her family in fish camp gathering food and other resources of the area. These memories were brought alive with her work on the place names project.

Esther and I spent many satisfying hours reviewing the Waterman texts trying to decipher the older Tlingit orthography used by Thomas Waterman in his reports from the 1920s. Esther had studied a newer orthography at Sheldon Jackson in the 1970s and would sound out the place names from the older report and rewrite them in the newer Tlingit orthography and then translate them into English. Many of these names were associated with places that Esther had visited over her lifetime of living in southern Southeast Alaska. These names often referred to events or natural resources that were associated with the site and frequently evoked strong memories of times spent in the area or stories told by her mother and uncles and aunties.

Field trips to some of the remote locations identified in maps of the area helped stimulate Esther's memories of the places located on these maps and charts. University of Alaska Southeast students and community members traveled on the Forest Service boat, the *Tongass Ranger*, to visit some of the sites located on the maps. The place names reflect the fact that each bay, inlet, and rocky outcrop was an integral part of the life of the Tlingit people. Walking the rocky beaches and gathering beach foods reminded Esther of the way her ancestors used to live. She frequently commented that they were a "tough people" gathering food, cedar bark, and other resources from the rainy, windy environment of Southeast Alaska. Unlike the current place names given by British explorers like George Vancouver that reflected the names of influential people, the Tlingit place names reflect the life of the Tlingit people as they made their living throughout the area of Southeast Alaska.

Esther Shea also consulted with her older sister, Martha Cosello, and Tongass-speaking elder Emma Williams on the meaning of some of the older Tlingit names that were not frequently used. She would sit for hours with her daughter, Martha Denny reviewing the Tlingit place names and their meanings. James Llanos, a Forest Service computer specialist, worked with Esther to correctly locate the places on the map. The work of preserving the knowledge of her elders was satisfying to her because of her lifelong commitment to teaching the Tlingit language and culture to the young.

Esther Shea frequently reminded us of the importance of knowing "who you are." Esther Shea's people, the Taant'a K̲wáan, are the people of southern Southeast Alaska and every social event is a reminder of who they are and the fact that they have been here since time immemorial. The place names serve to validate their long history in this area and reveal how their lives are intertwined with the places where important events, as well as day to day activities, took place. The place names reinforce the sense of who they are today as well as in the past.

gigedo Island, Gravina Island, and the other major islands in Revillagigedo Channel (with the exception of Annette Island) and Moira Sound on southeastern Prince of Wales Island.

Ketchikan (Kichx̲áan, "Near the [Eagle's] Wing," #396). Now the second largest city in the region, the name Kichx̲áan originally applied to Ketchikan Creek and the Native settlement there. The creek was esteemed for its king and humpback salmon runs. According to Reynold Denny Sr., the calm waters and ample supply of winter king salmon in its vicinity made Kichx̲áan a favorable winter village, and thus it became the principal settlement of the Taant'a K̲wáan. The Neix̲.ádi (or Naha.ádi, from Naha Bay) clan was the original owner of the townsite of Kichx̲áan. A man named Kichx̲áan was married to a woman of the G̲aanax̲.ádi clan of the Taant'a K̲wáan. When his wife passed away, he gifted Kichx̲áan to the G̲aanax̲.ádi, thus making Kichx̲áan G̲aanax̲.ádi clan territory. The story is recognized by both the Sanyaa K̲wáan and Taant'a K̲wáan. The Taant'a K̲wáan sing a love song to the Sanyaa K̲wáan to commemorate the gifting of this land and to carry on their close relationship to one another. In addition to being the founder's name, Kichx̲áan is said to refer to the calm water "spreading out like an eagle's wing" from whichever direction one approaches Ketchikan Creek.

Duke Island (Yéex̲, #839). This was the site of a large village and fort. Waterman's consultant, Pete Williams, told him the Tlingit landed first at Yéil X̲'ayik Àan (Raven's Voice Town, #217), near Cape Chacon and their leader took them around Cape Chacon (Tàan Lunáa, #959) toward Duke Island to find salmon creeks. Along the way, they built a camp at Stone Rock Bay (Kalgèeyi Ye, "Shining Place," #946). That night they heard noises, and saw an island way off (Duke Island). A strong-hearted man took canoes (which in those days were made of rotting logs soft and easy to work with stone tools) and landed at the island, where they encountered young men with drums, singing. The place had a fine sand beach on a point called X̲'éxkw.àan* (Sand Beach Mouth Village,* #893.1), so the leader said "Go back and tell all the people to move to this island." All the people came. Soon they saw strangers and so they made a fort about a quarter mile from the sand beach, at Cape Northumberland, where there's high rock. Here they saw Captain Cook, who stopped on his way up the North Pacific coast. They called the fort G̲ooch X̲'akanòow (Wolf Mouth Fort, #902.1). But they could get no fish, so they explored farther north and finally settled at Tamgas Harbor, where there was a good salmon creek from Tamgas Lake, called T'angàash (#650), from which they took their name (rendered in English as Tongass).

Pete Williams, whose Indian name was Nàawuskéitl (the Native name for Nowiskay Cove, #568), told Waterman of a solitary mountain on Duke Island, also known as Yéex̲ (Mount Lazaro, #839), which served as a weather beacon. Sometimes when the wind is blowing from the north, a cloud streamer extends northward from this peak. If so, this means "Lookout for southeaster [wind]! Go ashore." On the other hand, if a southeaster is raging, and they see the cloud streamer points southeast, they know a north wind will soon be blowing. They go right out, even if a southeaster is blowing, as they know it will soon quiet. If clouds cover the whole mountain, they know there will be no wind. The name Yéex̲ is said to mean "entering a room or something."

Esther Shea, too, remembers Duke Island. In the spring time her family used to go there by boat to dry seaweed, toast halibut with seaweed, and roast gumboots.

The late Esther Shea, Teik̲weidí, in her regalia. Photo courtesy of Priscilla Schulte.

Tongass Island Village (*Kadúk̲x̲uka, #931*). Located at the entrance to Portland Canal, this became a major settlement of the Taant'a after their relocation from Prince of Wales Island. According to one estimate (Bancroft 1886) there were nine hundred people here before the smallpox epidemic of 1836, which wiped out nearly a third of the population. George Kegan Williams, nephew of Pete Williams, testified to Goldschmidt and Haas in 1946 (1998, 167) about the movements of his people in Taant'a K̲wáan, and their preference for good sockeye streams.

> I belong to the Tongass clan and was born where Metlakatla is now, about fifty-eight years ago. My father lived there and had a log cabin at the present site of the town of Metlakatla; this was before the Tsimshians came there. I was born there about three years after the Tsimshians came there. I lived there with my father until I was about twenty years old. My father practically raised me at Kegan Cove [Yasyàat, #700, #711] and which was also claimed by my father. It used to be a very good sockeye stream and we dried fish there... There are four sockeye streams in Moira Sound; one at Port Johnson [X̲'áax̲, #559], North Arm [X̲áach Dana Héenak'w, #595] at Nowiskay Cove [Nàawuskéitl, #568], which is named after my uncle; he had a claim to the place.
>
> My father told me he was living at Tongass Village on Tongass Island when the first American soldiers came here. This village was claimed by our clan, the Tongass people. Our people moved from Village Island [Dàasxakw, #743] near Cat Island where there are still totem poles belonging to our people, and on Cat Island are some graves and totem poles, to Tongass Island and from Tongass Village to Ketchikan; this was way before the white people came here. Our family formerly had six cabins at Kegan Cove, of which about only four or five still stand. I go there every year to trap. Long time ago, we made good money at Kegan Cove fishing sockeyes but now it is not worthwhile for me to stay there as the runs are very poor. We never used to go anywhere else but fished only in this bay, but now I have to run all over with my gas boat to catch fish. I have a cabin at Nowiskay Cove where there is a sockeye stream. I trap here every year.

Port Stewart (*G̲àanax̲, "Sheltered Place,"* #149*) *and Helm Bay* (*Kiks, #197*). Port Stewart is the birth place of the G̲aanax̲.ádi and the G̲aanax̲teidí clans, among the oldest of the Raven moiety. Today these clans are distributed throughout Southeast Alaska. Similarly, Helm Bay is closely associated with another old Raven clan, the Kiks.ádi (though others suggest this clan's bay of origin lies further south in what is today British Columbia). A constellation of geographic names is built around the unanalyzable term Kiks: Kiks Tahéen (Stream at the Head of Kiks, #160), Kiks X'àa (Kiks Point, #208), Kiks Áak'w (Kiks Little Lagoon, #196), and Kikska X'áat' (Island on Kiks, #186).

Sanyaa K̲wáan

The Sanyaa or Cape Fox people were the southernmost Tlingit group. Their k̲wáan originally was centered above Cape Fox at a settlement called G̲àash (Powder, #730) below Kah Shakes Cove. In the 1890s they moved their principal village to its present location at Saxman, formerly part of Taant'a K̲wáan. Sanyaa territory includes vast portions of the coastal mainland from Cape Fox (Kuskaagi X'áat' Yadaa, #936) to the top of Behm Canal and the northern and western portions of Revillagigedo Island. Census records in the historic era, however, suggest a small population; even in 1838 (de Laguna 1990, 205), a half century before their removal to Saxman, the Sanyaa were estimated at only 363 people. The k̲wáan was composed predominately of three clans: the Kiks.ádi on the Raven side, the Teik̲weidí on the Eagle/Wolf side, and the anomalous Neix̲.ádi, which had no moiety affiliation (R. Olson 1967, 33). Based on evidence from Sir James Douglas's travel notes, Emmons (n.d.) suggests a possible origin for the Neix̲.ádi near Cape Fox.

Cape Fox Village (*G̲àash, #730*). Located below Point Kirk near Kah Shakes Cove, this was the most populous settlement in the modern era. Emmons documented seventeen communal houses among the three clans residing there in 1882. Within fifteen years of Emmons visit, this village was downsized considerably as people moved to Saxman for schooling and other services. This site provided access to the wealth of natural resources in Kah Shakes Cove and Foggy Bay, and rich halibut banks along the coast.

Kah Shakes Cove (*G̲unéik̲'an* [*K'ah Shakes*], *#660*). A large settlement, Àasgutu.àan (Village in the Woods, #670) was located at the head of this cove and was reported to be a winter settlement of all three clans before they were decimated by disease and the survivors moved to Cape Fox Village (Emmons n.d.). This area was especially dear to the Neix̲.ádi clan, who have many legends associated with it (e.g., R. Olson 1967, 34–36), along with the historic village, grave, and fort sites. In terms of its natural resources, the bay is especially prized for its herring spawn which has been gathered there since time immemorial, though severely depleted in recent years (Thornton et al. 2010). Sanyaa Ḵwáan members also harvested king and sockeye salmon, halibut, deer, furbearers, shellfish, and berries in Kah Shakes in addition to raising vegetables in gardens (Goldschmidt and Haas 1998, 166). The bay takes its English name from the Neix̱.ádi leader, K'ah Shakes.

Naha Bay (Nàa.áa, #203). This bay and lake system is a productive habitat for sockeye and other salmon. The main village was at Loring. According to Emmons, the Nax̱.ádi (or Naa.aa.ádi) clan took their name from this place after migrating from the Interior down the Unuk River in western Behm Canal. However, Ronald Olson's (1967, 34–36) informant had the clan migrating from a settlement in Karta Bay on Prince of Wales Island called Gaxate'h* (after a creek, not mapped but perhaps related to #301), and Garfield and Forrest (1961, 44) link them to Nakat Bay near Tongass Island, from which they took

their name after migrating from Kasaan. It may be that they were but one segment of the Neix̱.ádi, as both Olson and Goldschmidt and Haas suggest.

Unuk River (Joonák, "Dreaming," #2). With its neighbor the Chickamin, the Unuk extends far into the Interior and provided an important travel route to and from the coast (hence it was also known as Héen Tlèin, "Big Stream"). Though it is now considered Teiḵweidí territory, all the Sanyaa clans claim to have been there from the earliest times (R. Olson 1967, 37). As Joseph Johns told Goldschmidt and Haas in 1946 (1998, 79):

> Our people started on the Unuk River and moved outside of Prince of Wales Island to Dall Island, from there to Klinkwan on Prince of Wales Island, in Hydaburg territory, then down to Cape Chacon, then to Annette Island at a place between Deer and Tent points. From there, the Tongass people moved to a place on the outside of Duke Island and then to Village Island and Cat Island just to the north of

Chickamin River Camp
by Esther Shea

After the fishing season was over in the summer, my father got his seiner ready for a trip up the Chickamin River [X̱èel, #99] to our camp. Everyone in the family had to help. My six brothers packed our camping outfits and household things. My mother must have taken along half of our household; big cast iron pots, fry pans, enamelware, big crock containers, and jars. My brothers packed huge traps for bears and smaller traps for beaver, marten, and mink.

The trip started from Saxman and went through beautiful Behm Canal. We saw what is known now as the Misty Fjords. We saw waterfalls coming from the mountainsides into the canal. It took us nine or ten hours to get to the river. We had to catch a big tide to go up the river, otherwise the boat would go dry on the sandbars.

Our house was about three miles upriver. It was built like a community house with a fireplace in the middle and platforms for living quarters. The house was two stories. It was built that way so that the salmon could be hung up in the rafters. Salmon was smoked right in the same house. Sometimes the salmon numbered six hundred that were drying in the rafters. There were coho, dog salmon, sockeye, humpy [pink], and even king salmon.

We picked wild crab apples by the bucketfuls. My brother, Louie, would tie the branches down for us so it would be easy for us to pick. These my mother put up for winter use. She steamed some crab apples which were put down in eulachon grease. She made apple butter and preserves. We also picked blue currants and that was made into Indian jam.

My father and brothers would go up the mountain near the glacier for mountain goats. The goats were brought down in canoes. The meat was salted, smoked, and canned. They trapped black bear and the meat was smoked. The fat was rendered out for use. My brothers trapped and brought home beaver, marten, and mink. Their skins were dried on forms.

We all had a chore to do. My chore was to pack wood for the fireplace every day. We packed water about a half mile from our house by buckets from a cold spring.

Fall was a busy time for all of us. Sometimes we missed the first part of the school year in Saxman. We came back from camp when all of the food was put up and all the skins were dried.

Duke Island. There are still totem poles and graves at this place, and my own parents lived there. Some of the people came directly to Ketchikan from there and others first went over to Tongass Village. This was before the American soldiers came up there. I was born in Tongass Village, and soon afterwards we moved up here to Ketchikan.

The three clans were living at Unuk River at the time of the Flood. According to Ronald Olson (1967, 36) each clan sought refuge on a different mountain, the Teiḵweidí on Mount Stoeckl (near the U.S.-Canada border above Unuk River), the Neix̱.ádi on a mountain called Gweka'h* (Kwéiy Ka,* not mapped) at the head of Rudyerd Bay, and the Kiks.ádi on a mountain called Watsdék* (not mapped) in Boca de Quadra. The people fashioned anchor lines to prevent them from drifting away from their homelands. Reportedly, one such line, now petrified, can still be seen on the mountain above Rudyerd Bay, but, as is often the case with such sacred mountains, attempting to scale it brings fog or bad weather.

The Unuk River supported one of the area's few large eulachon runs and Natives traveled there to harvest them each spring in late March and early April. It was also used as a base from which to hunt bear and mountain goat and to harvest salmon, all of which were dried in smokehouses along the Joonák (#2), Shàax̱ Tá (#4), and Sháa Héeni (#7) rivers (Goldschmidt and Haas 1998, 81).

Chickamin River (X̱èel, "Foam," #99). Like the Unuk, the Chickamin River was an important settlement and Interior corridor associated with the Teiḵweidí clan. This river also was another important source of eulachon, and Sanyaa Ḵwáan clans maintained seasonal camps there for the harvest (see "Chickamin River Camp" box). In addition, salmon, mountain goat, and cranberries were taken at this place. Emmons (n.d.) notes that the X̱eel Ḵwáan, now centered in Wrangell in Shtax'héen Ḵwáan, previously dwelled on the Chickamin and take their name from the river. There is a long story associated with their migration to the coast.

Yes Bay (Yèis Ǥeeyí, #54). This was another productive sockeye salmon system and former village site. Today Saxman and Ketchikan Natives use this area to harvest sockeye for subsistence. Originally, Yes Bay was owned by the Sanyaa Ḵwáan Teiḵweidí. Yes Bay Johnny, whose Tlingit name was Yèis, was a caretaker of the bay.

Rudyerd Bay (X̱eenáa, #227). Claimed by the Neix̱.ádi, the mountains above this bay served as a refuge site for the clan during the Flood, and when the waters receded they established a village at the bay. Although the village has long been abandoned, sockeye and other salmon are still harvested there. The area was also favored for hunting bear, goat, beaver, marten, and porcupine (Goldschmidt and Haas 1998, 81).

Final Thoughts

The Taant'a and Sanyaa ḵwáan place names project reveals, perhaps more so than any other area, the density and wealth of indigenous names in Lingít Aaní. The outstanding work of Waterman and his four Tlingit consultants in 1922 provided a sounding board and resonant chamber for contemporary elders, like Esther Shea, to reflect upon their own deep memories of named places and their cultural associations.

Today, Taant'a Ḵwáan and Sanyaa Ḵwáan are using the results of the place names project to maintain tribe members' ties to the land through education, culture camps, and appropriate management of local natural and cultural resources. The results of the SENSC place names project are being used to build teaching units for primary, secondary, and post-secondary education as well as in the work of local Native groups (Saxman, Ketchikan Indian Corporation, and Tongass Tribe) with the Forest Service to protect sacred sites. Cape Fox Corporation's NAGPRA (Native American Graves Protection and Repatriation Act) repatriation program has used the place names to help identify clan property associated with particular named sites, so that the property may be returned to its rightful owners.

Dreaming of Places: Thomas T. Waterman and the Unuk River Story

Anthropologist Thomas T. Waterman was an important figure in the documentation of Native American place names. A colleague of well-known anthropologist Alfred Kroeber, with whom he worked to document the place name inventory of Ishi, "the last Yahi Indian," Waterman spent most of his career at the University of California, Berkeley, and traveled widely in the Pacific Northwest. He confessed to an obsession with Native place names, noting that "Whenever sojourning among a tribe, I have endeavored to get every geographical name they knew, the 'meaning' of it, and the exact spot on the map to which it referred" (Waterman 1922a, 175). These three requirements — getting the name, its meaning, and precise location — remain the essential hallmarks of toponymic investigation.

Waterman was impressed by the high density of Native names on the land. So thick were they, he once observed, that the nautical charts could hardly accommodate them all. Waterman also developed one of the first taxonomies of place naming to analyze patterns in semantic references. He celebrated Native names as richly descriptive of both the natural and human geography.

By contrast, Waterman decried the lack of descriptiveness in English place names that overlaid the indigenous nomenclature.

> The way we have of ignoring the Indian place names and plastering on the map such atrocities as Brownsville (English and French) Hydaburg (American Indian and German) and silly names like Cloverdale and Bella Vista, from novels, mythology, poetry, and geography of the old world and the new is to be deplored. There is some reason for the use of the names of great men, Columbus, Washington, Madison and (most popular of all for some reason) Franklin, but even this has been carried to extremes. The chief engineer of a railroad, an acquaintance of mine, was once sitting in a bunk house naming the stations of a railroad he was surveying. Running out of names his roving eye chanced to light on a package of breakfast food. Unhappy town which lacked a name at that moment, has been Ralston ever since. Such a way of naming places is certainly unsystematic and meaningless, indicating to the outside world merely that we have no ideas and certainly no place names of our own. The primitive names of every region *always* mean something, and there are countless thousands of them. Primitive geography is precisely characterized by a wealth, a redundancy of names. (1922b)

Waterman's only foray to Southeast Alaska was a brief trip in the spring of 1922, when he was assigned by the Bureau of Ethnology to "scrutinize certain native towns in southeastern Alaska . . . to ascertain how many totemic monuments exist there, and to get information regarding the carvings." Remarkably, this brief trip yielded some 856 place names in southern Southeast Alaska.

Waterman realized that art, including "totemic monuments," are ultimately derived from the land. As evidence of this, he recorded a Unuk River story in shorthand, which may be paraphrased and matched with our list of place names as follows:

> A man dreamed of going to the daylight, when the people were still living in darkness at a village at Shrimp Bay, across from the waterfall [X'áas Kèeka Àan, #89]. He heard a loud "holler" and so the group grabbed their bows and arrows and gave chase. The sound lead them to the mouth of the bay [Kagit Shàa Sèiyi, #90], where they saw daylight for the first time.
>
> The same man dreamed of a river "like milk." He went there and discovered the Unuk River [Joonák, #2] with its milky waters.
>
> Then he dreamed of a river of foam coming down. He went there and discovered the Chickamin River [Xèel, #99].
>
> Then he dreamed of a bay, which up at its head, always stinks. He went there and discovered Smeaton Bay [Xaan, #435], where his group settled and from there populated the Lingít Aaní.
>
> These were the Teikweidí "Bear People." The pole at Cape Fox village has this story. (1922b)

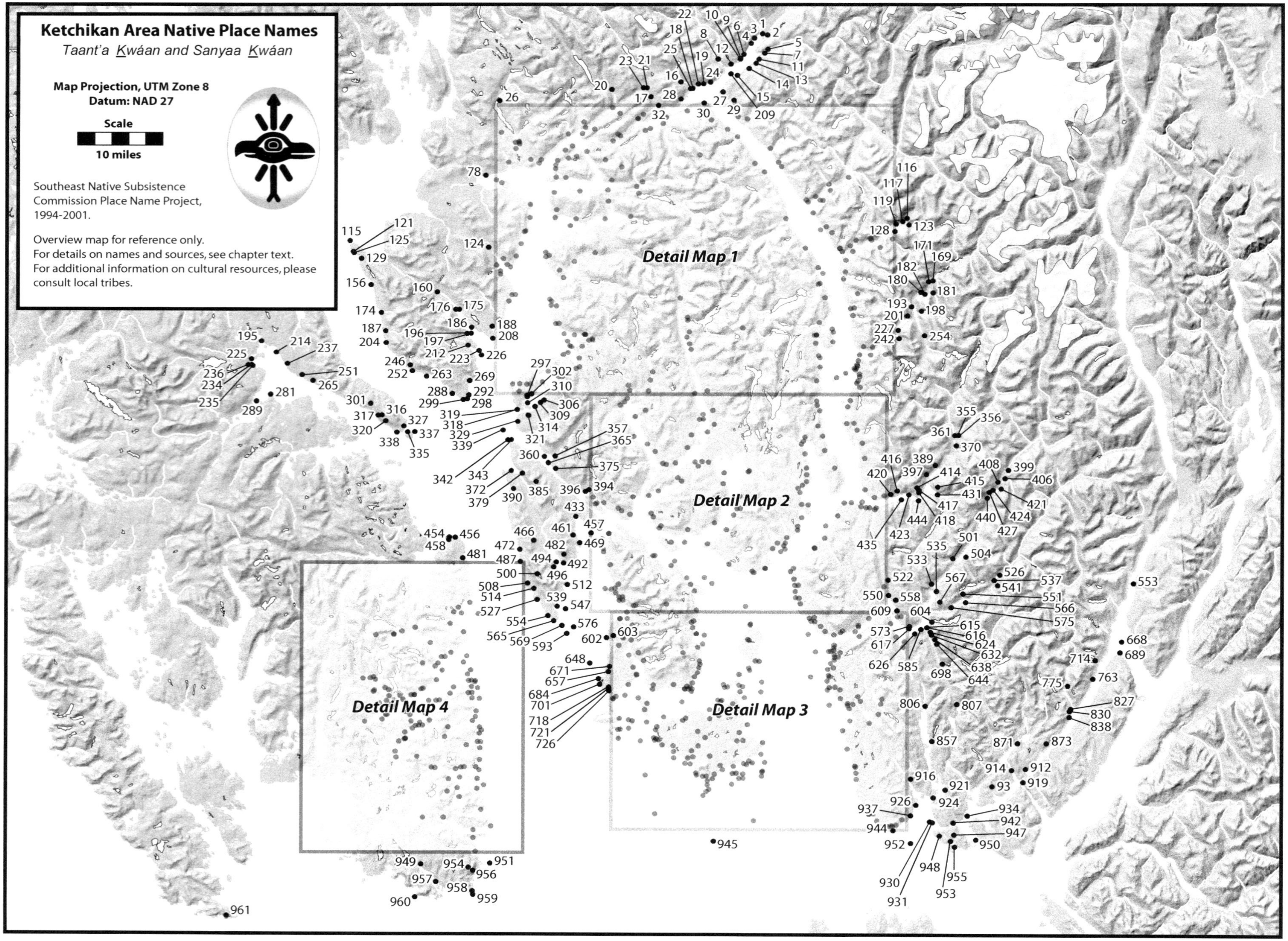
Ketchikan Area Native Place Names
Taant'a Kwáan and Sanyaa Kwáan
Map Projection, UTM Zone 8
Datum: NAD 27
Scale
10 miles
Southeast Native Subsistence Commission Place Name Project, 1994-2001.
Overview map for reference only.
For details on names and sources, see chapter text.
For additional information on cultural resources, please consult local tribes.
Detail Map 1
Detail Map 2
Detail Map 3
Detail Map 4

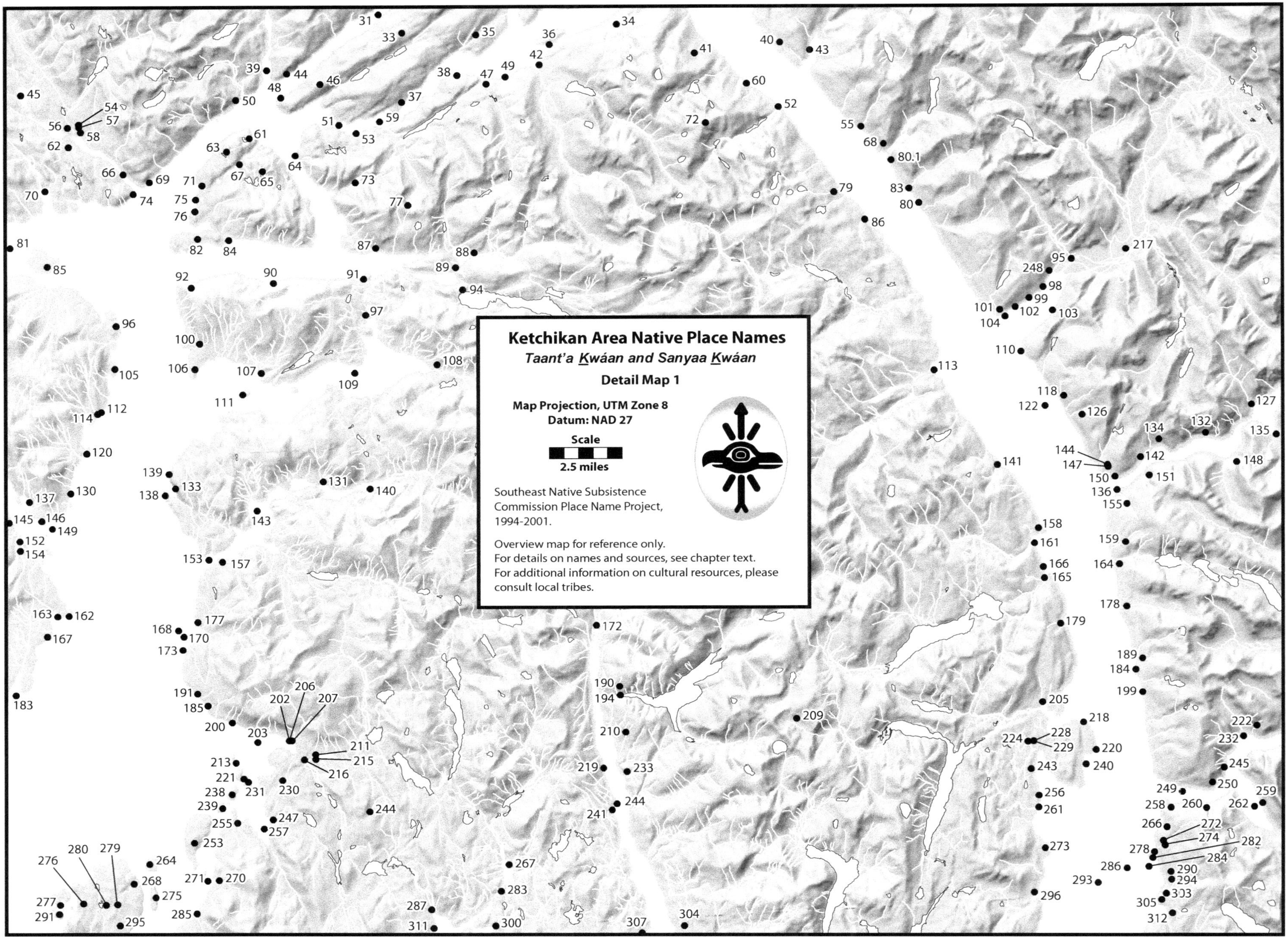
Ketchikan Area Native Place Names
Taant'a Kwáan and Sanyaa Kwáan
Detail Map 1
Map Projection, UTM Zone 8
Datum: NAD 27
Scale
2.5 miles
Southeast Native Subsistence Commission Place Name Project, 1994-2001.
Overview map for reference only.
For details on names and sources, see chapter text.
For additional information on cultural resources, please consult local tribes.

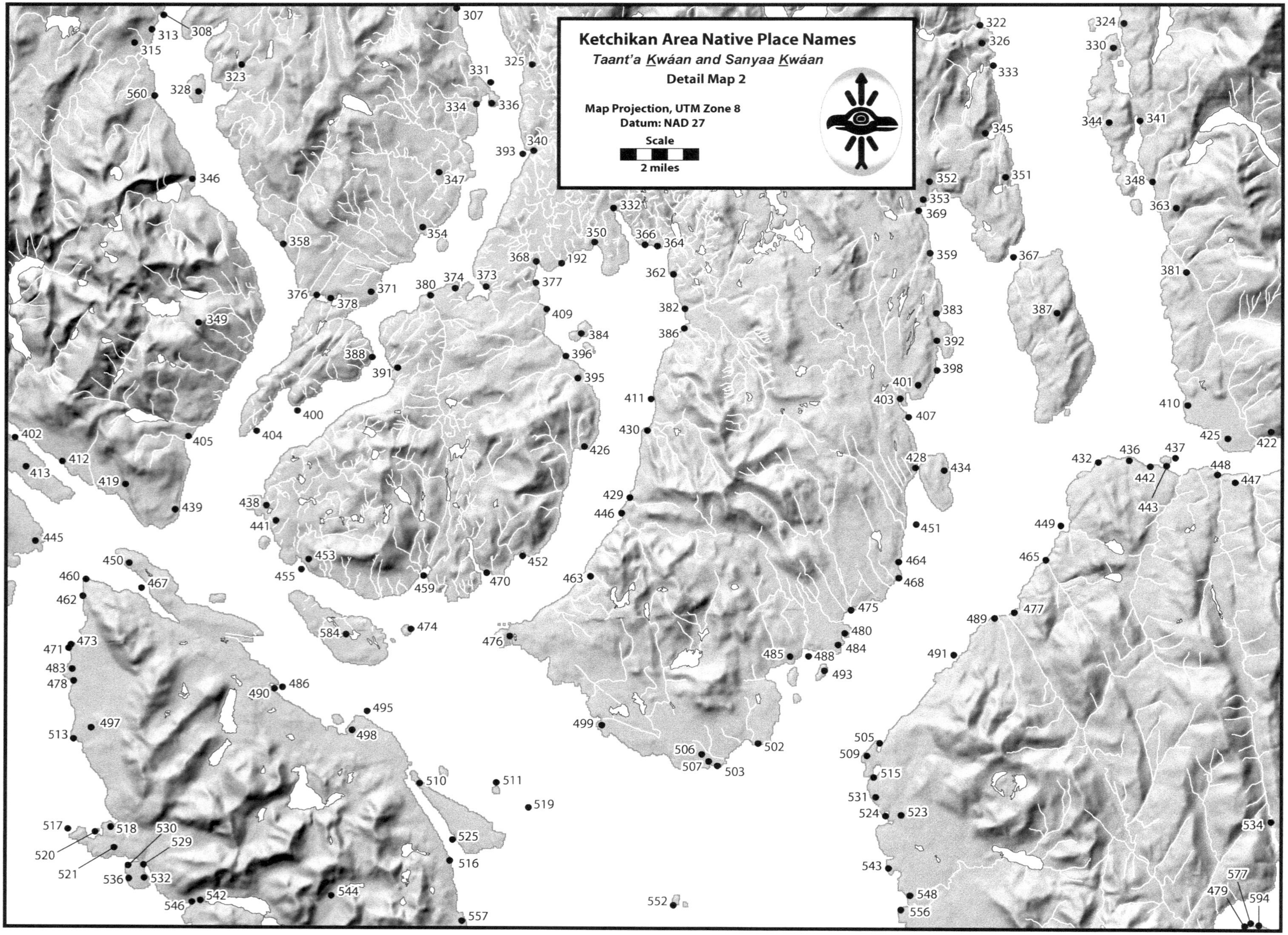
Ketchikan Area Native Place Names
Taant'a Kwáan and Sanyaa Kwáan
Detail Map 2
Map Projection, UTM Zone 8
Datum: NAD 27
Scale
2 miles
307
308
313
315
322
323
324
325
326
328
330
331
332
333
334
336
340
341
344
345
346
347
348
349
350
351
352
353
354
358
359
362
363
364
366
367
368
369
371
373
374
376
377
378
380
381
382
383
384
386
387
388
391
392
393
395
396
398
400
401
402
403
404
405
407
409
410
411
412
413
419
422
425
426
428
429
430
432
434
436
437
438
439
441
442
443
445
446
447
448
449
450
451
452
453
455
459
460
462
463
464
465
467
468
470
471
473
474
475
476
477
478
479
480
483
484
485
486
488
489
490
491
493
495
497
498
499
502
503
505
506
507
509
510
511
513
515
516
517
518
519
520
521
523
524
525
529
530
531
532
534
536
542
543
544
546
548
552
556
557
560
577
584
594
192

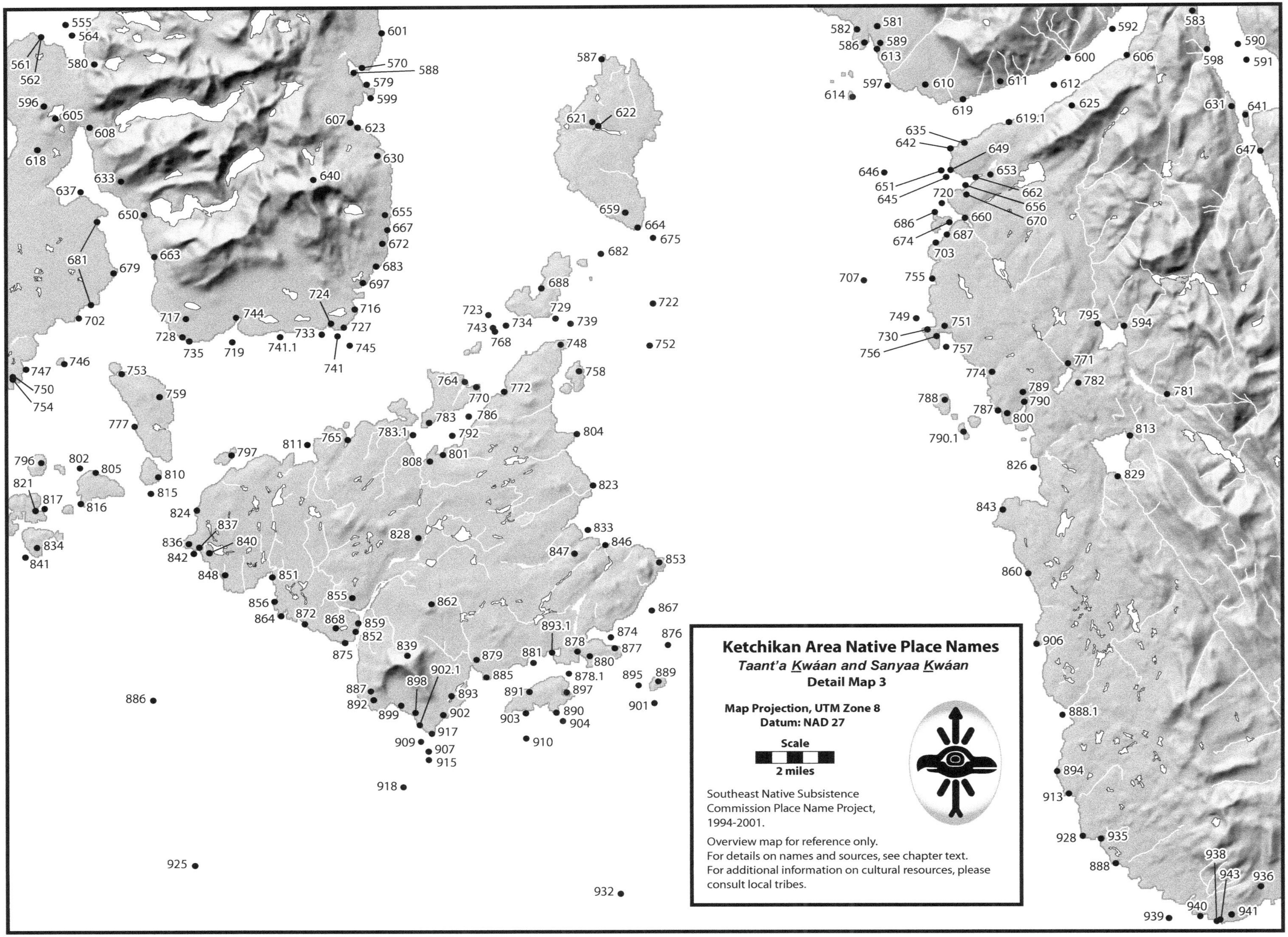
Ketchikan Area Native Place Names
Taant'a Kwáan and Sanyaa Kwáan
Detail Map 3
Map Projection, UTM Zone 8
Datum: NAD 27
Scale
2 miles
Southeast Native Subsistence Commission Place Name Project, 1994-2001.
Overview map for reference only.
For details on names and sources, see chapter text.
For additional information on cultural resources, please consult local tribes.

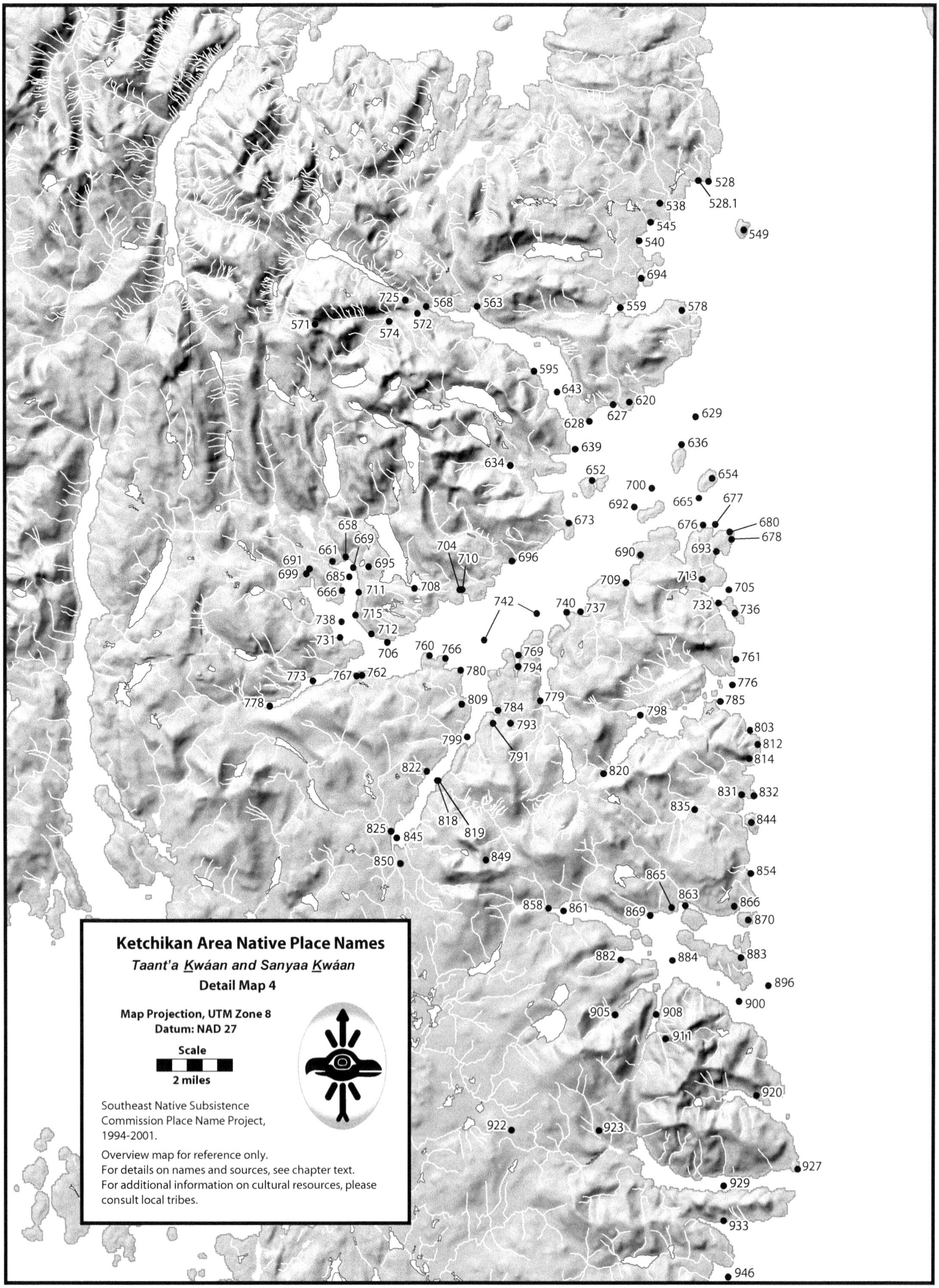
Ketchikan Area Native Place Names
Taant'a Kwáan and Sanyaa Kwáan
Detail Map 4
Map Projection, UTM Zone 8
Datum: NAD 27
Scale
2 miles
Southeast Native Subsistence Commission Place Name Project, 1994-2001.
Overview map for reference only.
For details on names and sources, see chapter text.
For additional information on cultural resources, please consult local tribes.
528
528.1
538
545
549
540
694
725
568
563
559
578
571
574
572
595
643
627
620
629
628
639
636
634
652
654
700
692
665
677
673
676
680
678
658
669
704
710
661
695
696
690
693
691
699
685
666
711
708
709
713
705
742
740
737
732
736
738
715
712
731
706
760
766
769
794
761
780
776
773
767
762
779
785
778
809
784
793
798
803
799
791
812
814
822
820
831
832
818
819
835
844
825
845
849
850
854
865
863
858
861
869
866
870
882
884
883
896
900
905
908
911
920
922
923
927
929
933
946

Taant'a Kwáan and Sanyaa Kwáan Place Names

Asterisk indicates uncertain, unconfirmed, or partial; NM = not mapped.
Some names have more than one pronunciation or translation.
Bracketed words in the name column are supplied by original sources (in most cases Waterman 1922b).

Map #	*Name*	*Translation*	*Location*
1	Dagiyge Héen	Middle Stream	Unuk River, north shore of Burroughs Bay
2	Joonák (Héen Tlèin)	Dreaming (Big Stream)	Unuk River, Burroughs Bay
3	Su Éix̲'i*	Long-Seaweed Slough*	North shore of Burroughs Bay
4	Shàax̲ Tá	Back of Gray Currants	North shore of Burroughs Bay
5	K'òonax̲ Aan	*	Point by Klahini River, Burroughs Bay
6	Jig̲èix̲latult Tlèin	*	North shore of Burroughs Bay
7	Sháa Héeni	Women's Stream	End of Burroughs Bay
8	Neechi*	*	Small cove, north shore of Burroughs Bay
9	Jig̲èix̲latult Yadi	Dry Alongside	Small cove, north shore of Burroughs Bay
10	Shàanax̲ Héeni	Valley Stream	North shore of Burroughs Bay
11	Chéex̲' Àan*	Shady Village*	End of Burroughs Bay
12	Kawchxidi G̲il'	Written-On Cliff	North shore of Burroughs Bay
13	Chéex̲' Àan Kunag̲i'y*	Shady Village Cove*	Southeast shore of Burroughs Bay
14	Lgàawu Héen	Noisy Stream	Southeast shore of Burroughs Bay
15	Néex̲' Héeni	Marble Stream	Point on southeast shore of Burroughs Bay
16	Dáadzi Héeni	Pyrite Stream	North of Point Whaley
17	Katnax̲ Séet	Katnax̲ (#20) Pass	Anchor Pass
18	Shéix̲'w K̲àadi	Red-Alder Slide	Up inside Walker Cove
19	Yatt'ukt	[Cliff] Where They Shot at the Side/Face	North shore of Burroughs Bay
20	[Yèis Shakag̲èey] Katnax̲	[At the Head of Yèis Bay (#54)] Top Side Way Back	Short Bay
21	Kayéil'i	Calm Place	Anchor Pass area
22	Tax'àak'u	Little Rock Point	Ledge Point
23	[Katnax̲] ——* Tahéen	Stream at Head of [Little] Katnax̲* (#20)	End of Anchor Pass and Bell Arm
24	Tax'àak'u Jig̲èi	Crook (inside curve) of Tax'àak'u (#22)	North of Point Whaley
25	Dáadzi Kunag̲èey	Pyrite Cove	North of Point Whaley
26	Dèishu Àan	Trail's End Village	Northern Lake McDonald
27	Chèech Shàayi	Porpoise Head	Point Fitzgibbon

Map #	*Name*	*Translation*	*Location*
28	Yéil Kòowu Nòow	Raven's Tail Fort	North of Point Whaley
29	Shàayag̲èey	Mountainside Bay	Fitzgibbon Cove
30	Tux̲'al.us'kw	Washing the Anus	Point Whaley
31	X'ul'jàa T'ika	Outside of X'ul'jàa (#46)	Bell Arm
32	Áa Sagank'i Ye*	Place Small*	South Anchor Pass
33	X'ul'jàa ——*	*	Bell Island
34	Keiyak Gan* Shaká	——* Above	North of Claude Point
35	Lak̲t Yakatan Ye* Tlèin	Larger Lak̲t Yakatan Ye* (#37)	North shore in Behm Narrows
36	Keiyak Gan*	*	Claude Point
37	Lak̲t Yakatan Ye*	Place Where Bentwood Box Lies*	North shore in Behm Narrows
38	Tsàa X̲àay Héen X'àa	Tsàa X̲àay Héen (#47) Point	South shore in Behm Narrows
39	[Shak̲éen*] Yèis Shakag̲èey	Bay at the Head of [Shak̲éen*] Yèis (#50)	Bailey Bay
40	L'iwani Kaayayuwa*	*	Below Dew Point in Behm Canal
41	Nàa.áa Shayadàa	Around the Head of Nàa.áa (#203)	West shore in eastern Behm Canal
42	X̲aawa Héen	Driftwood Stream	Small cove in Behm Narrows
43	Tl'éix̲wani Ye*	Certain Edible Root Place*	Saks Cove
44	Kuts'èen G̲il'i	Rat Cliff	Entrance to Bailey Bay
45	Yèis Ta	Head of Yèis [Bay] (#54)	North of Yes Bay
46	X'ul'jàa	*	Bell Island
47	Tsàa X̲àay Héen	Seal Lodge Stream	South shore in Behm Narrows
48	X'ul'jàa Tuk̲dàa*	Bottom Surface of X'ul'jàa* (#46)	Snipe Point
49	——* Yayuwàa	*	South shore in Behm Narrows
50	[Yèis] Shak̲éen	[Yèis (#54)] ——*	Southeast of Bailey Bay
51	Nax̲.ishka*	Small Hole in a Stream*	Behm Narrows
52	Kwéiy Sáani Yadi	Smaller Landmark Freshwater Little Bay	West shore in eastern Behm Canal
53	——* Héeni	Visiting* Creek	Small cove in Behm Narrows
54	Yèis [G̲eeyí]	——* [Bay]	Yes Bay
55	T'einéech* Tlèin	——* Big	Small cove south of Saks Cove in Behm Canal
56	Yèis Héen	Yèis (#54) Stream	Middle of Yes Bay
57	[Xèitgwáls'] Yèis Ka	[Hits the Breastbone] On Yèis (#54)	Yes Bay
58	Yèis Wat Àan	Village at the Mouth of Yèis (#54)	Middle of Yes Bay
59	——* Héeni Yadi	——* Smaller Stream	Behm Narrows
60	Nàa.áa Shayadàa X'áat'	Nàa.áa Shayadàa (#41) Island	West shore in eastern Behm Canal
61	Séedak'w Shata	Head of Little Pass	North end of Black Island
62	Gunax̲at Shi	Always Singing	East shore in Yes Bay
63	Séedak'w T'ika	Place outside of Little Pass	Black Island
64	Shgix̲'gi Àan*	Creaking* Village	Near Curfew Point

Map #	*Name*	*Translation*	*Location*
65	L'èet	Tail	Hassler Island
66	[Dakdachóon Àan] Xèitgwáls'	Hits the Breastbone [of Dakdachóon Àan (#69)]	South Yes Bay
67	——* Séedi	——'s Pass	Blind Pass
68	——* (T'einéech*) Tlèin	——* (T'einéech*) Larger One	End of Weasel Cove
69	Dakdachóon Àan	Straight-Out Village	Syble Point
70	Yèis T'èigèey	Bay behind Yèis (#54)	Cove in Spacious Bay
71	——* Àan	——'s Village	Camp at Black Island
72	*	*	Unnamed mountain on maps
73	Ít'ch G̲èeyi	Glass Bay	East of Hassler Pass
74	Keiyayee*	*	Bluff Point
75	——* Néigani*	——'s Fish Trap*	Near Blind Pass
76	L'itt'ak̲kanòow	Fort alongside L'èet (#65)	Cape on Hassler Island
77	Kagit Shàa	Dark Mountain	Mountain north of Shrimp Bay
78	West'eka	Back of Wes* (#81)	Spacious Bay
79	Kwéiy Sáani Tlèin	Larger Kwéiy Sáani (see #52)	West shore in eastern Behm Canal
80	Shas.áax̲u Yadi	Smaller Child	South of Robinson Creek
80.1	T'einéech* Yadi	T'einéech* (see #55) Child	Above Robinson Creek
81	Wes*	*	Spacious Bay
82	Xwéix̲*	Rock Pile*	Gedney Island
83	Shas.áax̲u	Tied in Bundles	Mouth of Robinson Creek
84	Xwéix̲ Àan*	Rock Pile Village*	Camp at Gedney Island
85	Westa X'áat'	Island at Head of Wes* (#81)	Square Island
86	Kwéiy Sáani Yayuwàa	Between [the Two] Kwéiy Sáani[s] (#52, #79)	West shore in eastern Behm Canal
87	Làax̲ X'àayí	Red Cedar Point	Dress Point
88	Kagit Áak'w	Dark Little Lake	End of Shrimp Bay
89	X'áas Kèeka Àan	Village across from Waterfall	North of Shrimp Bay
90	Kagit Shàa Sèiyi	Area below Kagit Shàa (#77)	Gedney Pass
91	Gòonk' Shayik*	*	Cove in Gedney Pass
92	Chichtayèe*	Porpoise Below*	Brow Point
93	X'áat' Ka	Island On*	Fillmore Island
94	Kagit X'áas	Dark Waterfall	End of Shrimp Bay
95	Nèix̲kéitkw	Small Valley	Marshy area at mouth of Clear Creek
96	S'ix'gàanax̲	Snail Rocks	Snail Point
97	Shòogu* Áak'w	——* (frogs laugh there) Lagoon	North end of Neets Bay
98	Chòokan X'àayi	Grass Point	Mouth of Chickamin River, north side
99	X̲èel	Foam	Chickamin River
100	S'áaw Áak'u	Crab Lagoon	Cove near Chin Point

Map #	*Name*	*Translation*	*Location*
101	X̲ilx'àa	Foamy Point	Fish Point
102	Teka.àanak'w	Little Village on the Rocks	North side of Chickamin River
103	Kutkeitlshaa Seiyi	Hunting with Dogs Mountain Front	South side of Chickamin River
104	K̲àa Shàayi Héen	Human Head Stream	Inside of Fish Point Creek
105	S'ix'g̲àanax̲ Èegayaa X'áat'*	Island by the Beach below S'ix'g̲àanax̲* (#96)	Island south of Snail Point
106	[K̲ukwas'*] X'àayi	[Forked*] Point	Chin Point
107	Xakw G̲èeyi	Sand Beach Bay	North shore of Neets Bay
108	Guteenexti* Tahéen	Stream at Head of Guteenexti* (#109)	Head of Neets Bay
109	Guteenexti*	*	Neets Bay
110	X̲èel Áa	Foamy Lake	Near Trap Point
111	Guteenexti* Kax'áat'	Island on Guteenexti* (#109)	Bug Island
112	G̲il'àa Héeni	Grindstone Stream	South of Snail Point
113	Kwéiy Tlèin	Big Landmark	Portage Cove
114	Àasgutuhéen	Stream in the Woods	South of Snail Point
115	Chòonèit Xweis'*	Arrow Smallest	Tip of Lemesurier Point
116	Atahéenak'w	Little Stream at the Head of the Bay	Walker Creek
117	Shéix̲'w K̲àadi	Red-Alder Slide	Inside Walker Cove
118	Óoxjaa Séet Héen	Windy Pass Stream	Stream inside Channel Island
119	T'óok' K̲àadi	Nettles Slide	Inside Walker Cove
120	Xetá Héen	Sea Creek from Shape of Heckman Point	Heckman Point
121	Shinséet	Bailer Pass	West side of Lemesurier Point
122	Ooxjaa*	Windy*	Channel Island
123	L'óox̲'u Héen	Silty Stream	Walker Creek
124	G̲àanax̲ Tahéen	Stream at the Head of G̲àanax̲ (#149)	End of Port Stewart
125	Shèen	Bailer	Island, west side of Lemesurier Point
126	X̲èel Yayuwàa	Place between X̲èel (#99)	In front of Chickamin River
127	Kuyi*	Sound of Something Animate*	Inside Walker Cove
128	X̲'éen	House Screen/Mural	Opposite New Eddystone Rock
129	Shinsithéen	Bailer Pass Stream	Small Inlet By Lemesurier Point
130	G̲àanax̲ Shakax'áat'	Island above G̲àanax̲ (#149)	South of Heckman Point
131	Kòonax̲ Èey	Kòonax̲ (#140) Tide-Race	Point inside Traitors Cove
132	Tag̲anis K̲àadi	Pole Slide	Inside Walker Cove
133	Nalgèich	*	Bushy Point Cove
134	Tekakuwa Héen	Looks like Rock Stream	Inside Walker Cove
135	Kèinax̲t Tlèin	Big Kèinax̲t (#139)	In Walker Cove
136	Shàax̲ Kóog̲u	Gray Currant Pit	Walker Cove
137	G̲àanax̲ Áak'w	G̲àanax̲ (#149) Little Lake	Small cove in Port Stewart

Map #	*Name*	*Translation*	*Location*
138	Kalxaji Yè*	Can See Through*	Bushy Point
139	Kèinaxt	*	Inside Walker Cove
140	Kòonax	*	Inside Traitors Cove
141	Kwéiy Tlèin Ègayáa	[Beach] Below Kwéiy Tlèin (#113)	West shore in eastern Behm Canal
142	Nàak'al	*	West of stream in Walker Cove
143	Xòoxan	*	Inside Traitors Cove
144	Kèinaxt X'aka.àan	Village at the Mouth of Kèinaxt (#139)	Hut Point
145	Kóosh	Plenty Free	Near Granite Creek
146	Gàanax Nòow	Gàanax (#149) Fort	Port Stewart
147	Sukka Héen	Grass Creek	Moss Creek
148	Tekas' Neixi Tlèin*	Big Split Rock*	In Walker Cove
149	Gàanax	Sheltered Place*	Port Stewart
150	Kèinaxt X'aka	On the Mouth of Kèinaxt (#139)	At the mouth of Walker Cove
151	Tekas' Neixi Yadi*	Split Rock Child*	In Walker Cove
152	Lax' Héeni	Crane Stream	East shore of Port Stewart
153	Kòonax X'aktl'áak'*	Dry [Rocks] at the Mouth of Kòonax* (#140)	Entrance to Traitors Cove
154	Lax' Xagu	Crane Sand Beach	South entrance of Port Stewart
155	Tax'àak'u	Little Rock Point	Small cove, north shore of Burroughs Bay
156	Gil'yé	Cliff Place	South of Lemesurier Point
157	Kòonax X'akanòow*	Fort at the Mouth of Kòonax* (#140)	Entrance to Traitors Cove
158	S'áaw Héeni Yakax'áat'	Islands in Front of Crab Stream	Shore near Snip Island
159	Kukèekan X'àayi	Lookout Promontory	Grave Point
160	Kiks Tahéen	Stream at the Head of Kiks (#197)	End of Helm Bay
161	Gòoch Héeni	Wolf Stream	Creek from Yellow Hill
162	L'ux'shu X'àa	——* Point	Point Francis
163	L'ux'shu Gèey	——* Bay	Small cove near Point Francis
164	Kóosh	Plenty of Everything Free	East shore of Port Stewart
165	S'áaw Héeni Yayuwàa	Between Crab Stream	Shore south of Snip Island
166	S'áaw Héeni	Crab Stream	End of Wilson Arm, Smeaton Bay
167	L'ux'shu Nòowu	——* Fort	Below Point Francis
168	Tàan Tèiyi Yadàa	Around the Side of Sea Lion Rock	Escape Point
169	Chiwa Eyakw*	Turning Falls*	Rudyerd Bay
170	Tàan Tèiyi	Sea Lion Rock	Escape Point
171	Tsàa Tèik'i	Little Seal Rock	North end of Rudyerd Bay
172	Tsáats	Place Liked by Seal	Mouth of Carroll River
173	Tàan Tèiyi Nòow	Tàan Tèiyi (#170) Fort	South of Escape Point
174	Wòosh X'adàa Yaa Aduwadletlgi X'áat'*	Wagering Done That Island*	South of Lemesurier Point

Map #	Name	Translation	Location
175	Nandesawat	Having Mouth [of Stream] toward the North	Stream one mile south of White River
176	Teyat'aḵkahéen*	Little Stream Run Down Rock*	West shore in Helm Bay
177	Kich G̲èeyi	———* Bay	North of Escape Point
178	*	*	Unnamed creek on map
179	Neix̲[w]uteen* Yayuwàa	Between ———*	North of Skirt Point
180	Adaa X'áasi	Turning Falls	Rudyerd Bay
181	Kéitl.adi Héeni	Seagull Stream	Stream in north end of Rudyerd Bay
182	Héen Tlèin Áak'w	Big Stream Lake	North end of Rudyerd Bay
183	Dàalg̲àasiye	Place That Is Proscribed All Around	Raymond Cove
184	Watgadlaan	Deep Mouthed [Stream]	Three miles north of Point Eva
185	Kóokx̲'	Pits	Indian Point
186	Kikska X'áat'	Island on Kiks (#197)	Island in Helm Bay
187	Tuwawòoli Héen	Stream with a Hole in It	Small cove above Ship Island
188	Dàalg̲àasiye Yadi	Smaller Dàalg̲àasiye (#183)	Wadding Cove
189	Àas Kadayéis'i Tlèin*	Tree in the Shadow Large*	Four miles north of Point Eva
190	Lagsheey*	*	Falls Creek; comes out of Swan Lake
191	Xakw Tlèin	Big Sand Beach	North of Indian Point
192	Tuwawòoli Héen	Stream with a Hole in It	Northern Thorne Arm
193	Xwàas	Falls	Falls opposite Nooya Lake stream
194	Tsáats Yayix̲g̲àx̲	Crying for Tsáats (#172)	Northeast of Nigelius Point, Carroll Inlet
195	Naká	*	Salt Chuck, Kasaan Bay
196	Kiks Áak'w	Kiks (#197) Little Lagoon	Lagoon on the west shore of Helm Bay
197	Kiks	*	Helm Bay
198	Lnax̲duwa.òowu Ye	Place That Cannot Be Lived On	Nooya Lake stream
199	Àas Kadayéis'i Yadi	Child of Tree in the Shadow	Two miles north of Point Eva
200	Nàa.áa Shàa Sèiyi	Area below Nàa.áa (#203) Mountain	East of Indian Point
201	Tleilkee Ye	Place You Can't Go Through	Steep place south of Nooya Lake stream
202	Nàa.áa Èey	Nàa.áa (#203) Tide-Race	Dogfish Island
203	Nàa.áa	Nation Lake (Distant Lake)	Naha Bay
204	Shachx̲'àan*	Women Drying [Fish]*	Near Ship Island
205	X'àa Ta*	Head of [Bay behind] Point*	Cove north of Wart Point
206	Kax̲.àan	After Something Town	Loring
207	Dàax̲.anahèen	[Salmon] Swim around It	North of Donnelly Point
208	Kiks X'àa	Kiks (#197) Point	Helm Point
209	S'axt' Àani	Devil's Club Village	Point on southeast shore in Burroughs Bay
210	G̲il'i Shaaku*	Little Mountain Cliff*	Shoal Cove, Carroll Inlet
211	Te Nòowu	Rock Fort	Near Roosevelt Lagoon

Map #	Name	Translation	Location
212	Ḵakwnáx̲'i*	Basket Stay*	Smugglers Cove
213	Kalts'akwkal.aax̲*	Sound of Squirrel Island	Cache Island
214	Katkasa*	*	Kasaan Bay
215	Èey Tuḵyèe Héen	Stream below Where the Tide-Race Comes Out	Near Roosevelt Lagoon
216	Yéil X̲'éik'	Raven's Little Mouth	Near Roosevelt Lagoon
217	Yéil X̲'ayik Àan	Inside Raven's Mouth Town (Raven's Voice Town)	North Pass
218	——* Séedak'w	——* Little Pass	Wart Point
219	Kóoshdàa Góoni	Land Otter Spring	North of Nigelius Point
220	*	*	Unnamed point on map
221	Tawanyèe X̲'áat'	Close-By Island	Cedar Island
222	G̲ushká Sáani	Place Shaped like a Lap	North shore of Rudyerd Bay
223	Katgàawtan	Drum Lying on It	Island just outside Smugglers Cove
224	Shàak'w Sèiyi*	Area below Little Mountain*	Cove area west of Sargent Bay
225	Lugu* Nòow	——* Fort	Fort in Kasaan Bay
226	Kal.àasak'w	Having Small Tree on It	Just outside Helm Bay
227	X̲eenáa	*	Rudyerd Bay
228	Nage'kl* Tahéen	Stream at the Head of Nage'kl* (#229)	End of Sargent Bay
229	Nage'kl*	——* (probably Tsimshian)	End of Sargent Bay
230	Nàa.áa T'èi G̲èey	Bay behind Nàa.áa (#203)	Long Arm
231	Kéet Nòowu	Killer Whale Fort	Off of Cod Point
232	G̲ushká Tlèin	Big Lap	Rudyerd Bay
233	T'ahéeni	King Salmon Stream	North of Licking Creek
234	Salkwa*	*	Settlement in Karta Bay
235	Lnit'eek̲'a*	*	Karta Bay
236	Djiwas*	Rapids*	Karta Bay*
237	Shèishóox̲ Àan	Rattling Village*	Kasaan Bay
238	Ts'axwelx'áat'i	Crow Island	Moser Island
239	Shkwasxagu*	Having Sand Beach in Front*	Stack Island
240	——* Tuk̲dàa X̲'áat'	Island on the Bottom Surface of ——*	Island, east side of Cactus Point
241	Shax̲'wg̲èeyak'u	Alder Cove	Nigelius Point
242	Keilkatsk	A Bush That Looks like Blueberry	In Rudyerd Bay
243	——* X̲'aka	On the Mouth of ——*	Sargent Bay
244	Shax̲'w X̲'àa	Alder Point	Nigelius Point,* Carroll Inlet
245	Jánwu Ḵàadi*	Mountain Goat Slide*	North shore of Rudyerd Bay
246	S'òow Héen	Green Stream	Creek at Niblack Point
247	Tàalḵuhéen	*	Near Long Arm
248	Chòokan X̲'àayi	Fine Grass Point	North side in tidal flats of Chickamin River

Map #	Name	Translation	Location
249	X̱eenáa X'aka	On the Mouth of X̱eenáa (#227)	Mouth of Rudyerd Bay
250	Dag̱atch Héen	Dripping Stream	Stream one mile south of Point Eva
251	Tsunkitwu Táal	Beaver Upset Place (used his tail to hit)	Kasaan Bay
252	S'èeḵ G̱èeyi	Smoke Bay	Niblack Point
253	Shkaskèix̱i*	Tangled On*	Grant Island
254	Anax̱óoḵs	*	South arm of inner Rudyerd Bay
255	Téey Chan G̱èeyak'w	Yellow Cedar Smell Small Bay/Cove	Cove at head of Moser Bay
256	——* Kax'áat'	Islands on ——*	Sargent Bay
257	Te Héeni	Rock Stream	End of Moser Bay
258	Nandeix̱an	Facing-Up Inlet	Point Louise
259	Kéitl.adi G̱il'i	Seagull Cliff	Rocky side of Punch Bowl
260	Tayei X'aal	Bottom of Skunk Cabbage	In Rudyerd Bay
261	——* X'aka.àanak'w	Small Village at the Mouth of ——*	Tramp Point
262	——* G̱èey	——* Bay	Punch Bowl
263	Shaltlax̱séet	Lichen-Covered-Rock-Island Pass	Below Niblack Point
264	Yax̱keek Kaga*	Island Is Flat on Top*	Back Island
265	Witlk'i* Nòow	*	Bight at new Kasaan
266	Tsàa Yòowu Ta	Back-of-Bay of Seal Stomach	South of Porpoise Point
267	Èey Shakahéen	Stream at the Head of the Swift Current	Salt Lagoon
268	Yáay Áak'u	Whale Little Lake	Northeast side of Betton Island
269	X̱akw Tóode Nadàa	Runs into Sand Beach	North Bond Bay
270	L'òok Héeni	Coho Salmon Stream	Northeastern Clover Passage
271	S'ée X'áat'i	Salalberry Island	Small island, northern Clover Passage
272	Xixch' Òodag̱àayawu Ye	Place Where [Rocks] All Look like Frogs	Little bay south of Point Louise
273	Kals'éix̱wani Héen	Stream with Tree Moss on It	South of Tramp Point
274	X̱'éen	Wall Screen/Mural	In Walker Cove
275	Dàalgil'i*	Having Cliffs around It*	Hump Island
276	Sataay* Àak'w	Little Lake of Sataay* (#279)	West Side of Betton Island
277	Kuts'èen G̱il'i*	Rat Cliff*	Tatoosh Island
278	Daa G̱il'giye	Place with Cliffs around It	Stream on mainland near New Eddystone Rock
279	Sataay*	Tangled On*	Betton Island
280	Saataak*	Name Around*	Betton Island
281	G̱òoch Làakanòow	Inside Wolf's Mouth Fort	Inside Kasaan Bay*
282	Wooshkigi	Two (like twins) Coming Together	West rock of New Eddystone Rock
283	Èey	Tide Run	Rapids at Salt Lagoon
284	Kastayèidi	Having Yellow Bladder Seaweed on It	Halfway to shore from New Eddystone Rock
285	Wat.sa.àan Héen	Having a Village at the Mouth Stream	Northeastern Clover Passage

Map #	Name	Translation	Location
286	Cháatl Wàaḵk'i	Little Halibut Eye	East rock of New Eddystone Rock
287	Atahéenk'u	Small Stream at Head of Bay	Leask Cove
288	Yakwseejan*	Canoe Safe*	Near Caamano Point
289	——* G̲èey	——* Bay	Twelvemile Arm
290	A Yáx̲ Aa G̲alshuwu Héen	Stream with Some [Trees] Hanging Down on the Face [of the Bank]	Near Edith Point
291	Satayki Yadi*	——* (see #279)	Tatoosh Island
292	Wat.lax̲'àak	Having a Ravine at the Mouth [of Stream]	Bond Bay
293	Kashk'atl[']k'*	*	New Eddystone Rock
294	Kuskàagi Nòow	Thick Fort	One mile north of Edith Point
295	Dàaltèiyi	Having Rocks around It	East side of Betton Island
296	X̲asx̲wéint	*	Cove north of Ella Point
297	Satá Héen	Satá's (see #279) Creek	East side of Betton Island
298	Kadax̲tgut*	*	Caamano Point
299	Kóoshdàa Kóogu	Land Otter Pit	Near Caamano Point
300	Kaltl'áak'i Héen	Stream That Has Mica	Tea Cove
301	Gadeeya Eenwai*	Half of ——*	Karta Bay
302	Satá Nòowu	Satá's (see #279) Fort	Betton Island
303	Tuwawóoli Nòow	Fort with a Hole in It	North of Edith Point
304	Yakw Tak'x̲'áas	Fall alongside Canoe	Creek at Shoal Camp
305	Yéil T'òogu	Raven's Cradleboard	Edith Point
306	X'áas Yayuwàa	Area between Waterfall	Middle eastern shore of Clover Passage
307	Tsàa Èeji	Seal Rock	Rock opposite from Marble Creek
308	X'àakahéenak'u	Small Stream Point	South of Leask Cove
309	X'áas	Waterfall	Waterfall, Clover Passage
310	Likatsi	Sharp Points	Clover Island
311	Katl'ak'gèeyi	Mica Bay	South of Leask Cove
312	Shéik̲l	[Somebody's name]	Creek in Checats Cove
313	Nandesawat	[Inlet] With Mouth toward the North	Small cove in Helm Bay
314	Watx̲.agàan*	Mouth [of Stream] Keeps Burning*	South end of Clover Passage
315	Kax̲yik	Way of Going after Something	White River
316	Shaa	Mountain	Kasaan Bay
317	Éek̲ X̲'aakasxuk	*	Mouth of Kasaan Bay
318	Satá Yádi*	Smaller Child* (see also #279)	The Pup Island
319	Lik'ats' Nòowu	Sharp Point	North end of Revellagegedo Island, clockwise from Betton Island
320	Shàa Nòowu	Mountain Fort	Kaasan Bay
321	Takgwats'àan	Shallow Bottomed	Southern Clover Passage
322	Gòon Yadi	Smaller Spring	South of Ella Point

Map #	*Name*	*Translation*	*Location*
323	Watsegan	Burned Out	Coon Cove
324	Tax̲'nòowu	Snail Rock Fort	Entrance Island
325	Yakw Tak'x'áas Se Yadi	Child of Yakw Tak'x'áas (#304)	Carroll Inlet, above Shoal Cove
326	Gòon Tlèin	Larger Spring	South of Ella Point
327	Xik G̲il' Geey.aak'w*	Inside of Cliff Little Bay*	Grindall Passage
328	S'in X'áat'i	Wild Parsley Island*	Coon Island
329	Wòotsàagáa X'àayi	Cane Point	Point Higgins
330	Tàakw.àank'i Shatanòow*	Fort at the Head of Little Winter Village*	Fort at Winstanley Island, northern tip
331	Ushu* Héen	Sticks Tied Together* Creek	Creek near Island Point, Carroll Inlet
332	Tayèes T'éex̲'	Stone Wedge Pounding	Near Mop Point, northern Thorne Arm
333	Tsòonx̲'e Héeni	Water-Dog Stream	West of Winstanley Island
334	X'àa Shahéen*	Point with Stream at the Head*	South of Island Point
335	Kahta*	Deep Channel*	Grindall Passage
336	Lax̲x̲'áat'ak'u	Red Cedar Islet	Island south of Island Point
337	K'awdaxat*	*	Grindall Island
338	Xik G̲il'*	——* Cliff*	Grindall Point
339	S'èenáa X'áat'i	Light Island	Guard Island
340	Gut'te* G̲èeyak'w	——* Rock* Little Bay	Shoal Cove
341	Tàakw.àank'i Séet	Little Winter Village Pass	Shoal Water Pass
342	Lgòoji Shak.eet*	Notch/Gap in Mountain at Head of Lgòoji* (see #343)	Off Vallenar Point
343	Lgòoji Shàa Ta*	Hilly Mountain [Behind*]	Vallenar Point
344	Tàakw.àank'i	Little Winter Village	Small town on Winstanley Island
345	Xakw G̲èeyi	Sand Beach Bay	Wasp Cove
346	X'áas	Waterfall	Outfall of Mahoney Lake, George Inlet
347	Tatóok X̲'ayèe Héen	Stream below Entrance to Cave	Bay west of Osten Island
348	Xóots Héeni Yadi	Smaller Brown Bear Stream	Creek one mile north of Winstanley
349	Gus'ya Kashèekw*	Caresses the Clouds*	Mountain in George Inlet
350	Kaltóolk'i*	*	Northern Thorne Arm
351	Xakw G̲èeyi Yadi	Smaller Xakw G̲èeyi (#345)	Small cove south of Wasp Cove
352	In Shàayi Ta	Head of Flint Mountain	North of Princess Bay
353	In Shàayi	Flint Mountain	North of Princess Bay
354	Ch'èix̲' Nòowk'u	Thimbleberry Small Fort	Bay near Hume Island
355	Nandachóonhan	Stands Straight-Up Inlet	End of Wilson Arm, Smeaton Bay
356	Lnadàayi Héen	Stream That Doesn't Flow	End of Wilson Arm, Smeaton Bay
357	G̲èinak̲s'*	——* (trail, no mountains, low path)	Wards Cove
358	Yéilchèeji Héen	Raven's Porpoise Stream	Across from Mahoney Lake
359	G̲òoch Héenak'u	Wolf Little Stream	West shore of Princess Bay
360	*	*	Site mapped by Waterman; a small island in Tongass Narrows

Map #	*Name*	*Translation*	*Location*
361	Sukshahéen	Grass Head Stream	End of Wilson Arm, Smeaton Bay
362	Stàanu Héenak'u	Small Stream That Has a Navel	Northeastern Thorne Arm
363	Xóots Héeni	Brown Bear Stream	Winstanley Creek
364	Wankagèeyi*	Edgemost Bay*	Thorne Arm, near Pop Point
365	Kichxáan X'áak	Kichxáan (#396) Ravine	Tongass Narrows (whole)
366	Wat.las'eex'*	Fish Got Rotten*	Pop Point
367	Kaxt Séet	Kaxt (#387) Pass	Short Pass, near Wasp Point
368	Dèishuhéen Tlèin	Big Trail's End Stream	Northern Thorne Arm
369	In Shàayi Héen	Flint Mountain Stream	North of Princess Bay
370	S'áaw Héeni	Crab Stream	Shore near Snip Island
371	S'in[y]axéen*	Flies on the Side of Wild Parsley*	Carroll Inlet, opposite side of Glen Cove
372	Deikée X'àa	Land Sticking Out	Yakuk Point
373	Dèishu Gèeyak'w (Dèishu Héen)	Cove at End of Road (End of the Road Creek)	Gnat Cove, beginning of portage trail
374	*	*	Site mapped by Waterman near Spit Point
375	S'ik.héeni	Black Bear Stream	Creek at Charcoal Point
376	Tsàa Xàayi	Seal Lodge	California Head, George Inlet
377	Dèishuki* Yakw	End of the Trail Canoe There*	Portage at "Tramway" Cove, Thorne Arm
378	Tsàa Xàayi	Seal Lodge	Gem Cove
379	Yeekuka	Good for Nothing	Vallenar Bay
380	Óoxjàa Héen	Wind Stream	Creek at Spit Point
381	S'igèekáawu Héeni	Ghost's Stream	Eastern Behm Canal, southeast shore near Smeaton Island
382	Kaxwas'héen*	Joining Streams*	Sea Level
383	In Shàayi X'akagèeyak'w	Little Bay at the Mouth of Flint Mountain	West shore of Princess Bay
384	X'áat'x'	Islands	Snipe Island
385	Lgòoji Shaa	Hilly Mountain	High Mountain
386	Kaxwas'héen Neeyadi*	Very Smallest Joining Stream*	North inside Thorne Arm
387	Kaxt	*	Smeaton Island
388	X'ul'ka	On the Strong Tide	Rocky Point
389	Yatt'úkt*	Face [of Cliff] Is Shot At	North shore of Wilson Arm
390	Yiku* T'ika Héen	——* Outside Water	A small creek north of Smooth Mountain, Gravina Island
391	Te Áahas Shayawtwa Jali Ye	Rock Piled Up by Old People, High as a Man	East shore of Carroll Inlet
392	S'ikwanaxt	*	Small inlet near Sharp Point
393	Gut'te*	——* Rock*	Near Shoal Cove

Map #	*Name*	*Translation*	*Location*
394	Kichx̱áan Héeni	Near the [Eagle's] Wing Creek	Ketchikan Creek and winter village
395	X̱'altsèeni Héen	Expensive Stream	North of Eve Point, Thorne Arm
396	Kichx̱áan	Near the [Eagle's] Wing	Ketchikan and (originally) Pennock Island
397	Hinx'áasi	Stream's Waterfall	North shore of Wilson Arm
398	S'ikwanax̱t Èegayáa	[Beach] Below S'ikwanax̱t (#392)	South of Sharp Point
399	Atahéen	Stream at the Head of It	Creek at the head of Boca de Quadra
400	Yòoḵ G̱il'i	Cormorant Cliff	South end of California Cove
401	Tatóok X̱'ayèe Hèen	Stream below Mouth of Cave	South of Sharp Point
402	Kichx̱áan Ka	Ocean Side of Kichx̱áan (#396)	Pennock Cove
403	Akanéix̱ Áak'w	——* Lagoon	Small cove north of Narrow Pass
404	G̱èiwu X'àa	Seine Net Point	California Head
405	Chachkw	*	Herring Bay
406	Téel' Héeni	Dog Salmon Stream	End of Boca de Quadra
407	Akanéix̱ Áak'w Èegayáa G̱éeyak'w	Small Stream on Beach below Akanéix̱ Áak'w (#403)	Small cove north of Narrow Pass
408	Yéil Tatóogu	Raven's Cave	End of Boca de Quadra
409	Dèishuhéen X'áat'i	Trail's End Stream Island	Thorne Arm
410	L.ux̱.òohèen	[Salmon] Never Swim into It	Near Point Trollop
411	Kayéil'i	Calm Place	Cove above Elf Point, Thorne Arm
412	T'èesh Ḵwáan Xagu*	Tanning Frame Tribe's Sand Beach*	Saxman
413	Tàakw.àank'i	Little Winter Village	Near Snipe Island
414	Òode Gan Wòogàani Ye	Place Where the Wood Burned Toward	North shore of Smeaton Bay
415	Náaḵw G̱il'i	Octopus Cliff	North shore of Bakewell Arm
416	X̱an ——*	*	Small cove on north shore of Smeaton Bay
417	G̱unayéide Tèiwanòogu Ye	Place Where Rock Moved Over to Sit in a Different Location	West shore of Wilson Arm
418	Ḵàa T'èey X'àa	Human Elbow Point	Point of north shore of Smeaton Bay
419	Yòowatsisgi Nòow	Floating Fort	Northwest of Mountain Point
420	Teya ——* Ka.àan	*	North shore of Smeaton Bay
421	Lax̱x̱'àak'u	Red Cedar Little Point	Inside Boca de Quadra
422	L'ukhéenak'u	Coho Salmon Little Stream	Creek on north shore of Smeaton Bay
423	Nandesawatk'*	Little [Cove] Having Mouth toward the North*	South shore of Smeaton Bay
424	S'achx'áat'i	Fern Island	Inside Boca de Quadra
425	L'ukhéenak'u X'àa	L'ukhéenak'u (#422) Point	Point on north shore of Smeaton Bay
426	Naandaat*	Beyond ——*	Eve Point
427	Katláax̱	Moldy Surfaced	Inside Boca de Quadra
428	——* Séet	——* Pass	Narrow Pass

Map #	*Name*	*Translation*	*Location*
429	Shàa X̲òoni Héen	Creek Comes Down alongside the Mountain	East shore in Thorne Arm
430	——* X'áat'ak'w X̲òo	——* Among the Bunch of Islands	East shore in Thorne Arm
431	Snaank'*	*	Bakewell Arm, Smeaton Bay
432	Tèey X'àayi	Yellow Cedar Point	Point Nelson
433	Tsàa Héeni Ta	Back-of-Bay of Seal Stream	Inside Seal Creek
434	Neix̲t'eenax̲*	*	Rudyerd Island
435	X̲aan	*	Smeaton Bay
436	Tèey X'àayi Lunáa G̲èeyak'w	Little Bay on the Point of Tèey X'àayi (#432)	Near Point Nelson
437	X̲anx̲'akax'áat'*	Island on the Mouth of X̲an* (see #416)	Carp Island
438	Kawchxitk'i Ye T'ikahéen	Stream Out from Kawchxitk'i Ye (#441)	North of Carroll Point
439	Yòowatsisgi X'àa	Floating Point	Mountain Point
440	Lsòog̲u Ye	Grassy Place	Inside Boca de Quadra
441	Kawchxitk'i Ye	Signboard*	Carroll Point
442	Kal.àasak̲w	Treeless [Island]	In Cat Passage
443	X'at'séet Héen	Island Pass Stream	Creek inside of island, near Point Nelson
444	Wat.lax̲'àak	Having a Ravine at the Mouth [of Stream]	Inside Boca de Quadra
445	Kichx̲áan X'àak'u	Kichx̲áan (#396) Point	Gravina Point
446	Chani Héen*	Stinking Stream*	East shore in Thorne Arm, near Notch Mountain
447	Kaltsèitk'	Little Place with Edible Tubers (sweet vetch, *Hedysarum alpinum*)	South shore of Smeaton Bay
448	X̲anx̲'akahéen	Stream on the Mouth of X̲an (see #416)	Near Short Point
449	Tèey X'àayi Jig̲èi X'áat'	Island in the Crook of Tèey X'àayi (#432)	Near Roe Point
450	S'iknax̲ Ka	Black Bear [Community Passes by] on Top	Race Point
451	Wat.lax̲'àak	Having a Ravine at the Mouth [of Stream]	West shore of Bond Bay
452	Te Kunag̲èeyi	Rock Cove	North of Moth Point
453	Kèit Nòowu Séet*	——* Fort Pass	South of Carroll Point
454	Cháas' Héeni Nòow	Humpback Salmon Stream Fort	Chasina Point area
455	Shàa Nòow	Mountain Fort	South of Carroll Point
456	Cháas' Héeni X'àa	Humpback Salmon Stream Point	Chasina Point
457	S'èi Nòowu	Clear Fort	Blank Island
458	Cháas' Héeni	Humpback Salmon Stream	Chasina Point area
459	Shàaw Datéen*	Gumboots*	Coho Cove, west of Thorne Arm
460	*	*	Site mapped by Waterman; Walden Point

Map #	Name	Translation	Location
461	Tsàa Héeni	Seal Stream	Seal Creek
462	Tl'àadenòow	Sideways Fort	Below Walden Point
463	Laxsèiyi Àan	Area below Red Cedar Village	Southern Thorne Arm
464	Gil'àa X'àa	Grindstone Point	North of Fox Point
465	Wat.lax'àak	Having a Ravine at the Mouth	West shore of Narrow Pass
466	Lgòoji X'àa	Hilly Point	Gravina Island / Dall Ridge
467	S'iknax	Place Where Black Bear Goes Through	Annette Bay
468	Gil'àa X'àa Yat'aḵéen	Stream alongside Gil'àa X'àa (#464)	Near Fox Point
469	Ayayòowu	The Boys Got a Stomach	Blank Point
470	Kals'aḵsk'i	Little One That Has Yews	Moth Bay
471	Ḵóoshdàa X'àak'u	Land Otter Little Point	Northeast Nichols Passage
472	*	*	Site mapped by Waterman west of Dall Ridge
473	Ḵóoshdàa G̲èeyak'w	Land Otter Little Bay	Ḵóoshdàa X'àak'u (#471)
474	Nakws'àatk'i	Little Witch	Round Island
475	Xéen Héeni	Fly Stream	Near Fox Point
476	Yéik Séedak'u	Spirit Little Pass	Cone Point, entrance to Thorne Arm
477	Kayéil'i Tlèin	Bigger Kayéil'i (see #491)	Cove north of Point Sykes
478	Teyaḵàashka X'áak	Between Teyaḵàashka (see #483)	Nicholas Passage
479	Ḵàa Shàayi Xágu	Human Head Sand Beach	Head of sand beach, Orca Point
480	Xéen Héeni Yadi	Smaller Fly Stream	North of Ape Point
481	Cháatl Héeni	Halibut Stream	Halibut Creek
482	Yadatsisk'w	Dangerous Looking	Flat Mountain
483	Teyaḵàashka Nòow*	Fort on the Thigh on the Rock Face*	Northeast Nichols Passage
484	Gantaḵw X'àak'u	Lupine Small Point	Ape Point
485	Tsàa X'àaki G̲èey Séet*	Seal Ravine Pass*	Near Bass Point
486	Nàach Héen	Nation Creek	Point south of Reef Point
487	Tsàa Tèix'i Nòow	Seal Rocks Fort	West of Dall Ridge
488	Watkadadoos[']*	Front Rolling Over	Near Ape Point
489	Kayéil'i Yadi	Smaller Kayéil'i (see #491)	Cove north of Point Sykes
490	Neishaa* Héenak'w	——* Little Creek	Point west of Hassler Harbor
491	Kayéil'i Èegayàak X'áat'	Island at the Beach below Calm Place	Point Sykes area
492	Shàanax X'àa	Valley Point	Bostwick Point
493	Tsàa X'àak G̲èey	Seal Ravine Bay	Island in Alava Bay
494	Shàanax Ta	Valley Head-of-Bay	Bostwick Bay
495	Ḵòosh Séet G̲èeyak'w*	Ḵòosh Pass (#510) Little Bay*	Harbor Point
496	Watkaste	Rocky Mouthed	Creek, Bostwick Inlet
497	Su X'àayi Chg̲èi Héenak'w	Little Stream Sheltered in Su X'àayi (#513)	Northeast Nichols Passage

Map #	*Name*	*Translation*	*Location*
498	Yàanasháali K̲uta	Starve Fish Trap Inlet	Hassler Harbor
499	Yat'akw Héen*	Nothing There Creek*	Lucky Cove
500	Lgòoji Shàa G̲éel	Hilly Mountain Gap	Dall Ridge, Gravina Island
501	Nóoskw Shàayi	Wolverine Mountain	Inside Boca de Quadra
502	Yayee Katdóok X'àa*	Solid below the Face of It Point*	East of Point Alava
503	Yat'akw Àan	Nothing There Town	Point Alava
504	Kindachóon Yal.àas*	Having Trees on the Face of It Going Straight Up*	Inside Boca de Quadra
505	Nánde ——* Jig̲èi	*	Point Sykes
506	Yat'akw	Nothing There	Point Alava
507	X'at'k'.usyàa*	Similar to a Small Island*	Point Alava
508	Héen.uwàa	Something Resembling a Stream	Above Dall Head, Dall Ridge, Gravina Island
509	Nánde ——*	*	Point Sykes
510	K̲òosh Séet	Unlucky* Pass	Harbor Point
511	K̲òosh T'ika X'áat'x'*	Islands outside K̲òosh* (#525)	Walker Island
512	Tciate* Taléix̲'u	Ochre at the Head of ——*	Seal Cove
513	Su X'àayi	Kelp Point	Northeast Nichols Passage
514	S'ei Taka	Clear	Small cove above Nehenta Bay, Gravina Island
515	Gàanyak̲'isht'* Kakòoxti	Dry When Tide Goes Down*	Point Sykes area
516	X'áas	Waterfall	Cascade Inlet
517	Ts'ak̲l Nòowu Ka	On Ts'ak̲l Nòowu (#521)	Driest Point
518	Ts'ak̲l Nòow Tayèe Héenak'w	Little Stream below Ts'ak̲l Nòowu (#521)	North of Driest Point
519	Kalguk̲ch	——* (where fish are trapped with bag-like nets)	Hog Rock, Walker Island, Lewis Island
520	Ts'ak̲l Nòow Tahéenak'w	Little Stream at the Head of Ts'ak̲l Nòowu (#521)	Driest Point
521	Ts'ak̲l Nòowu	Black-Paint Fort	Driest Point
522	Jée Ká* ([Chée Ká*]) Tlèin	[Man's name*] Big	Badger Bay
523	Kat Yòo Lèik*	Place Gets Dry (low tide)*	Shore south of Alava Bay
524	Gàanyak̲'isht'*	Hollowed House Post*	Shore south of Alava Bay
525	K̲òosh	Out of Luck	Ham Island
526	Shax̲dóol*	Crane Head*	End of Marten Arm
527	S'èi Ta Nòow	Clear Fort	Nehenta Bay
527.1	S'èi Ta	Clear	Nehenta Bay
528	Káy* Áak'u	——* Small Lake	Opposite Adams Point
528.1	X̲'ax̲aaw Héen*	Middle Creek*	Outside of Port Johnson
529	Tèil X'áat'i Séet Héen	Pitch-Patch Island Pass Stream	Driest Point
530	Kèeyshatéitl' X'áat'i*	Kneecap-Fat Island*	South of Driest Point

Map #	Name	Translation	Location
531	Ḵóoshdàa Nòowu	Land Otter Fort	Fort, shore south of Alava Bay
532	Tèil X'áat'i	Pitch Island	Hemlock Island
533	Ḵugèi* Tlèin	Basin*	Inside Boca de Quadra
534	——* Yadi	Little ——*	Point north of Robinson Creek
535	Teiwaa* T'ika Héen*	Creek outside ——*	Inside Boca de Quadra
536	Kawsgàani X'áat'	Burnt Island	Hemlock Islands
537	Lak'ách' Nòowu*	Porcupine Fort*	End of Marten Arm
538	Saḵs Héeni	Yew Stream	North of Port Johnson
539	Shàayahéen	Creek in Front of Mountain	Dall Bay
540	Kat Yòollèik*	The Tide Keeps Going Out on [It]*	North of Port Johnson
541	Shaxtk'akw*	Head Owl Screech*	End of Marten Arm
542	Tan	Receptacle	Creek to Trout Lake
543	Ch'aatein* Yadi	*	Above Black Island
544	Lxwéint	Dipping*	Annette Island (whole)
545	——* Héen	——* Creek	North of Port Johnson
546	Kéitl.adi Héeni	Seagull Stream	North of Metlakatla
547	Duḵ Nòowu Tlèin	Big Cottonwood Fort	Island east of Dall Head
548	Àashat Héeni X'áat'ak'w	Steelhead Stream Little Island	Above Black Island
549	Naḵnòow	Stand Fort	Wedge Island
550	Jée Ká* (Chée Ká*) Yayuwàa	Between ——*	Point between Badger Bay and Weasel Cove
551	Yéil Lòowu	Raven's Beak	North shore in Marten Arm
552	Xwenaxdàa	*	Twin Island
553	K'ahna.àan	*	Portland Canal
554	Dawóotlk'	Little Confusion/Trouble	Dall Head, point west of end
555	Tan Ka	Right Next to (on) Tan (#542)	Port Chester
556	Àashat Héeni	Steelhead Stream	Inside Black Island
557	Kanat'a Héeni	Blueberry Stream	Small creek, not on map, by Cascade Inlet
558	L'àaḵw Nèeji	War Canoe Beach	South of Badger Bay
559	X'áax	Go Between	Port Johnson
560	Nandesawatk'*	Little [Stream] That Has Its Mouth to the North*	Stream inside Coon Island, George Inlet
561	Tàakw.àani	Winter Village	Metlakatla
562	Tàakw.àani	Winter Village	New Metlakatla
563	Xakw Gèeyi	Sand Beach Bay	Nowiskay Cove
564	——* X'àayi	——* Point	Port Chester
565	S'áaw Áak'u	Crab Little Lake	Dall Head
566	Téel' X'áat'ak'w*	Dog Salmon Little Island*	South shore in Marten Arm
567	Shaachxaanak'w*	*	Inside Boca de Quadra

Map #	*Name*	*Translation*	*Location*
568	Nàawuskéitl	Dead Dog (treating each other like a dog)	Nowiskay Cove
569	Geetx̱ (Gitx̱*) X'áat'i	Fall* Island	Bronaugh Islands
570	Lxwéin[t] Nòow	Lxwéin[t] (#544) Fort	Near Kwain Bay
571	Nas'k Èey Shàa	Three Shallow Channels Mountain	Eudora Mountain
572	Hintakx'was'g̱i Áak'w	Bufflehead Duck Little Lake	Aiken Cove
573	K̲aax̱'eiḵux̱ti Àan*	Feeding Town*	Near Porpoise Point
574	Gòonk'	Small Spring	Aiken Cove
575	Oot'einak'w*	*	South shore in Marten Arm
576	X̲achx̱i L'éiwu	Pull Sand Beach	Point McCartey
577	Lustax' X'àa	Nose Biting Point	Orca Point
578	S'òok Éet'i Lunáa	Soaked Barnacles Promontory	Adams Point
579	Tatóok	Cave	Near Kwain Bay
580	Gakx̱ Kadàa	Current Runs Out into the Open	Creek seen from Ketchikan, near Metlakatla
581	Weiheen*	That's the Stream*	North of entrance to Boca de Quadra
582	Èechk' Tawanyèe	Alongside Little Shoal/Rock	North of Slate Island
583	Lustax' Héen	Nose Biting Stream	Orca Point
584	Shachka X'áat' (Shachkkax̱*)	Swamp Island (——*)	Bold Island
585	K̲utàan Nòowu Yakax'áat'	Island on the Face of ——* Fort	Entrance to Mink Bay
586	Shkax̱g̱asdàa	Flows on Top of Itself	North of Slate Island
587	Liyat'i Nòow Shata	Long Fort at the Head	Giant Point, Mary Island
588	Lxwéint ——*	Dipping* ——*	Crab Bay, Annette Island
589	Ch'aatein*	*	Cove north of Slate Island
590	Ts'axwelnòowu	Crow Fort	Fort by Kestrel Island
591	Yáay X'áat'i	Whale Island	West of Porpoise Point
592	Wat.lax̱'àak	Having a Ravine at the Mouth [of Stream]	South shore of Smeaton Bay
593	Duḵ Nòowu	Cottonwood Fort	Bronaugh Island
594	Watayalookei*	*	End of Very Inlet
595	X̲áach Dana Héenak'w	Little Stream That War Party Drinks	North Arm, Moira Sound
596	Suḵkahéen	Stream on the Grass	Small creek north of Smuggler Cove
597	[Ux Kw!Eteyet Kwa]*	Delivering Island*	Entrance to Boca de Quadra
598	Kèi Kawts.hayi Nòow	Dug-Up Fort	South of Orca Point
599	Katsgank'i Ye	Little Translucent Place	Promontory between Crab Bay and Kwain Bay
600	Kayéil'i Yadi	Smaller Kayéil'i (#609)	Inside Boca de Quadra
601	Òonax̱ Te Nàashuwu Ye	Place Where Rock Stands	Islet north of Kwain Bay
602	*	*	Site mapped by Waterman at Cedar Point

Map #	*Name*	*Translation*	*Location*
603	Adàax̱i Héeni	Making-Canoe Creek	Cedar Point
604	X̱eiy Áa* ([Xeyaa*])	*	Sockeye Creek, Hugh Smith Lake
605	Kaséiḵ'w Gòoch	Dyed/Colored Hill	Yellow Hill
606	S'èek Shàayi Sèiyi	Area below Black Bear Head	Mountain behind bay, below Orca Point
607	Te Wòol	Rock Hole	Near Kwain Bay
608	G̱òoch Héeni	Wolf Stream	Creek at head of Tamgas Harbor
609	Kayéil'i	Calm Place	Near Porpoise Point, Boca de Quadra
610	Kalséiḵ'w Nòow*	Colored Rock Fort*	Fort, entrance to Boca de Quadra
611	Yalchòokan Sèiyi	Area below Place with Fine Grass on the Face	Inside Boca de Quadra
612	G̱èey Tlèin	Big Bay	Boca de Quadra
613	Kalséiḵ'w Xakw	Colored Rock Sand Beach	North of entrance to Boca de Quadra
614	Ch'aatein* Yakax'áat'x'	Islands on the Face of Ch'aatein* (#589)	Slate Island
615	S'ax̱.àanak'u	Little Marmot Village	East shore in Mink Bay
616	Tlèikde Àanak'w	Little Village to One Side	Island at entrance to Mink Bay
617	Kóoshdàa X'àak'u	Land Otter Little Point	Porpoise Point
618	G̱uwakàan Héeni	Deer Stream	Smuggler Cove
619	Yalchòokan Seiyi G̱èeyak'w	*	Quadra Point
619.1	Kal.àasak'w	Having Small Tree on It	Boca de Quadra
620	Te Kunag̱èeyk'i	Rock Little Bight	North Arm, Moira Sound
621	Liyat'i Nòow Áak'w	Long Fort Lake	Lake on Mary Island
622	Liyat'i Nòow	Long Fort	Mary Island (whole)
623	Ch'aaxashant*	——* (they wished that a certain one kind of fish would go in)	Salmon creek in Kwain Bay
624	Yèesh G̱il'k'i	——* Little Cliff	East shore in Mink Bay
625	Ḵàa Kóol [Te*] Yadi	Small Human [——*] Navel	Northwest of Kah Shakes Point
626	Tsàa Yòowu Ta	Back-of-Bay of Seal Stomach	Cove east of Vixen Bay, Boca de Quadra
627	Nande X̱àayk'* (Nande X̱ànk'*)	Northward Little Lodge*	North Arm, Moira Sound
628	Nandeix̱áa	Further Up Lodge	Point Halliday
629	S'awan X'áat'i	Puffin Island	Moira Rock
630	Kalkèishishk'	Little [Bay*] Having Alder	Near Kwain Bay
631	Hóoch'i Xagu	Last Sand Beach	Sand beach south of Orca Point, inside Gannet Island
632	Shux'àa Héen	First Stream	Creek, entrance to Mink Bay
633	Xakw X'àayi	Sand Beach Point	Yellow Point
634	Óonàa Ka	On Gun	Niblack Anchorage
635	Ḵàa Kóol Tlèin*	Large Human Navel*	Northwest of Kah Shakes Point
636	X̱áaw	Drift Log	Moira Island
637	Óot Xwáa Ta Ye	Place Where Young Man Sleeps	Tamgas Harbor
638	Kóoḵ Àan Yadi	Smaller Pit Village	East shore in Mink Bay

Map #	*Name*	*Translation*	*Location*
639	Kaltl'áak'i X'àa	Point with Mica in It	Crowell Point
640	Lxwéint Shàa	Lxwéint (#544) Mountain	Tamgas Mountain
641	Dóol G̲èeyi X̲'akax'áat'	Island on the Mouth of Crane Bay	Cannen Island
642	L'éiw Ka Nòow	Fort on the Sand	Fort, Kah Shakes Point
643	Nas'k Èey	Three Shallow Channels	North Arm
644	Kóok̲ Àan	Pit Village	East shore in Mink Bay
645	Àasgutuwadi Yakax'áat'	Island in Front of Àasgutuwadi (#649)	Island off of Kah Shakes Point
646	Lunéesht	*	White Reef
647	Dóol G̲èeyi	Crane Bay	Vixen Bay
648	Tàay Shòowu	Fat Half	Hidden reef near Smuggler Cove
649	Àasgutuwadi	Smaller Woods	Kah Shakes Point
650	T'angàash	*	Creek from Tamgas Lake
651	Wéix̲' Nòowu	Bullhead Fort	Fort, two rocks near Kah Shakes Point
652	Uwax'agi X'áat'	Diving Island	Egg Islands
653	Wéix̲' G̲eey	Bullhead Bay	Bullhead Cove, Kah Shakes area
654	Kée X̲àay	Above Beaver Lodge	White Rock
655	G̲áatl	Bracket Fungus	Creek
656	X̲áa X'áat'i Yadi	Smaller War Party Island	Rock north of Kah Shakes Cove
657	Óox̲ Tix' Kawdwayèeg̲i Ye	Place Where Rope/Line Has Been Stretched Out	Point south in Smuggler Cove
658	Tsàa Kunag̲èeyi	Seal Bight	Dickman Bay
659	Liyat'i Nòow Àan	Long Fort Village	Near Edge Point, Mary Island
660	G̲unéik̲'an (K'ah Shakes)	——* (——* [from Tsimshian*])	Kah Shakes Cove
660.1	Taiyakaska Héen*	*	End of Kah Shakes Cove
661	K'akw Èeyak'w	Owl Little Tide Run	Dickman Bay
662	G̲unéik̲'an Héenak'u	G̲unéik̲'an (#660) Little Creek	Creek inside Kah Shakes Cove
663	Shàanax̲ Héenak'w	Valley Little Stream (Little Stream That Goes Underground)	East shore in Tamgas Harbor
664	Liyat'i Nòow Teikwi*	Long Fort ——*	Edge Point
665	X̲'éen X̲'awòol	House-Screen Door	Near Menefee Anchorage
666	Watx̲.agàan	Mouth [of Stream] Gets Burned Repeatedly	Dickman Bay
667	Tsàa X̲àayi	Seal Lodge	North of Annette Point
668	Ts'àanak̲l	Going in Behind	Pearse Side
669	X'óol'i Héen	Mixed-Up Stream	Continuation of West Arm
670	Àasgutu.àan	Village in the Woods	Point in Kah Shakes Cove
671	Kwas Tayèidi	Aged-Urine Bladderwrack	Small cove, southern Smuggler Cove
672	Chèech X'àak'u	Little Porpoise Point	North of Annette Point
673	Tàagan Layex̲ Àan	Poles Making	Black Point

Map #	*Name*	*Translation*	*Location*
674	Wuls'ixi Xakw Èegayàa Èech	Shoal/Rock in Front of Wuls'ixi Xakw (see #751, #755)	South of Kah Shakes Cove
675	Tl'anaxéedak̲w X'áat'ak'w	Wealth-Bringing Woman Little Island	Near Danger Passage
676	Anóoshi Nòowu	Russians' Fort	Menefee Anchorage
677	Làax̲ Sèiyi Àan*	Village below (in shelter of) Red Cedar*	Near Menefee Anchorage
678	Tl'ak'x'àa Lunáa*	Over Mica* Point	North of Chichagof Bay
679	Ch'èix̲' Àani	Thimbleberry Village	Deer Point
680	Anóoshi G̲èeyi	Russian Bay	Menefee Anchorage
681	Chòokan Àan	Grass Village	Deer Point or Seal Cove*
682	Xòonax̲nèxt	*	Lane Island
683	Tlax̲anes'tèiyi	Kingfisher Rock	North of Annette Point
684	At X̲àatk'i	Small Root	Promontory above Davidson Point
685	Yéesyat At Sèiyi	——*'s Shelter	Dickman Bay
686	X̲áa X'áat'i Tlèin	Larger War Party Island	Small island outside of Kah Shakes Cove
687	Shdat'ix̲'di Héen*	Self-Hammering Stream*	Just inside Kah Shakes Cove
688	S'áaw G̲èeyi	Crab Bay	Crab Bay
689	Ts'àanak̲l Shata	Ts'àanak̲l (#668) Head-of-Bay	Tree Point
690	T'ax̲'jàa Àanak'w	Exploding-Ember Little Village	Near Menefee Anchorage
691	Yàaw Héeni	Herring Stream	Dickman Bay
692	Tsèináa	*	Mouth of Moira Sound
693	Shàak̲ Kunagèey	Drift-Log Bight	Chichagof Bay
694	Kat Yòollèik G̲èeyakw*	The Tide Keeps Going Out on [It] Little Bay*	Bay at Dolomi
695	Yasyàat Góonnax̲ Héenak'w*	Little Stream over the Isthmus of Yasyàat* (#700)	Dickman Bay
696	Òodenikdug̲ich Àan	Village toward Which They Throw the Nets	North Moira Sound
697	Nàa G̲èeyak'u	Little Bay of the Nation	Creek with little bay, above Annette Point
698	Shux'àa Héen Kik	Other Side of Shux'àa Héen (#632)	Deep inside Mink Bay
699	X̲'éix̲kas.ax̲w*	Tied Together at the Mouth*	Dickman Bay
700	Yasyàat	Walk Fast	Moira Sound (whole)
701	Yàana.èit X'áat'x'i	Wild Celery Islands	North of Davison Point
702	Dixkunati Xagu*	——* Sand Beach	Moss Point
703	Shèey T'ani Héeni*	Limb Branches Stream*	Just inside Kah Shakes Cove
704	Neegaaxwk̲u*	News Duck Little Lake*	North Moira Sound
705	X̲àay Nòowu Séet	Yellow Cedar Fort Pass	Chichagof Bay
706	Xíxch' X̲'èiyàak'w*	Little [Place/Thing] Resembling a Frog's Mouth*	West Arm, Moira Sound
707	Lgòoshi X'áat'	Island with a [Killer-Whale's] Dorsal Fin	Black Rock

Map #	*Name*	*Translation*	*Location*
708	X'atgu Gòon	Dogfish Spring	North Moira Sound
709	At.ltsàa Nòowu*	Belching Fort*	Near Chichagof Bay
710	X'áat'ak'w T'èi Àan	Village behind Small Island	North Moira Sound
711	Yasyàat [G̱èeyakw*]	Walk Fast [Little Bay*]	Kegan Cove
712	Yalkèishish	Having Alders on the Face/Side	Dickman Bay
713	Áak'w Kakuxti	Dried-Up Little Lake	South Chichagof Bay
714	S'òow Héen	Green Stream	Cove south of Blaine Point, Pearse Canal
715	Tax'àak'u	Little Rock Point	Dickman Bay
716	Nàa G̱èeyak'w [Du*] Yadi	Nation's Young Little Bay*	North of Annette Point
717	Seitsa.kweinli*	Seal Swims Past*	Survey Point
718	Yàana.èit G̱èeyi Yádi	Wild Celery Bay*	Near Davison Point
719	Ḵugwas'héeni Yaka.èech	Reef/Shoal in Front of Frog Stream	Near Survey Point
720	Àasgutu.àan Yakax'áat'	Island on the Front of Àasgutu.àan (#670)	Island outside Kah Shakes Cove
721	Yàana.èit G̱èeyi	Wild Celery Bay	Above Davison Point
722	Kattsàa Ki*	Seal upon There*	Whale Rock
723	Dàalḵèedi X'àak'w	Little Point with Dams around It	Village Island, southwest of Cat Island
724	Kàag̱áa Héen	Basket Creek	Small creek by Annette Point
725	Kóoshdàa Nòowu	Land Otter Fort	Point in Aiken Cove
726	Yàana.èit G̱èeyi Yadi	Smaller (Child of) Yàana.èit G̱èeyi (#721)	Near Davison Point
727	Kàag̱áa Héen X̱'aa	Point of Basket* Creek	Annette Point
728	Tsax̱gwanli*	Seals Swim Past*	Survey Point
729	Kal.àasaḵw	Devoid of Trees	Near Point Nelson
730	G̱àash	Powder	Beach below Kah Shakes Cove
731	Kóoshdàa Áak'w	Land Otter Little Lake	Dickman Bay
732	X̱aynòowu	Yellow Cedar Fort	Inside Chichagof Bay
733	G̱òoch Héenak'w	Wolf Little Stream	Near Annette Point
734	Katk'walx̱i	Having Ferns on It	On Mary Island
735	S'óos'ani Àan	Pine Cone Village	Near Survey Point
736	X̱àay Nòowu	Yellow Cedar Fort	Polk Island
737	Tsàa Áak'u	Seal Little Lake	South shore of Moira Sound
738	G̱èey G̱il'wu	Marble* Cliff Bay	Dickman Bay
739	Dàasaxakw Séet	Having Sand Beaches around It Pass	*
740	Gitḵóo* Nòowu	[Haida man's name*] Fort	South shore of Moira Sound
741	——* Yayuwàa Héenak'w	Little Stream between ——*	Annette Point area
741.1	Kàag̱áa* Héenak'w Eejí	——* Little Creek Reef	Annette Point, Wallace Reef*
742	Kéitl.adi X'áat'i	Seagull Island	Moira Sound
743	Dàasaxakw Aan*	Having Sand Beaches around It Village*	Village Island

Map #	*Name*	*Translation*	*Location*
744	Kugwas'héeni	Fog Stream	Creek by Survey Point
745	Kàagáa* Héenak'w Niyàa Katlàax	Bald Rock toward ——*	Islands near Annette Point
746	S'igèekáawu X'áat'i	Ghost Island	Islet by Tamgas Harbor
747	Xàay Áayi	Yellow Cedar Lake	Cove with creek near Davidson Point
748	Kukèekan X'àayi	Lookout Point	Grave Point, Duke Island
749	Gàash Yaka.èech	Shoal/Rock on the Front of Gàash (#730)	House Rock, off Kirk Point
750	Walx'àa*	Hole Point*	Davison Point
751	Wuls'ixi Xakw Yadi	Smaller Putrescent Sand Beach	North of Kirk Point
752	Tàay Shu*	Fat End*	Little Rock
753	Tàakw.àank'i	Little Winter Village	Winstanley Island
754	Gáas'	Post	Davison Point
755	Wuls'ixi Xakw Tlèin	Large Putrescent Sand Beach	North of Kirk Point
756	Gàash X'àa	Gàash (#730) Point	Kirk Point
757	Gàash T'èiyinàa Gèeyak'w	Little Bay on the Back Side of Gàash (#730)	Cape Fox Village
758	Wakltateey* X'áat'i	Eye People* Island	Duck Island
759	Tàakw.àank'i Ka	On Little Winter Village	Hotspur Island
760	Sitxdashèex*	*	West Arm, Moira Sound
761	Àastanax* X'àa Yadi X'àayi	Àastanax* X'àa Yadi (#798) Point	Ingraham Point
762	X'us' X'áat'ak'w	Crabapple Little Island	West Arm, Moira Sound
763	Kéet Xagu	Killer Whale Sand Beach	Big sand beach, Pearse Canal
764	Yuxch' ——*	Sea Otter Pups*	Near Dog Island
765	Kalsaks Gèey	Bay That Has Yews	Tamgas Reef
766	Déix Nòow	Two Forts	West Arm, Moira Sound
767	X'us' X'áat'ak'w Séet Héenak'w*	Small Stream [in] X'us' X'áat'ak'w (#762) Pass*	West Arm, Moira Sound
768	Dàasaxakw	Having Sand Beaches around It	Village Island, southwest of Cat Island
769	Kalsaks Gèey[i]	Bay with Yews	Cove west of Johnsons Cove
770	Tagwàats'àan Ka	Shallow at Head of Bay Island	Dog Island
771	Gathéenak'u	Sockeye Salmon Little Stream	Very Inlet
772	Shachk Shuka.àan	Village in Front of the Marsh	Southwest of Grave Point
773	Nàsahéen*	Soaked Creek* (mouth of creek is a swamp)	Frederick Cove
774	Wéina Nòowu	Chalk Fort	Northern Foggy Bay
775	Gwéint	*	Hidden Inlet
776	Àastanax* X'àa Kax'áat'	Islands on Àastanax* X'àa (#812)	Just inside Ingraham Bay
777	Kàawsgàani Nòow	Burnt Fort	Islet, used to be fort, by Hotspur Island
778	Nats'héen Ta*	Head of ——* Creek	Frederick Cove

Map #	*Name*	*Translation*	*Location*
779	Sèenáa X̱'e	Going Past Something Hidden*	Johnson Cove
780	——* T'èigèeyi X̱'akax'áat'	Island at Mouth of Bay behind ——*	South Arm, Moira Sound
781	Dóol Áak'u*	Crane Little Lake*	End of Very Inlet
782	Shaḵ' Guyee.aa*	*	Very Inlet
783	Tagwàats'àan Àan	Tagwàats'àan (#786) Village	Dog Island
783.1	——* G̱èeyak'w	——* Little Bay	Pond Bay, Duke Island
784	Gul* Kax̱'ax̱'w	Cramped Cove Head*	South Arm, Moira Sound
785	Ashtanax̱ (Àastanax̱*)	Inside Passage* (Forested Inside*)	Ingraham Bay
786	Tagwàats'àan	Shallow at Head of Bay	Pond Bay
787	Kag̱éet Áak'u	Loon Little Lake	Loon Lake, near Foggy Bay
788	G̱àash T'èiyinàa X'áat'x'	Islands on the Back Side of G̱àash (#730)	De Long Islands, Foggy Bay
789	Nandayéen Àan	North-Facing Village	Entrance to Very Inlet
790	Yáay Dix̱'i Ta.àan	Village at the Back of the Bay from "Whale's Back"	Foggy Bay
790.1	Yáay Dix̱'i	Whale's Back	Foggy Bay area
791	Táḵu* T'èig̱èey	Bay behind Táḵu* (Hunter Bay)	South Arm, Moira Sound (linking to Hunter Bay)
792	A Yòok'u	Its Little Stomach	Pond Bay
793	G̱òoch Héenak'w	Wolf Little Stream	South of Davison Mountain
794	Ch'èet G̱èeyi	Murrelet Bay	South Arm, Moira Sound
795	T'ahéeni	King Salmon Stream	End of Very Inlet
796	Xóon Yatx'i	North Wind's Children	Cow Island
797	Sóoḵl	*	Vegas Island
798	Àastanax̱* X'àa Yadi	Smaller Àastanax̱* X'àa (#812)	Northern Ingraham Bay
799	Tsàa Èeji	Seal Shoal/Rock	South Arm, Moira Sound
800	X'àalkwèidi Àani	——* Village	Promontory, Foggy Bay
801	T'àawaḵ Áayi	Goose Lake	In Pond Bay
802	Tàakw.àank'i Séedak'u*	Little Winter Village Pass*	West of Hotspur Island
803	Dèikinàa Xagu	Haida Sand Beach	Entrance to Ingraham Bay
804	Tèey X'àayi	Yellow Cedar Point	Flag Point
805	S'axt' Àan	Devil's Club Village	Island southwest of Hotspur Island
806	Tàan Héeni	Sea Lion Stream	North end of Nakat Inlet
807	Kanax̱'áak Ká	With Middle	Willard Inlet (whole)
808	G̱òoch Héeni	Wolf Stream	Shore near Snip Island
809	Cháas' Héenak'w	Humpback Salmon Little Stream	South Arm, Moira Sound
810	T'àaḵsnéex̱'i Nòow	Marble-Sided Fort	Werlick Island
811	X'èesháa Ka	On Bucket	Ryus Bay
812	Àastanax̱* X'àa	Àastanax̱* (#785) Point	Entrance to Ingraham Bay
813	Lusayat' Héeni	Bird's* Long Nose Creek	Very Inlet

Map #	Name	Translation	Location
814	Ḵóok Nòow	Box Fort	North of Hidden Bay
815	Chilk Àan K'aak*	Cache Village ——*	Sealed Passage
816	T'aḵsnéex'i Nòow Yadi	Smaller ——* Fort	Island southwest of Hotspur Island
816.1	T'aḵsnéex'i Áak'w	——* Little Lake	Southern point of Hotspur Island
817	T'éexk'w	*	Percy Island
818	Gijukhéen	Golden Eagle Stream	South Arm, Moira Sound
819	——* Nòow[ú]	——*'s Fort	South Arm, Moira Sound
820	Shàak'w Sèiyi	Area below Little Mountain	End of Ingraham Bay
821	Wóoshdax ——* Àan	Divided ——* Camp	Percy Island
822	Suktuhéenak'w	Little Stream in the Grass	South Arm, Moira Sound
823	Àan Shóox Wudàa*	Water Runs at End of Town*	Point above Morse Cove
824	Chilk Àan	Cache Village	Outlying rocks in Sealed Passage
825	Kaxa* Héen	Merganser* Creek	South Arm, Moira Sound
826	Téil Ḡèeyi	Pitch-Scab Bay	Foggy Bay
827	Watkate Xé	On [Stream] Having Rocks at Mouth	Creek, Pearse Canal
828	Ḡil'i Shak'*	*	Duke Island
829	Kèixishtkanalhéen	*	Creek in Very Inlet
830	X'alinukdzi X'àa	Sweet-Tasting Point	Hidden Point
831	Yéil X̱'e	Raven's Mouth	Hidden Bay
832	Ásku.eey*	Strong Tide*	Hidden Bay
833	Layex̱.àa X'ayik Ḡèeyak'w	Little Bay in the Mouth of Layex̱.àa (#847)	Morse Cove
834	Xóon Tlèin	Big North Wind	East of Point Percy
835	Àasguwèe Èey Tahéen	Stream at Head of ——* Strong Current	Inside Hidden Bay
836	Kasx̱áawan X'àa	Feathers-On* Point	Point White
837	Yuxch' Yadi Héeni	Little Land Otter Stream	Small creek below Point White
838	Yéilnòow	Raven's Fort	Fort and little islets, Pearse Canal
839	Yéex̱	*	Duke Island (Mount Lazaro)
840	*	*	Site mapped by Waterman; south of Point White
841	Tèiḵw (Tèiḵu)	Among Rocks	Percy Islands reef
842	Kasx̱áawan	Feathers-On* Town	Old town by Point White
843	S'awan Lunáa	Noise of the Puffin* Point/Nose	Foggy Point
844	Àasguwèe Èey X̱'akax'áat'*	Island at Mouth of ——* Strong Current*	Hidden Bay
845	Kaxa* Héen Wat X'áat'	Island at Mouth of Merganser* Creek	South Arm, Moira Sound
846	Layex̱.àa X'ayik Héenak'w	Small Stream in the Mouth of Layex̱.àa (#847)	Morse Cove
847	Layex̱.àa	Making Lakes	Morse Cove

Map #	Name	Translation	Location
848	Àas Kadayéis'i	Blackened Trees (Shadowed Trees*)	Creek and pond below Point White
849	Gijòok Shàa	Golden Eagle Mountain	Mountain near Moira Sound, South Arm
850	Ḵàa X̱'us.èeti Héeni	Human Footprints Stream	Near Hunters Bay
851	Sht'àakanòow	Outside Fort	Bunch of islets along shore, near Duke Island
852	Lawáak*	Lower End*	End of Hall Cove
853	Saḵtanyik*	*	Duke Point
854	Te Kunagèeyi	Rock Bight	South of Hidden Bay
855	Naawan* Áa	——* Lake	Near Hall Cove
856	Gàant.àa Shaḵídi*	——*'s Drift-Log House*	West of Hall Cove
857	Gàat Héenak'u	Sockeye Little Stream	Salmon stream from Nakat Lake
858	Teey* Tahéen	Stream at Head of ——*	West Arm, Kendrick Bay
859	Wat.sa.áak'u	Having Little Lakes at the Mouth	Hall Cove
860	Te X̱'àayi	Rock Point	South of Foggy Point
861	Teey* Ta	Head of ——*	Inside Kendrick Bay
862	Yéex̱ Yadi	Smaller Yéex̱ (#839)	North of Mount Lazaro
863	X̱'ax̱aaw Héen*	Middle Creek*	North shore, Kendrick Bay
864	*	*	Site mapped by Waterman; west of Hall Cove
865	Shàaḵ Kunagèey	Drift-Log Bight	North shore, Kendrick Bay
866	Dàalgil' Gèey	Bay with Cliffs around It	North shore, Kendrick Bay
867	——* Yadàa X̱'áat'ak'w	Battle Island around the Face of ——*	South of Duke Point
868	Wanal'èet Góon*	——* Tail Behind	Near Hall Cove
869	Keshish.àan	Alder Village	Near West Arm, Kendrick Bay
870	X̱'éix̱w X̱eix̱	Blocking underneath Something	Kendrick Island
871	Aga Us'k Teix'	Splashing Rocks	Fillmore Inlet
872	X̱áa Ta	War Party Head-of-Bay	Cove at entrance to Hall Cove
873	Yat Tukt	They Shoot at the Side/Face [of Cliff]	Along Pearse Canal
874	Wat.sa.èey	Has Strong Current at the Mouth	Small inlet on Duke Island, near East Island
875	T'àawaḵ Séedi	Goose Passage	Passage inside of rocks, entrance to Hall Cove
876	Tlakwsatan	Long Branched Trees Always Lying There	Rocks east of Duke Island
877	Dàa.áax̱wk'u Yadàa*	Bundle Around*	Small promontory on Duke Island, near East Island
878	Ayandaguḵ* (Ayandakoox̱*)	Run-Away Island* (Turning Back [in boat]*)	Above Kelp Island
878.1	Ayandakoox̱ Séet*	Turning Back (in boat) Strait*	North of Kelp Island
879	Nèilk'*	Inside of Worm*	Northeast of Cape Northumberland

Map #	*Name*	*Translation*	*Location*
880	Náakw Áak'u	Octopus Little Lagoon	Above Kelp Island
881	Chkóol X'áat'i	Back-of-Hand Island	Point above Kelp Island
882	Tsàa Áayi	Seal Lake	Inside Kendrick Bay
883	X'éex'w*	Something Wedged In*	Island at entrance of Kendrick Bay
884	Teey K'ax Galshu*	*	Kendrick Bay
885	Kèi Kawt.s.hàayi Nòow	Dug-Up Fort	North of Kelp Island
886	Dàalagàaw	Hollow Sound	Bee Rocks, near Duke Island
887	S'axt' Àan	Devil's Club Village	Town by Cape Northumberland
888	Gilant*	*	North of Cape Fox
889	Kals'axt'	Having Devil's Club on It	East Island
890	Gichx.anagàat Nòow	Rainbow Fort	Fort on Kelp Island
891	T'àakdestan	Lying Crosswise	Kelp Island
892	Sukkats'áayi	Grass Perfume	Promontory on Duke Island
893	Kaa ——* Áak'w	One [Made*] Lagoon	Cape Northumberland area
893.1	X'éxkw.àan*	Sand Beach Mouth Village*	Beach at Judd Harbor, Duke Island
894	Tèet.lasàa	Waves Blowing [Through]	North of Cape Fox
895	Yées' Èeji	Large-Mussel Shoal/Rock	Near East Island, by Duke Island
896	Kóox X'áat'i	Wild Rice Island	Entrance of Kendrick Bay
897	Tináak'w Chgèi	Sheltered by Little Copper	East Kelp Island
898	Sukkats'áayi Nòow	Grass Perfume Fort	Point below Hall Cove
899	Sukkats'áayi Áak'w	Grass Perfume Little Lake	Pond inside promontory on Duke Island
900	Téey*	Trimmed-Down Patch*	Kendrick Bay
901	Kals'axt' Yadi	Smaller Kals'axt' (#889)	Near East Island, by Duke Island
902	Oonáx Dèi Nàashòowu Ye	Place Where the Road Goes Through	Cape Northumberland
902.1	Gooch X'akanòow	Wolf Mouth Fort	Cape Northumberland
903	Déesht Nòow*	Salmon Box Made Out of Cedar Bark*	South of Kelp Island
904	Yòok Te	Cormorant Rock	By Kelp Island
905	Àas Kéedi Yadi	Smaller Àas Kéedi (#908)	End of Shore Arm, Kendrick Bay
906	Làagakt* Áa	Eel Grass* Lake	North of Cape Fox
907	Yayéina	Whetstone	Vancouver Island
908	Àas Kéedi	Tree Flood-Tide	South Arm, Kendrick Bay
909	Nèixinte X'áat'i	Blue-Green Claystone Island	Vancouver Island
910	Kaltl'àak'wach' Shis'k	Having Fresh Wild Rhubarb on It	Sisters Island
911	A Yax Cháatl Kòowu Kèi Wut.syáayi Ye	Place Where They Used to Pack Halibut Tails Up along the Side	Mountain near Kendrick Bay
912	Kugéiyi Yu Àan	Big Village Town	Along Pearse Canal
913	Kagèet Áayi	Loon Lake	Loon Lake
914	Ax'éidax Yeil* Seet Nak	Raven's* Mouth from Pass	Edward Passage

Map #	*Name*	*Translation*	*Location*
915	A Yayuwàa Èech	Shoal/Rock between It	South of Cape Northumberland
916	Nakaat* Yadi	Little ——*	Harry Bay
917	Wóoshde Wòok'òodzi Te Yayèe*	In Front of Rock That Broke Apart*	Cape Northumberland
918	Keet*	Leader*	Club Rocks
919	Akulsaayi Seet	Narrow Pass	South of Edward Passage
920	Aak'wtáak	Little Lake Behind*	Gardner Bay
921	Tàan Wulsèeni Ye	Sea Lion Hiding Place	Nakat Harbor
922	Tàan	Sea Lion	Prince of Wales Island
923	Xwéinax̲ Tahéen	Stream at the Head of Xwéinax̲ (#929)	End of McLean Arm
924	Nakaat* X'àayi Yayuwàa	Place between ——* Point	Ledge Point
925	Néix̲éech	Place Where They Club Things	West Rock
926	Kuskàagi X'áat'	Thick Island	Slim Island
927	Xwéinax̲ X̲'akakatlàax̲	Bare Rock at the Mouth of Xwéinax̲ (#929)	Island Point
928	Katgòoni*	Having Spring on Top*	Tree Point
929	Xwéinax̲*	Rest*	McLean Arm
930	Taagwas'*	Skate*	Tongass Island
931	Kadúk̲x̲uka	Place on the Cottonwoods	Tongass Island Village
932	Kat.shàag̲i	Having Drift Logs Piled on It	Yellow Rock
933	Xwéinax̲ T'ika G̲èey	Bay outside of Xwéinax̲ (#929)	End of Mallard Bay
934	Ts'axwèil X'áat'i	Crow Islands	Rock north of Tongass Passage
935	Katgòoni Áak'u	Small Spring-Fed Lake	Boat harbor north of Cape Fox
936	Kuskaagi X'áat' Yadaa	Face of the Rounding Island	Cape Fox
937	Cháatl Héeni	Halibut Stream	Creek at Fox Hill
938	X̲'éide S'uwt.lg̲èech*	They Threw White ——* toward the Mouth of It*	Rocks off of Cape Fox
939	Yòolihashgi Èech	Floating Shoal*	Small island (rocks) near Cape Fox
940	Tuwawóoli X'áat'	Island with a Hole in it	Small island (rocks) near Cape Fox
941	Alk̲áa Xagu	Gambling Sand Beach	Sand beach near Cape Fox
942	Kèxashdi Yadi	——* Baby	Sitklan Passage area (similar to Cape Fox)
943	Yàakwyana X̲'éich*	Canoe Has to Twist to Get In*	Cape Fox area
944	Anax̲seik̲	Smoke from There	Island off of Cape Fox
945	X'áat'ak'w G̲èegi*	Poor Little Island*	Barren Island
946	Kalg̲èeyi Ye	Shining Place	Stone Rock Bay
947	Séet Tlèin Ka	[Island] on Big Pass	Sitklan Island
948	Kanax̲.ana.atk	Road to Walk Over On	Kanagunut Island
949	K̲eeku*	*	Head of Nichols Bay
950	Séet Tlèin	Big Pass	Tongass Passage
951	Tàan X'áat'i	Sea Lion Island	Stone Rock

Map #	*Name*	*Translation*	*Location*
952	Nakaat* X'akax'áat'x'	Islands at the Mouth of ——*	Lord Islands outside of Nakat Bay
953	Kéet Nòow	Killer Whale Fort	Old fort, east side of Lincoln Channel
954	Yàax K'èit Kagas'	Round Thing Slide	Mountain near Cape Chacon
955	Tlakw.àan Séedak'u	Ancient Village Small Pass	Lincoln Island, Lincoln Channel
956	Yaxk'èitgagas'ch Sèiyi*	Area below Where the Sprouts Slide Down to Rest*	South of Stone Rock Bay
957	Keeku* Dàaka	Around ——*	East shore of Nichols Bay
958	Tàan Yadi	Baby Sea Lion	Cape Chacon lighthouse
959	Tàan Lunáa (Tàan Àani Yadàa)	Sea Lion Promontory (Face of Sea Lion Country)	Cape Chacon
960	Óot Xóots Àa Ye	Where Brown Bear Sits	South of Nichols Mountain
961	Kéik'* Àan	Deep* Town	Cape Muzon
NM	Héen Tlèin	Big Stream	Stream in north end of Rudyerd Bay
NM	Watsdék*	*	Mountain in Boca de Quadra

11. *K'áyk'aanii*

Haida country (K'áyk'aanii) in Southeast Alaska encompasses large portions of the southern Prince of Wales Archipelago, including the present day communities of Hydaburg and Kasaan. Most scholars date the first Haida migration to Alaska some time within the last three hundred years, although there was undoubtedly a history of exploration and trade that brought Haidas to Southeast Alaska prior to that time. With migration, came Haida names for Southeast Alaska lands.

The Alaskan Haida became known as the Kaigani Haida after their first settlement in Alaska, at a "trading" village by Cape Muzon known as K'áyk'aanii (#72). Haida elders Robert and Nora Cogo (1983, 4) relate: "Haidas migrating to the north entered through K'áyk'aanii. The first Haida clan to reach K'áyk'aanii was the Ts'eihl Laanaas, the Eagle or Beaver clan. These people came from the north of Langara Island off the northwest tip of Graham Island. The Haidas called this place K̲'aysgwaayaay [#73]. K̲'aysgwaayaay then became the name of the Alaska Haidas. That was how they were identified. The Masset Haidas were known as G̲aw X̲aat'aay. The Skidegate Haidas were called Hlgayuu X̲aat'aay." As this statement illustrates, Haida clan names and place names cannot be understood solely within an Alaskan context. Ties stem back to Haida Gwaii, known in English as the Queen Charlotte Islands of British Columbia.

In contrast to the Tlingit system, Haida clan houses within a village tended to be dominated by a single (Raven or Eagle) moiety and were individually owned rather than communally owned. Alaskan Haida villages associated with the Raven moiety included Klinkwan (Hlankwa'áan, #55), Koinglas (K̲'wíi G̲ándlaas, #62), and Sukkwan (Saxk'wáan, #36), while the Eagle moiety predominated in Howkan (Gáwk'yaan, #58) and (old) Kasaan (K̲asa'áan, #8). However, as new clans and house groups developed and interactions with the Tlingit increased, Alaskan Haida social structure began to mirror Tlingit social organization in important respects. From the original K'áyk'aanii Eagle moiety came the Yaadas, Ts'eihl Laanaas, and Sgalans clans, each of which became further subdivided. Similarly, the original K'áyk'aanii Raven moiety divided into numerous clans, including the Yahkw Laanaas, Kwii Taas, Gaw Kaywaas, and Taas Laanaas and their subdivisions.

Our project was carried out in conjunction with the Hydaburg Cooperative Association and coordinated by Cherilyn Holter. Gail Dabaluz (formerly Nāpiha'a) served as the local research coordinator. Key contributors included Claude Morrison, Woodrow Morrison, Charles Natkong Sr., Delbert Nix, Robert Sanderson Sr., Helen Sanderson, and many others. We also benefited from the ethnogeographic work of others, including Robert and Nora Cogo, Nora and Richard Dauenhauer, Wilson Duff, Carol Eastman and Elizabeth Edwards (1991), Christine Edenso, Walter Goldschmidt and Theodore Haas, George Hamilton, Richard Hamilton, Louis and Alice Kitkoon, Ed Sanderson, John Swanton, Thomas Waterman, and others who documented indigenous place names over the years. Jordan Lachler, of the Sealaska Heritage Institute, provided linguistic review.

K'áyk'aanii Names

Few speakers of Haida with knowledge of indigenous names survive today in Alaska. For this reason, our work in Hydaburg was expanded to include both historic sites with Haida names and those without, for which it is assumed there were indigenous names. These missing names hopefully may be recovered through further research among Haida speakers in other communities. As a consequence, many Haida names for sites in this chapter are left blank or marked as uncertain. However, Haida cultural knowledge of these historic sites is vast. Some of this knowledge was documented in the Sealaska Corporation's historic sites and cemeteries survey conducted more than thirty years ago (Sealaska 1975). Our interviews and review of the literature added to this knowledge base, although it is still far from comprehensive.

Some important sites included the following places:

Essowah Harbor/Lakes (Lisuuwaa, #65).* The English name is derived from the Haida one. According to Robert and Nora Cogo (1983, 4–5), this was an important sockeye salmon system that was engineered to catch fish and marked by petroglyphs.

> There is a great red [sockeye] salmon stream called Lisuuwaa located a few miles up the outside coast of Kaigani. This was referred to as the "great store house of fish" for the Kaigani Haidas. It means that the fish was very plentiful there. All the salmon caught at this stream were divided by mutual agreement amongst all the Kaigani Haidas. A better way to utilize this resource could not have been accomplished without the cooperation of all the chiefs of each clan. Anyone visiting Lisuuwaa can still see the stone mounds and rock formations that were built to catch the salmon coming in the stream and lakes there. The entrance that leads into the stream and the lakes is a narrow chasm in the rocky ocean coast... Once you enter through the opening to the inside, you see a Haida wonderland. Everywhere you turn you will see some form of early occupancy of the area.

According to Claude Morrison (interview), the name refers to the lake system in particular.

Koinglas and Howkan (K̲'wíi G̲ándlaas, #62, and Gáwk'yaan, #58). K̲'wíi G̲ándlaas and Gáwk'yaan were major Haida settlements on Long Island, and their traces can still be found there, even in the anglicized place names which mark their locations. George Hamilton (Dauenhauer, Lang, and Natkong 1998) notes that K̲'wíi G̲ándlaas means "Muddy Bay," and Helen Sanderson (ibid.) relates the story of the two-finned killer whale, an important Haida crest, the origins of which are associated with this place:

> One of our chief forebears
> of the Yahkw Laanaas
> whose main village was situated on Long Island on Prince of Wales Island called K̲'wíi G̲ándlaas made a statement
> that if there is any truth to the belief of a drowned person's spirit
> entering a killer whale
> that he would prove it.
> They undoubtedly didn't believe.
> That was rather unusual
> since the people were very superstitious in those days.
> One day
> the chief went on a long expedition for the purpose of fishing for halibut and hunting seal.
> Somehow he became separated from the others
> and did not return to the village.
> Of course everything possible was done searching for him.
> After a long time they gave up.
> Mourning in those days took a whole year,
> especially for one of high caste.
> The village stood close to the water's edge.
> Remains of several of the old community houses still stand,
> some crumbling to the ground.
> One day the people were amazed
> to see the bay filled with killer whales.
> And right in the middle
> was a huge one with two fins.
> He was held
> slightly above water as though he was being shown to the people.
> While alive he told his people that to prove the belief he would return with double fins if ever he drowned.
> There was much wailing on the shore.
> And after a proper time had passed,
> a huge mortuary totem
> pole was erected by the successor of the clan.
> The customary
> ceremony took place with feasting,
> giving away of gifts,
> and tattooing of the royal family.
> Only after fulfilling this custom was a successor to a deceased chief regarded as high chief.
> On top of the mortuary pole is a beautiful killer whale with double fins.
> The original pole was moved from the village to Hydaburg,
> repaired, and now it stands in the Hydaburg totem park.
> The clan of the Raven tribe
> adopted the double finned killer whale as their crest
> and [it] is one of the most beautiful Haida designs.

Howkan (Gáwk'yaan, #58) is another famous village, also known among Tlingits, who sometimes call it Kátgaawtan (Drum on Both Sides). Sitka elder Herman Kitka Sr. (interview) explains the history of Tlingit-Haida interactions that gave birth to this name:

> The legend I know about the Haidas is that... when the Tlingits discovered them in Hetta Inlet, they had Tlingit fighting people all ready for war to wipe them out. But when they crawled up on the settlement, they saw those

red-haired Haida women and they forgot to fight. Instead they start helping them. I guess those red-haired women looked pretty good to those warriors. So nothing was ever done to them by the Tlingits. They were brought out of Hetta Inlet to Howkan. And they had them build their homes opposite the Tlingit winter village... And Howkan, the Americans, when they surveyed it, I guess they couldn't pronounce the Tlingit. The Tlingit name for that bay was Kátgaawtan; Howkan they called in English. At night you could hear the drums from both sides, the Haida side and the Tlingit side, over the bay. You can hear it from both sides. So they named that settlement Kátgaawtan, and the two settlements Kátgaawtan Aaní [see Hinyaa chapter].

Howkan became well-known as "Totem Pole City" for its handsome carved poles, many of which were removed or fell into disrepair when the settlement was abandoned as a winter village beginning around 1911. But strong memories of place linger. Robert Sanderson Sr. (interview), whose mother's roots are in Howkan, remembered that "every single year until the time she was eighty-three years old" she liked to walk with him "through this place."

We'd go from one end to the other. Start with the burial area where the boardwalk was at the harbor and go clean to the other end of town... my mother's old house, they'd moved it, but the foundation is still there where they picked the house up and they left them — there were steps made out of stone, slabs of stone; they're still there with bricks along the edge of it.

Hydaburg / Hydaburg Creek (Xikt'áa Gándlaay, #35). The English name Hydaburg is an unfortunate new hybrid, marrying an anglicized Native name (Haida) to generic Germanic term for settlement (burg). But, in fact, it is an ancient village, as Robert Sanderson Sr. (interview) explains:

It's right here. Right now, this place, this creek we used to call Hec-tah [Xikt'áa]. My mother said it had been settled about four times. Probably the original village was Tlingit.

Howkan (Gáwk'yaan, #58) is famous Haida village, which was also inhabited by Tlingits, who settled on the opposite side of the bay. According to Herman Kitka Sr., Tlingits called the settlement Kátgaawtan (Drum on Both Sides) because "you could hear the drums from both sides, the Haida side and the Tlingit side." Alaska State Library, Winter & Pond Photograph Collection, P87-0050.

> During 1911 or 1912, the Bureau of Indian Affairs and the local community leaders decided to form a new town basically to get an educational facility and get some schools and services that they didn't want to provide to three different communities. So they decided to move Klinkwan, Howkan, and Sukkwan. A lot of that move was done in the fall of 1912. Some people stayed behind and I think the last people moved back in about 1916...sometimes the people would pick up a house, put it on floats, get it all the way over to Hydaburg and pull it up. My mother's house was one of those that was moved three times. You can see the tremendous amount of labor that was involved in this. Now, when they got here, we had pictures of the town. We called it "Tent City," tents all along the beach. The first bridge was a big log that they fell[ed] across the creek and adze[d] the top of it; a real big spruce log right down here. They made boardwalks. Shortly after they came here they established a sawmill. As you see from the pictures, you can see how big the trees used to be right around Hydaburg, especially on the north side. They knocked everything down by hand and sawed them up by hand—drag those logs by hand to the sawmill and then put the roads and boardwalk in by hand. It was a tremendous amount of work. The pictures that we had, my mother had quite a collection...[In one] there's a big canoe about 1912 that was right in front of Mrs. Nix's house at high tide. There were about thirty people in it.

Woodrow Morrison (interview) remembers that Hydaburg was not the only option for the consolidated settlement. "Well, they picked three different sites: one here, one in Waterfall, and one in Seagull Creek. They had some men to go around the sites. The reason why they picked Hydaburg was because the creek is right in the middle of town and they can go right down the beach and pick clams. They didn't pick Seagull Creek because there's no clams there. The reason why they didn't pick Waterfall was because of strong tide...and here is Hydaburg, that's where they settled on for salmon and clams."

Klinkwan (Hlankwa'áan, #55). This may be adapted from a Tlingit name (Len<u>k</u>u.àan, "Tidal Flat Area Village," understood to be a reference to good shellfish beds; see Hinyaa <u>K</u>wáan #130), but the village became a Haida settlement. It was abandoned as a permanent village with the consolidation into Hydaburg.

Sukkwan (Saxk'wáan, or Su<u>k</u>ka.aan, #36). This is a Tlingit name that was adopted when Haidas established their community in the same locale. According to Charles Natkong Sr. (interview), it means "People [Village] of the White Grass" because there is "real thick, green grass in the summertime," but "it turns white in the fall time." Sukkwan Island takes its name from this place. Prior to the nineteenth-century smallpox epidemics, the village reportedly had a population of over two hundred, but the epidemic reduced it to about thirty. Archeological investigations suggest an antiquity of approximately fifteen hundred years. The village disbanded around 1911, when people moved into Hydaburg, although many continued to visit in order to commemorate ancestors, tend to property, and garden (Claude Morrison, interview).

Hetta Cove (<u>G</u>it'áa, #39) and Eek Inlet (Íik, #43)*. Both of these watersheds were important sockeye systems. Robert Sanderson Sr. (interview) notes:

> Eek Inlet, probably after Hetta, is the most productive sockeye system near Hydaburg. It would probably take about one-fourth of the amount of sockeyes you take in Hetta. That's still a pretty good size amount of sockeye. They're exceptionally large fish. They probably have a different age class than what you see in Hetta. It's a July run, Fourth of July up to the end of the month...Some [Haidas] fish in Hetta, some in Eek...There's a piece of land that's owned by the Natkong family...at Eek. That's where the camp is at now. They had a smokehouse there for years.

The English name for Eek Inlet is likely derived from the Haida name; which may refer to the abundance of halibut fishing holes (*éet* in Tlingit) in the vicinity.

Forrester Island (Gús<u>k</u>uu, #60). Forrester Island is an important cultural landscape for Haidas and Tlingits. Celebrated for its bird and sea mammal colonies, the island was regularly used for subsistence activities, including hunting, gathering, and gardening. In the following narrative, collected by Lisa Lang (see Dauenhauer, Lang, and Natkong 1998), Hydaburg elder Helen Sanderson offers a fascinating history of this important cultural landscape, which is now designated as a wildlife refuge and wilderness area.

> Thirty-five miles out of here on the Pacific
> outside Dall Island is an island they call Forrester Island
> and it has the Tlingit name Gús<u>k</u>uu.
> At one time the island was beautiful,
> with level, sandy beaches
> and it seemed like the island
> according to this story was owned
> by a woman,
> a woman owned it,

and she had a daughter,
and then on the island
also lived a couple,
a man and wife.
They had a small little hut they lived in.
Every day
the woman would go down to the beach
and dig clams.
And
every time she and her husband would
have a baby, when she'd give birth to a baby
he'd pick it up on the pretense of fondling it
and here
on his chest
was just like
red snapper fins.
It would raise up and he'd crunch—
crush the baby against it
and the baby would die.
And then the fins
would kind of settle down on his chest.
And his wife got tired of it.
And she started mating with the dog.
Eventually she gave birth to seven puppies.
And after that, what happened to the husband was never
mentioned in the story.
. . . .
And
every time she'd
go down and dig clams and as she neared her dwelling
she'd hear
a lot of children laughing and playing.
But when she'd go in there
in their dwelling
the puppies would be all curled up asleep.
And one day
she put her digging stick in the sand
and put her shawl over it and made a detour.
And when she peeked in through the dwelling
here the puppies
had discarded their skins
and they were
normal little boys.
She rushed in and gathered up the skins and she threw
them all in the fire.
And after that they were normal

Klinkwan (Hlankwa'áan, #55) was an important Haida settlement. It was abandoned as a permanent village with the consolidation of Natives into Hydaburg in the early twentieth century. However, the area is still used by local Haidas. Alaska State Library, Winter & Pond Photograph Collection, P87-0090.

little boys.
And when they got older
they started conquering the monsters
that inhabited the island.
And the first one was
a sea serpent that lived in a cave.
I've seen that cave, I had my husband circle the island
on our boat.
It's a huge cave,
right below a cliff.
And they start making plans on how they would kill that serpent.
They made all kinds of nooses from different materials and they climbed the cliff,
lower the noose
and when the serpent would
come out of the cave and stick its head through the noose
it would just strangle.
It would strangle it, it would thrash it apart.
They were in despair when they tried so many different ways of
gathering materials.
And one day
a little wren
trilled a little song and then ended by saying, "Use my sinews."
They looked at the little wren
and they couldn't see how they could get enough sinews to
make a big noose.
And after a time when they gave up on every kind of material available
they started
killing the little wrens.
And finally they got enough sinews
to make a noose.
And when it was done
they climbed to the top of the cliff
and lowered the noose.
And when the serpent stuck its head out
it went right through the noose
and that strangled it and that's how they killed it.
Now it's
murre ducks
lay their eggs there,
in that huge cave.
And then there's supposed to have been a huge crab there that
inhabited too,
but how they done away with that one, I don't know.
I never did hear it.
Anyway, the owner of the island had a daughter and she'd
go out in the current,
lay on her back, and her long hair would be streaming
behind her.
Why
the brothers wanted to do away with her it was never made clear.
Anyway,
they made
all kinds of crafts to get out to her
but every craft they rigged up
would break to pieces.
And one day
when they were trying to think of
what kind of craft to make again,
a little mouse
came up to them
and
the mouse said,
"Use my canoe."
And they followed her
to where she said her canoe was.
And here
there was a canoe there all right, in the bush,
but it was so old
the bottom
had big cracks and grass and weeds were growing through it
and they couldn't see how
a craft like that would float.
So, they just left it
and
tried some more
crafts that they
rigged up and
none would hold up.
Finally, they decided to try that old canoe.
And when they launched it, it floated real high.
And that's how they got out to that
girl.
They
beheaded her.
Why?
It was never stated why they wanted to do away with her.
And when the mother found out she was very, very angry.

She demanded her daughter's head and the brothers
wouldn't give it up.
And she told them that if they didn't give her daughter's
head to her she would turn the island upside down.
And she stuck her cane down
and the whole island started to wobble. Still they wouldn't
give up.
Finally,
she shoved her cane way down and the island turned
upside down.
And still the brothers were on it.
Anyway, that's why the island is so rocky,
there's no sandy beaches.
There's only one small little place they call
Eagle Creek.
Other than that it's all huge rocks.
And they keep the island, nowadays, for
all kinds of fowls.
They're protected.
Anyway
this belonged to the
Tlingits at one time.
And way back there were tribal wars all the time and the
Haidas finally took possession of it
and
they owned every part of the island.
Every spring
they'd
go out there in canoes to gather eggs
and they'd compose songs about the different sorts of
fowls that are out there.
And I truly wish I knew the whole story
. . . .
I'm just relating what
there is
that I know of it.

Cape Felix (Yáahl K'yúu Xagatdáa, #33). Yáahl K'yúu Xagatdáa is a mythic landscape, associated with Raven's mischievous activities. Perhaps not coincidently, as Robert Sanderson Sr. (interview) observes, Cape Felix also lies at the heart of a large area of volcanic activity and serves as a boundary marker between Tlingit and Haida country.

> That's the core of a volcano right there. Behind it there's a bunch of caves, lava caves... Cape Felix is generally, for the purposes of the land claims when they got going, it's what they usually accepted as a boundary between the Tlingit and the Haida... At the time that they decided to file a claim against the government... they decided that this would be the boundary line so they wouldn't be fighting each other, [and] at least be united... So I drew it through the watershed here on Suemez Island and came back clean around Cordova Bay. And everything you see here is a line that enclosed what is considered West Coast Haida and everything westward of that.

This is not to say that Haida enclaves did not exist elsewhere, as there were communities of Haidas that dwelled seasonally at places on Noyes Island, and also alongside Tlingits at places like Fish Egg Island near Craig, where herring spawn were harvested each spring. As Christine Edenso (1983, 40) emphasizes, herring egg time "was the time when a lot of people were intermingling with the Tlingits and they sort of coexisted there. There was never any trouble amongst the later Tlingits and the Haidas. They mixed together and they were occupied with their efforts to secure food. There was never any trouble."

Cape Flores (Ts'anuk̲'uu, #21). Christine Edenso (1983, 17) recalls camping at this place where the absence of seagulls served as a barometer of herring spawning activities elsewhere.

> In the summer months when they camped out around the food gathering places, there would be a day when there would hardly be any seagulls around. There was only one reason for that: They had all flown away to Fish Egg Island where the herring were spawning. Millions of seagulls went into that place. So it was no wonder that when we camped at Cape Flores called in Haida Ts'anuk̲'uu, we did not see any seagulls, and we knew that it was time for fish eggs.

Eastern Prince of Wales Island. The most well-known village on eastern Prince of Wales Island is Kasaan (K̲asa'áan, #8) which is from the Tlingit for "Beautiful Village." However, according Duff's (1971) informants, "Before they discovered Kasaan, the people lived on Chasina Island, just inside Cholmondeley Sound on the south side. The name was Chachini [Cháats' Híinii, #19], or 'humpback creek.'" This name was likely derived from the Tlingit Chás'héeni (Humpback Salmon Creek). In his testimony to Goldschmidt and Haas in 1946, elder Jacob Thomas referred to this island as "Skin Island," and both he and Duff's informants emphasize that this was a large settlement from which the Haidas moved to old Kasaan after a devastating smallpox epidemic (perhaps in the 1830s). The move to new Kasaan was completed by the early 1900s.

Jacob Thomas (Goldschmidt and Haas 1998, 173–74) further characterized the Haida seasonal use of eastern Prince of Wales Island as follows:

> I was born at old Kasaan around about 1886 or 1887. Same year Metlakatla was built. I have lived in this area all my life. My story is based on what I learned from my grandfather who lived to be 117 years old. He died in 1917. He was called "the history man" . . . I hunted with my grandfather from the time I was five years old.
>
> On left-hand side going in Skowl Arm we trapped and frequently hunted deer there too. In March and April we trapped there for mink mostly.
>
> We also used to trap and hunt deer just below old Kasaan Village [in a place] called Salt Chuck. This is a good place for clams. We used to trap all round islands in Skowl Arm and Polk Inlet. We lived in old Kasaan until I was about fifteen years old. Our people fished halibut around old Kasaan.
>
> From Tom Creek near Saltery Cove we used to get fish, highbush cranberries, salmonberries, humpies [pink salmon], and sockeyes. This creek was owned by Chief Skowl. Tom Skowl was his nephew. The stream was named after him. We go to High Island for black seaweed. All Kasaan people get their seaweed from there. There are also quite a few halibut banks on southern end of High Island. We had lots of gardens at Skowl Arm; we planted potatoes there.
>
> In the fall of the year most of Kasaan people would go to Cholmondeley Sound for dog salmon to dry and smoke here in the village. Some people claimed various fish streams around Kasaan. We respected these individual claims but often by asking permission from the owner, we were all allowed to use the place to hunt or fish.
>
> In August we would be through drying salmon and the rest of the month would be spent in gathering berries. In September and October we get our deer from Cholmondeley Sound. We hunt deer there every year. We also still hunt at Twelve-mile Arm and Skowl Arm. We also trap at Skowl Arm and use this area for fishing. We used to have gardens also at Skowl Arm but during the last few years the whites would pick them and so we stopped planting the gardens there. When I was a boy, Jones, Young, and I all had gardens there.
>
> We fish at Hadley Stream, south of Lyman Anchorage.
>
> We fish around Kasaan Peninsula; there are halibut banks there and seaweed.
>
> We used to go beaver hunting at Skowl Arm. We still do hunting there and at Twelve-miles . . .
>
> When I was a boy we went down to Cape Chacon for

The village of old Kasaan, near modern Kasaan (#8) on eastern Prince of Wales Island. "K̲asa'áan" is derived from the Tlingit name, meaning "Beautiful Village." It is an apt description of the locale and the name was retained by the Haidas who eventually settled there. Alaska State Library, Case & Draper Photograph Collection, W. H. (William Howard) Case, P39-0189.

> halibut, all the people of Kasaan. I was told by elderly persons now dead that the Natives from Kasaan went together to islands in Nichols Bay where they camped and got halibut. They also went to Brownson Bay. Some Haidas from Hydaburg were also allowed to come to Brownson Bay and Nichols Bay, but we never allowed a Tlingit or Tsimshian to go there or any place in Karta Bay, Skowl Arm, or along our coast.

Other Haida witness testimony confirms these general boundaries and patterns of use, and suggests that Haidas also had claims in Moira Sound and regularly ventured north of Kasaan Bay and east of Prince of Wales Island for certain foods (see Goldschmidt and Haas 1998).

Kasaan is also rich in mythological associations. A cliff cave in Kassan Bay was said to be the home of a giant rat (similar stories are localized elsewhere), which local Haidas warriors stalked and killed after the creature seized some women on their way to pick wild celery at Grindall Island. A version of the story by Alice Kitkoon was recorded and transcribed by Charles Natkong Sr. (see Dauenhauer, Lang, and Natkong 1998). And Paul Bight was known as "Wildman Fort" (Gagihit'taoch, #16) because it was inhabited by "Gagihit, or wild men," who "were people raised with no clothing. They became strong, hard and could stand cold... [and] lived on fish and rock cod. They say when they came around a person they would whistle loudly and throw some dry, rotten pieces of wood at him" (Duff 1971).

Final Thoughts

When the K'áyk'aanii Haida came to Alaska, they made it their home in part by laying down Haida names on the various places they settled on the southern Prince of Wales archipelago. They also adopted and "Haida-fied" Tlingit names and customs so as to facilitate interactions with their neighbors. The results of this project illustrate both of these processes at work.

Today, the Hydaburg and Kasaan tribes are using information on named historic sites to conserve and manage these areas in appropriate ways. Along with the Sealaska Heritage Institute and Canadian Haida First Nations, they also are working to revitalize Haida language and culture. Recognizing and documenting indigenous place names constitutes a vital part of these efforts. This project is just the beginning.

Reflections of 2000 K'áyk'aanii Historic Sites Fieldwork

Gail (Young) Dabaluz (S'eenaakw') was born in 1966 in Seattle, Washington, and raised in both Juneau and Sitka. Her family participates at Tlingit ceremonials and they harvest traditional food from the land and sea. Ms. Dabaluz has a bachelor's degree in anthropology conferred by the University of Hawai'i at Hilo. She completed her graduate studies in Alaska Native and rural development at the University of Alaska Fairbanks. Her master's thesis focused upon the cultural significance of the Alaska Native Claims Settlement Act section 14(h)(1) historic sites of Southeast Alaska. Ms. Dabaluz is the granddaughter of the late Judson and Selina Brown and her parents are James Young Jr. and Geraldine Williams. Her Haida grandparents are the late James and Florence (George) Young. They originate from Howkan and their ancestral homeland was Massett, Queen Charlotte Islands. Ms. Dabaluz credits her educational and professional successes to the unwavering support of her husband Leroy and their two children, Ke'alalakina Nāpua'oanamakuawahinemaka Nāpiha'a (Xíxch'i Sháan) and (Pietr Kalilōa'okeikikāne Dabaluz (Duksu.áat).

The month of December 2000 was a very remarkable and personally rewarding time for me. Cherilyn (Bell) Holter and I were provided the opportunity to work with Hydaburg Cooperative Association documenting the K'áyk'aanii (Kaigani) historic sites as conveyed by the Haida elders. The elders who instructed us were Claude Morrison, Woodrow Morrison Sr., Charles Natkong Sr., and Robert Sanderson Sr. The fieldwork captured their unique recollections of specific sites conveyed by their ancestors and their own first-hand experiences. The vivid expressions describe Haida life ways, communicating traditional use and occupancy of their homelands. The gathering captured reflections of tribal traditions, conveying inter-generational concepts. These concepts focus upon land stewardship, natural resource management, subsistence use and cultural practices revealing a uniquely Haida worldview.

The Hydaburg fieldwork was a professional and personal opportunity offering me a better understanding of my father's people and their inherent ties to Haida homelands. My tribal affiliation is Tlingit, Haida, and Tsimshian, directly following my mother's Tlingit lineage. Our family encouraged active participation at our ceremonials as both host clan and host family at cultural events.

It was apparent that embarking upon this project would accomplish two tasks. The fieldwork honors my father's heritage as well as creating a permanent record of the Haida tradition bearers whose recollections require documentation. It was very meaningful to me on a deeply personal level. In previous years, friends and family from Hydaburg invited me to visit and I declined to do so. The reason I declined was pragmatic. I did not want to visit my father's home community without his accompaniment. Because of this, my first visit to Hydaburg occurred when I was twenty-eight years old in 1994. While there, my father took me to various elders' homes for formal introductions to family. Those elders, some who are no longer with us, were the epitome of grace and humility. Their reception was both overwhelming and liberating. They allowed me into their homes and lives in a manner that instantly validated my Haida-ness. This was an area I had struggled with for so many years, not growing up near my father, his people or their territory. This was the first step in a journey of rediscovery.

The actual fieldwork was extraordinary, in that the elders were very lucid in the subject content and did not hesitate in any of their responses to the topic matter. It felt as thought they had been waiting to have the opportunity to participate in such a session. Although our daily work schedule contained an ambitious agenda, the elders were alert and cognizant throughout all aspects of the recordings. When the subject matter was sensitive, they answered the questions to their greatest ability without hesitation. Their sentiment shared with the field staff was that this project was long overdue and the resulting documentation necessary, to convey the importance of the Haida historic sites to future generations.

Various themes emerged as the week progressed. The most obvious theme expressed by the elders was the urgency that they felt in having their knowledge documented. The participants shared that they could identify a few community members who knew of the significance of cultural and historic sites in their region. This was of paramount concern for the elders, since some sites are culturally sensitive and cared for in the appropriate manner. The sites are comprised of previously occupied village sites, archaeological sites, cemeteries, and petroglyphs. The elders' fear was that the stewardship and oversight of such sites cannot be met, if the history associated with each site becomes lost.

Understanding one's history provides a firm foundation on how you are to conduct yourself as a human being. There are recognized protocols in our indigenous societies that codify how we conduct ourselves as individuals and in a tribal setting. The etiquettes have been in place since time immemorial and offer us the resiliency to overcome insurmountable challenges. Therefore, the instruction of our ancestors continues to serve as a guide in how we are to conduct ourselves on a daily basis. We are privileged to be born Haida, and with privilege comes responsibility. Our responsibility includes caring for our heritage in a respectful manner and sharing it with others.

Another theme that the elders touched upon was how adaptable we have been as a people. Their recollections of how the Haida moved from the Queen Charlotte Islands to Alaska offered us glimpses in the reasoning behind the relocation. It was very apparent that their ancestors strongly felt the need to provide a better life for their families and that when they moved it was with the intention of staying permanently. Families do not take lightly moving great distances in marginal weather for a temporary stay. The elders shared how the transition from the clan system in the Queen Charlotte Islands was adapted to a broader tribal system in Alaska, and its implications for contemporary society.

There were many stunning examples of indigenous life ways expressed throughout the week's sessions. The most relevant examples were those that touched upon the long history of tribal land stewardship that relied upon a consistent land tenure system. Agreements had to be made with the neighboring Tlingit in order for both groups to survive. Listening to the elders speak about the great Flood, migration stories, and how inter-tribal conflicts were resolved was mesmerizing. There were many clear examples of indigenous resource management that would be invaluable to implement today.

The potential application of the fieldwork conducted for heritage programs is immeasurable. The most important application is conveying the importance of the historic sites to the Haida people of that region. Becoming familiar with state, national, and international preservation laws in order to continue protecting these sites is necessary. Understanding the legal framework that can both protect and endanger the sites is critical. Indigenous language programs can benefit by learning more about each historic site. Entire curricula can be built upon the unique features of one site. Closer examination of the traditional Haida tribal system can be used comparatively, by reviewing existing Haida literature. Agency collaborations can be developed with the intent of protecting historic sites, benefiting both the community and agency. Protecting subsistence sites offers instruction for younger generations of why particular practices have been observed and remain intact. Development of indigenous research guidelines for the community can be finalized for future projects.

Many of these initiatives are being undertaken already in the community of Hydaburg. It is apparent that younger tribal members are fully participating in the process and their pride in who they are as Haida people is palpable.

Working with the Haida elders documenting their recollections of historic sites was personally enriching. It has been an extreme honor and privilege to be a member of the fieldwork team. It is a small token of my deep love and affection of my father's people.

Native Names for Places outside of Southeast Alaska

As this chapter shows, Haida place names are not limited to the Prince of Wales archipelago, but rather stretch back to Haida Gwaii in British Columbia. Haidas also incorporated and Haida-fied Tlingit names when they moved north. Similarly, we find other non-Tlingit names, such as Chugach, Eyak, Tsetsaut, and Tsimshian ones, in Southeast Alaska because the boundaries of cultural naming are not limited by culture areas, which are permeable, evolving, and shifting. At the same time, we have the phenomenon of Southeast Natives naming places outside the region with "nontraditional place names," which is the subject of this essay by Tlingit linguist James Crippen (Dzéiwsh).

The earliest recorded nontraditional place name used by a Tlingit speaker appears to have been for Victoria, the present capital of British Columbia, on the southern end of Vancouver Island. During the late nineteenth century Victoria was a place where numerous Northwest Coast indigenous people from many different tribes would gather for monetary employment in the burgeoning lumber and fishing industries. The Tlingit name for this town, as with many other early non-Russian loanwords in Tlingit, is derived from Chinook Jargon (CJ). The CJ name was Biktoli, and as recorded in Swanton's *Tlingit Myths and Texts* (Swanton 1909, 406) Gooshdutéen, the Naanyaa.aayí chief Shakes at the time, called Victoria in one of his songs Waktáni, transcribed by Swanton as "Waktâ'nî." A lamentation song from Yakutat calls the town Mektori, which is clearly similar (Hans Chester, pers. comm.). In addition, Vancouver Island has been called Deikee X̲aat, meaning "Faraway Salmon" (Harold Jacobs, pers. comm.).

The Tlingit language lacks a number of sounds which exist in English and Russian, and even in some neighboring indigenous languages like Haida and Tsimshian. Not to be left behind, Tlingit has perhaps four sounds which are not attested in any other language, these being *x'*, *x'w*, *x̲'*, and *x̲'w* (Crippen 2007). Thus when a word is borrowed into Tlingit from a foreign language it must be reshaped to fit the sounds of Tlingit. This is similar to the process by which words borrowed from one language are changed to fit another language, such as how Japanese *karaoke* is often pronounced by English speakers as "carry-okey." The patterns and rules by which sounds are transformed when words are borrowed from one language to another is called loanword phonology, and is an active area of research in linguistics. In the name Waktáni the *b* sound of Biktoli which does not exist in Tlingit has been converted to a *w* which is used in Tlingit. We can tell that the original was a *b*, as in CJ Biktoli, rather than a *v*, as in English Victoria, because the Tlingit conversion of the English name would probably be something closer to "Wiktáwya." Numerous other loanwords from CJ exist in Tlingit as well, such as *nakwnéit* from CJ *leplet* meaning "priest," originally from French *le prêtre* (Johnson 1978).

Another nontraditional place name that was borrowed into Tlingit was the name for Portland, Oregon. Frederica de Laguna recorded the Tlingit version of "Portland" in her book *Under Mount Saint Elias* (de Laguna 1972), said by a Yakutat speaker to be X'wáatlan. In this example we have the non-Tlingit sound *p* changed to *x'w* which is a rounded ejective fricative. The rounding approximates the labial quality of the English *p*, and the ejective frication approximates the noisy burst of air released in the English *p*.

The same Tlingit loanword phonology can be applied to other modern place names as well. For example, Seattle could easily become "Seeyátl," Anchorage could be "Áankawich" or just "Áankich," and Vancouver could be "Wankóowa." The object of using such Tlingitized place names is not of course to make fun of Tlingit pronunciation, as some might suppose, but instead to reduce the amount of language mixing of Tlingit and English when talking. While this may be unimportant to native speakers of Tlingit, as more people learn Tlingit as a second language and work to keep it alive, they will want to avoid mixing in English as much as possible. Using loanword forms of nontraditional place names is one method by which such language mixing can be avoided.

A method for nontraditional place name development which can prove useful is to borrow names from neighboring indigenous languages. For example, Tlingit people living in Anchorage may want to discuss places around upper Cook Inlet, but lack names for these places since this was never a traditional Tlingit territory. However, it was the traditional territory of the Dena'ina people and their place names of the region are well documented in the book *Shem Pete's Alaska* (Kari and Fall 2003). Dena'ina has some sounds which do not exist in Tlingit, but it is a much closer fit to the Tlingit sound system. For example, one Dena'ina name for Anchorage is Qatuk'e'usht meaning roughly "something drifts up to it" (p. 332), a name which is easily pronounced by Tlingit speakers and could be spelled "K̲atuk'e.oosht" in Tlingit.

An interesting Dena'ina place name in Anchorage is Chanshtnu, better known in English as Chester Creek. The Dena'ina name for this creek, from which the English version is derived, simply means "Grass Creek." Adapting this name to Tlingit could give "Chaansh Héeni," or even "Chaanshtnu Héeni," the latter an example of place name pleonasm since *-nu* in Dena'ina has the same meaning as *héen* in Tlingit. The Dena'ina people have developed new nontraditional place names to fit the many changes which have happened to the Cook Inlet area in the past century, one example derived being the name for Westchester Lagoon, a small lake created in 1973 when the mouth of Chester Creek was dammed. Kari and Fall offer Chansh Kaq' Bena, "Grass Mouth Lake," as a novel yet entirely genuine Dena'ina name, derived from the traditional Chansh Kaq', "Grass Mouth," which refers to the small Chester Creek delta that empties into Cook Inlet. A Tlingit adaptation of this is relatively simple, starting with any of the previous names for Chester Creek and adding the Tlingit term *wát* (mouth of a river), e.g., "Chaansh Wát," and then adding *áak'w* (little lake) to give "Chaansh Wát Áak'w."

An alternate method of deriving place names is direct translation. This method will tend to work better with names of Native American origin where place names are more commonly descriptive, rather than those of European American origin which are often taken from untranslatable personal names like "Baranof" and "Douglas." Working with the Dena'ina name for Chester Creek again, the Dena'ina word *chansh* (grass) might be translated into one of the Tlingit terms *sháak* (reed grass), *soo<u>k</u>* (wide grass), or *<u>x</u>aatl'* (freshwater grass). From one of these roots a number of new names can be created; using *sháak* we can produce "Sháak Héeni" or "Shaakhéeni" (Reed Grass Creek), "Shaakhéeni Wát" (Reed Grass Creek Mouth), and "Shaakhéeni Wát Áak'w," just for example.

Another method of developing new nontraditional place names in Tlingit is to create descriptive names from scratch using only Tlingit terminology. For example, Anchorage is well known for its extensive tidal mudflats around the head of the Cook Inlet, and could thus be named after this feature. The common Tlingit term for a tidal mudflat is *léin*, so Anchorage could be called "Léin.aan" or "Tidal Mudflat Town." Whitehorse is on the Yukon River and might be called "Héenwán.aan" for "Riverside Town" (*héenwán*, "riverside"), or perhaps because there is a good fishing hole (*ísh*) downtown, "Ishká.aan" for "At the Fishing Hole Town." Although these names are not traditional, they have a very close resemblance to the form of more traditional names and hence fit well with the existing place name system.

In sum, although the development of Tlingit place names has largely ceased with the declining population of native speakers and increasing loss of traditional knowledge, there is no reason that this situation should continue. This is especially relevant for Tlingit people who live outside their traditional homelands and who wish to maintain and invigorate their culture and language. There are a number of different methods by which new place names can be developed: by direct loans from European American languages with adaptation to the Tlingit sound system, by direct loans from indigenous Native American languages requiring much less adaptation, by translation from other languages into Tlingit, and by creation of completely new descriptive names using existing Tlingit terminology. Of course, various combinations of these methods are also possible and useful. And eventually, over enough time and with continuing use, these new, nontraditional place names may acquire the intricate cultural and geographic relationships that traditional names have as they are gradually adapted into the existing systems of Tlingit language and society.

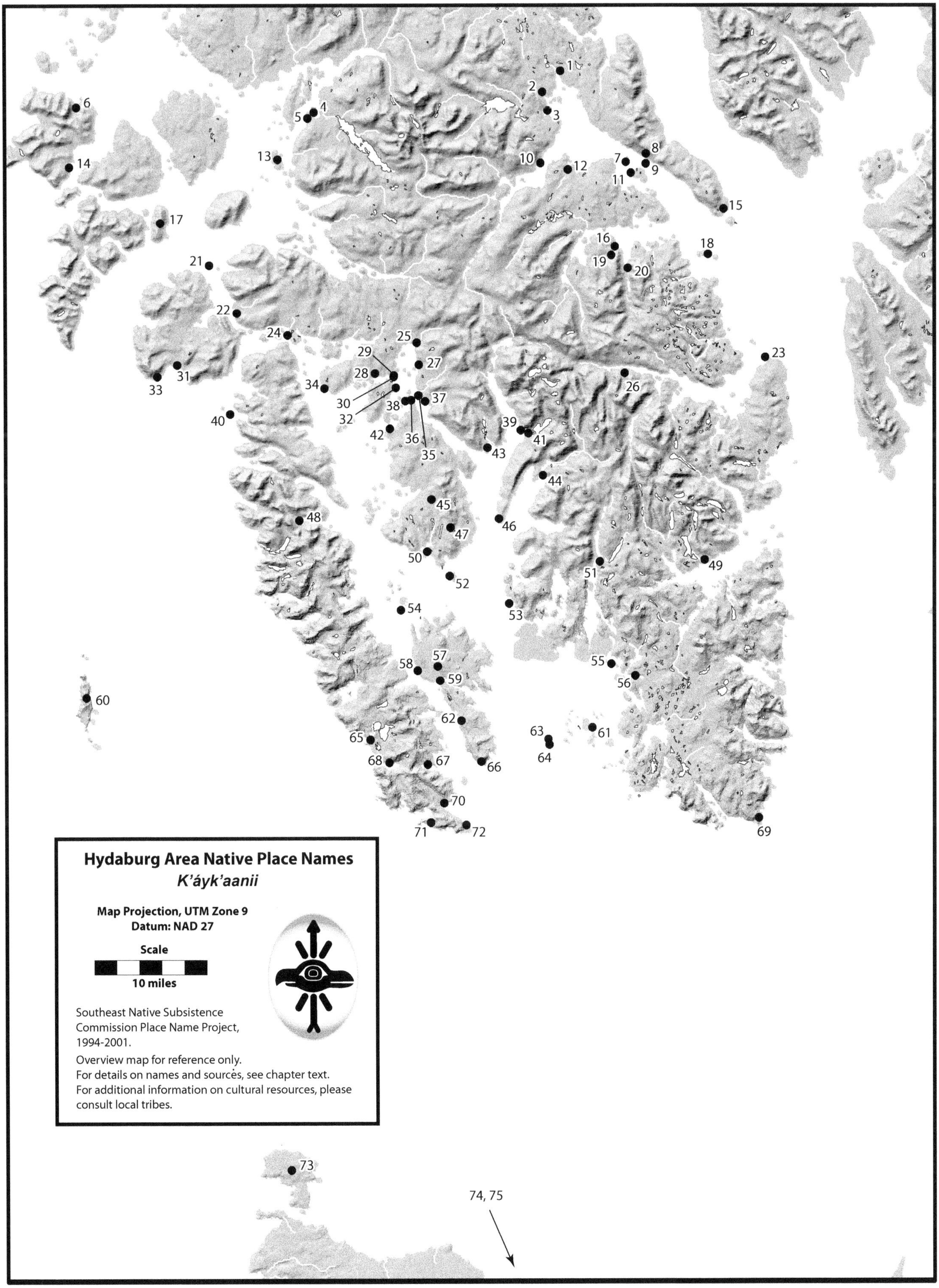
Hydaburg Area Native Place Names
K'áyk'aanii
Map Projection, UTM Zone 9
Datum: NAD 27
Scale
10 miles
Southeast Native Subsistence Commission Place Name Project, 1994-2001.
Overview map for reference only.
For details on names and sources, see chapter text.
For additional information on cultural resources, please consult local tribes.
74, 75

K'áyk'aanii Place Names

Asterisk indicates uncertain, unconfirmed, or partial; NM = not mapped.
Some names have more than one pronunciation or translation.

Map #	*Name*	*Translation*	*Location*
1	Sáahlaang Gwáayaas	Back of the Island	Salt chuck above Karta Bay
2	Kayán	*	Paul Young Creek in Karta Bay*
3	Gáadaa	Waterfall	Karta Bay
4	Hlaawáak	[Man's name]	Klawock
5	Yáahl K'íik (Yáahl Hlk'íik)	Raven's Herring Rake*	Village at Canoe Pass, near Klawock
6	*	Thumping Sand	Steamboat Bay, Noyes Island
7	Kulsíit Hat*	——* (from Tlingit*)	Smaller of two islands off Kasaan (Round Island*)
8	Kasa'áan	Beautiful Village (from Tlingit)	Kasaan and old Kasaan (Skowl Arm) villages
9	Q'eqdáxat*	*	Pass between Kasaan Island and Kasaan Peninsula in Kasaan Bay
10	Shíkada*	*	Cove inside Sandy Point, Twelvemile Arm*
11	Chaats Chuunii*	Humpback Salmon* (from Tlingit)	Berry Island, just above Kasaan Island in Kasaan Bay
12	Táng Suwáas	Salt Lake	Kina Cove, Kasaan Bay*
13	K'áaws Tláay	Fish Eggs Place	Fish Egg Island
14	Táas Dámptgaas	Noisy Sands	Kelly Cove
15	Kiichskwa.áan*	——* Village (from Tlingit)	Grindall Point
16	Gagihit'taoch	Wildman Fort	Paul Bight
17	Kúushdaa Shiit*	*	Saint Ignace Island
18	Kwedínas*	*	Paterson and High islands, Kasaan Bay
19	Cháats' Híinii	Humpback Salmon Creek (from Tlingit)	Old Tom Creek inside Paul Bight at entrance to McKenzie Inlet
20	Káinaxdá*	*	McKenzie Inlet
21	Ts'anuk'uu	*	Cape Flores
22	K'aax T'áay*	*	Waterfall Cannery/Resort, Ulloa Channel
23	Hitáa Gándlaay	——* Creek	Chasina Island, Cholmondeley Sound entrance
24	Júuts'iks*	*	Tlevak Narrows
25	Naats'uu* Híinii	Poison* Creek (from Tlingit)	Natzahini Bay/Creek
26	Cháats' Híinii	Humpback Salmon Creek (from Tlingit)	Chomly (abandoned town), West Arm, Cholmondeley Sound
27	Skúl Gawáas	Porpoise Harbor	Dog Salmon Creek above Hydaburg

Map #	*Name*	*Translation*	*Location*
28	Xúuts Híinii	Brown Bear Creek (from Tlingit)	Creek on North Pass
29	Kekwadaka*	*	Northeast end of North Pass, above Sukkwan Island
30	Shaa Noow	Mountain Fort* (from Tlingit)	North Pass area
31	Yáahl Híinii	Raven Creek (from Tlingit)	Suemez Island*
32	Gwáay Sg̱áanuwaay	Island Spirit	Goat Island
33	Yáahl K'yúu Xagatdáa	Raven is Keeping an Eye on the Door/Road*	Cape Felix
34	X̱akw In'wáay Kún (X̱agwáay Kún)	Half-Halibut Point (Halibut Nose)	Halibut Nose, north of Hydaburg
35	Xikt'áa G̱ándlaay	——* Creek	Hydaburg Creek, Hydaburg
36	Saxk'wáan (Suḵka.aan / Suḵw Àan [Tlingit])	White Grass Village (Grassy Village*)	Sukkwan Village
37	Stáw Suwáas	Sea Urchin Pond	Sea Egg Lake, Hydaburg
38	Yáahl T'áwts'	Raven's Fort	Near Hydaburg*
39	G̱it'áa*	*	Hetta Inlet
40	Náas	*	Diver Island
41	G̱it'áa'uu*	*	Hetta village site
42	Sg̱i K'udáas	Red-Lipped	Lone Tree Island
43	Íik*	Halibut Hole*	Eek Inlet
44	Náaxuwaa*	Halibut Hook*	Nutkwaa Inlet
45	Teukwitliisgam*	Rock Bear Claw* (from Tsimshian*)	Sukkwan Island (whole)
46	Tl'ahgáa*	*	Lime Point, south of Hydaburg
47	Tiuk'u*	Rock Concourse*	Sukkwan Island creek
48	K'úḵuu*	*	Coco Harbor
49	Yasyaat*	——* (from Tlingit*)	Kegan Cove
50	Kasúuk*	*	Kasook Inlet/Lake
51	Hlak'áas	Dry Land (Dry Waterfall)*	Klakas Inlet
52	Gwáay Ḵyáangulaas	Visible Island[s]	Jackson Island*
53	Gúlaa Gwaay	Abalone* Island	Abalone Island, above Kassa Inlet
54	Gwáay G̱ándlaa	Creek Island*	Aston Island*
55	Hlankwa'áan	Bark Village (from Tlingit)	Klinkwan, Klakas Inlet
56	Táaḵuu*	*	Hunter Bay
57	G̱waadúu Gwáay	——* Island	Long Island*
58	Gáwk'yaan (Kátgaawtan [Tlingit])	——* (Drum on Both Sides)	Howkan
59	K'áat G̱ándlaas	Deer Creek	Hunting camp near Howkan (Bolles Inlet*), on Long Island
60	Gúsḵuu*	*	Forrester Island
61	Gwáay Ts'aa Suu*	Islands ——*	Barrier Islands
62	Ḵ'wíi G̱ándlaas	Mud[dy] River	Koinglas, Long Island, Coning Inlet

Map #	Name	Translation	Location
63	Sgínaaw Tl'ajuwáas	Eggs*	Egg Rock, Barrier Islands
64	K'áalaay K'áaws Tláay	Sculpin's Fish Eggs Place	Dixon Entrance
65	Lisuuwaa*	*	Essowah Harbor/Lakes
66	Stla G̲udang Kún	——* Nose	Kaigani Point*
67	Dáats K̲uu*	*	Datzkoo Harbor
68	K̲uuk'iigaas*	*	Security Cove
69	Íntaan Kún*	Big Swell Point*	Cape Chacon
70	Déik̲uu*	——* (from Tlingit*)	Daykoo Islands, McLeod Bay
71	Siti Kún*	*	Chickwan Bight,* across from Cape Muzon
72	K'áyk'aanii	Crabapple* (Haida-Tlingit hybrid word) Country/Village (Tlingit)	Kaigani Village, Cape Muzon
73	K̲'íis Gwáay (K̲'aysgwaayaay)	——* Island	Langara Island, Haida Gwaii
74	Nai* Kún	Long* Nose	Rose Spit, Haida Gwaii
75	Gwáay Háanaas	Island ——*	Lyell Island area, Haida Gwaii
NM	K'áaw Núudaa	Fish Egg Season*	*

References

Ackerman, Robert E.

1968. *The archeology of the Glacier Bay region, southeastern Alaska.* Report of Investigations 44. Pullman: Washington State University, Laboratory of Anthropology.

Ackerman, Robert E., Thomas D. Hamilton, and Robert Stuckenrath

1979. Early cultural complexes of the northern Northwest Coast. *Canadian Journal of Archaeology* 3:195–209.

Arndt, Katherine L., Russell H. Sackett, and James A. Ketz

1987. *A cultural resource overview of the Tongass National Forest, Alaska.* Fairbanks: GDM, Inc.

Bancroft, Hubert Howe

1886. *History of Alaska, 1730–1885.* The Works of Hubert Howe Bancroft 33. Reprint, New York: Antiquarian Press, 1959.

Barnes, Robert D.

1968. *Invertebrate zoology.* 2nd ed. Philadelphia: W. B. Saunders Company.

Basso, Keith H.

1988. "Speaking with names": Language and landscape among the Western Apache. *Cultural Anthropology* 3(2): 99–130.

1996. *Wisdom sits in places: Landscape and language among the Western Apache.* Albuquerque: University of New Mexico Press.

Beardslee, L. A.

1882. *Reports of Captain L. A. Beardslee, U.S. Navy, relative to affairs in Alaska, and the operations of the U.S.S.* Jamestown *under his command, while in the waters of that territory.* 47th Cong., 1st sess., Senate Executive Document 71. Washington, D.C.: Government Printing Office.

Blake, William P.

1868. Notes upon the geography and geology of Russian America and the Stickeen River, from observation made in 1863. In *Russian America*, 40th Cong., 2nd sess., House Executive Document 177, pt. 2, 2–19. Washington, D.C.: Government Printing Office.

Bohn, Dave

1967. *Glacier Bay: The land and the silence.* Gustavus: Alaska National Parks and Monuments Association.

Bradley, Herbert

1990. Interview with Pat Green, Wrangell Museum. Audiotape in possession of John Feller, Wrangell, Alaska. Partially transcribed for the Southeast Native Subsistence Commission place names project by Nikki Morris.

Brady, John G.

n.d. Place names in the vicinity of Sitka. John G. Brady Papers. Yale Collection of Western Americana, Beinecke Rare Book and Manuscript Library. Microfilm copy on file at the Alaska State Historical Library, Juneau.

Campen, Brenda

n.d. Tlingit place names in the Angoon area. Manuscript in the author's possession.

Chaney, Gregory P., Robert C. Betts, and Dee Longenbaugh

1995. *Physical and cultural landscapes of Sitka National Historical Park, Sitka, Alaska.* Report prepared for the National Park Service, Sitka National Historical Park. Douglas, Alaska: Vanguard Research.

Cogo, Robert and Nora Cogo

1983. *Remembering the past: Haida history and culture.* Anchorage: University of Alaska Materials Development Center, Rural Education.

Crippen, James A.

2007. An embarrassment of riches: The proliferation of Tlingit writing systems. http://www2.hawaii.edu/~crippen/papers/orthography.pdf (accessed December 17, 2007).

Cruikshank, Julie

1981. Legend and landscape: Convergence of oral and scientific traditions in the Yukon Territory. *Arctic Anthropology* 18(2):67–93.

1990a. Getting the words right: Perspectives on naming and places in Athapaskan oral history. *Arctic Anthropology* 27 (1):52–65.

1990b. *Life lived like a story: Life stories of three Yukon Native elders.* In collaboration with Angela Sidney, Kitty Smith, and Annie Ned. Lincoln: University of Nebraska Press; Vancouver: University of British Columbia Press.

1991. *Reading voices, Dän dhá ts'edenintth'ę̌: Oral and written interpretations of the Yukon's past.* Vancouver: Douglas and McIntyre.

2005. *Do glaciers listen? Local knowledge, colonial encounters, and social imagination.* Vancouver: University of British Columbia Press; Seattle: University of Washington Press.

Dangeli, Joan Marie

1996. The Tsetsaut (Zit Zaow) Athabascan tribe of Portland Canal (Western Canada and southern-Southeastern Alaska). Manuscript in the author's possession.

Dauenhauer, Nora Marks, and Richard Dauenhauer, eds.

1987. *Haa shuká, Our ancestors: Tlingit oral narratives.* Seattle: University of Washington Press; Juneau: Sealaska Heritage Foundation.

1990. *Haa tuwunáagu yís, For healing our spirit: Tlingit oratory.* Seattle: University of Washington Press; Juneau: Sealaska Heritage Foundation.

1994. *Haa k̲usteeyí, Our culture: Tlingit life stories.* Seattle: University of Washington Press; Juneau: Sealaska Heritage Foundation.

Dauenhauer, Richard, Lisa Lang, and Charles Natkong Sr.

1998. Haida stories told in English. Haida elders recorded by Lisa Lang and Charles Natkong Sr., ed. Richard Dauenhauer. Working draft (December), Sealaska Heritage Foundation, Juneau.

Davidson, George

1901a. Explanation of an Indian map . . . from the Chilkaht to the Yukon drawn by the Chilkaht chief, Kohklux, in 1869. *Mazama* 2(2):75–82.

1901b. The tracks and landfalls of Bering and Chirikof on the Northwest Coast of America. *Transactions and Proceedings of the Geographic Society of the Pacific* (San Francisco), 2nd ser., 1:1–44.

Davis, Stanley D.

1996. The archaeology of the Yakutat Foreland: A socioecological view. Ph.D. diss., Texas A&M University.

de Laguna, Frederica

1960. *The story of a Tlingit community: A problem in the relationship between archeological, ethnological, and historical methods.* Smithsonian Institution Bureau of American Ethnology Bulletin 172. Washington, D.C.: Government Printing Office.

1972. *Under Mount Saint Elias: The history and culture of the Yakutat Tlingit.* Smithsonian Contributions to Anthropology 7 (in 3 parts). Washington, D.C.: Smithsonian Institution Press.

1983. Aboriginal Tlingit sociopolitical organization. In *The development of political organization in Native North America: 1979 proceedings of the American Ethnological Society,* ed. Elisabeth Tooker, 71–85. Washington, D.C.: American Ethnological Society.

1990. Tlingit. In *Handbook of North American Indians,* vol. 7, *Northwest Coast,* ed. Wayne Suttles, 203–28. Washington, D.C.: Smithsonian Institution Press.

Dennis, Si, Sr.

1998. Interview with Clay Alderson, April 17. Transcribed by Alice Cyr. Manuscript, Klondike Gold Rush National Historical Park, Skagway, Alaska.

DeWitt, Forrest, Sr.

1985. Tape recordings on Juneau history. Transcribed and translated from the Tlingit by Nora Marks Dauenhauer. Tapes in possession of the translator.

Dixon, E. James.

1999. *Bones, boats, and bison: Archeology and the first colonization of western North America.* Albuquerque: University of New Mexico Press.

Duff, Wilson

1971. Cultural heritage project — report on Kasaan. Contributing associates Walter B. Young Sr., William Burgess, Lydia Charles; ed. Andrea Laforet. Manuscript, Alaska State Museum, Juneau.

Eastman, Carol M. and Elizabeth A. Edwards

1991. *Gyaehlingaay: Traditions, tales, and images of the Kaigani Haida.* Traditional stories told by Lillian Pettviel and other Haida elders. The Thomas Burke Memorial Washington State Museum Monograph 6. Seattle: University of Washington Press.

Edenso, Christine

1983. *The transcribed tapes of Christine Edenso.* Trans. Robert and Nora Cogo, ed. Tupou L. Pulu. Anchorage: University of Alaska Materials Development Center, Rural Education.

Emmons, George T.

1911. Native account of the meeting between La Pérouse and the Tlingit. *American Anthropologist,* n.s., 13(2):294–98.

1916. *The Whale House of the Chilkat.* Anthropological Papers of the American Museum of Natural History 19(1). New York: American Museum of Natural History.

1991. *The Tlingit Indians.* Edited with additions by Frederica de Laguna and a biography by Jean Low. Anthropological Papers of the American Museum of Natural History

70. Seattle: University of Washington Press; New York: American Museum of Natural History.

n.d. The history of Tlingit tribes and clans. Manuscript (ca. 1916–45), American Museum of Natural History Archives, New York.

Garfield, Viola E.

1945. Fieldnotes from Kake, Alaska. Viola Edmundson Garfield Papers, 2027-001, box 10. Special Collections, University of Washington Libraries, Seattle.

1947. Historical aspects of Tlingit clans in Angoon, Alaska. *American Anthropologist* 9(3):438–542.

n.d. Ownership of food producing areas. Viola Edmundson Garfield Papers, 2027-001, box 1, folder 15. Special Collections, University of Washington Libraries, Seattle.

Garfield, Viola E., and Linn A. Forrest

1961. *The wolf and the raven: Totem poles of southeastern Alaska.* Revised paperback edition. Seattle: University of Washington Press. (Orig. pub. 1948.)

George, Lydia

n.d. Notes on Angoon place names. Manuscript in the author's possession.

Gmelch, George

1990. Caught in the middle. *Natural History* 99(9):32–37.

Golder, Frank A.

1922–25. *Bering's voyages: An account of the efforts of the Russians to determine the relation of Asia and America.* 2 vols. New York: American Geographical Society.

Goldschmidt, Walter R., and Theodore H. Haas

1998. *Haa aaní, Our land: Tlingit and Haida land rights and use.* Edited with an introduction by Thomas F. Thornton. Seattle: University of Washington Press; Juneau: Sealaska Heritage Foundation. (Report orig. pub. 1946.)

Grinnell, George Bird

1901. The Natives of the Alaska coast region. In *Alaska*, vol. 1, *Narrative, glaciers, Natives*, ed. C. Hart Merriam, 137–83. Report of the Harriman Alaska Expedition. New York: Doubleday, Page and Company.

Hall, George

1962. Report of a visit to Hoonah, Alaska, July 1960. Manuscript, Sitka National Historical Park, Sitka, Alaska.

Hammond, Austin

n.d. Papers. Sheldon Museum and Cultural Center, Haines, Alaska.

Harrington, John

n.d. Notes and vocabulary from George Johnson, Jack Ellis, and others, 1939–40. Manuscript, Alaska Native Language Center, Fairbanks.

HIA (Hoonah Indian Association)

2006. *Tlingit place names of the Huna Káawu.* Map. Hoonah, Alaska: Hoonah Indian Association.

Hinckley, Ted C.

1970. The canoe rocks — We do not know what will become of us. *Western Historical Quarterly* 1(3):265–90.

1996. *The canoe rocks: Alaska's Tlingit and the Euramerican frontier, 1800–1912.* Lanham, Md.: University Press of America.

Hope, Herb

2000. The Kiks.ádi survival march of 1804. In *Will the time ever come? A Tlingit source book*, ed. Andrew Hope III and Thomas F. Thornton, 48–79. Fairbanks: University of Alaska, Alaska Native Knowledge Network.

Hunn, Eugene S.

1994. Place-names, population density, and the magic number 500. *Current Anthropology* 35(1):81–85.

1996. Columbia Plateau Indian place names: What can they teach us? *Journal of Linguistic Anthropology* 6(1):3–26.

Hunn, Eugene S., Darryll R. Johnson, Priscilla N. Russell, and Thomas F. Thornton

2003. Huna Tlingit traditional environmental knowledge, conservation, and the management of a "wilderness" park. In "Multiple methodologies in anthropological research," supplement, *Current Anthropology* 44(S5):S79–S103.

Jackson, Clarence

2003. Migration history. Audio recording (February), Sealaska Heritage Institute, Juneau.

Jackson, Johnny C.

1971. Kaach.ádi history. Audiotape and transcript, Organized Village of Kake, Kake, Alaska.

1979. Transcript of oral history recording. Manuscript, Organized Village of Kake, Kake, Alaska.

Jacobs, Harold

2000. Inhabitants of the Burning Wood Fort. In *Will the time ever come? A Tlingit source book*, ed. Andrew Hope III and Thomas F. Thornton, 34–47. Fairbanks: University of Alaska, Alaska Native Knowledge Network.

Johnson, Samuel Victor

1978. Chinook Jargon: A computer assisted analysis of variation in an American Indian pidgin. Ph.D. diss., University of Kansas.

Joseph, Charlie, Sr.

n.d. Tlingit place names around Sitka. Map, audiotapes, and transcriptions on file at Sitka Native Educaton Program and Sitka Tribe of Alaska, Sitka.

Joseph, Phillip

1967. The history of Aukquwon. *New Alaskan*, December, 8–15.

Kan, Sergei

1989. *Symbolic immortality: The Tlingit potlatch of the nineteenth century.* Washington, D.C.: Smithsonian Institution Press.

Kari, James, and James A. Fall

2003. *Shem Pete's Alaska: The territory of the Upper Cook Inlet Dena'ina.* 2nd ed. Fairbanks: University of Alaska Press.

Keithahn, Beverly

n.d. The first people of the place that has everything. Manuscript, USDA Forest Service, Juneau.

Keithahn, Edward L.

1945. *Monuments in cedar: The authentic story of the totem pole.* Ketchikan, Alaska: Roy Anderson.

1966. *Alaska for the curious: Alaska centennial edition 1867–1967.* Portland, Ore.: Graphic Arts Center.

Kitka, Herman, Sr.

1998. Deep ties to Deep Bay: A Tlingit elder's training. *Cultural Survival Quarterly* 22(3):47–48.

Knowles, Tony

1999. The canoe still rocks. State of Alaska executive proclamation by Governor Tony Knowles, July 19.

Krause, Aurel

1956. *The Tlingit Indians: Results of a trip to the Northwest Coast of America and the Bering Straits.* Trans. Erna Gunther. Seattle: University of Washington Press. (Orig. pub. as *Die Tlinkit-Indianer*, 1885.)

1981. *Journey to the Tlingits by Aurel and Arthur Krause, 1881/82.* Trans. Margot Krause McCaffrey. Haines, Alaska: Haines Centennial Commission.

Krauss, Michael E.

1982. *In honor of Eyak: The art of Anna Nelson Harry.* Fairbanks: Alaska Native Language Center.

Kunz, Cecilia

1997. The story of how Yees Ga Naalx got his name. *Juneau Empire*, April 21.

Langdon, Stephen J.

2006. *Traditional knowledge and harvesting of salmon by Huna and Hinyaa Tlingit.* Fisheries Resource Monitoring Program, final report (project no. 02-104). Anchorage: U.S. Fish and Wildlife Service, Office of Subsistence Management.

La Pérouse, Jean-François de Galaup, comte de

1799. *A voyage round the world, performed in the years 1785, 1786, 1787, and 1788. . . .* Trans. from French. 2 vols. and atlas. London: Printed by A. Hamilton for G. G. and J. Robinson, J. Edwards, and T. Payne. (Orig. pub. as *Voyage de La Pérouse autour du monde*, ed. L. A. Milet-Mureau, 1797.)

Littlefield, Roby, Ethel Makinen, Lydia George, Nora Marks Dauenhauer, and Richard Dauenhauer, eds.

2003. Aak'wtaatseen, "Shanyaak'utlaax̱." Told by Deikeenáak'w, Sitka, 1904. Transcribed by John R. Swanton, 1904. Originally published in Swanton (1909), *Tlingit myths and texts*, as story 99, "Moldy-end," pp. 301–10. Working draft (February). Transliterated into modern orthography by Roby Littlefield and Ethel Makinen. http://www.ankn.uaf.edu/curriculum/Tlingit/Salmon/graphics/swanton.pdf (accessed April 20, 2007).

Maschner, Herbert D. G.

1992. The origins of hunter-gatherer sedentism and political complexity: A case study from the northern Northwest Coast. Ph.D. diss., University of California, Santa Barbara.

McClellan, Catharine

1975. *My old people say: An ethnographic survey of southern Yukon Territory.* 2 vols. National Museum of Man Publications in Ethnology 6. Ottawa: National Museums of Canada.

Mills, David D., and Anne S. Firman

1986. *Fish and wildlife use in Yakutat, Alaska: Contemporary patterns and changes.* Technical Paper 131. Douglas: Alaska Department of Fish and Game, Division of Subsistence.

Moss, Madonna L.

2004. The status of archaeology and archaeological practice in Southeast Alaska in relation to the larger Northwest Coast. *Arctic Anthropology* 41(2):177–196.

Moss, Madonna L., and Jon M. Erlandson

1992. Forts, refuge rocks, and defensive sites: The antiquity of warfare along the North Pacific coast of North America. *Arctic Anthropology* 29(2):73–90.

Muffler, L. J. P.

1967. *Stratigraphy of the Keku Islets and neighboring parts of Kuiu and Kupreanof Islands, southeastern Alaska.* U.S. Geological Survey Bulletin 1241-C. Washington, D.C.: Government Printing Office.

Muir, John

1895. The discovery of Glacier Bay. *Century Magazine* 50(2): 234–47.

1915. *Travels in Alaska.* Reprint, with a foreword by David Rains Wallace. Boston: Houghton Mifflin Co., Mariner Books, 1998.

Naish, Constance M., and Gillian L. Story
1976. *Tlingit noun dictionary.* 2nd ed. Revised and expanded by Henry Davis and Jeff Leer. Sitka: Sheldon Jackson College.
n.d. Excerpts from notebooks based on fieldwork in Angoon. Manuscript (ca. 1960s), Alaska Native Language Center, Fairbanks.

Nyman, Elizabeth, and Jeff Leer
1993. *Gágiwduł.àt: Brought forth to reconfirm; The legacy of a Taku River Tlingit clan.* Whitehorse: Yukon Native Language Centre; Fairbanks: Alaska Native Language Center.

Oberg, Kalervo
1973. *The social economy of the Tlingit Indians.* Seattle: University of Washington Press.

Olson, Ronald L.
1967. *Social structure and social life of the Tlingit in Alaska.* Anthropological Records 26. Berkeley: University of California Press.
n.d. Tlingit field notes, 1933–34. Ethnological Documents of the Department and Museum of Anthropology, BANC FILM 2216, reels 130(1–2), items 130.1–10. The Bancroft Library, University of California, Berkeley.

Olson, Wallace M.
1989. Warm Chuck Village report of 1989 research. Manuscript in the author's possession.

Orth, Donald J.
1971. *Dictionary of Alaska place names.* Geological Survey Professional Paper 567. Reprint with minor revisions. Washington, D.C.: Government Printing Office. (Orig. pub. 1967.)

Paul, William
n.d. The Alaska Tlingit: Where did they come from? Manuscript 7077, National Anthropological Archives, Smithsonian Institution.

Petroff, Ivan
1884. *Report on the population, industries, and resources of Alaska.* Part of U.S. Census Office, 10th Census (1880), vol. 8. Washington, D.C.: Government Printing Office.

Rabich-Campbell, Chris
1988. *"Raven's wrinkled foot": Cultural resources overview of Kupreanof Island, Southeast Alaska.* USDA Forest Service, Stikine Area, Tongass National Forest.

Sackett, Russell
1979. *The Chilkat Tlingit: A general overview.* Anthropology and Historic Preservation Occasional Paper 23, Fairbanks: University of Alaska, Cooperative Park Studies Unit.

Sealaska Corporation
1975. *Native cemetery and historic sites of Southeast Alaska.* Preliminary report prepared by Wilsey and Ham, Inc., Seattle. Juneau: Sealaska Corporation.

SENSC (Southeast Native Subsistence Commission)
1995–2002. Southeast Alaska Native Place Names Project, final reports. Maps and reports on file at the Central Council of Tlingit and Haida Indian Tribes of Alaska, Juneau.

Schroeder, Robert F., and Matthew Kookesh
1990. *Subsistence harvest and use of fish and wildlife resources and the effects of forest management in Hoonah, Alaska.* Technical Paper 142. Juneau: Alaska Department of Fish and Game, Division of Subsistence.

Scidmore, Eliza R.
1896. The discovery of Glacier Bay, Alaska. *National Geographic Magazine* 7(4):140–46.
1899. *Appletons' guide-book to Alaska and the Northwest Coast.* New York: D. Appleton and Company.

Shotridge, Louis
n.d. Tlingit geographical names. Manuscript (ca. 1930?), Alaska State Historical Library, Juneau.

Shiva, Vandana
2000. *Stolen harvest: The hijacking of the global food supply.* Cambridge, Mass.: South End Press.

Swanton, John R.
1908. Social condition, beliefs, and linguistic relationship of the Tlingit Indians. In *Twenty-sixth annual report of the Bureau of American Ethnology,* 391–485. Washington, D.C.: Government Printing Office.
1909, ed. *Tlingit myths and texts.* Smithsonian Institution Bureau of American Ethnology Bulletin 39. Washington, D.C.: Government Printing Office.

Thornton, Thomas F.
1995. Tlingit and Euro-American toponymies in Glacier Bay. In *Proceedings of the third Glacier Bay science symposium, 1993,* ed. Daniel R. Engstrom, 294–301. Anchorage: National Park Service.
1997a. Anthropological studies of North American Indian place naming. *American Indian Quarterly* 21(2):209–28.
1997b. Know your place: The organization of Tlingit geographic knowledge. *Ethnology* 36(4):295–307.
1997c. Traditional cultural property investigation for Auke Cape, Alaska. NOAA project no. 601.00, contract no. 50ABNA600056, Livingstone Slone, Inc. Unpublished report in the author's possession.
1998. *Tlingit traditional use of Sitka National Historical Park.* Sitka: National Park Service.

1999. Tleiḵw aaní, The "berried" landscape: The structure of Tlingit edible fruit resources at Glacier Bay, Alaska. *Journal of Ethnobiology* 19(1):27–48.

2000a. Building a Tlingit resource atlas. In *Will the time ever come? A Tlingit source book*, ed. Andrew Hope III and Thomas F. Thornton, 98–116. Fairbanks: University of Alaska, Alaska Native Knowledge Network.

2000b. Person and place: Lessons from Tlingit teachers. In *Celebration 2000: Restoring balance through culture*, ed. Susan W. Fair, 79–86. Juneau: Sealaska Heritage Foundation.

2002. From clan to ḵwáan to corporation: The continuing complex evolution of Tlingit political organization. *Wicazo Sa Review* 17(2):167–94.

2004a. The geography of Tlingit character. In *Coming to shore: Northwest Coast ethnology, traditions, and visions*, ed. Marie Mauzé, Michael E. Harkin, and Sergei Kan, 363–84. Lincoln: University of Nebraska Press.

2004b. *Klondike Gold Rush National Historical Park: Ethnographic overview and assessment.* Anchorage: National Park Service.

2008. *Being and place among the Tlingit.* Seattle: University of Washington Press; Juneau: Sealaska Heritage Institute.

Thornton, Thomas F., Virginia Butler, Fritz Funk, Madonna Moss, Jamie Hebert, J. Tait Elder, Robi Craig, Shingo Hamada, and Adela Maciejewski Scheer

2010. *Herring synthesis: Documenting and modeling herring spawning areas within socio-ecological systems over time in the southeastern Gulf of Alaska.* Final report, North Pacific Research Board Project 728. Portland, Ore.: Portland State University. http://herringsynthesis.research.pdx.edu/ (accessed December 10, 2010).

Thornton, Thomas F. and Harold P. Martin.

1999. What's in a name? Indigenous place names in Southeast Alaska. *Arctic Research of the United States* 13(Spring/Summer):40–48.

Thornton, Thomas F., Robert F. Schroeder, and Robert G. Bosworth

1990. *Use of sockeye salmon at Sitkoh Bay, Alaska.* Technical Paper 174. Douglas: Alaska Department of Fish and Game, Division of Subsistence.

Visaya, Bessie

1972. The story of Yees-cah-nalg. Letter to the City and Borough of Juneau administrative office, October 30. Copy in the author's possession.

Waterman, Thomas T.

1922a. The geographical names used by the Indians of the Pacific Coast. *Geographical Review* 12(2):175–94.

1922b. Tlingit geographic names for extreme Southeast Alaska, with historical and other notes. Manuscript 2938, National Anthropological Archives, Smithsonian Institution.

Willard, Mrs. Eugene

1884. *Life in Alaska: Letters of Mrs. Eugene S. Willard.* Ed. Eva McClintock. Philadelphia: Presbyterian Board of Publication.

Williams, Frank, and Emma Williams

1978. *Tongass texts.* Transcribed and edited with an introduction by Jeff Leer. Fairbanks: Alaska Native Language Center.

Williams, Judith

2006. *Clam gardens: Aboriginal mariculture on Canada's west coast.* Transmontanus 15. Vancouver: New Star Books.

Wood, C. E. S.

1882. Among the Thlinkits in Alaska. *Century Magazine* 24 (3):323–39.

YHMA (Yukon Historical and Museums Association)

1995. *The Kohklux map.* Whitehorse: Yukon Historical and Museums Association.

Young, S. Hall

1915. *Alaska days with John Muir.* New York: Fleming H. Revell Co.

Ingram Content Group UK Ltd.
Milton Keynes UK
UKHW052054300523
422598UK00004B/8

9 780295 988580